D1554968

In the Museum of Maya Culture

Touring Chichén Itzá

Quetzil E. Castañeda

University of Minnesota Press
Minneapolis
London

Published by the University of Minnesota Press
111 Third Avenue South, Suite 290, Minneapolis, MN 55401-2520
Printed in the United States of America on acid-free paper

Second printing, 1997

Library of Congress Cataloging-in-Publication Data

Castañeda, Quetzil E.
    In the museum of Maya culture / Quetzil E. Castañeda.
      p.   cm.
    Includes bibliographical references and index.
    ISBN 0-8166-2672-3 (hc)
    ISBN 0-8166-2673-1 (pb)
    1. Chichén Itzá Site (Mexico)   2. Pisté (Mexico)   3. Mayas—Ethnic identity.   4. Mayas—Antiquities.   5. Ethnology—Mexico—Yucatán (State)   6. Tourist trade—Mexico—Yucatán (State)   I. Title.
    F1435.1.C5C37   1996
    972'.65—dc20   96-4583

Contents

Part II: War and Its Topography

Illustrations

Note on Orthography

This English text uses many Spanish and Yucatec Maya words. While the written form of Spanish language words has been standardized, the varieties of currently and previously spoken Yucatec Maya has not. In use today as in prior centuries are several different orthographic systems that seek to make graphic the sounds of the language. I retain the use of multiple spellings of words—such as "Cucúlcan," "Kukulcan," and "K'uk'ulkan" for what is more commonly known by the Nahuatl word "Quetzalcoatl" or by the English "Feathered Serpent." These variations are maintained as traces of the writers' political, cultural, ethnic, linguistic, historical and other locations. Whereas the spelling of Mexico has been anglicized by the dropping of the accented "é," other proper names, such as Yucatán and Pisté are written in their Spanish form. Most Yucatec Maya names are written in their Spanish form (e.g., "Chichén Itzá"), but may also appear in Maya (e.g., "Chich'éen Itza'") or anglicized ("Chichen Itza"). In the case of Cancun, the Yucatec Maya spelling and pronunciation are used, which had been the norm in English until a very recent tendency in English to spell it in the Spanish form, with an accent: Cancún.

The major difficulty in transliterating Yucatec Maya is the problem of representing the glottal stop. Glottalization of vowels can be presented by an apostrophe (') following the vowel or at times by an accent (e.g., "é") if hispanicized; in the orthography of linguistics, however, accents on vowels indicate rising or lowering tone, not glottalization.

The glottalization of consonants is different and is the crux of different orthographies. While the glottalization of some consonants ("p," "ch") has been represented by a duplication ("pp," "chh"), others ("tz") are changed altogether ("dz"). The hard "c" or "k" is more complicated in that if a "c" is used for the k-sound, then a "k" may be used for glottalization of that value; otherwise the contrast is made between a "K" and glottal "K'"; but often both graphic forms are used and may not actually represent the difference of the glottal in any given word depending on the text. The "c" in the Yucatec Spanish words "cenote" and "cenotillo" is soft, or an s-sound.

The current tendency has been to use the apostrophe after the vowel to represent the glottal (e.g., "p'," "ch'," "k'," "tz' "), except in proper names whose spelling has been solidified by usage over the centuries (e.g, "Dzibilchaltun," not *"Tz'ibilichaltun"). In the case of colonial period P'izte', the modern form has dropped both the glottal of the "P" and that following the "e"; in addition, the "s" has substituted for the "z" value.

Note on Toponyms

The toponym "Chichén Itzá" means "[At] the Mouth of the Well of the Itzá," where Itzá has been translated as either "Witches" or "Magicians of Water" and the well or *chén* referred to is the Sacred Cenote of Sacrifice. Some argue that Chichén had a different name before the Toltec or Mexicanized Maya invasion, but others suggest that this alternative name, Uuc Habnal or "Seven Caves' Stones," was an honorific title of this capital city-state and not a prior toponym of a different Pure Maya settlement. This is a title that transfigures Chichén Itzá into the mythic place of origin from which came all Mesoamerican peoples.

Debates such as this on the history of Chichén Itzá are the necessary and unavoidable point of passage for any and all interpretations of the cultures and civilizations of the Yucatec Maya and Lowland Classic Civilization.

The toponym "Pisté" derives from *p'iz,* "to measure," and *te',* the numerical classifier for things made of wood; thus, Pisté is "measuring stick," but further, colonial dictionaries say it meant "seed of cacao" and was, therefore, also the unit to measure value. According to interpretations of the sacred Maya *Books of Chilam Balam,* Ah P'izté', the Itzá land-surveyor, "measured," *p'iz,* the lands and towns of the Itzá dominion "seated" at Chichén. After being measured, Mizcit Ahau, an avatar of the Feathered Serpent, "swept," *miz,* the lands clean for Itzá occupation. Here too, in this guidebook to the Museum of Maya Culture, Pisté measures the distance Maya cultures travels to and from the Mouth of the Well of the Magicians of Water, that fabulous and fabled city of K'uk'ulkan.

Acknowledgments

This study is inscribed with the passions, friendships, intellectual inspiration, learning, and concern of all the many who have shared their time and gifts with me. Of all those to whom I owe heartfelt appreciation I can only thank a precious few, and these persons with inadequate words.

Foremost of those to whom this work is indebted are the people of Pisté, so maligned and troubled yet intensely warm and alive with generosity and love. I especially mention Pepe and Yolanda Pat; Jaime Cen Puc; Eva Tus; Gina Puc Cauich; Víctor Olalde and Doña Monica Olalde; Silverio Koyok, Milquides Ucan, "Joven" Ucan; Don Edu Pat, Froylan Pat, Salomon Pat; all of the Mis families, especially Reynaldo, Edy Cime de Mis, Angelino, Ebelio, Luis, Fernando; Fidel Mex; Galdine and David Nahuat and *familias*; Don Domas Tun; Jorge Tun and Doña Munda; Hilario, Rubén and Lalo Briceño; Víctor Tun; Don Primitivo, Elieser Padilla and family; Don Popis and Sepo; Doña Pil; Sixto Mazon; Oswaldo Yam Puc, Doña Olga Argáez de Yam; Vitaliano Salazar, Doña Simiona and the late Don Felix Salazar; Nico Dzib, Valentín Dzib, Martín Dzib, Fernanda Tec de Dzib and *linaje*; Hiliberto Yam; Don Chumin; Tito Burgos, Bernardo Burgos, Tomás Burgos; Edy Garrido, Víctor Garrido, Alfredo Marrufo, Rey Pacheco, Ramona Hoil; Miguel Angel Vergara; Eduardo "el Viejo"; Dr. Eduardo Coeto and Agustín; "Kiki" Tun; Claudio Puc and Doña Gregoria; Don Olegario Cime, Doña Elda, Nandy and Sergio Cime; Víctor and Teresa Díaz; and all the members of the Comité de Lucha. Don Eraclio Olalde, the Halach Uinik of Pisté, whose fortitude lent the movement its successes, died of a heart attack in town hall while negotiating a community crisis regarding the long-awaited paving of the streets. It is to his memory and the memory of the community of Pisté that I hope this rendition of their struggles may lend some additional honor and visibility.

I want to express a profound appreciation for the guidance, training, and friendship that Jorge Klor de Alva, Gary Gossen, Bob Carmack, and Richard Leventhal have provided. Their influences are indelibly impressed upon this text and my thoughts. Antonella Fabri, Jay Indik, Kim Benson, Ed Cimafonte, Amy Gottleib, Dennis Phrayre, Jennifer Burtner, Abigail Adams, John Sosa Jr. and Sr., Tom Jamison, Lynette Leidy, Kathy O'Connor, Lisa van Eysden, Jan Gasco, Jim Boon, Tom Kirsch, Billie-Jean Isbell, John Henderson, Mario Ruz, Barbara and Dennis Tedlock, Jim Collins, Alicia Re Cruz, Carol Smith, Wendy Weiss, Joanne Rappaport, Victor Montejo, Benito Juarez, Carmen Varela, Eeva Jokinen, Soile Viejola, David Webster, and Colleen Barry, Ana Luisa Izquierdo, Manuel G. Oropeza, Miguel Angel Vergara, Juan Luis Bonor and Carolina, Carmen Morales, María Elena Peraza, Lourdes Rejón, Alfredo Barrera Rubio, Luis Várguez Pasos, Nancy Villaneva, Juan Castillo Cocom, Ella Quintal, Dulce Ramos, and Miguel Bojórquez have all significantly "impacted" my personal life and this project for which there are no adequate words to express my gratitude. A deep appreciation is reserved for Kay Warren for the generous and indispensable support offered at a moment of crisis. In Houston, I am indebted to Lawrence Hogue, Pauline Kolenda, George Marcus, Cynthia Freeland, Jan Lin, Susan Rasmussen, Norris Lang, Melissa Cefkin, Mazyar Lotfalian, Myanna Lawson, Laura Bunt, and Kathryn Milun for their friendship and intellectual engagement. I am honored by and especially thankful to Stephen Tyler and Jean-Paul Dumont for their critical yet luxuriant reviews of the manuscript as well their inspiration; their insights forced me to revamp. A special thanks to Janaki Bahkle for her faith in the text and to the staff of the University of Minnesota Press for their enduring patience and excellence. I hope these paltry words convey at least some of the many debts I owe; they certainly do not communicate the passion or significance with which they were given or the depth of my feelings for these persons and others I have not mentioned. Despite the support and advice of many, any remaining shortcomings are all my own responsibility.

Finally, I want to recognize my family that has shaped and sustained me: my siblings Xmucane, Hector-Neri, and especially Omar and Kicab, who kindly read the early manuscript; my mother, whose correction of my autobiography was none too late; and my father, whose unreadable comments written in the margins during his last months continue to resonate. I dedicate this endeavor to find myself to Miriam M Castañeda and Hector-Neri Castañeda, whose contrary styles of self set me on this trajectory.

I thank the Carnegie Institution of Washington, the Hartford Seminary Foundation, the Peabody Museum, and their staffs for access and guidance to materials essential to this study. Funding for this research was graciously provided by DeCormier Scholarship (I.M.S., SUNYA), 1985; Fulbright Hays Training Grant (#022AH70018), 1987-88; National Science Foundation Grant (#BNS 8716015), 1987-89; Fundación Cultural CECIJEMA, Chichén Itzá, 1990; a Research Initiation Grant (1992) and an L.G.I.A. Subvention Grant (1994) from the University of Houston.

Guidebook to the Archaeology of Chichén Itzá

About This Book

This study concerns the complex stratigraphy of discourses, practices, struggles, contestations, texts, and events through which the Maya have been and are (re)invented as a "culture" and as a "civilization." This book guides the reader through the historical contexts of Yucatec regionalism and Mexican politics to see how the interplay between local Maya society, tourism, and anthropology has invented the modern ruins of the ancient city of Chichén Itzá, Yucatán. Through different essays on ("tours" of) the archeological restoration and the concomitant development of a tourist complex at Chichén and the nearby Maya town of Pisté, we see how a museum of Maya culture and civilization was created. This guidebook then maps how this Museum of Chichén Itzá operates as the embodiment of Maya cultures and as a key site for the continual reinvention of the Maya within certain textual guises, forms, and tropes. We then revisit this tourist attraction to map a field of power relations that regulates the localized practices of tourism as well as the discursive production of knowledge about the Maya that occurs in and is linked to Chichén Itzá. Thus, these tours of the Museum map out ethical and political dilemmas of the intervention of anthropology in the world of the Maya.

This historical ethnography of a tourist/anthropological site is a guidebook to the invention of Maya culture in the Museum of Chichén Itzá. As such, this ethnography, like a guidebook, is composed of different maps and tours that serve to describe and analyze the places and texts of Chichén Itzá and Pisté; the production and contestation of the landscapes through which these places have been settled; the everyday practices of tourists, Mayas, archeologists, ethnographers, guides, New Age spiritualists, and so on, that are situated and enacted in those specific sites; the spatialization and temporalization of

1

these practices; the production of knowledge in and through these everyday practices; the fieldwork practice that produced the knowledge of the museum as "data" for this ethnography; and a biography of the ethnographer/"tour guide" as a factor that shapes this research. This "Guidebook to the Archaeology of Chichén Itzá"[1] serves as a map of the complex issues and problems under investigation within the encompassing ethnographic guidebook. A guidebook is ultimately judged by what it offers in terms of the multiplicity of departures by which to visit a place; modern guidebooks, it would seem, have always and only been a sort of hypertext. Like a guidebook, then, this ethnography seeks to multiply the "departures" by which to analytically visit a problem. The immediate task in this legend, however, is to describe what this book is about in terms of maps and tours, as well as to argue how this, and all, ethnography can be comprehended as a genre/species of guidebook.

The relation between tours and maps, concepts borrowed from de Certeau, can be understood as the relation that Geertz called "culture" when he imagined cultures to be models of and for behavior. One example in his discussion was the idea of maps and blueprints: not only are maps models of and for tours (i.e., behavior), but tours are models of and for maps. This terminology identifies a relationship that is also isolated by Sahlins (1985) in his notions of structure and event, by Bourdieu (1977) in his concept of habitus, by Giddens (1984) in his theory of structuration, and also by Derrida (1978a) in his analysis of the hinge or free play between event and structure. For his part, de Certeau contributes to this theoretical and philosophical pursuit two concepts that are brilliantly rooted in and tooled for ethnographic tasks of description.

De Certeau (1984: 118–30) inspects stories of everyday life on the assumption that they are both stories about travel, that is, quotidian or extraordinary travel, and a practice of travel in both word and act. He notices that the spatial anchorage of the everyday world is narratively mapped out as everyday life is itself enacted as a tour occurring in and around the spatial anchors of this lived-in map. A tour is simply an organized series of acts of going, doing, seeing, saying, consuming, and exchanging in defined space. As a mode of knowledge, tours rely on these activities and on the partiality of individual subjectivities: tours exemplify subjective and intersubjective knowledge motivated and produced in experience as experience. Maps are models of totalized and totalizing knowledge based on the primacy or premise of an all-seeing, objectivist eye and a summary composite of multiple sources/experiences; as such, maps exemplify and are a critical tool of scientific knowledge since they are representations of the known that exhibit accumulated and objectified knowledge derived from individual tours, whether quotidian or scientific. In this sense, a museum is a complex map, a place, to be toured. The same holds for ethnographies. Maps correspond to strategies of power and places, whereas tours are composed of tactics oriented to the momentary use of space. As historical forms, techniques of narrative and action, and rhetorical figures, maps and tours are everywhere in evidence both in combination and as dominant tropes. For example, dialogical ethnographies would seem to be predominantly a kind of tour, that is, of a culture in the guise of a dialogical encounter; functionalist ethnographies, in contrast, are primarily maps of a cultural totality that chart out the subsystems and their interrelations (cf. Boon 1983: ch. 1–2).

Cultural anthropology, like tourism, makes use of combinations of these two narrative and rhetorical structures and techniques. Guidebooks are a mediation and composite of the two forms of knowledge. Derived from the multiple "goings," "doings," "seeings," and "sayings" of multiple subjects, guidebooks present a composite and summarized knowledge; but this map is dual since it also charts out the possibilities of future travel/tours as a heterologic and multiple itinerary in both tour and map modes. This is a "how to" kind of knowledge that charts the possibilities of individual, subjective experience as a "unique" species of the general structure and modes of travel experience. If the modern map of the world was the historical product and synthesis of multiple voyages of exploration, then the guidebook reverses the process: knowledge is already totalized and can thereby dictate and chart the truths already known, experienced, and located in their proper place. The use of both the tourist scriptures of guidebooks and the Holy Scriptures of medieval Europe had the objective of an individual rediscovery of truth. Yet the rediscovery of God's truth always already inscribed in the world approached the form of revelation that would lead to a spiritual unification with the divine (Campbell 1988; Clifford 1983); in tourism, the rediscovery is an individualizing experience of identity with civilization in opposition to the cultural other(s). These truths, known and revealed to the reader-traveler, contain their own moral imperatives; the guide describes where to go, what one ought to do and say, what to see and how to consume. In both senses, the tourist guidebook functions again like scriptures that reveal the already existent imperative truth of God's creation (de Certeau 1984: 131–39).

Ethnographies, then, are guidebooks that function to reveal a truth about a society. Such truths are always already there; they are *posited* as *there* hidden in the cultural reality that is to be explored and discovered by the authorial ethnographer. This is not a divine truth, but the profane truth, in general, of anthropological knowledge: the knowledge of otherness testifies not only to the existence of the Other, properly located in history, but to the truths of the given theoretical-analytical model that is deployed against the Other by the ethnographer according to the methodological rules of replication and reproduction of truths. Maps are constantly converted into tours just as tours slide and slip into maps. The guidebook, in the narrow sense of literary genre of touristic discourses, is a conventionalized form of that structure of reciprocal slippage between tours and maps; and thus it offers another name of this movement between structure and event. From this angle, guidebooks are indeed ethnographies and ethnographies are guidebooks. Further, like all other guides of and anthropological discourse about Chichén Itzá, this ethnography participates in the scriptural economy that is mapped out below in a series of tour(ist) essays. This guidebook is another artifact in the "archaeology" of the Museum of Maya Culture.

Getting There by History: Of Maya, Tourism, Anthropology

This work was conceived as a historical and ethnographic study of the Maya Indians of Pisté, Yucatán, in relation to the tourist complex of nearby Chichén Itzá. The result is an investigation of the relations of power and knowledge that are deployed in and regulate the production of knowledge of Maya culture and civilization at Chichén Itzá. The problem is to understand and explain the articulation between three different series of sociocultural entities, that is, Maya culture(s), anthropology, and tourism. Here, then, are the three legendary figures—Maya, tourist, and anthropologist—whose historical intercalation, complicities, appropriations, and differentiations are the subject of study.

Chichén Itzá proves to be a unique place to investigate this problem because of its being an important site in the long history of intensive interaction between Mayas and non-Mayas, specifically anglophone anthropologists and traveler-chroniclers of different types (Sullivan 1989). John L. Stephens, the U.S. diplomat to Yucatán and Central America in the mid-nineteenth century, "rediscovered," for the anglophone world, the Maya, both ancient and contemporary, with the publication of his travelogues, *Incidents of Travel in Yucatan* (1843; cf. 1841). In these texts, he cleared a field for both modern Mesoamerican studies and tourism in the Maya world: in conjunction with the illustrations, the narrative images formulated an enduring vision of Maya civilization for Western, specifically anglophone and Yucatec, imagination.

A critically important element in the power and effect of these texts is that they conjoined with the interests and motives of the intellectual and political movements then current in Yucatán. Campos García (1987, 1989) shows how Stephens's *Incidents of Travel* was incorporated into the agenda of Yucatec intellectuals, which sought the reformulation of the (Spanish-speaking world's) vision of the Maya in order to establish a cultural heritage or patrimony that would legitimize the goal of a politically independent Yucatán (Morales Valderrama 1987; Barrera Vásquez 1980). Led by Sierra O'Reilly, the Yucatecos turned to the Mayas just as the criollos of colonial central Mexico had turned to the Aztecs and appropriated this indigenous past in their legitimization of an independent Mexico (Lafaye 1974). Much like Texas, Yucatán had been an independent nation in the mid-nineteenth century and even sought to join the United States on several occasions. Thus, the Spanish-language studies of the Aztecs and the Maya have served nationalist interests, whether of the Mexican state or of Yucatec regionalism (Bernal 1980; Klor de Alva 1992; Campos García 1987).

At the turn of the century, Edward Thompson, Stephens's heir in politics and Maya studies, bought the Hacienda Chichén, which encompassed much of the ancient city, in order to conduct his studies of the Maya. In the course of his stay he became initiated as a Maya shaman-priest and fathered a family with a Yucatec woman (E. H. Thompson 1932; Willard 1926). Prominent among his anthropological endeavors was what some call the "exploration" and others the "pillaging" of the Sacred Cenote in search of the ritual offerings sacrificed in the waters of this large sinkhole (see Coggins and Shane 1984;

Ewing 1972; Ramírez Aznar 1990). With the rise of revolutionary Mexico on the embers of the Porfiriato, he became embroiled in a controversy with the Mexican government about his Chichén property and the antiquities he recovered there. As a result of the litigation, the ancient Maya city became split into two properties: the buildings and adjacent land were bought by a prominent Yucatec family and the remainder was appropriated as cultural patrimony of the new nation-state. During the court battles, however, Chichén became the target of a massive scientific intervention sponsored by U.S. and Mexican interests.

After nearly a decade of conducting both U.S. naval intelligence and archeological reconnaissance in Central America, Sylvanus G. Morley organized the Chichén Project in 1923, a long-term, multidisciplinary study of the Maya and Yucatán with his base camp located at the famous Hacienda Chichén. This research was arranged with the socialist governor of Yucatán, who granted permission for the research under the condition that the major part of the site be restored. This, it was thought, would be a monument to the ancient Maya and would stimulate the formation of Maya class consciousness and identity: Chichén Itzá would be a monument of and for, to borrow from Geertz, a revolutionary class coming into being. Climatological, geological, medical, historical, ethnographic, anthropometric, linguistic, and other studies were conducted in conjunction with the excavation and restoration of the monumental architecture of the central parts of the site.[2] Eighteen years later, the investment of hundreds of thousands of dollars by the Carnegie Institution of Washington and the Mexican government in these investigations had converted Yucatán into a scientific laboratory and the ancient city into a virtual factory of knowledge, the products of which formed the foundation of Maya studies and the local tourist industry. In short, the ancient Maya city became a modern ruin. Chichén Itzá was invented as a tourist attraction to showcase not only an "ethnic-class" identity, but the modern science of archeology (Kidder 1930; Sullivan 1989). Underlying the motivations of both socialist governor and archeologists was the explicit recognition that Chichén would be a monument of and for tourism.

From this synoptic history, it should be apparent that the relations between Maya societies, anthropology, tourism, and the politics of nations have great historical depth and complexity. The stereotypical question, which is asked in any social scientific or lay conversation, about tourism — "What is the impact of tourism," in this case, "*on* the people of Pisté and other nearby villages?" — is an inappropriate and inadequate line of investigation. It is not simply tourism that has shaped the communities of Pisté and Chichén, but anthropology. Moreover, tourism is not that which impacts, but is the desired culmination, result, and means of something else, here, of anthropology in relation to the politics of identity construed at regional, national, local, and international levels. The intervention of this discipline at a time of its professionalization was only in relation to yet other political and economic interests and processes of national and regional scope. In turn, the regional context reflects and expresses a history of regional nationalism and the socialist nationalism of the Mexican nation-state. The relevance of the problem of the "impact" of tourism dissolves under the complicated intertwining of different factors; that is, to focus on "tourist impact" is to forge an ahistorical study that misses key forces in the shaping of social reality. Implicit in the assumption of impact is a synchronic view, an ahistorical explanation, and the ability to isolate unilinear causes; furthermore, it assumes that the local Maya were and are passive objects whose summation equals an objectlike society that lacks internal dynamics, on the one hand, and that has a defined exterior surface that can be scratched or transformed by "external" factors in a moment's intrusion by Western institutions, on the other hand. The ethnographers' fear that their presence may alter the studied other is wrought from the same assumptions. Both the insidiously pompous concern of the field-worker and the question of tourist impact are paternalizing tactics that maintain the Other in a museum diorama, that is, in allochronic elsewhere as described by Fabian (1983). Both are generalized forms of violence that are epistemologically central to the making real of culture.

This problem of epistemological violence waged against the other/object of anthropological inquiry is a source of that heterogeneous movement that can be labeled dialogical anthropology. Despite the often extreme variations, points of contestation, and levels of operation between the different attempts to constitute dialogical tools, all, it seems to me, are in response to the challenge that Fabian so nicely phrased:

> If we can show that our theories of their societies are *our praxis* — [that is,] the way in which we produce and reproduce knowledge of the Other for our societies — we may... put anthropology

back on its feet. Renewed interest in the history of our discipline and disciplined inquiry into the history of confrontation between anthropology and its Other are therefore not escapes . . . [but] are practical and realistic. (Fabian 1983: 165)

However successful or unsuccessful dialogical approaches are, they "are ways of meeting the Other on the same ground, in the same Time" (ibid.). If this challenge is taken seriously in the study of the social history of Pisté in relation to Chichén Itzá, anthropology is necessarily a significant part of the object of study; that is, in order to study the everyday operations of tourism at an archeological site of Maya civilization, the history of anthropological discourses and practices must be critically evaluated, including the present ethnographic practice. If rigorously pursued, this means that I must continually deconstruct this text or textual representation even as I compose it, dismantle my own authority even as I forge an authorial voice, and question my analyses even as I set the argument. However unsettling this may be for the reader, the purpose is to bring anthropology, anthropologists, and their others (both the subjects of study and homologous institutions) under interrogation in the "same moment." It also aims to unsettle and dismantle our structured blindness to the ethical and political quandaries that undergird the anthropological intervention in the world.

If anthropological practices of the nineteenth and twentieth centuries invented Maya *culture and civilization,* then the tourist industry of the region must be understood as the "product" and extension of our science. Further, it has appropriated part of the scientific task of continually reinventing the Maya, but now in other forms and derivative contexts. But anthropology and tourism have not simply imposed "culture" onto Maya peoples as the frame through which they and we experience their sociality; rather, it should be added that the Maya have invented the anthropology (and tourism) of Yucatán. Maya participate in this invention as active agents or subjects in the guise of informants, workers, and "real culture-bearers," as objects engaging and contesting Western knowledge, as the pretext of investigation, and as ideal representations of alterity that are refashioned in Western imagination. The Maya are likewise active agents involved in the invention of the region's tourist industry. Not only through events as momentous as the Caste War,[3] whose side effect was the shaping of a future tourist landscape, or activities as mundane as the construction of the luxury resorts within that topography, the Maya have participated in the formation of the existing tourist geography and political landscape.

What I suggest, then, is that there is no "impact." There is absolutely no "tourist impact" to study. It is the wrong concept by which to adequately understand the complexities of tourism in Yucatán or elsewhere. Even the idea of studying tourist impact on ecology is an erroneous notion: as any environmentalist will explain, the natural world has an internal dynamism that has always already been in interaction with humans; thus, even nature itself is a historical agent and subject of complex historical change (cf. Haraway 1989), even though the environmentalist may not concede this conclusion. What this implies is that the discourse of "tourist impact" is itself an artifice of modern tourism and requires a deconstruction of its rhetorical forms, political ramifications and social bases. The idea of impact implicitly and explicitly argues that the society or culture being impacted is a static, ahistorical, agencyless, solidly bounded, noninteractive object, whether conceptualized (imagined by social scientists) as an organism, a system, a structure, or a text. To identify impact is to impose rigidified borders on an entity whose defining boundaries have always been violently contested not only in theoretical debates but in so-called real life. Historical perspective demonstrates that society—not even ecology!—was never an ahistorical, pure object that could be impacted; rather, "impact" consists of multiple reworkings and contestations of the ways collectivities imagine the contours of the social forms they inhabit.

The particular situation of Chichén and Pisté suggests that Maya society, anthropology, and tourism have become interwoven over a long history of interaction, collusion, mutual influence, and even opposition. These three "variables" form a single social fabric, however patchwork- and mosaic-like. But this statement is simply academic rhetoric since these "variables" are quite fluid, indefinable, and easily transpose into other rhetorically constructed "variables," such as regional politics, national economy, Yucatec regionalism, and international relations. In any case, it is clear that "anthropology" and "tourism" are glosses for a heterogeneous ensemble of practices, institutions, politics, econonomic processes, and so on, that operate at multiple levels and contexts, from the local, regional, and national to the international. Ultimately, the identification of variables is just a rhetorical device to fix domains of activities and events that necessarily interpenetrate and historically intercalate. In my case, "three variables" seemed to have the magical aura of scientific rigor required to attain funding.

Getting There by Theory: Of Imaginary Machines

Such an extension of the notion of a text beyond written material, and even beyond verbal is, though metaphorical, not, of course, novel.... But the idea remains theoretically undeveloped; and the more profound corollary, so far as anthropology is concerned, that cultural forms can be treated as texts ... has yet to be systematically exploited.
        Clifford Geertz, *The Interpretation of Cultures* (1973: 449)

More than twenty years later, the notion of culture as text seems to have run its course. This concept has been worked out, critiqued, rethought, extended, transformed, substituted by related models, left aside, and pushed into that zone of "exhausted" (or exhausting) assumptions that are inherited as part of the dowry of the theoretical tradition of the discipline. The notion, however, retains value not as the end point of analysis, but as one tool among a series by which to weave cultural analyses (e.g., Tedlock 1983). Boon (1977, 1983, 1989), for example, has indicated that culture is, indeed, a text and text a culture, if we understand those entities to be a result (side effect?) of or a momentary pause in what he has recently termed the "crisscrossing" of institutions, discourses, languages, translations, rituals, histories, hierarchies, biographies. This study takes this idea and casts it within an explicit rhetoric and problematic of power.

The dual thesis that "culture is text" and "text is culture" not only defines a unit or tool of analysis, but a problem, as well as an approach. Ethnographically, my concern is with the (re)invention of an Other, specifically, the "Maya," through the production of knowledge about this entity in (a range of) everyday practices within the tourist complex of Chichén Itzá and the dissemination of such knowledge in and through what I call the Museum of Maya Culture.

To pose this question, I borrow tools from well-known poststructuralist methods: my versions of archaeology, genealogy, and deconstruction are located within an analytics of discursive practice inspired by de Certeau. Given this panoply, my task is to (de)construct (what could be called) a *regime of writing*: the substitution of writing in Foucault's famous phrase opens, on the one hand, to the use of Derrida's idea of *arche-writing* to analyze tourism; on the other hand, the addition of the idea of writing in relation to truth and practice leads me to de Certeau's notion of a *scriptural economy* as the master trope by which to excavate the power/knowledge relations that inhabit Chichén Itzá and its Museum of Maya Culture. The scriptural economy (de Certeau 1984: 131–53), then, is an instance of the general regime of truth in which we are situated. But here it needs to be emphasized that this trope and the analytical tools and metaphors it marshals form what Adam Smith called an "imaginary machine"; that is, this model of the social world, like all scientific models, does not so much reflect the world as highlight, reshape, and rearrange worldly matter into pieces, called data, that fit the image of the model and thereby legitimate or "prove" the explanation. In other words, if the scriptural economy describes and explains the invention of Maya culture, it is because that object has been invented and imagined to fit the machinery of this imaginary model.

The genealogy of the Maya as culture begins in medieval cosmography, where the East and its marvels constituted a primary domain against which Europe was fabricated: the categorical ambivalences of this marvelous Elsewhere cleared a space — a blank page, as it were — in which the West, in its moment of wonder, inscribed its difference as presence, that is, as a positivity (Greenblatt 1991; Campbell 1988; Mason 1990). The explosion of the European cosmos by the Americas and its cannibals (see Hulme 1986) immediately stimulated the multiple efforts to reformulate a totalizing vision or topography of alterity, which was reassembled in the Enlightenment dream of the museum: this was a *place* envisioned as coincident with the systematic and true ordering of the exhaustive knowledge of the universe. The Museum of Natural History embodies this dream by institutionalizing in real architectonic space an "art" and "theater of memory" (cf. Yates 1966; Hooper-Greenhill 1992). It is this muse of a total history of nature constituted as a theater of knowledge that inhabits, I suggest, all museums. Having replaced the medieval *mappae mundi,* these Enlightenment cosmographies operate as testaments of and monuments to modernity. Chichén Itzá is one such museum, that is, locus of the strategic organization of knowledge and deployment of practices in which the multiple guises of the West are realized (made real) through the "mysterious" difference of a Maya otherness textualized and experienced as culture and civilization. In the Museum of Chichén, the marvels of the East live on in the Mystery of the Maya. And the mysterious Maya live on in Western imagination as a marvel of survival that is positioned as a puzzle whose decipherment divulges a moral of how and who of Western civilization can live on into the future.

In terms of this ethnography, this archaeology transcribes as a study of a place—specifically, the contemporary Yucatec Maya town of Pisté and the nearby ancient Maya city of Chichén Itzá, Mexico. This topos is composed, conceived, and analyzed as the articulation of multiple strata of phenomena. Briefly, I distinguish three layers in the stratigraphy that correspond to three sets of questions: What is the history of the political and economic processes that have constructed a landscape in which Chichén/Pisté are situated and that have intervened in this local context so as to structure, shape, and intercalate these two communities? How is the *Maya* invented as culture in the daily operations of the tourist sight/site and what is the epistemic strategy that governs this production of knowledge in these runes of modernity? What is the apparatus that orchestrates everyday touristic activities and that constitutes the place of Chichén/Pisté as a battlefield of ongoing struggles? These three strata—the historical mapping of a topography, the Museum of Maya Culture, the tourist apparatus—form the topos and object of this archaeological study, which aims at both the historical events that condition the possibility of *Maya culture* and the ongoing reinvention of such an entity. This text, then, just as the museum itself, is part of the scriptural economy that it seeks to describe. Thus, the analytical framework of the scriptural economy turns in two directions: this *ethnographic representation* points toward the production of *Maya* as a natural-technical object of knowledge (see Haraway 1989), but it also reflexively refers back to the discursive formation from which the trope of culture derives. In brief, the imagining of culture and the invention of national communities as coterminous with state apparatuses belong to the horizon of modernity.

The very semantic shift that Mesoamericanists and Mayanists will notice (and may protest) in the preceding indicates the problem under investigation. To what specific group of people in what geographic area and period of history do I refer with the term "Maya culture"?

Is it the Yucatecan Maya, Tzotzil, Quiché, Jacaltec, or another group of Maya people? Or am I lumping all these possibilities together and erroneously not using the word "civilization"? Who is it that identifies as the "bearer" of this—or any other—putative culture? In terms of self-identification, the term seems to have once been relatively less problematic. "Maya" or "Mayab" referred collectively to those people of northern Yucatán (the Xiu, the Itzá, and others) that organized their society, polity, history, landscape, and so forth on a calendrical system in which the *may* (Yucatec Maya for "hoof" as well as a period of approximately 260 *tuns* or years composed of 360 days) was the privileged unit for calculating time. Over the course of the last centuries, "Maya" then became an ascriptive term used to designate heterogeneous peoples and societies that nonetheless shared certain religious, historical, aesthetic, social, and linguistic forms in a geopolitical space called Mesoamerica. It seems that the category of "Maya culture" has become embodied with meanings and references—with a life all its own—that take the notion beyond any temporal, spatial, and social (i.e., ethnographic) anchorage. The surplus of referents or signifieds is exactly what is under interrogation. Of course, this surplus is one hinge on which Maya as a *civilization* is constituted. But this investigation must necessarily suspend designation of the Maya and resist the seduction to define who or what is Maya, since it is precisely my task to critique and contest how this has been done in anthropology and tourism relative to Yucatán. On the other hand, my operating assumption is that *Maya culture and civilization* (in contrast to whomever might be designated as the referent of the terms) are in the first case a function of a complicitous history of discursive practices in which Maya alterity has been appropriated for use in Western constructions of what it is to be "civilized" as measured against non-European-derived social forms. The analyses that follow presuppose that categories of Maya, Maya culture, and Maya civilization are not at all empty of meaning or reality, but that these are fundamentally contested terms that have no essential entity outside of the complex histories of sociopolitical struggles.

This does not mean that there are no Maya, even if no one or everyone were to identify themselves as such. Indeed, relative to the approximately six million Maya by ascription, there are substantially fewer who use this term as their primary self-identification. In Guatemala, indigenous people use other terms that refer to a combination of linguistic, town, or sociopolitical communities; however, there is a group of indigenous intellectuals who are forging a postcolonial Mayan identity that operates in the difficult space between Indian nationalism and pan-national Indianism (see C. Smith 1991; Warren n.d., 1992; Fabri 1994). In Mexico, indigenous people of Yucatán refer to themselves as Maya in the first instance (see Sosa 1985; Gossen 1986); in Chiapas, the primary identity is in reference to community (e.g., Zinacantan, Chamula, Cancuc), to linguistic group (e.g., Tzotzil, Tzeltal, Chol), and then to a cultural-ethnic group (Maya), although the Maya Zapatista movement may be altering this style of self-identification. In Pisté, indigenous locals refer to themselves as Mayas, Mayeros, Yucatecos, Mestizos, and Mexicans, depending, of course, on context. Ironically, there is another small group of people who identify themselves as Maya; these "racially" non-Indian, New Age spiritualists from Mexico and the United States are discussed in chapter 6.

Thus, to argue that Maya cultures are invented and continually reinvented does not mean that Maya cultures are not real or do not exist. "Cultures" are very real, but have become real: this category of Western thought emerged in the "anthropological" discourses of the nineteenth century and became progressively rooted in the material world as the totalizing frame of reference through which much or all social life is experienced and constituted. In other words, anthropology has invented culture because it has been foremost in using this category as the central idiom to think about and experience otherness. The other side of this coin is that through culture anthropology was invented, since the particular debates about and systematic practice of the term were what constituted a scientific community of disciplined practitioners that sought to fashion an object of knowledge from non-Western peoples:

> Since anthropology exists through the idea of culture this has become its overall idiom, a way of talking about, understanding, and dealing with things, and it is incidental to ask whether cultures exist [or to "whom" does it refer as its "culture-bearers"?]. They exist through the fact of their being invented and through the effectiveness of this invention. (Wagner 1981: 10)

On the one hand, the reality (what Wagner refers to as the "effectiveness") of this invention, that is, culture, cannot be attributed to the powers of anthropology alone. Indeed, the task of this ethnographic guidebook is to illustrate the multiple forces that intervene in the invention of Maya culture. On the other hand, the effectiveness of culture or the reality of invented cultures derives from its being what Haraway calls a "natural-technical object of knowledge." Indeed, the very notion of culture is precisely the theorization and concept of the border zone between human nature and human artifice, between facts given and facts manipulated. And, if we return to classical rhetoric, as we do in chapter 3, it can be discovered that invention is also a notion defined by the ambivalences of what is given by nature and what is manipulated by human artifice. Thus, Wagner is very clearly correct when he states that "invention is indeed the most crucial aspect of our understanding of other cultures [and] the way in which all cultures operate. Invention *is* culture" (Wagner 1981: 35). And, culture is invention, which brings us back to the culture is text thesis.

Geertz's famous formulation held that culture is an assemblage (that is, text) of (performative and prescriptive) texts. Criticism against this interpretivist tradition in anthropology placed attention on that which was held to be the culture of a people or community. Various (often conflicting) camps showed that culture was a text, not because it referred to what a collectivity "out there" feels, thinks, or does, but because the interpreter had constructed, that is, invented, "the culture" — an ideal order and imaginary totality in the various guises of "system," "structure," "logic," "habitus," or "mode of production" — as a text in the representational form of a text, which otherwise is known as an "ethnography." Fabian (1983) has argued that this trick is not monopolized by interpretive-symbolic anthropologists, but that it has been essential to the way the discipline has constructed its object of study. In other words, the ethnographer, by employing the available theoretical models and "applying" them to the "data," authored an imaginary object in the form of a text, which was somehow to refer beyond the author-ethnographer and outside the text. Instead, anthropology has authored a house of mirrors or museum and modern cosmography that interpolates the modern Self in the various guises of displayed and textualized alterity.

Anthropologists, however, *are not the only ones* who reify the lifeways of a community, collectively refer to these as "culture," or situate that object in an atemporal elsewhere of the Other. The concept of "culture" has become generalized in the everyday thought and languages of people throughout the world, from the caves of the Tasaday to the Sorbonne. Curiously, at a moment when many trained experts of the discipline have either jettisoned the concept as unworkable or make great (rhetorical) efforts to have it refer to "really real" people (as Geertz might say) that are located somewhere "on the ground" or "outside of (an ethnographic) text," those people the world over who have not been attuned to these rarefied debates assume the reality of the concept and its referent: culture in general and their or another's specific culture is manifested everywhere in objectified gestures, styles, habits, and so on. Tourism has made this fact undeniable, but it is my proposition that anthropology (in the widest historical sense) is complicit with this commoditization of culture because it provided certain conditions of possibility by which culture(s) became objective and a true or effective dimension of reality.

In 1956 Linton (1988: 199–202) distinguished between the "real culture pattern" and the "culture construct pattern." On the one hand, culture is produced and reinvented in the everyday life of a group of people as the everyday logic, forms, and practice of activities. This is the *real* culture, the living and lived-in phenomenon, a *pattern* so intrinsic that it is mostly invisible to untrained reflection. Granting theoretical variation, this is the subject that anthropologists investigate, that is, obviate as text in various approximations whose representations, needless to say, fail to attain the plenitude of the real pattern. On the other hand, culture is produced and reproduced as these reified representations and totalizing tropes of a group, people, or community. This is "the culture of" a people, that *pattern constructed* and objectified in discourse as an imaginary embodiment of an imaginary collectivity. This constructed totality has numerous synonyms and objectifications (e.g., tradition, myth, high society, customs, ethnicity, tribe) to which it refers and makes sense, but whose reference either dissolves under pressure or comes to rest on material objects as the manifestation of "the culture." In this second sense, culture is always an argument, that is, the effect of a rhetoric and a will to authenticate. From this perspective, culture is indeed a text and a discourse. But, is there in fact a *real culture pattern* outside of its own constructed pattern? Even if a "native" or even all of the native bearers of a *real culture* were to articulate a unified vision of what their culture was, is this not a construct, that is, a textualized representation of itself? A culture-text and text-culture? The real pattern, the "lived-in culture," is an abstraction *embodied* in its own representation of an imagined world and not in the supposedly real world outside of *its* reification. Here too the autoethnographized real culture is also a simulacrum in Baudrillard's sense. The "lived-in" culture and the "culture of" melt into air in the moment they are cast into the die of objects and texts. Culture and its two subspecies, then, are always already *simulacra* and live a *hyperreal* existence. In other words, all cultures are imaginary machines: real representations of identities, communities, and belongings forged in contestations of power, but whereas the anthropologist used to believe in the unconstructed reality of cultures, now we tend to understand them as social constructs; and, whereas the culture-bearers lived their reality oblivious to the existence of their or any culture, now their lived experience tends to be framed by and constituted through this notion. Both cultures are really real no less so for being hyperreal and imagined understanding of experience.

The imaginary separation of these two "cultures," then, snaps shut, but is forever opened again in and by the discourse of culture, whether in the mode of theoretical practice or quotidian struggles. This *oscillation* between two series of relationships (the world and its text[s], on the one hand, and the world entexted, on the other), opens up questions that have only begun to be posed with the profound multiplication and extension of the new technologies of communication. The issue is not simply the relationship between a "lived in" culture (a culture "lived in" or imprisoned in an ethnographic locality) and the general circulation of these as "the culture of" within globalizing systems of communication and representation. Anecdotes abound that tell of informants reading to an ethnographer from the classic ethnography of their "culture" in response to questions of "native tradition" or of the revitalization of a culture according to the ethnographic or even touristic canon. It is important not to deny either the authenticity of the "culture" in such encounters or the reality of such inventions: the modernist denigration and the postmodernist exaltation of such incestuous mirroring of identities obscures what, it seems to me, is a human trait. After all, the knowledge embodied in those culture-texts is effected through a dialogical process of reflective intercalation, however effaced and power-laden or politically imbalanced. This suggests that the idea of dialogue should be discarded for *complicity* and *collusion,* since the inscription of cultures always already occurs within an interconnected social field crisscrossed by multiple series of economic, social, political, historical, and *even* cultural vectors. Granting the variations among theories, it seems to me that anthropology has understood this, even if we have often ignored or forgotten this critical supposition in practice.

What seems to me to be at stake is the problem of culture, not only as a practical issue but as a theoretical/critical question in relation to modernity: What is the invention of culture (in the register of truth) and the culture of invention (as an economy and technology of the real)? The analytical problem, then, concerns the circuits by which *culture travels.* How are cultures transported, imported, exported, deported, reported across topoi (i.e., the textual spaces of discourse and ethnographic localities)? As it—culture, that is—traverses landscapes of imagination, how does culture constitute topographies, by which I mean the multiply contested differentiation and mapping of space into sociogeographic units of identity, belonging, and power? Also, how do topographies shape and constitute culture(s) as these imaginary communities traverse space? These are issues in an *economy of culture,* which I refer to as a scriptural economy, to borrow from de Certeau.

Getting There by Autobiography: Of Travel

What is the genealogy of this questioning of culture? If this archaeology of Chichén Itzá is a kind of biography of that topos, then my personal and intellectual autobiography can offer insights as to why this study is composed as it is. Fables of the Self traverse risky grounds, so I limit my discussion to the personal factors and motivations that led me to insert myself into the discipline of culture. This turn to anthropology has disciplined both my Self and my pursuit of that elusive form of identity and community. But also, I have sought to carve out a politico-ethical position within the disciplinary institution and norms from which to "do anthropology" that resonates with that Self and that continues to be shaped in part by the field.

Alienation, in a loose sense, or the distantiations, fragmentation, dispersal, multiplicities, and hybridities within identity, is often a general, if variable, experience and phenomenon. Gloria Anzaldúa's work is one highly touted elaboration of this crisscrossing of identities constituted on borders. In my case—and not unlike my siblings and perhaps relocated peoples generally—I have felt caught between multiple sociocultural identities or "primordial" roots of cultural-national belonging; these three were the one I was born and socialized into (the midwestern United States) and those to which my parents and ancestors belong (the mestizo/ladino worlds of Mexico and Guatemala).[4] A tension between a double not-belonging between three possible homelands or heritages, on reflection, seems always to have haunted me, all the more so as I was growing up. My name had always been emblematic of my social dislocation and fragmentation of identity: my consciousness of not-belonging was inscribed in my name, an unpronounceable oddity in English and often as perplexing in Spanish, given that it is a word "corrupted" from a term indigenous to Mesoamerica, specifically of the Nahuatl language of central Mexico.

In 1970, and with some awareness, I had invested a family trip to Mexico and Guatemala with the special meaning of finding a homogeneous origin and secure identity; I hoped for an antidote to my estrangement of growing up in a predominantly white supremacist southern Indiana town. However, I was unprepared for this encounter that induced a "culture shock" typically attributed to tourists. MacCannell (1976) has argued that "to be a tourist" is the structure of being and alienation that the modern world capitalist system provides. But it was not until twelve years later that I definitively identified "tourist" as the sign of the betweenness and not-belongingness that I had been experiencing in both North and Central America. This is perhaps a playful way of saying what some postcolonialists have more famously said about their double differentiation from "home." As for me, although the "tourist shock" is over, I am still a tourist and, I argue in this text, anthropology is still tourism, if in rarefied form. From this angle I can agree with Lévi-Strauss, who says that anthropology is indeed a vocation.

I had expected Guatemala to be a full, happy, and homogeneous presence to which I could belong; after all, this is the plot of ethnic/racial identities coming to terms with its otherness in the context of U.S. marginalization ever since Alex Haley or Rudolfo Anaya (1976). Instead of unproblematic roots, I found the mosaic of culture, class, race, and nations to be a shock. My familial, cultural, and national belongings were fractured and contradictory: there was not a singular origin, but I could trace myself back to (fabulate my identity through) different heritages. My solution was to dedicate myself to the fully archaeological task of discovering the original and authentic Maya, as a sublimated resolution. The grandeur of the ancient Maya—as opposed to the legendary black and bloody roots of Hispanic America—appealed as a compensation for an uprooted life in Indiana.[5] I became a Maya hobbyist, reading archeology and translations of native books from the colonial period. In a typical kind of maneuver, I used anthropology and the study of the Maya as the means to invent myself by creating a structure of identity through the recovery of a lost social history of civilization. The Maya provided me with an (imaginary) "primordial origin" (see Geertz 1973: 255–69), not to create an ethnic essence, but to first stabilize a strategic sense of or security in self. A parallel is evident in the Chicano invention of a Chicano identity, community, and national consciousness through the use of the myth of Aztlán (e.g., Anaya 1976; Anaya and Lomelí 1989; Klor de Alva 1986, 1992), or more recently la Malinche and related figures (Anzaldúa 1987). Notice, however, that this strategy that I chose—was able to choose—as an individual derived from my specific socioeconomic location in a "borderland" of the United States, a space between the myriad institutions dedicated to inscribing the boundaries and identities of self in racial-ethnic terms.

In the course of my readings on the Maya and Guatemala, I became disconcerted by the lack of any indisputable "truth" about the Maya. Further reading on the Aztecs and Mexico only increased my confusion. In particular, I was concerned about the status of the "Mexican influence" on the Maya, which seemed to me to be made out to be too monolithic and too imperialistic (see Schele and Miller 1986: 18–33; Schele and Freidel 1990: ch. 9; Sabloff and Andrews 1986; Carmack 1981). This was disturbing at another and contradictory level. This pre-Columbian "influence" of anthropological lore seemed to be a symbolic repetition or displaced allegory of contemporary U.S. intervention in Guatemala, which, from my family upbringing, I understood as brutal neocolonialism. Contemporary Mexico also stood in the position of an oppressor or threat to Guatemala, just as ancient Mexicans did to the ancient Maya. I wanted to hear a different story, the muted yet true story about Guatemala and the Maya. I wanted an unfiltered, pure voice, yet I sensed that the speech of the carved stones, glyphs, and living Maya was the result, and could only be the result, of various forms of ventriloquism.

My whole intellectual and psychological problem really hinged on the status of the feathered serpent, since this symbol seemed to embody these relationships. This, I felt, was the key to understanding the pure root of Maya religion and thus societies, and therefore also Mesoamerican polities and history in general. I did not know what to do with the different Mesoamerican myths and histories of the personages and deities referred to as Quetzalcoatl, Kukulcan, Gugumatz, and Topiltzin.[6] There were two sources of confusion and contradiction in the knowledge. On the one hand, different ancient Mesoamerican peoples each had their own narratives, symbology, and even name for a personage-deity that had particular import for their different societies and cultures. On top of these variations of mythical history and cosmology, different students of Mesoamerica added their interpretations, which, it seemed, indiscriminately mixed and matched variants from across all the different Mesoamerican groups and time periods. I wanted cultural and historical analyses to identify the particular meanings for particular people instead of boiling or melting everything down into a Mesoamerican culture or a pan-Maya civilization. The reality that I had encountered resounded with the multiplicity and the heterogeneity of Maya and central Mexican peoples. It seemed that reality, not just meaning, was plural. In this way, the crisis of personal identity slid into an intellectual problem, a posture that allowed a distance between the ideological and sensory poles of experience[7] that paralleled the distance between—and my distance from—Indiana (where I lived) and Guatemala/Mexico (where I longed to be rooted).

Another intellectual-experiential question concerned the name of the national bird of Guatemala, which is the quetzal. It seemed to me that it should not be a Nahuatl word, this being the language of central Mexican peoples, but that it should be a word from a highland Maya language. This loan word indicated, according to the scientific mythology of "influence," the political and cultural hegemony of Mexican peoples over Maya. I took this question in relation to my name (Quetzil) as emblematic of my situation: until just recently I thought that the spelling was changed from the letter "a" to "i" as a way to make a "feminine" name "masculine" in Spanish. Actually, my father, with a wisdom only parents have, thought to change the spelling of the name my mother gave me as a way to lessen the stigma of an ethnic-indigenous name and to assist in my assimilation to the Anglo world.[8] In other words, my name itself indicated an identity not only in and across national borders (Guatemala/Mexico), but also complicated cultural, racial, and gender borders. Conceivably, I could affiliate my identity to three nations: Guatemala (as homeland of my parents), the United States (as birth and socialization place), and Mexico (because of the linguistic affiliation of my name and various Mexican relatives from both sides of the family). Yet in the Anglo context in which I lived, the fact of my name reduced these theoretical options to one: not Anglo. While my great-uncle and other Guatemalan relatives always called me "Quetzal," one of my brothers would always mimic the Indiana Hoosier pronunciation of my name, which rhymed with "pretzel." I was caught between two extreme mispronunciations or two paths of self-invention: one path flattered because of imaginary associations with the symbols of a glorious antiquity in which I might cast my identity of self; the other path was a double parody, from the mouth of the dominant culture — "kwetzel" assimilated my otherness as it defaced the rival alterity from which "quetzal" derives and, from the mouth of my brother, "pretzel" condemned both that imposed assimilation and the artifice of any appropriated authenticity. From the view of 1992 and the debates on the Five Hundred Years, this double binding simulates the general quandaries of being "American," which we can take to mean an identity forged in hybridization, and to be from "America," which we can take to name a topography of hybridity forged in a specific history of cultural conflagrations and collisions.

This is an ironic otherness and marginality, because the word is equally unknown as a personal name in Guatemala and Mexico as it is in the United States. Eventually I learned to feel better about this double lack of roots in either Guatemalan or American culture, since I could invent my self-identity through selective reappropriation. I understood my name as a hieroglyphic allegory for my Self. It presented a series of appropriations, substitutions, misbelongings, dislocations, dominations, and duplicities through which I could understand the legends of Quetzalcoatl and the relations between Mayas and Toltecs (or pre-Columbian Mexicans), Guatemala and Mexico, Yucatán and central Mexico, Guatemala and the United States, Hispanic and Anglo America as powerful allegories of community formation and contestations.

If "tourism" is one mode of alienation in the modern world (MacCannell 1976), then it seemed that anthropology was its opposite and antidote, given the latter's goals of cross-cultural communication and its method of creating "community" in the field. Inflated with Lévi-

Strauss's (1978) parodic proclamations about the vocation of anthropology,[9] I gave myself this self-assuring yet troublesome label when in 1982 I traveled the "Ruta Maya" (cf. National Geographic Society 1989): it was reassuring because I could pretend to differentiate myself from the denigrated savagery of the tourist (and even the mythical figure of the traveler from which the ethnographic ideal derives); it was troublesome because I recognized both the colonizing ramifications of anthropology and the self-deluding arrogance of this legitimated mode of intervention in people's lives. Being a gringo with the ability to speak Spanish and having both Mexican and Guatemalan parentage did not assuage my anxiety; rather, it was this that problematized my positioning in these borderlands. Caught in this crisscrossing, it was my experiences at Chichén Itzá and Palenque that planted the seeds for this study.

At the famous "Maya-Bell Campground" adjacent to the archeological zone of Palenque, I watched would-be "Yaquis" from California and Texas being led by a "Yaqui shaman" from, I suspected, Mexico City, in search of hallucinogenic mushrooms in the cow pastures of Chiapas. Under the influence of the texts of Carlos Castañeda, these tourists would "go native" in search of an authentic self as they sat in restored temples of the ancient Maya ruins. This curious technology of self struck a chord. It appeared to me to be ludicrous and insulting, all the more so since it was so obviously homologous with (if distinct from) my own form of self-invention through the practice of anthropology. I decided that I would study tourists, Mayas, and anthropologists because it would be a kind of shifted if not inverted, and metaphoric, autobiographical study. In any case, it is common enough that anthropology is about the reflections of the Self that are constructed through the refinement of practices by which an Other is choreographed into a position adequate for mirroring.

I imagined this still-to-be-designed study to take place at Chichén Itzá, the most famous Maya city of Quetzalcoatl and Kukulcan. I acclimatized perfectly to what seemed like the ideal combination of the storming humidity of Indiana summers and the suffocating aridity of the winters in my father's Zacapa, Guatemala: it offered a viable "home" in contrast to the war-scorched mountains of Guatemala. My attention was focused on the Yucatec Maya, who seemed not to have received much ethnographic attention since Redfield, at least in comparison to the highland Maya. Perhaps this can be attributed to the lack of colorful dress and customs, that is, to the *seeming* "accultur-ation" of these Maya. I found this problem of ethnicity, plural cultural identity hidden by assimilation, to be a stimulating question because it reflected upon my personal situation of "being without culture" (see Rosaldo 1989). Sociologically, Chichén was clearly a privileged site because of the economic importance that the regional tourist in-dustry invested in it. Further, this archeological site is of critical, if not seminal, importance in the history of Maya and Mesoamerican studies within anthropology. I chose not to study these issues at Tikal, in northern Guatemala, because of the civil war that Guatemala had been undergoing. In 1983, when I began designing my graduate pro-gram, the most intense period of military repression and genocide had just ended with the substitution of the Ríos Montt regime by an-other. My choice was to investigate Maya culture in relation to both tourism and anthropology (as opposed to questions of violence) in the wider contexts of politics and economy (as opposed to contexts of self and the cultural construction of self.)[10]

This decision to focus not on issues of selfhood, but on institu-tions and the construction of social realities, involved my decision to leave archeology, which had enticed me since my first visit to Tikal. From archeology I moved into cultural anthropology to study arche-ology as a social institution that, in turn, eventuated in this step to-ward an *archaeology* of anthropology.[11] The incidents during this, my fourth, trip through the world of the Maya, which culminated in an archeological field school in Honduras, ended with two questions.

First, I was troubled by the fact that although it might seem to be a neutral act to study eighth- or thirteenth-century Maya, such activ-ity carries profound political effects and implications. Some of these effects stem directly from the ideological assumptions that undergird the research paradigm and interpretive models, whereas others derive from secondary manipulations by persons other than the researcher. Once the archeologist produces an interpretation of the past, that knowledge has a political life of its own.[12] What drove this point home was having heard a Maya guide debunk, in a scientific manner, an Atlantis origin for the inhabitants of Palenque in favor of diffusion from ancient astronauts. Second, I was concerned that anthropology, or at least my own work as an anthropologist, should have a certain ethic of engagement with the people with whom research is con-ducted. Ethnography allows the great opportunity for one to produce knowledge about society that can have practical value and importance, if not direct use, for the people with whom one engages. How can ethnography produce knowledge according to its disciplinary canons that enables our collaborators to appropriate this knowledge and use it in ways that can empower them?

From the inception of research, this question was a motivating issue. In this, Foucault's notion of the *specific intellectual* became my framework by which to pursue a style of fieldwork that would be politically and ethically engaged. Within anthropology, related concepts have been developed. For example, Rosaldo's idea of "researcher positioning" offers tangible if partial examples of how Foucault's notion might get expressed in the realm of fieldwork. Rosaldo, through a critique of the objectivist and value-free style of social science that derives from Weber, argues that the individual subjectivities and subjective experiences of investigators are critical for the production of more comprehensive understandings of cultural situations and communities. Although this formulation does not explicitly elaborate on the political and ethical dimension of ethnographic engagement, Myers's (1988) notion of "applied hermeneutics" does. In this ethical style of research, the ethnographer consciously intervenes with an explicit (versus implicit) political and practical agenda in the politics of knowledge in which a cultural community is situated. The difference between this and a paternalist ethic typical of colonialist anthropology — see, for example, Clifford's (1983) discussion of Griaule — is that the goal here would be to reveal the political dimensions of and the power relations underlying the representations of culture that are produced in and through ethnographic practices. Still, as this study exemplifies, there are definite contradictions and problems that emerge if ethnography is formulated as the tactical struggles of knowledge (cf. Haraway's discussion of feminist primatology/primatologists [1989: 278–383]). One significant problem for such an ethical style inheres in the institutionalized construct of research itself and the logic of the ethics that generally guides modernist anthropology.

Six elements of a generic ethic in ethnography can be isolated for comment so as to identify a problem that continually reemerges in this study. The first three rules of thumb are essential to the scientific ethos in general. First, the investigator must create scientific neutrality through the elimination of political postures both in the formulation and in the conduct of research. Second, the investigator must practice *nonintervention* in the "culture" of the community being studied. Third, objectivity in research and analysis must be practiced so as to prevent the biases associated with various forms of subjectivity. I refer to these rules as commodity ethics or an *ethics of the "doughnut hole."* This uncanny pastry is a presence defined as absence and an absence materialized as presence: thus, the presence or intervention of the anthropologist effaces or distantiates itself from the subject of study so as to be formally defined as an absence (one or another form of objectivity), which in turn allows for the objectification of this "absence" as a positive presence not only as moral/political neutrality, but as the necessary conditions for disclosing, transmitting, and scientifically producing truth. Just as doughnut holes come in different flavors, so does the ethical style of fieldwork; that is, different theoretical frameworks provide distinct mechanisms and procedures to guide fieldwork so as to maintain these three criteria of engagement. Thus, in the production of a commodity that can be bought and sold in the scientific market of knowledge, neutrality, nonintervention, and objectivity combine to conceal, if not obfuscate, other dimensions of research, specifically gift exchange.

The second set of rules are particular to those sciences that deal with human subjects; they are also of recent date and somewhat specific to the United States: I suspect that the three stem from a federal law that requires a *contract* between ethnographer and informant in which written consent of subjects ironically establishes a *gift relation* as the formal mode of interaction in the economy of ethnographic production. Thus, the fourth ethic by rule of the contract is the dissimulation or concealment of the identities of the informants, who individually and collectively embody the entire community of research, which must therefore also remain officially anonymous, at least in "classic norms" ethnography (Rosaldo 1989). Fifth, the contract legally establishes the voluntary exchange of information by the subject as a reciprocated service exercised without coercion or threat of danger and regardless of any wages that may or may not be paid. Thus, the document of informed consent actually conceals mechanisms of commodity production: in the transmission of knowledge the producer, the scene, and the act of production are effaced. In this erasure knowledge becomes constituted in a three-staged modality in which knowledge passes from a "raw good" to "collected data" amenable to a manufacturing process (scientific analysis) that results in the finished commodity form of a book or article. Concomitantly, the informant is literally de-authorized by giving up the right of ownership and authorship at the same time that the ethnographer becomes authorized as "owner" of "data" that can be transformed into a commodity, which then transforms the owner into a new status, that is, author. Thus, the legal document reasserts the ethical value of *nonimpact* on both individual and collectivity through regulated intervention that is construed as even/equal reciprocity, but that actually provides key procedures to commoditization of knowledge.

The sixth rule, then, is a more profoundly experienced norm that relates to the gift production of knowledge: the ethnographer is obliged to make a communal return prestation in addition to any monies or services paid in kind to individual informants. This gift, stereotypically a copy of the completed manuscript or book, is given symbolically "to the whole community" in a gesture that is intrinsically a philanthropic attempt to have the manufactured knowledge of the Western world circulated and distributed within the community for the collective good. In other words, the very notion of intervention is ethically bifurcated: it is not supposed to generate any *immediate* social, cultural, or individual change through *direct* contact; yet, at the same time, the presupposition and desire of all anthropological intervention is that a lasting and *positive aftereffect* of contact is to occur in the long or short run. Of course, the criteria by which the "goodness" of the aftereffect is judged derives from Western norms and contexts. Deeply embedded within the anthropological endeavor is the powerful ethic that some "good" should, must, result from our intervention in the lives of those we study. This is indeed the case whether the ethnographer in question has a colonialist mentality in which the anthropology is understood to contribute to the general civilizing of the native; whether the anthropology is "applied research" in which sociocultural change is explicitly pursued according to a model of assimilating modernity without "negative impact"; or even whether anthropologists simply have a general and altruistic sympathy for those with whom they do research such that they desire nonspecific "good" things to stem from the anthropological intervention. It is for this reason that the task of "studying up" immediately raised *ethical issues regarding the alliance of the ethnographer.*

The general ethics of anthropology, or strictly speaking ethnography, is inherently paradoxical, as is the notion and pastry of a doughnut hole. Our ethics is also *scandalous* in that we dream of a simultaneous presence and absence in the place of the Other. The solution that I explore here, which I am led to by biographical factors as well as theoretical considerations already discussed, is based on the ideas of complicity, collusion, and reciprocal appropriation for different, if not antagonistic, purposes. If, in fact, the invention of cultures, that is, the self-fashioning of individual and collective identities, occurs through a thick history of complicity and antagonistic collusion, then reworking ethics from such an appreciation would force a dramatic rethinking of the ethnographic endeavor, particularly our construction of research.

If the biography of the Self is constituted at the intersection of the institutions that impinge on it and if the goal of such narratives is to define that space of identity as an ethical substance, then my turn to the ethics of the institutions through which my Self has become defined is a projection and an extension of the autobiographical matter. Indeed, the ethnography that follows is the continuation of my autobiography, but metamorphosed and complicit within this guidebook to anthropology and tourism at Chichén Itzá. Thus, I am compelled to recite, but also resituate, Montaigne's apologia in the preface to his *Essays* (1958): "Thus, dear Reader, myself am the groundwork of my book. It is then no reason why thou shouldest employ thy time about so frivolous and vain a Subject. Therefore farewell [to the Self]."

Travel Itinerary

This "Guidebook to the Archaeology of Chichén Itzá" has sought to multiply the points of departure from which to understand the complex stratigraphy of practices, discourses, texts, events, and histories that comprise the places of Pisté and Chichén. Thus, the text abides by a logic that resists linear argumentation. The organization of material seeks to accentuate not the continuity, but the junction (conjunction, disjunction) of data and analyses at the same time as it assembles alternative angles for understanding the myriad ways in which worlds juxtapose, overlap, intersect, resonate, conjoin as they simultaneously fissure, dislocate, conflict, disrupt, and erupt. Concerned with these multiple constructions and practices of a place, this historical ethnography is divided into two parts that correspond to two perspectives on the problem of space. "Part I: The Scriptural

Economy" inspects a variety of primarily discursive and textual ways in which a space has come to be differentiated, invested with meaning, bounded, ordered — that is, become particular places — and linked up into wider spatial networks or topographies. "Part II: War and Its Topography" is concerned with the temporalities and spatial orchestration of practices that constitute the spaces of Chichén and Pisté as tourist attractions, as well as the power relations that inhabit and the politics that erupts from this apparatus. If the perspective on space in Part I is discourse and text, the lens from which space is studied in Part II is practice. The artifice of the analytical separation of these two angles is manifested by the sort of stereovision that results from their "combination," as evident in the middle chapters (5–6) where the analyses seek to describe the articulations of discourse and practice, text and vision, time and space. As these visual metaphors suggest, there are blind spots or exclusions built into the layout of the book, but the rationale of the study has been to pursue connections that are otherwise obscured by more standard categories of analysis.

Part I is in turn divided into two sections. The first section, "Inscriptions of Travel in Yucatán," is composed of two chapters that are concerned with locating Pisté and Chichén Itzá in two travel-oriented discourses, anthropology and tourism. Chapter 1 considers the history of the anthropological intervention on Yucatec Maya communities, specifically Pisté and Chan Kom, in order to reveal a scandalous dimension of the way in which these communities and Maya culture have been envisioned. Chapter 2 explores not so much the history of the intervention of tourism in Pisté but that which is commonly assumed to be the result of the way tourism has become a part of the community. Together these two chapters deconstruct the question of tourist impact and problematize anthropological intervention. These two analyses, then, direct us toward the complicity and collusion of anthropology and tourism with community, region, nation.

Chapters 3–6 compose the second section of Part I, which concerns Chichén Itzá as "The Museum of Maya Culture and Civilization." Chapter 3 presents a genealogy of the modern museum as a trope and strategy of knowledge; a framework for analyzing the museum economy of discourse and images is elaborated so as to inspect Chichén as a museum of Maya culture. Chapter 4 provides a genealogy of the vision and discourse of mystery through which the Maya have been invented in Western, specifically, anglophone, understanding. Chapter 5 is an analysis of the construction of the tourist sight and site via a mapping of the tour of the Museum of Chichén Itzá. Chapter 6 is an analytical description of the government-sponsored tourist ritual of the spring equinox phenomenon of light and shadow that occurs at Chichén. While chapters 3–4 bring into focus the complex stratigraphy of discourses that constitute Chichén, chapters 5–6 put into tension and motion those layers by inspecting the practice or performance of certain of those discourses. Together the chapters of this section inspect the (re)invention of the Maya as culture and civilization in the archeological and tourist site of Chichén Itzá.

Part II is an ethnographic exploration of different relations and kinds of power (authority-control, discipline, resistance, struggle, politics) that constitute Chichén and Pisté as places of tourism. Chapter 7 maps the spatial and temporal orchestration of the touristic practices that make up the tourist apparatus. Chapter 8 analyzes a grid of power/knowledge in which both the practice of selling handicrafts at Chichén and my own ethnographic practice of fieldwork were situated. Chapter 9, "Departures from the Museum," concludes the book by revisiting the intersecting problems of ethics, complicity, collusion, appropriation, espionage, and invention. It begins with the story of an event of a role "reversal" in which the ethnographer became an informant for the political leaders of the town, but that in the telling becomes a story of "town politics," which necessarily includes stories of telling ethnographic stories. In this way, the narrative of this scriptural economy of Maya culture at Chichén Itzá returns "home" to the question of culture and texts but departs, perhaps, from the Museum that has its home there between texts and cultures.

Part I

The Scriptural Economy

Inscriptions of Travel in Yucatán

1 / The Progress That Chose a Village

Measuring Zero-Degree Culture and Other Scandals

GILLIN: *The question of values is very fundamental. As long as the old values appear more rewarding they'll stick with them. We used to think that all you have to do is to expose people to education and they'll change their ways . . .*

TAX: *Dr. Redfield has a new book in press concerning a revisit to Chan Kom. I would like to ask Villa how different is Chan Kom from other villages that didn't choose progress?*

VILLA: *That point has been taken into consideration by Redfield. Chan Kom is very similar to other villages of the region, but the historical process—the appearance of new leaders, the proximity to Chichén Itzá where the Americans were working—all those accidental factors gave them an opportunity to change their point of view.*

From the concluding discussion in Sol Tax, ed.,
Heritage of Conquest (1952: 275)

The cumulative effect of these contacts was to catalyze the development of an awareness on the part of the Kayapo of the potential political value of their "culture" in their relations with the alien society by which they found themselves surrounded. . . . to publish or otherwise communicate publicly about Kayapo culture was to become, willy-nilly, a part of both the political and cultural

dimension about which one was attempting to speak as an
anthropologist.... One not only becomes part of the process one is
trying to record, but directly affects it in numerous ways, some
intended and some not.... In the process, we had become
coparticipants in a project of resisting, representing and
rethinking, and both their "culture" and my "theory" had
become, in some measure, our joint product.

Terence Turner, "Representing, Resisting, Rethinking"
(1991: 301–12)

The Coke Theory of Culture

Anthropologists have always been concerned about their intervention in the object of study. On the one hand, there has been a "fieldwork" approach to the formulation of this problem, which has yielded
responses ranging from methodological formulas for scientific neutrality and objectivity to critical-reflexive postures such as dialogical
anthropology (e.g., Tedlock 1983; Crapanzano 1980) and "researcher
positioning" (Rosaldo 1989). On the other hand, there has been an
"institutional" approach concerned with the history of anthropology's
intervention in the world as a *translocal* or *transnational* enterprise
working in an uneasy complicity with (neo)colonialisms, nation building, and even postcolonial projects. The urgent question, it seems, concerns how to integrate both dimensions of the problem of anthropological intervention into a single investigation.

One way to begin to reconceive research *from its inception* is to
take into account that the imaginary object called *culture* exists not
so much out there in communities localized in geometric space but in
the textual productions (or discursive space) of anthropological practices. By "culture" I refer to a generalized mode of imagining the identities and differences of communities. Our ancestral (proto-)anthropol-
ogists were the "original," but now no longer the only, culture-bearers.
In their travels, they carried this concept, category, construct of "culture" around the globe and planted it so that all the communities of
the world (of whatever dimension) have begun, or could begin (however unevenly and differently), to envision reality and imagine their
own or other communities *in terms of this filter,* the always already-
contested concept of culture. From this angle, our ethnographic object of study would be the transculturation of culture (cf. Pratt 1992),
which would include the intervention of anthropology in the world.

Coca-Cola offers a way to "theorize" this approach to research:[1] in the capitalist metropolis, two goods (the coca leaf and cola nut) are imported from the periphery; they are transformed into a product which is then — after an astounding marketing success in the core that definitively associates the concept of the object to its metropolitan site of production and consumption — exported back to the periphery, where it variously supplants indigenous beverages in contexts ranging from recreation to ritual. As a result, the natives in the peripheries of capitalism have incorporated Coke into their life as part of their reality (often) without any contradiction in their own eyes, just as they have done with countless other Western artifacts and ideas, such as metal utensils, radio, TV, the modern nation, and so on. Because Coke has become a synecdoche for a specific culture, this situation is often nostalgically or angrily lamented by some culture-bearers of the metropolitan core as cultural rape or loss in the encounter with an inevitably advancing modernity. The analogy is not that Coke is Culture, but that Culture is like Coke: And what is missing from this imperialist nostalgia (Rosaldo 1989) that screams "cultural rape" when Bushmen drink Coke is a historical analysis of the complex apparatuses that produce, market, distribute, disseminate, consume both Coke and its concept. Thus, we might analyze the invention of Culture whether locally or globally as if it were Coca-Cola: a heterogeneous entity constituted in and through the contested crisscrossing of borrowings across boundaries forged by such transcultural traffic. The place to begin such an analysis is our own fundamental involvement in those inventions and the complicity of our scientific practices of culture with other agents, not just including the subjects with whom we conduct research, but the various economic, political, and social agents that also intervene in the life of both anthropology and its *subject* communities.

A Tale of Three "Cities": On the Topography of Culture

Redfield was hired part-time from the University of Chicago by the Carnegie Institution of Washington (CIW) to direct a comparative study of Yucatec society. At the time, the CIW was already conducting archeological, historical, epigraphic, medical, botanical, anthropometric, genetic, and climatological studies of Yucatán under the supervision of

Sylvanus G. Morley. Since the central focus of these endeavors was the excavation and restoration of the pre-Columbian city of Chichén Itzá, they were known collectively as the Chichén Project (1924–41). The nearby cattle Hacienda of Chichén was restored as the project headquarters. Redfield's study, which became a long-term collaborative project with four researchers, was actually adjunct to the Chichén Project, which, strictly speaking, referred to the archeological studies, as was the research of Morris Steggerda (1941).[2] Steggerda, a physical anthropologist employed by the Genetics Department of the Carnegie, made the town of Pisté his home base and focal point for his diverse studies.[3] Thus, the ethnographic mapping of cultures that the Carnegie sponsored included five communities (Mérida, Dzitas, Chan Kom, Tusik, and Pisté) and was based in a sixth, the archeological city of Chichén. Yet the Redfieldian topography excludes (in significant ways to be demonstrated) the last two places in order to base itself on only the first four, which were said to form a single continuum of Yucatec Maya culture-civilization (R. Redfield 1941: 338).

This brilliant synthesis of then current sociological theories of modernity depended on three procedures: first, expand the ideal types of Primitive versus Civilized to four, not disjunct but interpenetrating, types whose interrelations were said to be like that of a spectrum; second, both localize the ideal sets of relations that comprise each type and spatialize the spectrum of relations that link the four into a series; third, ascribe to the spatial order between the four types a historical value and status of a totality. In this way a space between Primitive and Civilized was opened yet immediately truncated by the weight of emphasis given to the Folk-Urban "poles" of the Continuum and then closed by subsuming the *continuum* of culture-communities into a singular, totalizing trope of the "Folk Culture of Yucatán," which happens to be embodied in Chan Kom. My task, then, is to analyze this Redfieldian topography anchored in that village and its ethnographic representation by retelling the story of Chan Kom in relation to the two other places, Pisté and Chichén, that were left out of or peculiarly put into the Continuum of Maya Culture.

In so telling this tale of three topoi, I aim first to reveal certain rhetorical operations in Redfield's discourse that led him to imagine and construct Maya Culture in a very specific way. Second, I disclose aspects of the political economy of these rhetorical-discursive procedures through an understanding of why and how Redfield localized

Maya Culture in one geographic-social space and not another. The story concerns the anthropological intervention in Chan Kom, Chichén, and Pisté: on the one hand, it is about the scandalous way in which this intervention was portrayed as a positive event; on the other hand, it is about the censorship of the scandal that this intervention had no or a negative impact.

Postmodern Scandal: Pisté as Antiprogress

Many villages in Yucatán have some industry like hammock or hat making, the manufacture of pottery, baskets, candles, or chocolate mixers, but Pisté has none of these *(emphasis added).*
　　　　　Morris Steggerda, *Maya Indians of Yucatan* (1941: 21)

Although generations of anthropologists, Maya scholars, and sociologists can easily picture Chan Kom in their minds, few have any knowledge or image of a town some twenty kilometers to the north, called not Chichén Itzá, but Pisté, which is two kilometers to the west of those modern ruins of an ancient city. Pisté, unlike its neighbor, has not entered into anthropological memory and its imagination of culture. Indeed, it has been erased from the ethnographic *mappae mundi* through which anthropology plots its contesting classifications of sociocultural forms to their proper space-time localities via the operations of theory building. Why is Pisté absent from the anthropological museum of cultures? My argument is that "it" represents zero-degree culture and, thus, a scandal.

Those who have an interest in nineteenth-century travel writing about Yucatán may recall brief passages that describe Pisté just before the author-traveler spots the stones of the Castillo or Pyramid of Kukulcan towering above the scrub forest. For example, Le Plongeon, Charnay, Maudslay, Maler all note briefly the desolation and destruction that the Caste War inscribed on and in this town before offering extended descriptions of the ruins of Chichén. Morris Steggerda contributes to this discourse of depreciation:

> During my observations in the village, I have never seen any evidence of hobbies among the men. No one carves stone or wood; no one is interested in learning to play a musical instrument well; no one has made a collection of archeological material.... No one seems to feel the need of such diversion. It is true that the women care for flowers under all the adverse conditions of Yu-

catan, and they do embroider tablecloths and dresses purely for enjoyment. But there is an apparent lack of interest, as far as the men are concerned, in most forms of recreation. There is no tendency among them to form clubs or organizations. Piste has no band, although it might well have one considering its size. There are no outstanding leaders, priests, ministers, or doctors. In 1933 there were two yerbateros [herbalists], but accusations of witchcraft forced them to leave the town. The town is not particularly religious, being indifferent to Catholic and Protestant and, apparently, to the remnants of its own Indian beliefs. (Steggerda 1941: 24–25)

This is a description not of a *community*, but of a *town*, a geographic and geometric space in which the social life of the inhabitants is so apathetic and minimal that there is hardly a trace of that magical attraction and cohesion that makes human groups a society and that distinguishes such hordes from the world of nature. Depicted here is an indifference that defines the community as deviant for it constitutes a collective *anomie* and *anarchy*: the listless apathy is a threat to the orderly imposition of control, norms, regulation. This town, to apply MacCannell's phrase (1992) toward an opposing objective, is an "empty meeting ground," a space filled with a nonsocial order and an order of nonsocialness.[4] "This town"—that is, its *ethnographic depiction*—is in deep contrast to that "Village That Chose Progress" (R. Redfield 1950): here, an "apparent lack of interest" is so pervasive and imposing it constitutes an "indifference" not only to European religions, but to the "remnants of its own Indian beliefs." As Steggerda tells us, even those technicians of the sacred and natural world, that is, the herbalists and other ritual specialists, were run out of town—run out, we are led to suspect, by indifference. In Steggerda's view, it seems that not only has the Folk Tradition disintegrated but so has the sticky spirit, or in Spanish, the *ánimo*, of the social bond.

Yet, Steggerda himself contradicts his *assessment* of indifference, which is stated with the authority of a fact as if validated by science. In contrast, his published monograph and unpublished field notes document a bustling economy comprised of a surprising ethnic heterogeneity, religious pluralism, and complex class relations in a situation of economic boom that at the time was unmatched in this microregion and many rural areas of Yucatán. This was a community composed not simply of subsistence farmers, but of proletariats, seasonal semiproletariats, small-sized ranchers, petty entrepreneurs and merchants, recently freed hacienda debt-peons, chauffeurs, hotel workers, lower-level "managers." Local economy was based on small mixed cattle and maize production for export, transportation service of goods and tourists, several cantinas, cooperatives and general stores, a match factory, two hotels, road construction, gasoline sales, corn-grinding mills, and chicle trade. At the center of this booming economy was the factory of knowledge at Chichén Itzá operated by the Mexican government and the Carnegie Institution of Washington. It was this factory that made Pisté a significant site of migration as Chinese-Korean, Lebanese, ex-hacienda Maya, central Mexicans, and Yucatec mestizos migrated to (and sometimes through) Pisté in search of employment or commerce. The establishment of the first Evangelical Protestant sects in a sister hamlet six kilometers to the north of Pisté was also not a fortuitous occurrence. Although Steggerda said little about local politics per se, his unpublished descriptions of family and personal histories suggest that this economic diversity and ethnic-religious pluralism correlated to a local situation that was in high relief from most of the Yucatec countryside: here the ethnographic record indicates an absence of the power mongering or bosshood known as *caciquismo,* which is exemplified by the leadership of the famous Don Eustaquio Ceme, a leadership Redfield dressed up as "progressive." To phrase it differently, the diverse bases of economic power made it difficult or impossible for a single political faction or family to become hegemonic at the local level; or, at least, there were no overt struggles over the structures of authority, as was actually the situation in Chan Kom. Is it not reasonable to suspect, then, that the general prosperity of the community provoked a disinterest in politics or political action per se and, in turn, that it was this *dis*interest that blinded Steggerda and that he translated into an anarchic and apathetic *in*difference of the collectivity?[5]

Steggerda's description is peculiar, and it is this peculiarity that points toward a secret comparison not so much with Chan Kom as with Redfield's description of Chan Kom. The traits he listed presuppose that Pisté is categorically not a village type of culture-community—whether idealized as Redfieldian Folk or as a peasantry struggling against proletarianization—but an urbanized modern type of collectivity. Indeed, hindsight shows that Pisté was as economically and ideologically significant as the nearby Dzitas (Redfield's ideal-type "town" community). How surprising, then, to discover that Pisté was only a village of between three hundred and 450 inhabitants.[6] Thus, despite the greater socioeconomic importance of Pisté as a modern center of a microregion, it did not even have the requisite population size necessary to become an independent *municipio libre* according to the 1917 Revolutionary Constitution, as did Chan Kom (see Castañeda 1991: ch. 2). Furthermore, despite this economic vitality, Pisté could not be understood as a village (such as Chan Kom), yet it could not be considered a city/urban form of life, what with there being no clubs, no bands, no hobbies, no leaders, no recreation, no artisanry, and no collections of pre-Columbian artifacts. Some of these traits that Steggerda lists, such as the last, are in explicit contrast to what R. Redfield has identified for Chan Kom (1932); but still other diagnostic traits of urban modernity are also missing (alienation, anomie, fragmentation, individualism, conflict, enlightenment). Elsewhere, Steggerda notes the presence of dances, sports, bullfights, and other collective rituals of sacred and social life that characterize rural as distinct from urban life. Nonetheless, if Pisté is not an Urban-Modern Culture, it is also not a community of Folk Culture. The sign of Indifference again marks the Pistéleños as anomalous: is not this indifference an individual and collective "alienation," "apathy," or "anomie" from Indian vestiges *and* Christian church disciplines? Even so, we are led to believe that this is neither an urban situation nor a modern condition of culture. Thus, this Indifference may have the status or value of apathy, anomie, anarchy, alienation, but it is not those modern forms of culture. Pisté, then, is anomalous and deviant: here is a non-Folk folk that is also non-Modern modern; neither vestige nor new and "not hybrid," Pisté is a nonculture community, a noncommunity culture.

Can we not call this town *postmodern*? In a categorical sense it is *post*modern since it—like all communities we have discovered—wreaks havoc on the ever-pervasive *modern* discourse of culture that was so brilliantly formulated by Redfield. Might a different modern theory accommodate the commonly uncommon difference of Pisté? Perhaps, but then Pisté is not a Tepoztlán, that is, it was never a privileged topos of culture or of the anthropological discourse that maps "cultures" into their proper space-time dioramas. Pisté, like hundreds of other villages, including Chan Kom itself, could have been used as a privileged example of how and why Redfield's Folk-Urban Continuum was too simple, misleading, historically naive, and so on. Instead, Pisté is erased from anthropological memory. Why? Because it was and is still today a scandal of many dimensions. I shall call this scandal that I suggest Pisté embodies, and thus refer to Pisté as well, by the term "postmodern." Here, then, is the first scandal of the many mapped in this book: in my critique of how anthropological discourse "imposed" a classification on the "community"?/"culture"?/"town"? of Pisté, there is no alternative but to impose on this entity another metaphor for a mode of life that is also necessarily embedded in a value-laden theory and discursive formation. Because my task in this and later chapters is to point out the ironies and complicities by which "Pisté" is imagined as a social form, I am here stuck with ironically reproducing in form what I critique in substance. Thus, Pisté is postmodern in that it scandalously escapes modernist discourse of culture in a very specific way: it presents a difference (social, collective, cultural, theoretical) that must be understood in relation to the possible ways of assimilating its distinction to theoretical forms.

Pisté is not a Tepoztlán: Why did not Steggerda use Pisté as the foil to Redfield's theoretical edifice? Is the difference of Pisté (which is being isolated in this text) a difference that was located in Pisté or was it a facet of Steggerda's *way of seeing*, that is, of his social-scientific perception? It seems clear by reading Steggerda's ethnography and field notes that the socialness of Pisté is unrecognizable and imperceptible to "its" ethnographer: Steggerda cannot seem to fathom the social bond or agency of Maya individuals. But is this an inadequacy on his part? Is it *he* that cannot perceive the moral integrity and political wholeness of the town, that *we*, his readers now, are always already predisposed to posit as existing? In other words, is Steggerda, unlike the anthropology-bearers of his day and today, so *scientific* (or sociocentric) that he does not believe in what Herbert (1991: 1–28) identifies as the *superstition of culture* and therefore cannot "see" the ghostly coherence that animates and integrates the collectivity of *inhabitants*? Certainly, the title of his ethnography, *Maya Indians of Yucatan*, exposes the fact that the phenomenon constructed as his object of study—which with irony might be read like a postmodern list of arbitrarily selected topics that were all quantitatively investigated—was not imagined as a "culture," a "community," a "case study," a "society," an "ethnic group," but rather as a class or category of humans known as a "race." When Steggerda did imagine the Maya *sociologically,* his view was so marked by a kind of Christian diffusionism that he speculated that the Maya were so docile and dull-witted as individuals and as a race as to be incapable of historical agency in general and particularly with regard to their achievements as a civilization; he theorized that these achievements were initiated and directed by superior outsiders who formed the "mind" of the Maya "body." This type of "theory" was completely unacceptable to the scholarly directorship of the Carnegie's Division of Historical Research. Alfred V. Kidder, who responded to this idea in a personal letter written to Steggerda, stated that this "opinion" was "wet all over" and most likely ensured its censorship from the Carnegie publication.[7] However much Steggerda's *individual* opinion was blinded, the difference of Pisté, whether "indifference" or booming economy, was also blinding to those such as Redfield (as we shall see) who did have the proper *modernist* "superstitions" of culture. Pisté embodies the negative spaces between and the exclusions of Redfield's discursive construction of culture in the form of a Folk community embodied by Chan Kom.

The indifference of Pisté is its *deviance,* a difference that resists assimilation, comprehension, and categorization by the anthropological imagination. Pisté embodies a deviance (non-Folk folk, non-Modern modern) that can only be localized *betwixt* nature and culture and *between* the ideal types of culture as theorized in modernist typologies of social forms: this is an *anticommunity community* that stands scandalously outside, beyond, and against modern discourses of culture. In this sense Pisté is *post*modern, that is, a topos of *postmodernity,* because its difference is undomesticable: it is neither a culture "with culture" nor a culture "without culture" (Rosaldo 1989), but—according to *my* theoretical machinery—a zero-degree culture. Ironically, my use of the term *postmodern* is obviously a truncated and even *erroneous* version of all the polemics that this term has come to signal; and, therefore, it is also scandalous. Postmodernity, as I am arguing about culture, is like beauty, narrated landscapes, culture, and the emperor's new clothes; that is, they are such in the eye/I of the beholders (cf. Pratt 1992).

The *spatialization* of *zero-degree* culture (in Pisté and elsewhere) is the underbelly and girding of an apparatus of knowledge through which culture is territorialized in Yucatán, that is, through which the topography of Yucatán is inscribed, practiced, and imagined as a system of cultural sites (and citations). Just as Chaos enables Order (see Taussig 1987: 209–20) and Nature supplements Culture, zero-degree culture is for us here the figure of a rhetorical operation that constitutes a notion and modern discourse of "culture."[8] Consider the strategic role of anarchy within the theory of culture composed by Mathew Arnold (cf. Williams 1983; Herbert 1991). The function of *desire unbound,* that is, of *unbridled desire* and *freedom* that results in anarchy, anomie, and deviance, is overwritten and occupied, in the modernist theorization of Mesoamerica, by the rhetorical operations of "acculturation," "ladinoization," and "culture change" as loss (e.g., Tax 1952: ch. 2, 3, 9–14). Anarchy is the *moment* of *loss* itself, that is, the *temporality* of shifting/shifted identity and disciplinary control that creates a space or gap in the grid of theory through which the object of study falls beyond and outside the web of knowledge. Neither Indian nor ladino, neither authentic nor acculturated, having neither culture of Civilization nor Culture of Folk, the Indian-not-Indian embodies a zero-degree culture that originates and propitiates the discourse of culture in a scandal that is endlessly erased, concealed, retraced.

"Progress" Revisited: A Mysterious Cultivation

Robert Redfield continues to cast a deep shadow on Yucatán. His sociology of modernity and popular understandings of Indianness seem to still inform and ignite the imagination through which Yucatec Maya culture and the Yucatec landscape are known. This is evident when an internationally renowned scholar chooses — in the fifth edition of a famous introductory book on the Maya written for both lay and academic readers (Coe 1993) — to represent the Yucatec Maya with a discussion of Chan Kom as depicted in 1934 by Redfield and Villa Rojas. As if the passage of sixty years had not altered either Maya societies or anthropological understanding of them, *the ethnographic representation of Chan Kom* stands in the place of Yucatán as the quintessential Yucatec Maya culture.

Let us return to that ethnographic topos to see how the authority of this representation of exemplary ideal is constructed. The book opens with a description of the ecological zones of Yucatán under the label of "Gradients of Civilization" and takes the reader directly to Chan Kom, which lies in the geographic middle of this not yet *continuum-gradient* and is

> neither large nor small; but in respect to the effects of the recent outside stimulus and in the disposition deliberately to welcome these changes and to modernize the community, Chan Kom is the extreme deviate. Other villages in the area assist their school-teacher and evince an interest in reform and in new public works, but none so much as has Chan Kom in the three or four years preceding and during the period of these observations. During this period it has been distinguished among its neighbors for industry, sobriety and internal harmony. (Redfield and Villa Rojas 1934: 4)

Passing over the putative industry, sobriety, and harmony for which this village is distinguished, we might ask, how is it that this supposedly "deviate" community becomes, not simply typical, but the exemplar of Yucatec Maya culture? The ethnographic depiction of Chan Kom construes it as fitting the ideal model of a Folk Society whose deviation from the normal and typical village is its relation to reform and modernity. Is it that Chan Kom becomes more like other Yucatec villages (i.e., stops "modernizing"), or is it that other communities, which came to be studied in terms of this issue, therefore became like Chan Kom? Are they now also reforming and modernizing, which makes them all atypically typical and Chan Kom the most typically atypical? It should be noticed that sixteen years before Redfield conducts his "restudy" of Chan Kom in which he discovers that this "village chose progress" (Redfield 1950), the community was already being framed as progressive and modernizing. Thus, it needs to be asked how exactly this Folk Culture of Chan Kom and its Progress are constructed: What are the scriptural (textual and rhetorical) procedures by which a place is constructed as the proper habitat for a community that is also produced as the proper Culture of a Folk such as the Maya of Chan Kom?

Our task is parasitic—to "see" how Progress and thus Culture and its Folk version were localized in one place and not another—and repeats that of Redfield and Villa Rojas. As if in response to the questions I have just posed to Redfield and Villa Rojas but that remain a shadow dialogue in their text between the excerpt just quoted and their next sentence, they tell us on page 6 of the famous ethnography that an "explanation of the fact that Chan Kom has, *more than any other Maya village in the region* defined 'progress' for itself lies in a complex of circumstances that can be only *imperfectly* understood" (Redfield and Villa Rojas 1934: 6; emphasis added). Why imperfectly? What is this blind spot, this anthropological scotoma, that conceals the critical operations by which culture is constructed as an ideal form, embodied in a community, localized in a privileged place, and spatialized in a system of topoi?

In the corpus of the sociological study of Yucatán that Redfield orchestrated, Pisté—as in the colonial Maya *Books of Chilam Balam*—is alluded to, but without a direct reference to the community: unnamed as a culture-community and not discussed in the text (except in the brief historical section that situates the places of this native landscape), Pisté secretly organizes a *contrast* unlike the explicit culture *comparisons* with Mérida (the City), Dzitas (the Town), Tusik (the Tribal Village), Chan Kom (the Peasant Village with a Folk Culture) (see R. Redfield 1941). Why is Pisté *not* a part of the *comparative study*? A first guess might suggest that since Pisté "is" Morris Steggerda's "village," Redfield did not want to "steal" his colleague's data, which was, strictly speaking, not part of the *sociological research project* within the Carnegie's Chichén Project. However, this does not really explain why he could not have discussed Steggerda's sociological findings as he did Villa Rojas's or that of Asael Hansen, who conducted research on Mérida. Certainly, there may have been a personal difference that matched the intellectual-scholarly divergence, but the only conscious rationale that would eliminate *comparative discussion* of Pisté (or any other Yucatec community) would be the forbidding rigor of methodological, controlled, and scientific comparison of ideal social scientific types.[9] Yet, how could some attention to Pisté not slip into the text? How could Redfield's insightful sociological curiosity have been blinded to or by Pisté?[10] Although the renowned blindness and insight of his sociology are discussed by others, it still needs to be asked: Why the absence of Pisté? Why avoid a village that smacks of the "culturelessness" of Redfield's modernity and that is located smack-dab between his ideal points of the Town (Dzitas) and the Village (Chan Kom) but that traverses and spins off his Continuum: it is *matter out of place*, a pollution and danger to a (fragile, indeed) theoretical edifice.

Out of place, but Pisté is still in the text: How does this thriving *anti*community become inscribed within the Redfieldian topography of Maya culture, but erased from the Continuum? That Chan Kom "defined progress *for itself*" tells us that other *unnamed* communities, such as Pisté, did not. Thus, the text traces simultaneously the specter of an *anti*progress as it recontextualizes how Chan Kom was constructed as a village that "chose progress." Three "circumstances" are given for why Chan Kom was chosen among all the possible villages to study, and thus constitute the "imperfect" explanation: "One of these circumstances is certainly the unusual sympathy and guidance the people have had from certain of their schoolteachers, especially from the junior author of this monograph [i.e., Alfonso Villa Rojas]" (Redfield and Villa Rojas 1934: 6).

The identification of the *junior* author is a recognition of the *authors,* not simply schoolteachers, as a "circumstance." By association, the senior author is simultaneously implied and recognized, but then immediately erased and forgotten as a factor. Reading further, we find that in the ethnographic text Redfield hides his presence in Chan Kom as author, as sociological authority, *as circumstance of progress.* Not only does this duplicitous presence/absence work to construct the aura of objectivity and neutrality for the "collection" and "dissemination" of ethnographic knowledge, but this structural opposition of scientific ethics also grounds the discursive shaping of the object to be known: pointing to one but not both authors insinuates but then erases the *textual production* of "progress" and of the "Chan Kom" that "defined" a progress "for itself." After all, what do authors, especially anthropological ones, do? They write. They write the "culture construct pattern" or the text of the culture, that is, the Culture as Text, which is here *defined* as progressive. And, as they write the Culture-Text into the (form of) ethnography, they simultaneously erase the named presence of one of the authors so as to construct an authorial legitimacy planted on the traces of a fieldwork presence (Villa Rojas) in oscillation with an absence (Redfield) that provides the necessary distance for a *scientific* and *objective* description. The insinuation or trace of the textual production of the "definition" of progress is then confirmed as it is sidestepped and effaced in the next line:

> Another [second circumstance] is the particular attention given the village by Americans at Chichén Itzá, where the Carnegie Institution maintains its center for archeological work. [Given Redfield's status as a sociologist, he again elides his presence in this

factory of knowledge.] Contacts with *the* Americans at Chichén began to be significant through the distribution of medicines and medical advice from the clinic [which are so deeply associated with modernity and modernism] extended to the visits of scientific investigators in the village [who are cited in a footnote, but which again excludes the senior author]. A third circumstance is, probably, the chance occurrence in the village of Maya [here referring to the truly extraordinary Don Eustaquio Ceme] with unusual gifts of leadership and temperamental disposition to *enterprise*. The presence of Villa, the teacher, drew the Americans at Chichén to Chan Kom; on the other hand, Villa's contacts with these Americans increased and partly shaped his interest in the village where he worked. Villa's advice and help supported the leadership native in the village. (Ibid.; emphasis added)

Three circumstances are identified: the junior author, the Americans but primarily the American medical staff at Chichén (i.e., the now folkloric Nurse Miss MacKay who is cited in the acknowledgment), and the "native leadership" of Don Eustaquio Ceme. What are the dynamics of these factors? The maestro Villa Rojas, again, not Redfield, becomes identified as the key: the explanation positions Villa Rojas as the primary mechanism—call him the "culture-broker"—in this event of cultural transmission construed as a "diffusion of progress." Contact between the three circumstances channels "progress" through a synaptic network that constitutes its diffusion, but is itself constituted through a kind of natural or magical attraction: "The presence of Villa, the teacher, drew the Americans at Chichén to Chan Kom."[11] Thus, the "external" intervention of two circumstances is dissimulated and naturalized: the presence of Americans at Chichén is narrated as unsurprisingly "natural" and coincidental. Given their deep association with modernity, "Americans" typically travel and sojourn in places other than their U.S. home for a variety of economic and scientific purposes; by the same token, the teacher, sent from the Mexican metropolis by the new revolutionary government to educate the rural masses, is at "home" in the rural village-as-classroom. In contrast, the Maya are localized to the space of the "community" that Redfield is at pains to isolate and demarcate through a series of scriptural procedures of which this is one.[12] It might be said that the villagers of Chan Kom are "chained" to the ethnographic scene of investigation through scientific description.[13]

Notice that it is not the Maya themselves of Chan Kom that drew the attention of the Americans to Chan Kom, but the *teacher*: here, the magical attraction and vehicle of diffusion is the identity relation (like to like) embodied in education, which, in turn, roots these agents to the locality of contact as if they were natural or organic extensions of the Yucatec landscape.

This rooting and naturalization is important because it implicitly construes and shapes the Progress not as an "impact" on the Folk community *caused* by external forces, but as a local, *internal* event of change construed as a conscious, rational, and natural development chosen by the villagers themselves. "The reforms have not been imposed upon the community from outside; they have arisen out of the conviction of the village leaders and have been put into effect by the efforts of the people themselves" (Redfield and Villa Rojas 1934: 4). Neither were "the Maya of Chan Kom attracted to the Americans" nor were "the Americans attracted to the Maya of Chan Kom." This relation, then, is already inscribed in the nineteenth-century division of labor between ethnologist (Redfield) and ethnographer (Villa Rojas): the schoolteacher is cast as the key culture-broker, who is already planted in the field site that attracts the attention of the Americans. This contagious attraction then causes an increased contact with the presupposed superior "teachings" of the metropolitan *other,* which in turn causes an increased interest in the "village classroom field lab." Consequently, Villa advised and supported the "leadership native" *in* the community, which is also a tactical phrase: neither "native leaders" nor "native leadership," the selected pronominal phrase implicitly emphasizes the presence of communal leadership versus individual leaders. Further, the word choice fabricates the idea in the reader's mind that the leadership is organic, natural, and rooted in consensus versus political imposition: "No considerable opposition to this leadership has appeared; the inhabitants have, on the whole, supported the reform policy" (ibid.). Thus, all the circumstances turn out to be aboriginal and in *this* sense organic; but, as the Redfieldian interpretation argues later in this book and in Villa Rojas's ethnography, this is not an organic leadership in the sense theorized by Durkheim. The Maya Folk are said to be without internal differentiations that constitute classes or castes: Chan Kom leadership, then, in Durkheim's phrase, is a *mechanical solidarity* based on ethnic homogeneity, economic likeness, and political sameness. The native leadership, then, is supported and advised by the schoolteacher: the leadership learns the superior ways of the modern world outside its boundaries. The unusually gifted leadership is able to learn, to cultivate the associations, the contacts, with the other two—not agents, but—"circumstances" of progress.

This elaborate circuitry that explains the defining of progress by Chan Kom is depicted as an organic and natural *cultivation of education*. It forms an ethnographic fable that complements the more legendary allegory narrated later by Lévi-Strauss in "The Writing Lesson."[14] There Lévi-Strauss philosophizes on the invention of writing when a tribal "chief" imitates the ethnographer's note taking as a way to (presumably) augment his power. The chief is later sacked by his band of Nambikwara for his presumptuous use of the "totalitarian" and "Western" means of alphabetic violence that marks civilization. In other words, the Primitive reject, resist, block the diffusion of the cultivated traits of Culture. On the one hand, the Chan Kom story has a certain parallel: already among the leaders of Chan Kom is a literate man who in a way conducts himself as the Nambikwara chief; however, as the primary informant of the researchers, he does not merely imitate ethnographic writing, but writes his autobiography for inclusion as appendix within the original, unabridged ethnography.[15] This life document then becomes the evidence for Redfield and Villa Rojas to narrate a different story, a fable of how Chan Kom embraces the seeds of culture, that is, education itself, and how the villagers cultivate *themselves* as a Folk, that is, "define progress for themselves."

It needs be underscored that underlying this fable is a relation of identity between culture and education that is mediated by progress: progress *is* the cultivation of education-culture. Here, then, is a trace of a logic that is associated with Mathew Arnold and others: culture is cultivation/education (cf. Williams 1983: 110–29) and thus already embodies the notion of progress. In other words, the folk of Chan Kom are found to have had a community, but more significantly this is also already "Culture-Progress" in which progress (cultivation) implied culture (education) and vice versa. That these Folk were "found to have" Culture-Progress is what distinguished this ideal type of social form from both the Primitive and the Civilized-modern because it combined elements from both; as well it distinguished this specific community from the neighboring villages—among which is Pisté.

Or, it might be said that this contrast is what puts into high relief the progress of Chan Kom, which is precisely its qualification as a culture in the modernist sense of the term. It is also ultimately what constitutes the attraction between "the Americans"—meaning Redfield—and the village: education (teaching the folk community) and science (learning from the folk through research on them) are the two poles of this magnetism. Redfield's genius for synthesis allows him, on the one hand, to then *spatialize* the ideal types into the theory of Folk-Urban Continuum and, on the other hand, to narrate the ethnographic particulars as a fable of progress in both the 1934 and 1950 texts: The Chan Kom "leaders have determined upon a program of improvement and progress and have manifested a strong disposition to take advantage of the missionary educational efforts of the government and of the advice and assistance of the occasional American or Yucatecan visitor" (Redfield and Villa Rojas 1934: 4).

What are these reforms exactly? "The principal of these reforms involves matters of public hygiene [*sic*] and construction of new and more modern public and private buildings, and support of the school" (ibid.: 6). How were these reforms put into practice?

> Villa's advice and help supported the leadership native in the village. And the traditional Maya institution of *fagina* [that exploitative system of tribute used by colonial Maya elite to maintain the stratification and integrity of indigenous communities against the colonial regime], whereby membership in the community is conditioned upon faithful performance of labor tasks for purposes decided by the local leaders, has gradually *eliminated* those families who were least disposed to cooperate in the *program of reform and improvement,* and attracted to the village new families to whom the reforms were congenial. (Ibid; emphasis added)

How is it that a centuries-old mechanism for the extraction of *obligatory tribute* that is readapted to effect centralizing (if not totalitarian from the perspective of those Maya who left!) control of a community could be associated with *reform* or with *improvement*? This is the question asked, for example, by Goldkind (1965, 1966), who shows how these "reforms" were part of a "traditional" gambit for local power. It is also addressed by Joseph (1982), who shows how the socialist movement in Yucatán relied extensively on caciques such as the "leadership native" to Chan Kom to build a grassroots

power base. Further, this political strategy was connected to an ideological struggle to aggrandize and promote the Ancient Maya civilization, that is, the educational strategy of Felipe Carrillo Puerto,
the socialist governor, to create an ethnic class consciousness via the
restoration of archeological monuments such as Chichén Itzá.[16] Thus,
this "reform" of a tributary mechanism was (narrativized as) an "improvement" because it was *complicitous* with two aspects of modernism: a socialist program of nation building and (anthropological)
science. In other words, Redfield's construct of Progress entails a contradictory relation to power whereby one form of domination is replaced by another. On the one hand, Chan Kom is founded by set-
tlers as a frontier hamlet outside of the political sphere of the "unjust"
fagina demands of the mother town of Ebtun; thus, the first step in
Progress is the escape from "domination." On the other hand, the village leaders struggle for the village to become legalized as a township
and politically wired into the new revolutionary Mexico; thus, the
second step of Progress is reinsertion under domination of the modern apparatus of the nation-state. Redfield's notion of Progress is the
substitution of Traditional with Modern forms of control facilitated
by education and medicine.

Three observations can be made. First, one goal here has been to
suggest how Redfield's ethnographic discourse participates in a wider
episteme (or discursive formation) organized around the trope of culture. Many have already analyzed this discourse and its invention
and their arguments need not be reviewed here (e.g., Wagner 1981;
Williams 1983; Boon 1983, 1989). Instead, note that the "Progress"
(that Redfield asserts has been) defined by Chan Kom (and not his
sociology) "more than any other village in the region" abides by the
modernist trope of culture; specifically, I have suggested that it shares
affinities to Mathew Arnold's idea of culture even though he is not
among those Redfield (1941) recognizes as his theoretical inspiration.
No doubt there are significant differences between them, but there is
also another connection: in a sense they shared the "same" benefactor.
Andrew Carnegie, among his many philanthropic endeavors, founded
the Carnegie Institution of Washington in 1901, which sponsored
Redfield, Morley, and several other archeological projects up until
1956; Carnegie also patronized Mathew Arnold, whom the former
appreciated in spite of having a different posture toward the poor
(Lagemann 1989: 12–28). Thus, all three shared assumptions about

the necessary and *illuminating* role of education in the cultivation of Culture-Progress, which in turn provides for the moral holism or holistic moralism that constitutes a culture (see Williams 1983: 110–29). Chan Kom's "Progress" is Chan Kom's "Culture" and both are a form and function of modernism, that is, artifacts of the culture of modernity: progress is culture and culture is progress when the future (modernization) is organically rooted and conjoined to the past (tradition) to form a present moment that is hypostatized as an *oriented movement*. This, then, is the model of the Folk type of society that Redfield constructed; that is, the Folk is a collectivity midway — "midway" in the geographic and discursive space of the Continuum — between Primitive and Modern/Urban.

Ultimately, the ethnographies, specifically their theoretical architecture, must be read in light of the wider context of Carnegie philanthropy; that is, they must be read as propaganda promoting Carnegie philanthropy and the Carnegie Institution of Washington through the promotion of the civilizing effects of the American (over and against the Latin-Mexican) civilization. This is particularly evident in his 1950 ethnography where, for example, Redfield discusses the "Road to the Light," in a chapter with that title, that the villagers built to Chichén while serving their compulsory labor duties:

> "The road to the light" starts out toward Chicago rather than toward Mexico City. The changes in Chan Kom are in the direction of North American or cosmopolitan urbanized life rather than in the direction of Latin culture.... Apparently the spirit of this people is not favorable to the adoption of Latin manners or mores.... None of the aesthetic sensibility of Latin culture has found lodgement in the Chan Kom people.... The practicality, the exaltation of hard work, and the acquisitive rather than the expressive spirit — these qualities of the villager lead him away from Latin culture toward another, perhaps a predominating stream of world-wide expanding influence. Before progress came to Chan Kom, Chan Kom had a life-view of its own, not at all Latin in nature, and Chan Kom has shaped the progress it has won in conformity with this ethos. (R. Redfield 1950: 153–54)

The underlying assumptions about racial and national character types need not detain us here, except to point out how the quote operates as ideology justifying Anglo-Western world domination and its vehicle, projects in economic modernization. Thus, the Redfieldian sociological project in Yucatán, just like the Carnegie's archeological projects, is part of a wider political economy in which scientific knowledge is used to target Mexico as an inferior society, culture, and civilization. Together they formed one small campaign within the Carnegie's larger war to control the production of knowledge both nationally and internationally (see Lagemann 1989; Patterson 1986; Helm 1984; Hinsley 1981, 1984).

Second, Redfield's ethnographic-theoretical discourses on Chan Kom are also dependent on the scriptural operation through which the anthropologist-author is erased to leave an authenticated native Maya in their designated text-field topos (which is a reversal of the touristic discourses that eliminate the Maya so as to substitute and interpolate the reader-tourist into the topos of travel). In this case, the Maya native who stands out from and in the text, the man to whom Redfield is constantly directing (deserved) applause for his skilled *cultivation* of both (modernizing) progress and (traditional) culture, is Don Eustaquio Ceme. The genius of this man cannot be doubted: here was a man who was able to play the language games of Redfield's sociology, Mexican socialism, and Maya politics so well that he easily reflected back to his interlocutors the images that they desired as he manipulated both image and interlocutor according to his own interests (see Jones 1977).

Third, it must be noted that this collaborative ethnography, as Redfield himself confesses and cites the complicity, is a truly *dialogical, transculturative,* and *autoethnographic* text (or culture-text) through which culture is invented and then *re*invented as it is reread here in this text and the shadow texts produced in the readings formulated by its readers. Although the dialogical dimensions of the text are evident,[17] what should be underscored is what Pratt has called "transculturation" (1992: 6), or the multidirectional adaptation and selective borrowing between super- and subordinate groups, whether in the "same" place or across localities marked as hegemonic center/ dominated periphery. Thus, *Chan Kom: A Maya Village* might also profitably be understood as an autoethnography, that is, a text of self-representation by subordinated subjects that is constituted through the *struggle* between and *engagement* with non-Eurocentric and Western/ colonialist forms of discourse. This autoethnography *is* the *contact zone* of the heterogeneous discourses and vectors of power that the text articulates as its referent, product, context, practice, and event.[18]

This (autoethnographic) text can be understood, then, in two other ways. First, the deconstructive analysis enacted here reperformed the mechanisms by which the analyzed text reads and writes culture, that is, culture-texts designated as "Maya culture" and as the modern discourse of culture; what has been isolated is a machine of reading and writing (other texts, other cultures) that is text itself.[19] Second, this imaginary machine or machinery of recitation and engagement is also, from another angle, the *economy* of those texts (or readings/writings) and of those vectors of power that articulate these *scriptural productions.* Let us call this/these text(s) a *scriptural economy* devoted to the invention of culture and, in this situation, of Maya culture: here is a scriptural economy put into motion again (reinvented) by and enacted in *Chan Kom,* itself a discursive and sociogeographic topos for a moment and tactic of engagement.

The sociological study of Yucatán that Redfield directed marked a significant moment in the invention of Maya culture. It is an invention that has been criticized for the theoretical framework that it supports and for the dissonance between the "data" and the interpretive portrayal of *the* culture. The village outside the text did not quite correspond to the village depicted within the text. The community was not as homogeneous or class- and conflict-free — not as happy, in other words — as the "culture construct pattern" made the "real culture pattern" out to be.[20] Yet, does this not presuppose, first, that ethnographic representations can adequately portray a community as a complex whole, and, second, that such patterned, moral wholes exist out there outside their textual representation? Research in various fields has answered that neither proposition is tenable.

It would be better to understand ethnography as the presentation (not representation) of a culture, that is, a simulation in Baudrillard's sense. Here a privileged culture is invented in discursive and geographic space through an ethnographic complicity. *Chan Kom,* whether explicitly as in Coe (1993) or implicitly (Kintz 1990), became the paradigm of Yucatec Maya culture in the guise of a Modernizing Maya Folk. In turn, this paradigmatic understanding of the Maya as modernizing — which is even the theme of a recent photojournalist book (Everton 1991) — is the secondary Western construct and trope in complementary opposition to the dominant view of the Maya as mystery, that is, the Mysterious Maya, as the National Geographic Society designates them (cf. Stuart and Stuart 1977).

On the other hand, I suggest that the ethnography is adequate as a representation if the referent is inverted or redirected from that imaginary community south of Chichén to the situation of engagement that produced the text. The text *is* an adequate representation *of a transculturated and negotiated image* or imagining of a Maya community with which "everyone" who was concerned (the Carnegie, the sociologist, the socialists, the federal government, the Ceme family, the schoolteacher) was *happy*! Here *was* Progress! And all those who were not happy with it—for example, those "malcontents" of Chan Kom—left. Unlike contemporary Chan Komeros, who, I have been told, flaunt the text as a self-representation, those malcontents did not love their community, and thus migrated to Pisté, that "unhappy" town whose uncanniness was way out of place, especially since it was right *in* the way, that is, right in the "middle" of the road from Mérida to Chichén.[21]

We must now return to Pisté to further understand why "Chan Kom, more than any other village in the region, defined progress for itself." If the preceding discussion elaborates on how and why the geographic space of Chan Kom was the site in which "Maya culture" was localized, we need now ask why the Folk Culture of Progress (or is it the Folk Progress of Culture?) was not located in other villages such as Pisté.

A Measured "Postmodernity": The Scandal of Zero-Degree Impact

April 3, 1939. Dear Mr. Gilbert [administrative secretary of CIW]:
    Relative to our conversation of a few days ago, dealing with the money spent in Piste, may I quote a paragraph from [the draft of] my [forthcoming] manuscript:
    "In 1924 Carnegie Institution rented the Hacienda at Chichén Itzá as headquarters for its investigators. Naturally, this had its effect on the Piste population.... the Institution paid to Maya laborers an average annual sum of [blank space], most of which was paid to the Piste inhabitants...."
    I quote this paragraph in order that you may know the effect that I think the Institution has had upon the inhabitants of Piste. If you can supply me with a figure for the space I left blank, I would be glad to have it.... If you think this is not expedient, I, of course, will change the text relative to this point.
        [Signed Morris Steggerda; emphasis added][22]

On April 6 the bursar provided Mrs. Harrison, the Carnegie editor, with the requested amount: the total sum paid *in local wages* by Sylvanus G. Morley during the eight-year period between 1927 and 1934 was $80,703.93 or a *yearly average of $10,087.99*. The smallest amount spent in any of these years was just over $4,000 for 1934; the greatest amount was over $15,000 in 1927 and 1932.[23]

Four days after the initial request for information, the administrative secretary answered Steggerda:

> The data now in hand concerning cost of labor at Chichen between 1927 and 1934 indicates great variation in amounts and in number of men employed in various years. It seems to me that a better way of stating your case might be the following, or something like it:
>
> "The Institution employed the services of a large number of *natives* [sic] as laborers, sometimes as many as fifty or more being engaged for a season, and most of these men were Piste inhabitants. In addition the Mexican Government employed many of Piste's men in work of restoration at Chichen Itza. The large amount of money paid in wages for such service, most of which was probably spent in Piste, did not *materially change the mores of the community*."
>
> If we were to try to arrive at an average for annual expenditure it would probably be between seven and eight thousand dollars. In some years, however, it did not amount to more than two or three thousand. Of course, this is entirely your party. I have taken the liberty of expressing a possible form of statement only in order to put my thoughts on the subject concisely. Sincerely yours.
>
> [Signed by W. M. Gilbert on April 7, 1939; emphasis added]

Here is a curious, if scandalous, dissimulation and passing of the blame. First, no figures were requested, tabulated, presented, or relayed concerning the number of workers under Morley. My own research led me to the proposed budget for 1925, which entails a wage-labor expense of more than $10,000 for a hundred workers divided into about eighty excavators ("tram-men, day laborers, etc.") at 75¢ a day and twenty masons at $1 a day; this does not include the ten to fifteen persons who for eighteen years comprised the house staff of the Hacienda (among whom were Chinese-Koreans, Maya, and both Mexican and Yucatec mestizos). Thus, budgets of $4,000 and $15,000 correlate to approximately forty and 150 laborers, respectively, calculated on an average $100 per worker (skilled and unskilled) for

four months of work: Considering that Pisté had a population ranging from three to four hundred inhabitants, this represents between
10 and 25 percent of the total population, or virtually all of the men
in town for most years. Yet Gilbert suggests that Steggerda mention
no more than fifty as the usual number of workers, that is, from half
to a third of my estimated figures. Second, the secretary of the CIW
deploys, and suggests that Steggerda use, a tactic of distraction that
sloughs off some of the responsibility: the Mexican government also
hired locals and is, therefore, also responsible for whatever "impact"
may have resulted. Third, Gilbert sidesteps the question with obfuscation. He tells Steggerda that in essence the accounts are so confusing (!) that it is just not possible to really know how much money
was spent. Certainly, Steggerda assumed (and so should we) that the
Carnegie kept (and keeps) precise financial records of its monies—
how could it not? How, then, could the message be other than that
this is a delicate and dangerous issue? Imprecision is the recommended
path: "Do not mention any numbers, not even the deflated and misleading figures we give to you to assuage your concerns."

Why did the Carnegie directorship feel it necessary to dissimu-
late—not only to the world, but to its own researcher—this situation of *zero-degree impact*? There is a powerful assumption and moral
framework operating here: Pisté *should have progressed*. The town
should have *cultivated* the American presence; *should* have *improved*
its standard of living with a "wise" investment of wages earned; *should*
have *reformed* its indifference into a naturally forward-looking, cohesive, and holistic community. But, "Pisté did not"—or so asserts
one Carnegie scientist. Here is Steggerda's scandalous, if revised, paragraph, published in 1941 by the Carnegie, which attests to the an-
tiprogressive indifference of the town:

> In 1922 *a new road* between Dzitas and Chichen Itza was begun
> under the administration of Felipe Carrillo Puerto. . . . the new
> highway gave Piste, for the first time, free access to the railway.
> Two years later Carnegie Institution rented the hacienda at Chi-
> chen Itza as headquarters for its archeological and other investi-
> gations. During the eight-year period between 1927 and 1934,
> when excavation and repair work were at their height, the Insti-
> tution employed per season as many as 50 Indian and Yucate-
> can laborers, mostly from Piste. The Mexican government also
> engaged many Piste men in its restoration at Chichen Itza. *The*

large amounts of money paid in wages, most of which was probably spent in Piste, did not materially change the mores of the community. People continued to cultivate their cornfields and to eat the same kind of food as they had before. A few effects, however, were noticeable. The number of horses probably increased in that period, or rather, they conspicuously decreased after the Institution activity ceased. It is possible also that more Maya women wore gold chains, although no actual count was made. No automobiles or house luxuries were purchased, nor was extra food for the table observed, and I believe that *by 1938 the temporary effects of the money influx were completely obliterated.* (Steggerda 1941: 11; emphasis added)

Pisté, in a secret opposition to Chan Kom, is truly, then, the topos and trope of *antiprogress*. This is due not simply to Steggerda's ethnographic representation of it, but to some of the manifest (if not well understood) characteristics of this town. Redfield himself could not (or for some reason did not bother to) imagine Pisté as a progressive community, much less a Folk Culture. Even the construction of a road—which is the Euro-Yucatec symbol par excellence of the intrusion of modernity and the diffusion of its light into the Primitive Darkness of Other Folk—does not here cultivate enlightenment in Pisté. There *should have been* "enlightened change," which in the discourse of the Carnegie, Redfield, and Arnold, means/equals/*is* Culture; there should have been Culture here. Instead, there is only zero-degree impact and a zero-degree culture: a nonimpact on a nonculture. In this way, the Yucatec landscape is made blank or wiped clean. The obstacles to anthropological science, socialist reforms in education, and government are removed, "erased" as it were, from the topography to provide a tabula rasa for a new inscription of culture localized in a new spatial order.

Pisté *should have progressed*: it should have improved itself and reformed its community through a "wise" investment of the material benefits gained through the benevolent association with the modern Americans. But it "did not." Situated in a space deterritorialized by war, Pisté enjoyed a freedom of a frontier: sacked at the beginning of the Caste War and then again in 1862, a small population only slowly refounded a town in the 1880s, which endured yet another reign of violence known as the Mexican Revolution. Afterward, it became a place of refuge for Maya liberated from slave-peonage on henequen haciendas and, even later, from the violent struggles of nearby Chan Kom. This frontier allowed a relative political *freedom from*: authority structures that were being planted at the time; attempts at local appropriation of these mechanisms as in Chan Kom; political ideologies and practices imposed from the metropoles or from age-old systems of tributary labor like the *fagina*. As well, there were "*freedoms to*" in terms of economics, religion, social relations—for example, freedom *to* subsist within traditional economies of household production and *to* explore entrepreneurial endeavors opened up by an expanded wage economy; *to* abide by three different religious traditions (Catholicism, Protestantism, and Yucatec Maya); *to* spend the profits from work in a myriad of ways (for example, commerce, hoarding, and in the consumption of alcohol—that sin which has always triggered decadence and anarchy in the Western Christian imagination). Whereas the various forms of *un*freedom (i.e., *socioeconomic control* or *discipline*) of Chan Kom were perceived, understood, categorized, analyzed as Progress and as Culture, the "freedoms *from* and *to*" that were enjoyed in Pisté were excessive, in excess, anarchic, anomalous, and ultimately a *danger* to both the Redfieldian theory and the Carnegie image of itself and the world it attempted to know and shape.[24]

This was a freedom that *resisted* insertion into metropolitan typologies of social forms: it was a community that practiced, as it were, an "indifferent" self-imaging, as Steggerda noted. And why not? After eighty years of war beginning with the Caste War (1847–1901) through to the Mexican Revolution (1917–1921 in Yucatán), the threat of destructive raids or random violence was constant. Here is a collective sensibility—an ethos—that would "define" Pisté in the minds of its observers as indifferent to metropolitan notions of "goals," "ethos,"[25] and modernist *schemes of social types*. Thus, it could be, has been, and is said that Pisté, more than any other town in the region differs, abstains, resists *from defining itself* to itself and for Others. It positions itself in tension with or even outside the grids and discourses of modernity (the nation, state, anthropology): it is knocked *loose*; it is *loose space*. Community can be neither imagined nor cultivated here—except, of course, by those secret bonds of integration that rerouted Pisté refugees from a war zone back to their plots of corn and stone hearths that they *once owned*. These are bonds that have remained *savage* to scientific domestication.

Pisté was not simply the opposite of Culture, whether Urban-Modern or Folk-Traditional, but the unspeakable supplement to Culture that ruptures its categorical forms. Is there surprise, then, that Chan Kom was the topos marked as and by (Maya, Folk, Traditional, Progressive) Culture because it was a place of *un*freedom? After all, the concept of culture develops as the name of that underlying and pervasive social control (variously defined as "norms," "tradition," "rules," "civilization") that makes humans social animals over and against "nature" (cf. Herbert 1991; Cottom 1989; Rosaldo 1989). In contrast, Pisté, as a nonplace of nonculture, was erased from anthropological memory, leaving only the telltale traces of an immemorial anarchy, anomie, anomaly on the topography of Maya Culture.

What, then, is the scandal of this mysterious impact and zero-degree culture? The operative assumption in the Carnegie correspondence is that the intervention of anthropology and its culture-bearers (that is, anthropologists) must necessarily and automatically lead to progress, which is conceived as a duplicitous event of *directed change* linked to nonchange and allochronic stasis (Fabian 1983). Imagined here is a modernizing of the Other that maintains tradition. This is a dream of a difference that remains the same, that is, remains in the *same place* within the anthropological cosmography of cultural forms. Thus, the glory of the Carnegie, which Redfield triumphed, was the "modernizing" that effectively represented stasis as tradition. The scandal of the Carnegie, however, was that it triggered (putatively) no change, but, nonetheless, planted the future alteration of the community-town of both Pisté and Chan Kom. The scandal that is named by Pisté is a community that remained the same in its alterity or difference from the categories and systems of knowledge that would securely situate it as a topos among the ideal types of culture-localities within the ethnographic *mappae mundi*. The alterity of Pisté was not "conquered" by anthropological knowledge: it was not inscribed within the economy of culture invented through anthropology.

The resistance and resilience of this alterity to anthropological inscription would be later explained by the concept of *impact* and its agent, tourism. Burdened by expanded economic opportunities—increased economic freedom, no?—Pisté becomes fully "impacted" by tourism: by the 1980s, Pisté is held to be a quintessential case of the "cultural destruction" of Maya communities that is perceived to occur through the supposedly "external" intervention of development, modernity, tourism-capitalism. Can there be any surprise that some of the more vociferous critics of the culturelessness, community-lessness, and Mayalessness of Pisté are "Mayan" archeologists, that is, those whose disciplinary ancestors explicitly and consciously created Chichén Itzá as a monument to the science of archeology in the form of a tourist attraction and site? The invention of culture is, indeed, a complicitous web of practices.

But the scandal is not simply this discursive distortion and textual inadequacy. The issue is not at all the white lie told to Steggerda by the directors of the Carnegie to hide a zero-degree impact; rather, it is the dissimulation of an ethics of knowledge that is necessarily in practice a politics of science. At stake here is that same ethic of scientific intervention that Paul Sullivan (1989) has already brought to light in his account of the conversations between Cruzob Maya and S. G. Morley. The scandal here is the dissimulation of a highly charged moral and political agenda that passes and is disguised as the "objective," "neutral," and "value-free" collection of "facts" and "truths" (cf. Rosaldo 1989). The scandal, I argue, is not so much that what we hold to be objective and neutral is actually not—the fact that there is a politics to all knowledge is now a well-known truth. The scandal is rather that we continue to *conceal* the intricacies of this politics. This scandal is also an *error,* for that politics (and its history) is not extraneous to either the object of study or social-scientific method, but it is part of the object. The politics of knowledge is that which constitutes the phenomenon as an object and thus must be a part of the method that makes the study of that object science. The "object" of study is indeed a complex web of contested meanings and of complicitous practices.

The Progress That Chose a Village

The question then arises as to whether we want to fill in the broad picture of anthropology's growth that is already familiar to us or to illuminate through anthropology aspects of the transformation of which this discipline was a small part.
        Talal Asad, "Afterword," *Colonial Situations* (1991:315)

In a volume devoted to the relations between anthropology and colonialism, Asad (1991) warns us that the role anthropology has played in consolidating imperial domination was usually trivial. Although this seems to be very true at the most immediate levels of political and economic action, I—as a believer, bearer, and observant practitioner in the superstition we call "culture"—have a suspicion that this may be too fast an assessment of the "impact" of anthropology in the world.

Terence Turner, as·Asad even approvingly notes, suggests that the ramifications of anthropological practices and discourses of culture may be profound, pervasive, and a mostly imperceptible reformulation of the way human groups imagine themselves, others, and the relations between self and other. The situation that Turner describes for the Kayapo is, he argues and I agree, cross-culturally generic:

> If the Kayapo are any indication, the processes of cultural and ethnic self-conscientization that have been catalyzed by the new media and their use in worldwide networks of communication are becoming more important as components of "culture" (or, by the same token, "ethnicity") and more central to basic social and political processes in many "primitive" and "traditional" as well as "modern" cultures. This comes to the same thing as saying that the nature of "culture" itself is changing together with the techniques we employ to study and document it. (T. Turner 1991: 310)

What I find curious about Turner's argument is the way he truncates the historical depth of the transculturation that he has so nicely isolated: Why does the seemingly most recent and "advanced" technology of the West cause this change in the "nature of culture"? If we take Turner's own conclusion seriously—that is, that through their coparticipation in a series of films on the Kayapo "their 'culture' and my 'theory' had become, in some measure, our joint product" (ibid.: 312)—then are not "cultures" themselves a joint and ongoing production begun in that fabled moment of contact between "Europe" and the "rest of the world"? Asad addresses this point when he suggests that "the role of Western technologies in transforming colonial subjects" needs to be studied more systematically, if, "however, [we] extend the concept of technology to include all institutionalized techniques that depend on and extend varieties of social power" (Asad 1991: 323).

Although it is now an old myth, is not the "first" such technology of power that of textual inscription, which includes the techniques of writing, reading, reproducing, circulating, interpreting texts (texts in the widest sense)? Might we refer to this technology as scriptural, not only because it indicates procedures of writing and reading of texts that are held in high regard, but because what is produced (scripts, texts, scriptures, images) are vehicles for constituting, communicating, asserting, manipulating, and altering the truths accepted by communities? Anderson (1991) points out that the significance of this technology, specifically in the form of print-capitalism, is not so much what truths are being produced, but the forms (languages, newspapers, etc.) in which they are being consumed. This is also what Asad argues when he directs our attention to the colonial situation through which "customary law" was invented. In turn, de Certeau (1984) calls the economy of truths that emerged from transformations in the sixteenth century in relation to print-capitalism, a scriptural economy.

This notion seems to be a useful concept by which to think through several problems. First, it is a vehicle by which to conjoin the political economy of social practices with the economy of "cultural" or ideological practices and effects. Second, it provides angles by which to inspect the intervention of anthropology (or any scientific discipline) within that which is being studied. Third, it provides an image or concept by which to imagine the multiple levels and contexts of cultural-ideological productions, from the microphysical and local through to the most global. In other words, it provides an analytical model to think through questions about so-called transnational cultural communities, institutions, and their interrelationships. Fourth, in providing a comprehensive image to think of relations between local and global as well as political and cultural, the idea of scriptural economy allows for the heterogeneity of and conflict between practices and interests while nonetheless comprehending their complicity and articulation. Fifth, although this concept as an analytical model of reality tends toward more inclusive comprehension, within the notion itself it acknowledges and deconstructs the procedures by which it synthesizes and integrates phenomena into reified abstraction: like the nations, cultures, and communities that it may be used to analyze, the scriptural economy is also an "imaginary machine," that is, a fiction we make real by envisioning its utility and using it effectively.

(Unconscious? of) The Scriptural Economy: Blindness in Citation

The question of values is very fundamental. As long as the old values appear more rewarding they'll stick with them. We used to think that all you have to do is to expose people to education and they'll change their ways.
    John Gillen, in Sol Tax, ed., *Heritage of Conquest* (1952: 275)

In closing I would like to return to the Coke Theory of Culture, which might be a more tangible image of the scriptural economy. From Redfield on, the Maya of Yucatán have been understood, studied, and represented as the Modern or Modernizing Maya—with exceptions, as argued here. Consider the closing paragraph of a recent ethnography dealing with "tradition and change among the Yucatec Maya":

> It was late afternoon when Nicolas and Maria returned to the village. Nicolas had a load of corn he carried on his back by a tumpline crossing his forehead. Maria carried a load of wood for the hearth. As they entered town, they walked past the cemetery. A new tomb had been placed there for Silvestre May Balam, who represented the past as Nicolas and Maria represented the present. They saw their young son Jose Feliciano and their daughter Reina squatting by the side of their yard. The two children were chewing on small ears of corn, biting into the kernels, and in their other hand, they each held a bottle of Coke. These children represented the future. (Kintz 1990: 147)

Although the text ends ambiguously indeed on this note, it is accompanied (and the message repeated) by a photo (ibid.: 146, fig. 7.5) of these barefooted Maya children with their bottle of Coke: Culture and Coke, Tradition and Modernity. As for them, the future is the modernizing of tradition. Coke and Culture: as if to ensure the endless circularity of the reference, the text accompanies the photo and the photo accompanies the text and forges a hermetically sealed cosmology based on statements of symbolic equivalences. The reading movement between photo and text reproduces the movement between Coke and Culture as each supplements the other with its oppositional value. Locked into this circular movement to decipher the meaning or implications of this scriptural economy, one realizes that there is no escape, no outside referent, no future. Time and history are hypostatized, frozen, into the image of the modernizing of tradition that never fully becomes modern nor fully returns to a prior, supposedly "authentic," tradition.

In *Chan Kom* and Chan Kom, that atypically typical village that chose progress, a topography of Yucatec Maya culture was inaugurated. But this complex strategy for the representation and practice of Yucatec Maya culture conjoins with another encompassing topography. These Modernizing Maya—rather, this ideal (romanticized) type and trope of Yucatec Maya—complement the famously Mysterious Maya (chapter 4). Here the reference is to those Maya of the pre-Columbian civilization that disappeared for "mysterious" reasons and to those Maya of Guatemala that for other, but nonetheless still "mysterious" reasons, refuse to give up their "traditional" culture— that is, to disappear, ladinoize, and "modernize," for the "greater good" of building a *modern* nation-state (see Smith 1990; Carmack 1988). And, there is yet another image of the Maya that, like the Cheshire cat, scandalously escapes these tropological types since this variety is already not modern/Western and not folk/Indian.

Erased from anthropological memory and its museum of theory-loci, Pisté embodies an anomalous indifference to the popular and scientific imagining of culture-communities. With no community, no cultivation, and no progress toward culture in either modernist or folk forms, Pisté is always already depreciated as a zero-degree culture. Ironically, this alterity of the Maya refuses and has refused comprehension within the anthropological discourse of cultures and cultural forms as it, nonetheless, scandalously inaugurates that discursive formation and topography of Maya Culture. Yucatec Maya culture, which is imagined to reside elsewhere (Chichén, Chan Kom, Mérida, etc.), can only be *measured from* Pisté, it seems, that is, from this topos inscribed by multiple practices and discourses as zero-degree.

2 / Measuring Tourist Impact at *P'iz-te'*, "La Antesala de Chichén Itzá, Patrimonio de la Humanidad"

*Maya studies, save for those carried out in distant villages by
intrepid ethnographers, have been predominantly studies of
civilization. . . . Those regions and time periods that have been
perceived, rightly or wrongly, to fall outside these criteria have
been largely ignored. Remaining beyond the limits of the known
and the readily apprehensible, they have simply not challenged our
interest and imagination.*
    Grant D. Jones, *Maya Resistance to Spanish Rule* (1989: 3)

Pisté is one of those zones of "savagery" that have resisted colonization by anthropological knowledge. It is one of those places of darkness where "tradition" and "modernity," "culture" and "civilization," "Indian" and "European" have always already hybridized into
social forms, identities, and ways of life that fall through the dominant categories of Western comprehension. It is this betwixt and betweenness that marks Pisté with disinterest by its visitors, whether
scientific or otherwise; it is a disinterest intimately connected to the
putative indifference of its inhabitants. Tellingly, the authenticity of
Chichén Itzá is its specific hybridization of Classic Petén Maya, Gulf
Coast Mesoamerican, and ancient central Mexican cultures. But the
hybridity that Pisté names is its inauthenticity, anomaly, and indifference. From one perspective, it is indeed arbitrary and historically con-

tingent that the hybridization of one community—for example, the cultural-racial *mestizaje* of Yucatán—becomes a primordial identity while for another collectivity it becomes a sign and stigma of culture loss, as in Pisté. But then, such contingency "proves" or is evidence that there is a determining political context that motivates the different values ascribed to hybridity in different communities.[1]

In the context of the tourism that has developed in the last four decades of the twentieth century, Pisté has become especially clothed in an aura of an "inevitable" cultural corruption that capitalism, Western consumerism, and touristic commodification entail. Thus, the anthropological and popular (or touristic) indifference that "Pisté" *confronts* is due to its being not modern, not traditional, and even not ex-primitive, to use MacCannell's label of the way some Fourth World natives, who, such as those memorialized in O'Rourke's film *Cannibal Tours,* dress up as exotic primitives for the tourists or who, as in the legendary *Farside* cartoon, hide the TVs and VCRs when the anthropologists arrive in the thatched village. The objective in this essay is to dismantle the perspective by which one could believe that there is such an event or process as impact and that Pisté has been impacted by tourism and anthropology. To do so, I critically assess the mythology of tourist impact in this situation by mapping out several dimensions of the problem: first, we revisit the scandal that Steggerda's ethnography revealed about the "effects" of anthropology on the town; second, we tour the urban underdevelopment of Pisté in search of the elusive and imagined impact of tourism; third, we map, on this situation, the politics of tourism that has settled in on Pisté.

The Nonimpact Impact of Anthropology

The large amounts of money paid in wages, most of which was probably spent in Piste, did not materially change the mores of the community. People continued to cultivate their cornfields and to eat the same kind of food as they had before. A few effects, however, were noticeable. The number of horses probably increased in that period, or rather, they conspicuously decreased after the Institution activity ceased. It is possible also that more Maya women wore gold chains, although no actual count was made. No automobiles or house luxuries were purchased, nor was extra food for the table observed, and I believe that by 1938 the temporary effects of the money influx were completely obliterated. (Steggerda 1941: 11)

Missing from among of all the things Steggerda studied was the issue that some would name from *today's* perspective as the impact of anthropology. He treated Pisté as a town "containing," as it were, subjects to be measured, weighed, tested, and dated according to their birth, menstruation, birth giving, personality, and death; or whose productive activities and material resources could be quantified so as to be rated for efficiency, productivity, and utility. The title of his book, *Maya Indians of Yucatan,* keys us in on the fact that his is not a study of the sociocultural bond and bonding of a collectivity, but of disparate dimensions of a category of individuals that together somehow comprise a "race." Furthermore, there was not only no comparative research that charted a "before and after" with regard to some diagnostic trait of exogenous influence, but there was no research on the town as a social collectivity, that is, as a coherent, integrated, and *bounded* entity against which a before and an after could be traced. From this angle, Steggerda is not burdened with the problem that is being discussed; since he has not imagined a community that could be impacted, *there is already no impact.* Nonetheless, his published opinion about the effects of anthropology must understood and scrutinized as an informal assessment informed not only by his eight years of experience "in the field" but his cultural and theoretical baggage. And, of course, all of this applies to my commentary on Steggerda's comments, since I, like Steggerda before me, did *not* conduct research on the "impact" of anthropology or tourism and did not study Pisté as a *community* per se.

A widely shared assumption then and now about the causal relations that constitute society can be identified in his observation. It is an assumption that undergirds not only the paradigm of acculturation but the spirit of capitalism, the ethic of Protestantism, the ideology of missionary work, the legitimation of imperialism, the logic of philanthropy: contact with money (or: civilization, knowledge, true God, television, asphalt roads, etc.) triggers an automatic and contagious change in value (or mentality, culture, tradition, community, ritual, belief). Ironically, although decades of materialist social scientists have not been able to *prove* beyond question this equation, it remains a popular truism held by many when debating the ills or benefits of "acculturation" and "culture change" in the contact between Western culture and its Third, Fourth, *and First* World Others. In other words, the moralist debate and the theoretical contest about material versus ideal causes only presuppose the validity of the premise of an inevitable, one-way alteration of life forms. The ethnographically reported Pisté is scandalous because it does not contribute evidence to nor substantiate the terms of the discussion: on the contrary, the most material effects of the Carnegie had no consequence on material or cultural conditions "after 1938."[2] Or so asserts Steggerda.

There is a certain irony as to how the Carnegie leadership was scandalized by this revelation: they had no alternative but to trust in the science of their scientist. Not only the logic of Carnegie philanthropy was thereby challenged, but also a modern aesthetic of social causation. Thus, incredible as it may seem, the people of Pisté did not become clones of middle-class North Americans: no automobiles or luxuries for the home were bought, just as no Redfieldian progress was manifested. Yet, Steggerda is clearly wrong in his opinion about the long-term effects of archeology.

In the long run of this century, the Carnegie and Mexican archeology projects have had profound ramifications, in that a modern tourist attraction was built on, in, and as the ruins of an ancient Maya city. Furthermore, this was indeed the intended result of the archeological leadership of the Carnegie (see chapter 3). By the same token, archeological factories of knowledge spread throughout the region to other sites as these loci of Maya civilization became the targets for (re)construction as potential tourist attractions; these archeological sites, of course, became organized into a network of tourist sights. Thus, we might say that the "impact" of anthropology on both local and regional communities is the creation of tourism, *except* that the notion itself is inadequate to describe, analyze, and comprehend the long history of collusion and complicity between these two entities and the specificity of their interaction with local and regional societies. The invention of the modern ruins of Chichén Itzá attests to the fact that anthropology and tourism do not merely mutually reinforce but *inhabit* each other; that is, there is already a complex interweaving and sharing of practices, goals, strategies, contexts, resources, and frameworks. To argue that one determined the other or that one impacted a culture is to already assume the absolute difference and boundedness of these heterogeneous practices and strategies.

Regarding the putative impact of anthropology on the town, we have already suggested, on the basis of information provided by Steggerda, that the community entered into a kind of economic boom; that is, there was an expansion of and experimentation in commercial activities spurred by a dramatic increase of wealth in the form of wages. This suggests two points. First, we could agree with Steggerda that the most immediate *effect* of the Carnegie was the local economic depression that was triggered by the closing down of the archeological projects in 1941; but such a depression must be understood in the context of encompassing crises in henequen monoculture and the chicle trade as well as of national and international politics. Second, this is not a town transformed from a peasant-based economy to one of wage labor; rather, there was already a mixed productive base that dated to before the Caste War and that shifted and grew with the opening of the archeological factory of knowledge. Nonetheless, it is here where the ramifications of the anthropological endeavor can be most clearly identified and could be mapped out in a historical study of the composition and organization of class relations. But again, this should not be understood as "impact" but as the historical contingencies by which individual and familial participation in the archeological industry reshaped existing social, political, and economic relations.

In general terms, it can be said that there was a shift in the composition of the Pisté "elite." In the first two decades of the century, there were two major landholders. One was E. H. Thompson, who had bought up the Hacienda Chichén and developed it with both cattle and archeological looting. The other was a man who lived in neighboring Dzitas who produced both cattle and maize. The few men who worked as their principal foremen and labor managers seem to have formed the political elite of the town of two to four hundred persons. The Revolution forced both landowners to abandon their possessions. As for the managers, two families (Maya, but with Spanish names) developed into large (by local standards) and well-to-do landowners with mixed maize-cattle production; afterward, their influence or participation in town politics seems to have been minimal. Two other families were not able to retain economic position in the same way, although one man did become the town registrar (*registro civil*) for the greater part of seven decades.

A new managerial class emerged as other individuals entered positions of *mayordomo, capitáz,* and *guardián* not only for the Carnegie and the Mexican Monumentos Prehispánicos but for the Barbachano family, who had constructed the first hotel, the Mayaland, in 1930. Thus, it was among these families that a new economic middle class and political elite emerged. The history of two families is illuminating: The men were originally hired by the Mexican government as archeological laborers and then, with the closing down of excavation, they became the principal guardians of the site; over time, their steady income allowed for their descendants to gain educations and become teachers, to gain employment with the Instituto Nacional de Antropología e Historia (INAH), to become among the first tour guides, and, eventually, to diversify in commercial endeavors. These two families are among the five or six that formed the political elite of the town from the latter half of the 1970s to the present: one family provided two town mayors (1981–83 and 1986–89) and the other family controlled the potable water system for sixteen years (1972–88). Together with the Pat/Padilla families who were exiles of the Progress that Chan Kom chose (see Goldkind 1966), these families have dominated political life in Pisté since the tourist boom triggered by the development of Cancún; these families, however, were never involved in archeology, but were split between campesinos and petty entrepreneurs owning a corn mill, a store, and a truck used for transportation of basic commodities.

The political dominance of these families cannot be said to be a result of anthropology or tourism. Rather, I suggest that it stems more directly from participation in state agencies such as the Partido Revolucionario Institucional (PRI) and labor unions, as well as from successful careers in education: more than six persons from these families became educators in the last twenty years, among whom is the two-time mayor and principal of the high school. Between the closing down of archeology in 1940 and the rise of tourism in the mid-1970s, these families were not dominant; rather, the majority of the population allied itself with other factions whose socioeconomic base was rooted in either agricultural production or wage labor. For this period, virtually all household economies were based in maize production on *ejido* land that may have been supplemented with small, private holdings that in some cases supported livestock. Seasonal and part-time wage labor had always been an option for Pistéleños, either in agricultural production or sectors such as construction, hotel/restaurant service, and even archeology.[3] Interestingly, a political alliance between the agricultural and service sectors of the local economy has developed because the older generation males who have maintained employment in the hotels and restaurants have typically also maintained milpas and ideological solidarity with campesino life; thus, the custom developed that continues today whereby these wage earners, and later *artesanos* and *vendedores,* would either work their *ejido* or private plots during off days or hire seasonal agricultural laborers. My sources indicate that it is this allied socioeconomic sector that provided the political leadership of the town between the 1940s and the mid-1970s.

Beginning in the 1960s, employment in construction work expanded as new hotels and restaurants were built in the Pisté-Chichén area. Many of these *albañiles* became part of the massive labor force that constructed Cancún in the state of Quintana Roo during the 1970s. As was typical for Maya males between the ages of eighteen and thirty-five or so throughout the Yucatán, individuals would contract out on specific jobs for several months at a time, usually sleeping in the building under construction during the week and returning to their village every other weekend; depending on individual temperament, this lifestyle could be maintained for a greater part of the year for several years. In this way, some capital could be accumulated and residence in Yucatán maintained. With the major construction phases ending at the time of the Mexican debt crisis in the early and mid-1980s, and with the growth of tourist influx at Chichén Itzá, a majority of these workers "came down" from Cancún;[4] although there were by this time a variety of economic options available outside of Pisté, a great number of persons began to traffic in handicrafts and to make artisanry themselves. In this way, the invasion of the archeological zone of Chichén Itzá by three to four hundred vendors was initiated. As a synopsis of the occupational histories of many men, an example is one man approaching his sixties: he had been involved in handicraft sales since 1983, when gave up work in construction as a skilled mason and foreman; his father and uncles were all chief *albañiles* or assistant masons for the Carnegie and he himself had assisted in the building of the Villas Club Med at Chichén as well as hotels in Cancún and Cozumel.[5]

As the infrastructure for this restructured regional tourist industry was laid out, the population of Pisté continued its dramatic increase (see tables 1 and 2). The town grew from five hundred persons in 1940 to almost four thousand in 1989. Also significant is the growth in relative size compared to other communities of the county. While Pisté accounted for only 16.5 percent of the municipal population in 1940, it claimed 39 percent in 1982 and an estimated *44 to 55 percent in 1990.*[6] Tinum, the capital of the county, on the other hand, has remained since the nineteenth century at a fairly constant population of between one and two thousand and its relative size began to diminish in the 1980s from a mid-twentieth-century norm of 30–31 percent to under 25 percent in 1990. The combined population of the remaining rural communities has also decreased in relation to the whole *municipio* (from 44 percent in 1960 to 31 percent in 1990) while increasing in absolute numbers. These figures reflect the fact that Pisté, which had been developing into a socioeconomic center, had, in the 1980s, consolidated its dominance over a microregion that included not only the *municipio* of Tinum but seven other neighboring counties that are economically linked to the tourist apparatus of Pisté-Chichén.[7] Wage laborers and petty entrepreneurs from fifteen different communities up to two hours away (depending on proximity of the main highway) regularly commute or migrate to Pisté. Only a few come to sell handicrafts to tourists, while a significant number commute to sell food in Pisté not so much to tourists, but to locals, for example: a man from a town thirty minutes away who commutes daily to Pisté to sell his handmade ice cream at the high school; a group of women who live within twenty minutes of Chichén who sell oranges from their household "gardens" (*solares*) and other wild fruit (*guaya*) to the *vendedores* and workers at Chichén; an itinerant vendor of popcorn and *chicharrón* (fried pork rinds) who spends the day traveling between Kantunil and Valladolid selling his wares on the second-class bus and, of course, stopping at Chichén for an hour or two in the afternoon. There is a small group of persons who transport goods or persons to and from Pisté and its peripheries. The great majority, however, come to Pisté in search of seasonal agricultural wage labor or other unskilled employment. It is from this group, most often campesinos from severely depressed rural areas nearby, that come the migrants who have relocated in Pisté. These migrants form a new underclass of proletarianized peasants who have contributed to a

Table 1. Population of Pisté, Tinum Pueblo, and Tinum County, 1811–1990

	Pisté	Tinum Pueblo	Tinum County	Current events
1811[a]	1,433	?	n/a	
1821[a]	882	1,525	n/a	Mexican independence from Spain
1846[a]	1,172	1,600	n/a	Census just prior to Caste War
1862[a]	308	326	n/a	Second Cruzob Maya attack on Pisté
1883[a]	0	?	1,496	Pisté is abandoned, refugees in Tinum
1900[a]	85	616	1,735[b]	Slow repopulation of town begins
1910[c]	233	782	2,227[b]	after 1888, continues until the Revolution
1918[c]	474	?	?	Mexican Revolution is "imported"
1921[c]	332	1,092	1,817	to Yucatán (Joseph 1982)
1930[c]	295	?	2,116[b]	Morley begins projects in 1924
1933[c]	307	?	?	Steggerda conducts eight yearly census
1934[c]	364	?	?	
1935[c]	415	?	?	Highway from Mérida to Chichén is
1937[c]	433	?	?	completed in 1936
1940[c]	500	?	3,028[b]	Carnegie project ends in 1940
1950[b]	820	?	3,350[b]	
1960[b]	974	1,149	3,757[b]	30,000 visitors to Yucatán in early 1960s
1970[b]	1,308	1,289	4,171[b]	Mass tourism begins in region
1980[d]	2,471	1,776	6,725[e]	Cancún ten years old
1982[d]	2,718	1,954	6,958	Closing of highway sets off invasion
1988[f]	3,774	?	?	Presidential elections
1989[g]	3,979	?	?	Lucha 107 de Pisté begins in March
1990[f]	4,196	?	?	Pisté wins municipal elections
1990[h]	3,124	1,723	7,111[i]	

Sources:
[a]Figures for 1821 from Rodríguez Losa (1985a); 1846, 1862, 1900 from Rodríguez Losa (1989: 190, 206, 219).
[b]Figures for the *municipio* 1910–70 from the Censo General del Estado de Yucatán.
[c]Figures for Pisté 1910–37 are unpublished (Steggerda n.d.); 1811 from Steggerda (1941: 5 n.14, 233).
[d]Figures for 1980 and 1982 from Gobierno Estatal de Yucatán (1982: sec. 5.2).
[e]Alternate figures for 1980 are 4,986 (Rodríguez Losa 1991: 349).
[f]Figures for Pisté in 1988 and 1990 (Pinto González et al. 1989: sec. 3) based on survey and projected growth rate.
[g]Figures for 1989 from census of the Comisaría de Pisté and the Comité Pro-Lucha, April 1989.
[h]Official figures for 1990 by INEGI (1991: 13, 32) appear to be underestimations of populations.
[i]County population in 1990 by Rodríguez Losa (1991: 349) is 7,131.

Table 2. Distribution of Municipal Population of Tinum, 1940–90 (in %)

Pueblos	1940	1950	1960	1970	1980	1990
Pisté	16.5	24.4	26	31	37	44
Tinum	–	–	30	30	26	24
Other communities	–	–	44	39	37	31
Municipio	100	100	100	100	100	100

housing problem. Although there has been a dramatic increase in the number of homes, from 193 in 1970 to 640 in 1988 (Pinto González et al. 1989: 5.1), twenty-four families out of 664 had to rent in 1988 (ibid.: 5.4). In 1989, seven migrant families were granted house plots from the *fundo legal,* or town land grant, by the *comisario* (mayor) in a demonstration of openness to newcomers and of solidarity with the sister communities that would form part of a new county based in Pisté (see chapter 9).

At the end of the twentieth century, then, Pisté became a thriving socioeconomic center with its own hinterlands. It is in this sense that nothing has changed with the advent of tourism that was not already going on in the 1920s and 1930s, although it is clear enough that everything indeed has altered. It is too easy to attribute what is visible to the eye in Pisté to a mythical impact of tourism; but I have suggested that it makes better (or just as bad) sense to understand tourism as one of many contingent ramifications of anthropology and its intervention at the local level. As this ethnographic mapping has suggested, it is certainly not possible to talk about the social, economic, and political changes in Pisté as being the result of tourism without first comprehending the multiple ways in which tourism was already inscribed within the anthropological project and how both were always already interwoven within the social fabric of the regional and local communities. Still, we must look at Pisté itself to see what material changes have resulted "from tourism" and how these changes constitute its local infrastructure.

A Tour of the City:
The Underdevelopment of Tourist Impact

Among the principal services with which this settlement counts are the following: one airport located in the archeological zone of Chichén Itzá, eighteen taxis pertaining to the FUTV of Mérida, one secondary [or high] school, a CBTA 87 complex [or vocational school], two elementary schools (for the morning and afternoons), two kindergartens, one cultural center (CECIJEMA). Between Pisté and Chichén Itzá are twelve tourist accommodations with services rated at all categories and more than 249 total rooms, a total of twenty restaurants in the whole zone, six food stands, seventeen general stores, three pharmacies, one magazine store, two soda shops, thirteen private trucks for heavy transport, four *loncherías,* one general parts store, a gasoline station, ten handicraft stores, two shoe stores, six butcher shops, two poultry outlets, two fruit shops, three professional auto mechanic shops, two *tortillerías,* three corn mills, three ice-cream shops, three bars, three beer outlets, a soda warehouse/outlet, three stores for construction materials, a billiard hall, one bank, a money-exchange house in Chichén Itzá [operated] by BANAMEX, 120 independent *vendedores* in the handicraft market of Chichén Itzá, a toy store, a beauty salon, two book and paper stores, three video clubs, a cinema, three satellite disks, telephone service in the major hotels and six simultaneous international lines servicing the town, three CB radio services, a subregional office of the federal electrical commission, a postal service office that will be expanded into the administrative center for the area, a private hospital-clinic, a government health center, three sewing workshops, six workshops for the production of clothes, a video film service, and resident correspondents from two major newspapers, the *Diario de Yucatán* and *Novedades,* plus there are other [unspecified] businesses under construction. (Author's translation)

With this summary of activities, businesses, services, and facilities, the Comisario of Pisté sought to impress the governor of Yucatán with the economic vitality of the town. But, at the same time, the writing of this letter of May 5, 1989, was motivated by the concerted attempt to remedy the striking urban underdevelopment of the community. In order to elaborate, in later chapters, the politics that emerged from this situation, I here sketch this combination of and contradiction between the infrastructural underdevelopment and the economic vitality of Pisté. Since the "impact" of tourism is a negatively tainted notion, perhaps this tour can reveal something about the unsavory and modernizing effects of tourism on Pisté.

To assess local industriousness, we can consider the results of two different socioeconomic studies of Pisté. One study, commissioned by the state government in 1988 and conducted in the spring and summer by a team of five architecture students (Pinto González et al. 1989),[8] found that 29.9 percent of the population, or 1,130 persons ranging in age from fourteen to sixty-eight years, were actively participating in the local economy. While this economically active population (EAP) is broken down according to three sectors of production by the architects, the widespread mixing and overlapping of activities put into question the numerical values of categorical types. Nonetheless, the *conflicting data*[9] suggests that about 30 to 40 percent were mainly involved in the primary sector, principally agriculture (37.66 percent) but also apiculture and cattle production; 10 to 20 percent were involved in the secondary sector, principally handicraft production (10.82 percent), construction, and processing; 40 to 50 percent were involved in the tertiary sector, principally service related to tourism (27.27 percent), commerce, and transport (Pinto González et al. 1989: sec. 3.6–7).[10]

The second study was a survey conducted by the Comisaría de Pisté and the Comité Pro-Lucha in April 1989. The purpose of this survey was to collect hard socioeconomic data that would be used to prove the importance of the community as a dynamic center of a microregion so as to justify the community's political lobbying to become a county seat. To this end, the Comisaría and the Comité de Lucha surveyed all local businesses to calculate the amount of taxes that the community generates for the state. Despite the inaccessibility of information from official sources, we were able to make the reasonable estimate of 1,766,285,790 pesos paid in 1988–89 by the commercial and tourist sector of Pisté to the Hacienda in business taxes;[11] this would be about US$735,952 at an exchange rate of 2,400 pesos. This figure does not include the tax that was imposed that year on the handicraft vendors of the Tianguis, which would add another 9,312,000 pesos (US$3,725) for 1989 and 18,624,000 pesos (US$7,760) annually thereafter; but it does include estimates on the taxes that should be paid by the major hotels and restaurants of the tourist complex. In order to understand the value of Pisté commerce, this figure, first, needs to be compared to the total municipal business tax collected by the federal Hacienda; second, it needs to be determined how this amount gets redistributed back to the state and county governments and how this hacienda money compares to the municipal budget of Tinum; and, third, these latter figures would have to be compared to the amount of money that Tinum, the county seat, gives back to Pisté for its budget. Unfortunately, answers to the first two questions were unattainable.[12] With regard to the third question, the Ayuntamiento of Tinum, or county government, provided the 1988–89 budget for the Comisaría of Pisté with a bimonthly allotment of three hundred thousand pesos, that is, US$120 (2,400/1 rate).

This amount is impressive for its poverty and provides a departure for understanding the sociopolitical unrest of Pisté: this budget could not cover the basic operating costs of electricity, water, and salary for one policeman. Certainly it is true that other rural towns of similar size receive(d) as little and less in direct government support—after all, this sort of thing contributed to the crises that threatened the overthrow of the PRI in 1988. However, with regard to Pisté this injustice is all the more striking given that Tinum county has ranked (1980–83) and surely continues to rank among the fourteen most economically significant of the Yucatec *municipios*; further, the per capita rate of state income that the county generated was more than twice that of twelve of the other *municipios* and *second only to Mérida* in 1985.[13]

The observable importance of Chichén Itzá as a tourist attraction to the state can be quantified with some basic figures.[14] It consistently captured around 50 percent and 55 percent of all tourism to archeological zones in Yucatán between 1977–81 and 1981–87, respectively; despite the loss of four months of tourism in 1988 because of Hurricane Gilberto (September 14–15), this figure increased to 61 percent. In turn, Chichén captured 36–43 percent and 44–55 percent of all tourism to the state for the years 1977–81 and 1981–88. Furthermore, Chichén accounted for 91 percent of the increase of tourism to all the state's archeological zones; also, the increase of tourism to this site alone exceeded the increase of that to the state by 126 percent. Despite this importance as an attraction, the state and federal governments do not receive substantial direct income from the site; and thus they are not financially able to reinvest significant amounts in the maintenance and conservation of the archeological patrimony, which has been a constant and loud complaint of different sectors throughout local and regional society. My research on the state revenue that Chichén generates through CULTUR, the Patronato de las Unidades de Servicios Culturales y Turísticos del Estado de

Yucatán (one of the three state tourist agencies),[15] provides an estimate of 1,255,379,960 pesos for 1988, or US$523,075; this gross is
primarily based on ticket sales, but also parking and rental of commercial space within the Parador Turístico; it is not at all clear how
much of this low figure remains after operating costs, nor who has
access to it. The high profits generated by tourism go, instead, to the
major hotels and restaurants, which are being fed in turn by the travel
agencies in Mérida and Cancún, and only indirectly do they reach
the state through taxation.

It is here where a contradiction comes to light. Despite the attraction of Chichén for the tourists who visit Yucatán, only 13–15
percent of the overnight visitors to the state spend one night in Pisté
or Chichén Itzá (based on 1984–88 figures).[16] Although this makes
Pisté-Chichén second only to Mérida, it indicates that this tourist
complex operates as a day trip within the regional network. Yet we
should expect a convergence of interests between different economic
agents that would not only seek to increase tourism but to do so
specifically by expanding the local share of the overnight market.
The residents of Pisté, which recognizes that its communal and individual interests have been intimately connected to Chichén since the
1920s, are definitely in favor of increased tourism. The state and private capital should also be in favor of this to the extent that their
tourist endeavors elsewhere (e.g., Mérida, Cancún, Valladolid) are not
adversely affected by the development of tourism locally; whether
this interest in the local situation is actually in contradiction with
other interests or simply not recognized, no strategic efforts have
been made to develop Pisté into an attraction in its own right capable of pulling in an increasing number of overnight visitors.

In the 1980s the state government began to devise more coherent
tourism strategies and to implement these in different projects, however limited in scope. Although part of the state's general 1981–82
"Municipal Plan of Urban Development," the socioeconomic analysis
of Tinum county included a project relating to tourism at Chichén
and Pisté (Gobierno Estatal de Yucatán 1982a). It is at this time that
the major changes that situated the invasion of the archeological zone
by three hundred vendors were conceived. Specifically, these are (1) the
closing of the road that passed through the center of Chichén and
making the *desvío* so that the highway between Mérida and Cancún
would pass alongside the airport to the north of the Sacred Well; (2)

the construction of a new entrance with touristic services, the Cuber-tizo, just to the west of the Ball Court, which was not thought to be replaced by a more modern Parador Turístico until 1985, when a new state office of tourism (CULTUR) was created; and (3) the installation of a nighttime Light and Sound Show on the pyramids. Other projects of a more social and urban aspect, such as the construction of a lighted "boardwalk" between Chichén and Pisté, were also planned; however, not all were carried to completion, nor did they constitute a comprehensive plan to create an urban infrastructure. Because the county government was not dedicated to investing its budget in social works projects in communities other than Tinum, urban improvements then and now require intervention by the state or federal government. But that was not forthcoming, since the projects initiated by CULTUR in 1985 were at Chichén.

The inadequacy of the urban infrastructure of Pisté increased with the growth of tourism and the community as a socioeconomic center. The local *perception and image* of its inadequacy grew as well in relation to the increased investment in and development of the tourist complex. For neighboring communities, of course, Pisté provides a destination of migration because it is more developed as an urban, economic, and social center. Nonetheless, the profound community frustration with the inadequacy of the urban infrastructure reached a threshold of protest in 1987 and 1988 and motivated the new congressional deputy of District 13 (to which Tinum belongs) to initiate a multiphased project of development in March 1988. The first phase was a comprehensive analysis of the socioeconomic situation by a team of architects, as already mentioned. Their study quantifies the characteristics and problems that stimulated intense social agitation that in turn officially motivated the deputy to initiate the development project.

The urban zone comprises 166 hectares of the *fundo legal,* of which 116.2 or 70 percent are residential, giving an average population density of 32.48 persons per hectare; 26.25 hectares or 15.81 percent are occupied by services such as schools, clinics, and churches; and 23.55 hectares or 14.19 percent are used by commercial enterprises. But, of this urban area only 85 percent was connected to the water supply system; nonetheless, most of the population was forced to haul buckets of water from wells or from the neighbor's house down the street whose water connection was functioning. Even when working, water only trickled through the pipes for two hours in the early morning and in the afternoon. This situation was severely aggravated when the pump broke in early 1987 and ran at less than full power until October 1989 because of lack of support from the municipal and state governments. Further, although the system was rated for a population of 4,607 persons at 150 liters per person, the team of architects estimated that 250 liters per person was necessary because this source of water is also used for household gardens and animals; in turn, this use by those who received water nearest the pump diminished its use by others at higher elevations or a greater distance (Pinto González et al. 1989: 34, sec. 6.1).[17]

Only 2 percent of the residences, but all the hotels, restaurants, and posadas, have septic services (ibid.: sec. 6.2). There is a complete absence of a water drainage system, which results in daily flooding of the streets during the rainy season.[18] This combination results in the increasing contamination of the water table, which is only between twenty-two and twenty-five meters below ground, from the surface disposal of human waste of a steadily increasing population. Despite the existence of a large transformer and electrical substation located on the road between Chichén and Pisté, only 40 percent of the urban zone had public electricity; 72 percent of all households and only 60 percent of the households in the residential "downtown" were connected (ibid.: sec. 6.4–5).

With regard to roads, there are 15.5 kilometers that service Pisté, which makes up 12.64 hectares or 7.6 percent of the urban zone (ibid., sec. 6.3). Of this only 3 kilometers or 19.35 percent of the total road length is paved, which corresponds to the federal highway that runs from Dzitas in the north through the center of town past Chichén to Valladolid in the east and to the road that runs west out of town toward Mérida. The remainder is composed of *terracería* or rubble fill (4.9 kilometers or 31.61 percent of the urban zone), *pedragosa* or uncut bedrock (6.6 kilometers or 42.58 percent of the zone), and *brecha* or footpath (1 kilometer or 6.46 percent of the zone). Thus, 86.65 percent of the road surface is unpaved (as compared to nearly 100 percent paved in Tinum), and virtually unpassable by motor vehicle. There is no public transportation system. In 1988, there was no bus terminal for the regional bus lines and no post office; both were constructed in 1990–91 as a result of the politics discussed in the next section of this chapter. The study noted other aspects of the town that, for a socioeconomic center of Pisté's stature, were deficiencies, such as the fact that the only athletic field, used for soccer and baseball, was located in the side of an old quarry and that the CONASUPO, or *ejido*-based agricultural store, was of inadequate size. Another issue that was and continues to be of major significance is that what little sidewalk existed in town was severely damaged, disrupted in places, and often accompanied by holes where large mud puddles would form during the rains: the protests about the sidewalks follow the commonplace rhetoric of positioning outside interests above local needs by noting that this gives a very bad image to and is very dangerous for the tourists who visit. This same logic is used to protest the high volume of traffic along this road, at the time the only major east-west thoroughfare, which caused an amazing and constant drone of buses, cars, and eighteen-wheel trucks. Further, unlike most of the other towns and villages that lay along this route, Pisté counted only two *topes* (the infamously large concrete speed bumps) located to the immediate east and west of the *zócalo* (town plaza). The lack of these is significant, because without them there is nothing to cause traffic to slow down from highway to urban speed. This not only contributes to the noise pollution, but has resulted in a high number of accidents involving pedestrians or bicyclists going to and from Chichén. And the lack of speed controls is a threat to tourists who might wander unknowingly across the street in search of a souvenir and get smacked by a speeding car or a two-ton truck.

In summary, the underdevelopment of Pisté is relative, even though it presents a *striking image* to outsiders as a run-down, commodified, and westernized society and, to locals, of unjust infrastructural inadequacies. The major problems, for the architects and locals alike, were lack of water, electricity, paved roads, sidewalks, an athletic field, a bus station, a post office, and *topes* (speed bumps). To argue that this could be a symptom or result of the *uneven* or *under*development triggered *by tourism* is to ignore the fact that these urban problems were and continue to be part of a more general and severe crisis throughout Yucatán and the nation as well. On the contrary, Pisté has unquestionably developed because of tourism into a major socioeconomic center whose material and urban advantages distinguish its standard of living quite dramatically from larger and older towns within a broad surrounding area. Instead, the inadequacies in the infrastructure that have gone unabated with the growth of both local and regional tourist industries are not so much the result of tourism as a function of a political *abandonment* by county, state, and federal governments. At least, this is the crux of the issue for the people of Pisté and many other Yucatec communities whose social and economic dissatisfactions became a widespread, if mostly localized, political protest by the end of the 1980s.

The Impact of Politics on the Impact of Tourism: In the Contact Zone

The problems of development and economic diversification that have troubled Yucatán derive from a successful monoculture based on henequen that emerged in the 1880s but that decayed into a long-stagnant, dependent, and peripheral economy after the collapse of the world henequen market in 1918.[19] By the end of the 1960s, the failure of the state-controlled production of henequen motivated a series of government diversification projects, primarily in agricultural products such as fruit in the Puuc zone of Yucatán, which have had varying results. The corn belt in which Pisté is located was never targeted by such projects, for even the governmental institutions and agencies that sought the promotion of traditional artisanry and crafts bypassed much of this zone, with the exception of rural places such as Dzitnup or major towns such as Valladolid. Instead, tourism developed slowly and without any strategic regulation or supervision both regionally and locally throughout the 1960s and 1970s. This is in significant contrast to the tourist development of Cancún and the state of Quintana Roo, which originated in a famous computer search of ideal sites and was orchestrated by FONATUR (Fondo Nacional de Fomento al Turismo) and SECTUR (Secretaría de Turismo).[20]

Without much planning or effort, then, tourism to Yucatán peaked out at more than nine hundred thousand visitors in 1980. But this figure would not be approached again until 1987 when one million visitors were registered. Among the principal factors that led to this decline throughout the 1980s is Cancún, which, at ten years of age, had begun to reorient the whole Mexican tourist endeavor and to restructure the regional market. Notice, however, that this loss of tourist dollars for Yucatán did not primarily affect the upper levels of private capital, which had invested early on in Cancún. The state, for

its part, was mostly unconcerned; after all, although the 1981 municipal projects for urban development did entail consideration of tourism
for specific localities, there was no overarching conceptualization of
the state as a network of tourist attractions apart from the Cancún
circuit or of such a system of sights that required orchestration. Such
a strategic understanding would not emerge until 1984–85 and was
manifested in the creation of CULTUR as the governmental agency of
the state that would not simply coordinate and plan tourism, but
would essentially operate as a state-run tourist business. The recuperation of tourist flows to Yucatán in 1987 and continued growth in
subsequent years, which the hurricane devastated for 1988, represents
successful state-level management and planning of this institution.
These two events—the 1981 municipal plan of urban development
for Tinum and the creation of CULTUR—had profound ramifications
not only for the region, but specifically for Pisté and Chichén. In many
ways, these two political interventions shaped the course and practice of tourism to the present day.

First, as already mentioned, the 1981 plan called for the closing
of that part of the Mérida-Cancún road that entered the archeological zone and the construction of a new entrance, the Cubertizo (which
turned out to be temporary). This entailed, of course, the destruction
of the old entrance under the Castillo, as well as the dozen or so homes
that had been built along the road by the INAH custodians. Thus, this
state action forced the relocation of these families who comprised
the village of Chichén (population 100+) to Pisté. Because the families of the custodians were allowed to build their homes within the
heart of the site, homes from which they had begun to sell artisanry,
food, books, and guide service, the INAH employees were compensated
for their losses with the privilege of maintaining one *palapa*[21] in the
zone (near the Temple of the High Priest) for commercial purposes.
The agreement held that the custodians could form a cooperative to
sell food, beverage, handicrafts, guidebooks, postcards and other items.
Thus, the *palapa* was organized as a *cooperativa* or co-op run by the
INAH custodians and soon provided the circumstances that were to
fuel the invasion of the archeological zone by three hundred vendors
of food and artisanry.

Second, this invasion in turn became a crisis of multiple dimensions.
This illegal activity could not be controlled by the INAH wardens,
who were not simply disinterested authorities but commercial com-

petitors. Having superior location and mobility for their sales, these invaders also threatened the profits of all handicraft stores that were situated in Pisté, Chichén, or on the charter bus route from Mérida or Cancún. The loss of sales by these stores in turn implied the loss of commissions by the tour guides who would take their groups to specific stores to buy artisanry. The state, for its part, lost if not revenue from sales tax, then the ability to control commerce. Beyond these economic issues that tied different groups into a war over tourist dollars, there were aesthetic and ecological problems. The massive intrusion of *vendedores* who converted the sight into an open-air handicraft market gave tourists a "bad" *image* of Yucatán and Mexico: the aggressive sales tactics were said to be unappealing, typically rude, deceitful, tacky, and so on. In short, it was all but explicitly stated that it was aesthetically polluting because it was definitively too Third World. Further, the high volume of sales threatened the ecology, specifically the survival of a tree that was used to make *ídolos* or wooden figurines. This invasion and its crises were able to develop because of the lack of an effective preexisting authority structure that controlled commercial activities in the archeological zone. Thus, despite police and military efforts to put a halt to the invasion, no resolution of the conflicts emerged until 1987 through the intervention of CULTUR. This agency was legally constituted at the height of the invasion and was immediately given the jurisdiction to intercede so as to establish *order.* Order was indeed established through the coerced relocation of the illegal and itinerant *vendedores* into a handicraft market constructed just for the purposes of extracting the invaders.

Third, although some two hundred *vendedores* and *artesanos* did enter this new market called the Tianguis, many refused to become part of that disciplinary institution and continued to sell, no longer within the archeological zone, but still illegally, on its outskirts and in the streets of Pisté. Thus the invasion became refashioned into a political and social crisis for the town. In turn, this ongoing crisis is one significant reason why the state-level authorities have maintained a "hands-off" position with regard to requests by Pisté for socioeconomic assistance. As was the case during the invasion, this shift in the tourist war involved everyone in town, not simply the store owners and *vendedores de artesanía,* in a complex series of long-standing, mobile conflicts and alliances.

One of these store owners (whom we will revisit in chapter 9) is a man who, as a tour guide, developed some capital and, through his investments in a restaurant and a handicraft store, became a capitalist of regional scope. His entrepreneurial success catapulted in 1985 when he was able to buy land for these two businesses from the *fundo legal* via an illegal transaction with the mayor that was not and would not have been approved by the community. When the community became aware of the sale, the mayor was nearly lynched before agreeing to resign. Given the antagonism between the capitalist and the street vendors (and even much of the town), there is no doubt that it was his influence on the new political leadership of the mayor (*comisario*), county president (*alcalde*), and district deputy (*diputado*) that ensured that one of the objectives of the 1988 development project was the creation of a handicraft market that would accomplish for the streets of Pisté what CULTUR's Tianguis succeeded in doing for Chichén. Thus, politics and tourism "impact" each other repeatedly as they intersect yet again within a space defined as the problem of the inadequacies of the urban infrastructure of Pisté.

In other words, instead of comprehending these agents and forces as constituted and differentiated entities named "state politics," "tourism," and "local society" that "effect" one another, we must break down these fixed and asphyxiating categories to understand the fluidity of social action and events. Let us understand the political struggle and protest over the underdevelopment of Pisté that emerged in 1988 as a site of engagement for local, regional, national, and international agencies, and not as a preexistent space called the town of Pisté that would be "impacted" by some putatively exogenous forces of tourism, state politics, and so on. The differentiation between local and nonlocal has no stable nor absolute borders. Indeed, even the alliance of persons that comprised the group of officials that entered the authority structure in 1988 with the intention of correcting local underdevelopment should be understood as a contact zone of contesting interests. Some had said that the deputy was interested in actually having a positive effect on the community through *mejoramientos,* or urban development projects, because this would provide him a plank on which to pursue higher political posts. The *alcalde*, in contrast, would never allow for municipal funds to go out of his or Tinum's pocket for the improvement of Pisté; his support of *mejoramientos* was an order given from above with the promise that he could go home with a welcome percentage of whatever budget would be approved for construction work.

In turn, the newly elected *comisario* would have to play off his own self-interest and that of his superiors in order to attain some measure of successful improvement of the urban situation. This turned out to be very difficult for him to achieve: although his election might not have been based on fraud or bought votes, as claimed by the opposition, the first nine months of office were very unstable. The opposition, which had been politically dominant throughout the latter 1970s and early 1980s, did not take losing authority lightly and created an intensifying political antagonism for the new mayor that centered around his inappropriate and unsuccessful resolution of the water crisis. Thus, within the first three months of 1988 the new *comisario* was already under strong and constant attack by a highly agitated community that was demanding water and/or his removal from office. As a result, many of the key advisers of the mayor's political entourage of subordinates were forced to resign in February, and then another set of assistants resigned in March. But by this time the deputy had called a town assembly to announce the 1988 development projects for Pisté; the critical issue of the water was quietly resolved with a new pump that would continue to be sporadically dysfunctional and a public accounting of its operating costs.

In this way the opposition was smothered temporarily and the "Anteproyecto del desarrollo socio-económico y urbano del pueblo de Pisté" (Pinto González et al. 1989) was initiated in the spring and summer. It was at this time that it became clear that this project, although prophesying resolution of the many inadequacies already noted, was truly about the *vendedores ambulantes de artesanía* and the *bad image* they gave to tourists. The months of April through July were filled with discussion of Pisté as a tourist *sight* and of the many ways to improve the tourist aspect/attraction of the community. These, of course, revolved around getting the vendors and artisans off the streets and into their own cooperative, community-operated, traditional handicraft market. Such an entity, by the way, never existed in Pisté or in Maya culture; such traditions only and always already exist as a function of modernity and, here, of tourism (see Canclini 1993 and chapters 7 and 8). Not only was this market explicitly modeled on the recently constructed Tianguis, but many of the other projects were developed from the recommendations made by a team of INAH anthropologists for resolution of the invasion (Peraza López et al. 1987). For example, with the new handicraft market was to be a restaurant and a workshop where tourists could see the artisans making idols; and, more, there was continuing talk of an *ejido*-owned and -run hotel/posada conjoined with the market. All of this was to be for the "benefit" of the handicraft vendors and producers and in their "best" interests. The *vendedores,* for their part, pointed out the fact that the travel agencies and their proxies, the tour guides, control the flow of tourists and, thus, nothing would be successful without the payment of commissions; however, no deal with them could be trusted because they are allied with the large handicraft merchants that can afford to buy off the guides through the commissions game. Thus, the question of urban development returned and returns to the problem of the tourist body, its trajectories in time, and its durations in space. Scores of private meetings, work-group reunions, town *asambleas,* and informal discussions were organized to debate not only the possibility that some of these projects would be actualized, but how to shape or subvert them if they were to be put *en camino,* "on the path," and where best to situate oneself on this dual path of development and tourists so as to direct or have access to the body of the tourist.

Consumed with the practical problems and politics of *tourist* development, public and private discourse assumed a rhetoric of community good that was dominated by the trope of the *image* of the town as an attraction for tourism: How might Pisté refashion itself as a sight beyond its functional role as the service center for Chichén? This figure of *image* as the attraction of tourists operated not only as a yardstick by which to evaluate *mejoramientos* but as a moral code to judge the actions of individuals and economic sectors that were and are involved in tourism. Specifically, *tourist image* targeted the *artesanos* and *vendedores* who were blamed for breaking aesthetic values of self-presentation with Third World-style street vending, for ecological destruction of trees and forest habitats, for lack of education and consciousness about the cultural patrimony that the archeological ruins represent, and, finally, for loss of "traditional" forms of communal-collective versus individualized, entrepreneurial economic action. In short, the vendors and artisans were the root and image of all underdevelopment, whereas in truth they were and are simply seeking to exploit, as rational individuals in competitive and conflictive activities, the massive tourist development that chose their village. This discourse of blame fell short of placing responsibility on the vendors for the broken sidewalks and mud puddles of the town in which a group of alcoholics (*teporochos*), among whom are many artisans, are often found strewn about in drunken stupors. After all, is not the lack of progress in Pisté due to the cultural backwardness and lack of modern education that compels *some* Maya artisans, construction workers, and agricultural proletarians to squander their (no longer archeology silver, but) tourist dollars on liquor instead of "luxuries for the home"? Here, indeed, is the *mal imagen* of Pisté *under*development but also of the *over*development of *tourist impact*.

In the image and figure of the *teporochos* lying in puddles between broken slabs of concrete sidewalk is the conjoining and complicity of two discursive practices and (re)colonizing politics, both of which situate Pisté and the inhabitants of this topos as simultaneously too Maya and too modern and at the same time as both too untraditional (culture loss) and too unmodern (not yet civilized). Here again is a zero-degree culture in a postmodern topos that refuses and yet conflates the measuring of the impact of tourism, of anthropology, of modernity, and of traditional culture.

From this perspective, the problem of the infrastructural inadequacies is revealed as a rhetorical vehicle for gambits for power not only by the authorities of 1988, but by the local opposition that lost the election. Even the political agitation that flowed from the crisis of potable water was submerged in the spring of 1988 with the minor adjustments of the physical system and forgotten about during the summer struggles over the fate of the street vendors. The summer also saw the emergence of a new issue that put underdevelopment politics on the back burner. As is the common strategy in municipal politics, the Pisté opposition had patiently waited for a series of flagrant "irregularities" of graft and corruption on the part of the *comisario* to come to light so that it could denounce these illegalities and foment community outrage. Thus, at the end of August, began denunciations of the *comisario*'s illegal use of *ejido* lands with the intention of "privatizing" very specific plots that would be of high commercial value; many suspected that his construction of permanent features (an animal pen) was a ruse that would allow him to sell this to the store-and-restaurant-owning capitalist already introduced. The town was again embroiled in a major dispute that climaxed on September 9 with a town assembly in which the *comisario* was verbally and physically assaulted in an attempt to have him removed from office and desist from any illegal land sales. It is emblematic of the composition of the factions and of the other underlying issues at stake that the man who did approach the mayor to hit him was a *vendedor de artesanía* who operated stalls legally in the Tianguis and illegally at the Mayaland entrance to Chichén. An irony of this event is that this *vendedor* is known for illegally appropriating communal lands to sell them. The subsequent five days were extremely tense as the two sides—one the legal civil authority backed by the state government and the other led by the *ejido* authorities backed by the federal government—maneuvered their nonlocal allies and prepared for a long, drawn-out battle.[22] However, Hurricane Gilberto put a definitive stop to the party.

The hurricane devastated the peninsula. Although this is not the place to detail the social and economic wreckage, it can be noted that tourism was completely shut down for four months in Cancún and only hundreds of visitors from Mérida and Cozumel passed through Chichén during that time. Everyday life on the peninsula became devoted to the immediate tasks of survival and recuperation of losses. The reterritorialization of Pisté in the subsequent months did not include a return to the old political scenarios. Instead, the opposition took effective action in leading the regeneration of the town but in a necessary solidarity with the twice besieged mayor. In this context, in January 1989 he initiated petitions for federal assistance that could resolve the infrastructural problems of Pisté, which, as the *antesala* (antechamber) of Chichén Itzá, was deserving of special attention and *mejoramientos* in the aftermath of Gilberto. The *comisario*, whose independent support had eroded completely, was forced to ally himself with his opposition and a Comité de Lucha was formed as an adjunct community leadership that would pursue no longer simply urban development, but now the juridical status of an independent county (the 107th of the state), or *municipio libre*, according to the state and federal laws of the Mexican Revolution (see Q. Castañeda 1991: ch. 2, Appendix G).

In this way, the Movimiento 107 reinitiated the struggle of earlier comisarios during the previous twenty-eight years to attain a more permanent political resolution of the problems of development that Pisté has experienced as the *antesala* or service center to Chichén. Although there is much more to say about the Lucha 107, we can note that the community and leadership alike sought to strategically resolve their problems through political independence from Tinum; this would grant greater local control over the financial surplus generated by Chichén, which in turn would be a means to rectify infrastructural inadequacies, to improve the community's tourist image, and therefore also to intervene directly in the management of the tourist body. In this way, Pisté dreamed itself more than simply the *antesala* of Chichén; it began to imagine itself in the seat of political, economic, and social power as the *cabecera* (county seat) of a new county that would be the *municipio* of Chichén Itzá. However, when, on May 9, 1989, the town's leadership and supporters submitted to the state congress their formal request to become a *municipio libre,* it had become obvious that this was just the beginning of a long struggle that would be prolonged through to the municipal elections of 1990 (see *Diario de Yucatán* 1989e, 1989f; de los Reyes 1989; Góngora Navarette 1989; ch. 9 below). Pisté was allowed to win these elections and to have our friend the mayor positioned as *alcalde* or president of the county. Yet, politics being what it is, he lasted not a year before being jailed for corruption and other charges. Thus, it seemed that Chichén was destined to be a day trip and Pisté, the Antesala de Chichén Itzá, would be only a lunch stop on a three- or seven-day itinerary of beaches and ruins.

In closing, note that it was only through the successive and reciprocal "impacts" of anthropology, tourism, state politics, modernity, and even traditional culture that Pisté, or local society, finally chose the path to progress that Chan Kom had so easily pursued some fifty-two years earlier. But *this* path did not lead to Chicago: it leads to Mexico City.

*Chichén Itzá: The Museum of
Maya Culture and Civilization*

3 / On the Museum's Runes, the Ruins of Modernity

A Genealogy

Writing is a strange invention.
Lévi-Strauss, "The Writing Lesson," Tristes Tropiques (1978: 298)

The art of memory is like an inner writing.... "For the places are
very much like wax tablets or papyrus, the images like the
letters, the arrangement and disposition of the images like the
script, and the delivery is like the reading."
Yates, quoting the *Ad Herennium*, in
The Art of Memory (1966: 6–7)

An Easy Guide to the Museum of Chichén Itzá

Chichén Itzá is a fabulous place. This city of fables is inscribed on the scrub forest of the imagination as well as carved out of the effervescent limestone of Yucatán. First invented by Mayas over many centuries, refashioned by the colonial and criollo imagination, and then later reconstructed by archeologists according to their early twentieth-century vision, the ruins form a complex layering and interweaving of signs, symbols, representations, texts, discourses, spaces, time and timing, practices, legends, meanings, and memories that are all invisibly "heaped up" on the ancient buildings. Here is a complex stratigraphy of contesting knowledge and struggles put into motion in an economy of scriptural practices. It is a kind of space that Foucault termed "heterotopia" (Foucault 1986). The task in this section, devoted to the Museum of Maya Culture and Civilization, is to ethnographically map, understand, and analyze the multiple dimensions and operations of this heterotopia.

The Museum Palimpsest: A Strategic Place

Chichén Itzá is, in the first place, the name of a strategy and apparatus of knowledge embodied in the form of a museum. Materially, this "episteme" (Foucault 1972) exists, that is, is embodied, in the form of "ruins," which are not simply the physical remains of ancient buildings and artifacts that have been excavated, restored, and reconstructed in a scientific calculation, but also all the trees selectively left standing, discarded stones, paths, weeds, tourist stands, rest areas, waste disposal sites, and boundary-marking roads and milpas. The ruins are a palimpsest on which "Maya" is continuously read, written, rewritten, and overwritten by diverse practices in multiple texts of heterogeneous media. It is a palimpsest that operates like a "text," in the sense that Derrida has defined it: a text is a giant machine for reading and writing other texts (1979). The Museum of Maya Culture, then, is a strategic orchestration of both knowledge of the Maya and of the production of this knowledge; it is an apparatus (Foucault 1979, 1980b; cf. de Certeau 1984) through which Maya culture is invented and continually reinvented in text.

The purpose of this chapter is to arm a panoply of tools and tropes that can aid in the description and analysis of this apparatus, which Foucault has defined as a "heterogeneous ensemble of discourses, institutions, architectural forms, regulatory decisions, laws, scientific statements, philosophical, moral and philanthropic propositions...inscribed in a play of power" (1980b: 194–96). While the preceding and subsequent chapters (1–2, 7–9) chart dimensions of this apparatus that from a different theoretical framework would be its "context" or "process," in this section I am concerned with the manifestation of this strategic orchestration of practices in the mode of the museum ruins of Chichén Itzá. In order to scrutinize the heterogeneous operations, historical complicities, and multiple articulations of practices that comprise this Museum, I am compelled to offer a conceptual model and series of terms that might strike the reader as a mixing of metaphors (e.g., machine, text, economy, palimpsest, wax slab, factory, reading, travel). However, it is through this panoply of terms that I have been able to envision the complex stratigraphy of discursive practices that constitutes what appears as a relatively unproblematic tourist attraction based on Maya ruins. By the same measure, this language should reveal not only the contestation and artifice that inhabit Chichén, but the analytical machinery that seeks to comprehend—to read and to write—this entity as a facet of a wider scriptural economy.

A Genealogy of the Museum as Figure of Modernity

The general history of museums, especially in relation to the rise of anthropology and modernity, is well known. The following genealogy underlines certain conjunctions between travel practices and the emergence of nations as they pertain to understanding museums and Chichén Itzá as a museum.[1]

The arts of memory required the speaker to mentally associate ("deposit") words and things of discourse with mental images of objects and/or personified qualities; in turn, these images were mentally located in specific places (loci, topoi) that were spatially arranged in a determinate order provided by a remembered building. Through a mental tour of these topoi to "see" the images, the speaker recalled the topics embodied therein and performed the discourse that was already scripted as an architectural system. This art of memory, as centuries of advocates have noted, is a form of writing that occurs in the mind. However, this analogy with writing needs to be further drawn out. First, notice that it is not so much the mind that comprises the space on which the writing occurs, but, according to the rhetoricians, the imagined places located in an actual building that are like wax tablets on which are inscribed the images. If "the arrangement and disposition of the images [are] like the script" (Yates 1966: 6), then the building is both the space of the composite text and a library analogue that houses a series of tablet-texts. The building is, thus, an intertextual space—the space of a page as well as of a book—that conjoins an inscription of images as if on wax that is understood as a literal writing. Second, but because the architecture has a duplicitous nature, being both real and mental, it is writing in a larger sense: an actual building is selected and must be visited and revisited not only so that all of its architectural (structural) details can be recorded in memory, but so as to empty it of any incidental artifacts that would occlude the orator's memory-writing. Thus, abandoned buildings—ruins, that is—seem to be favored. It is as if a new building were reconstructed in the mind and swept clean of the artifacts of others' image-memories so as to be occupied by the orator's own images. In other words, this art of memory abides by the three facets of what de Certeau called writing: (1) the preparation of a blank space on which (2) are practiced the gestures that create a system of meaning, and (3) the operations of the text by which it imposes its meaning/law over an outside. Third, the practice of this memory-writing is, in its critical gestures, travel: the art of memory is a spatializing practice through which space is sighted, traversed, created/carved, inscribed with value, bounded, extended, linked up, imagined, communicated. Thus, while Yates's term "local memory" emphasizes this spatial aspect, we can also understand the classical art as travel or travel-memory, to emphasize the procedures and practice of this scriptural economy.

Yates (1966) argues that the art of memory informed the Enlightenment project of modernity in that rationalist methods of knowledge developed from Renaissance elaborations of the art. These divide into occult and rationalist versions that offer differing styles of totalizing knowledge. First, as Hooper-Greenhill (1992: 91) notes, although the occult arts and theaters of memory have been discussed in the emergence of the modern museum, their exact role has not been substantially elaborated.[2] The imaginary building that housed memory was "transcribed" from an existence in the mind back into a physical, material form; thus, a prototypical architectural model for the display of objects is established: the museum. But more, the spatial rhetoric of images (objects and mythic persona) arranged and displayed as a cosmology does inform the museum logic: the occult arts and theaters of memory provided the cosmovision—understood in terms of micro/macrocosm similitudes—on which the wide variety of cabinets were organized (cf. Hooper-Greenhill 1992: 78–132).[3] Thus, these occult cosmologies shared the generic and gendered Renaissance view of a man-centered universe, which becomes one of the pivots, along with its macrocosmic double, civilization, of the modern museum.

Second, Renaissance rationalism, exemplified by Ramus, refashioned the memory systems into "arts" of knowledge in which order is comprised of a simplified, image-less hierarchy conceived as a logical continuum between "generals" and "specifics" (Yates 1966: 231–43, 266–86). As Yates points out with regard to Ramus, this rationalizing occurs in the context of political and religious struggles from which modernity and the modern nation-state emerge (see Toulmin 1990). Before the modern institution comes into existence, however, rational methods of ordering and producing knowledge are reworked, first, into the eminently modern classifications of eighteenth-century botany and zoology and, second, into the nineteenth-century geological and archeological ways of knowing. In these shifts, human history became naturalized and amenable to representation in rational systems of display in theaters of knowledge: The modern museum is born as an idea and institution in the form of a natural history in which Man is simultaneously centered in the universe yet decentered through naturalization. In other words, the modern museum is forged out of a combination of and tension between these two occult and rationalist styles of memory/knowledge. One style explicitly operates a moral-mystical representation of a man-centered universe through metaphoric/allegorical images; the other style explicitly conceals these cosmological functions within a rational representation based on a realist aesthetic of metonymic/synecdochic images ("artifacts").

From this angle, then, we can understand how the museum embodies the Enlightenment project for totalized, rational knowledge (cf. Crimp 1983; Haraway 1989). Donato (1979) points out, however, that the museum has not been generally recognized as the emblematic figure of knowledge for the episteme of modernity; this status has been given to the library-encyclopedia (think of Borges), which as heir of the medieval *Book of Nature,* has a longer claim in Western culture as repository of knowledge and truth. Bacon, in a well-quoted passage, for example, suggests four key tropes of knowledge for the modern episteme: library, garden, "cabinet" (or museum), "still-house" (or laboratory). Interestingly, Donato's reading of Flaubert's subordination of the library as one figure of knowledge belonging to a series located within the museum resonates with our discussion of the classical art of memory. The library is within the museum as that collection of texts inscribed as striking images on the waxy memory places housed within an imaginary building. Yet, as embodied architectural systems, the library and the museum are also already coincident. From the angle of text (writing in the narrow sense), the memory building is library, whereas from that of representation (displayed image), it is museum. This (irreducible?) hinge of text/representation (writing/image) can account for vacillation between different ways of construing the modern episteme. Read, for example, Foucault's juggling of notions:

> In seeking... to write a history of the *episteme,* I was still caught in an impasse. What I should like to do now is to try and show that what I call an apparatus is a much more general case of the *episteme*; or rather, that the *episteme* is a specifically *discursive* apparatus, whereas the apparatus in its general form is both discursive and non-discursive, its elements being much more heterogeneous. (Foucault 1980b: 196–97; emphasis in original)

This dilemma invokes another aporia, the debate between materialist and idealist theorizations. It also suggests the resolution that has been sought through the notion of practice:[4] From the angle of practice, what would be the relation between library (episteme) and museum (apparatus)? In a word: travel, that is, the spatializing and discursive practices that comprise travel.[5]

The travels and travelogues of the age played a critical role in the dream of totalizing knowledge contained in a visual-spatial architecture that does not merely record and recommunicate, but ceaselessly accumulates new information. For example, Stagl (1990) shows how certain students of Ramus developed his techniques in the field of travel to produce travel methodologies that were, in effect, sixteenth-century manuals on how to do ethnography, ethnographies not of cultures, but of nations and peoples. These travel methodologies derive from the same humanist tradition from which the Spanish *Relaciones Históricas-Geográficas* originate; these are questionnaires about the peoples, places, geography, economy, politics, and histories of the colonies that the Crown required colonial administrators and *encomenderos* to file (de la Garza et al. 1983). However, instead of being reports from the colonies by those located in the periphery, Ramus's students developed not only (very similar) questionnaires but methods through which travelers from the center would go to the peripheries to collect exhaustive knowledge of other nations. Thus, these manuals served as models for later developments in social-scientific method as well as tourism (e.g., the Grand Tour [Stagl 1990; cf. Klor de Alva 1988, Urry 1984]). As Stagl points out, these manuals also served as guidebooks for intelligence gathering in both diplomacy and espionage. To anticipate issues explored in Part II, "War and Its Topography," a genealogy of ethnographic practice and tourism would demonstrate the incestuous complicity of these practices and would necessarily pass through espionage to a matrix of travel methodologies.

"National politics" emerges as a critical context within which travel, its practices, and its products are situated. Just as Toulmin (1990) argues that the sixteenth-century struggles in Europe do not merely *contextualize* modernity but inhere within its operations, so too must we locate the nation and its struggles within the practice of travel and the museum as a driving force and fundamental mechanism:[6] Ramus-inspired travel methodologists planned to create a museum/library of the *vitae humanae*—called "Musaeum Generis humani Blotianum"—in which the accumulated knowledge of "tourists" would be processed in a center of documentation that would be organized as an argument for the natural superiority of one "nation" (the Holy Roman Empire) as the universal center and pinnacle. In other words, the nation comes to insert itself within the dual classificatory schemas of the museum *as the central pivot* around which the meanings, values, and identities are effected through the representational inscription of memory/knowledge. The nation becomes the privileged category of human community against which other forms of collectivity are imagined, represented (for example, as "cultures," "races," "tribes," "civilizations"), and then hierarchized into a political cosmology shaped as a genetic continuum (called "progress") of a unitary Civilization. But notice that Civilization and Nation are different levels of a more basic entity: Man. The modern museum might, then, be understood as a "theater of the real" (versus of memory-images) in which the representation of the world is triangulated by the categories and qualities of Nation, Civilization, and Man that are not displayed directly in images, but *evoked* through realist images of objects.

This genealogy of the museum as Western artifact provides a map by which to model the heterotopia of Chichén Itzá. It allows an understanding of the multiple facets of the ongoing historical invention of Chichén Itzá, which is discussed next, and of the scriptural operations that constitute this Museum.

Invention of Chichén Itzá

In 1921, a ten-year, renewable contract was signed between the Carnegie Institution of Washington, the state government of Yucatán, and the federal government of Mexico. Sylvanus G. Morley was given permission to conduct the Carnegie-sponsored Chichén Project in conjunction with archeological work, under the directorship of Erosa Peniche, conducted by the Monumentos Prehispánicos, a federal agency that was later to become Mexico's Instituto Nacional de Antropología e Historia. Thus the modern invention of Chichén Itzá began. The archeologists literally carved Chichén out of *puro monte* (out of the "pure jungle"), as the locals today proclaim, and inscribed their vision of the Maya onto the jungle, creating "ruins." It is exactly what Mircea Eliade would identify as a foundation act, the re-creation of cosmos—that is, ordered and sacred space—from the chaos of the undifferentiated and profane. Putting it in this context, we can remember that within the museum, that quintessential image of rational order, is a cosmological order organized around a sacred principle that governs in the realm of human collectivities.

The ruins are clearly an artifact of (primarily) Western science. They are a representation of the ancient city, constructed through the techniques of early twentieth-century archeological science. Chichén Itzá is a life-size scale-model replica of "itself": it is *hyperreal*. The traces of the constructed authenticity of Chichén are scandalously and continuously concealed and effaced in memory even as they are brought to consciousness. For example, naive tourists at Chichén Itzá often confuse and invert restored and unrestored ruins: they assume that the beautifully (re)constructed buildings are in their "natural" state, whereas the mounds of rubble emerging from the underbrush or backsides must be where the archeologists have destroyed the ruins in the course of their excavations. This naive understanding is a kind of parody of archeologists' concern about their destruction of data through present-day excavation when a future generation may develop a technique for "salvaging" unknown forms of would-be data. On the other hand, there are tourists who wish that the archeologists would restore either more or less of the site as way to more authentically and fully re-present the ancient Maya culture; in other words, the popular criteria of authenticity can be satisfied with *either* more extensive clearing of the jungle *or* extreme jungle growth. Regardless of which of the two logics/criteria of authenticity operate in a tourist encounter, both are representations based on a constructed image that can only approximate an original that is absolutely not there, that is lost.

Not only is the original lost, but the pristine and authentic original never existed. When in its more than fifteen-hundred-year history, and in which of its cultural forms, is to be found the authentic Chichén? Who says so, and why? The imposition of a social convention that would differentiate a given moment as the authentic, original, fully present phase of a society, building, art style, civilization, institution, or city is an inherently contested act of power in the register of knowledge. Representation or a representational system, however, is ruled by specific criteria and logics of authenticity. Because the original is lost and there is no uncontested authentic representation, all representation is evaluated by what can be called the rules of "authenticity." The better it abides by such necessarily contested rules, the more "authentic" the representation. Thus, when imitations and copies of the lost "original" are made, they must be forged on a resemblance to the "authentic" representation, which stands in the place of the "original" that never existed. This idea of "never existed," however, must be understood in terms of an authentic and original moment of full presence. Therefore, a representation that is valued as authentic (however contested the evaluation) is privileged as original, a situation designated by Derrida's term "originary."

At this point, it may seem that I am using invention in its commonsense meaning—but also in the rhetorical sense of *inventio*. After all, the Maya did build and live in Chichén; otherwise there would not have been a representation of a Maya city of legendary proportions. *Inventio* refers to a complex process including the study of the facts of the case, determination of the issues of the matter, the organization of proofs, and the elaboration (versus arrangement) of an argument; it is the disclosure of the logic of *what is*, of what actually exists, so as to present this understanding/truth in persuasive discourse. In the sense of classical rhetoric, nothing new is created in the realm of material existence or truth; the newness is in terms of a perspective, an understanding, and an arrangement of the given facts/knowledge.[7] The centuries of debates about the status of *inventio* in relation to logic, facts, and truth/falsehood were no doubt involved in transforming the meaning of invention from organization of proof to that of completely novel creation. In fusing these two concepts, the *inventio* is understood as an ideal order (whether a "culture," episteme, rhetoric, text, individual mind-set, or even descriptive sentence) of the world that seeks to account for the world; through embodiment of that order in actual material form, the *inventio* "proves" itself and thus becomes marked by truth so that its statements circulate within the true, the real, the factual.

This point may seem a tedious elaboration, but it allows us to isolate those obscure shifts in the perspective/arrangement of the "facts" of the "case" as the history of the ceaseless (re)invention of the Maya and of Chichén. This notion of invention directs attention to the nuanced differences by which the "Maya" have been and are repeatedly reinscribed in memory/knowledge. In this sense, the invention of the Maya, of Maya culture, and of Chichén Itzá as an ancient Maya city that embodies/exemplifies Maya civilization is not the false fabrication or ideological obfuscation of some other more real and authentic truth, but an ongoing practice situated within a regime of contesting practices and contested truths.

Having stated this, the contrast between this argument and another recently published argument about the invention of Chichén Itzá as a museum can be appreciated. In this widely disseminated book, the authors "are forced to acknowledge that our perception of the past is always a prisoner of the present [and that] our [scientific, Western] reconstruction of the mountains inside the Maya mind is . . . an interpretation and not the true original" (Freidel, Schele, and Parker 1993: 36). In other words, they accept the idea that Chichén is an artifact of contemporary agencies and cultural rationalities, yet they proceed to argue against the historical contingencies of scientific, even Maya, truth: "Once we have discovered the rationalities of the Maya — through the words and actions of the Maya themselves — it is our heartfelt belief that we will also discover a central truth" (ibid: 37). This truth — that Maya words and actions "are all symbols of the Creation of the cosmos" (ibid.) — is rhetorically positioned as a transcendental axis that can then anchor the Western and scientific interpretations that occupy the subsequent five hundred pages of their text. This point or truth, on the one hand, seems trivial, contentless, and "obvious" — obvious at least to those superstitious anthropologists, such as Redfield, who presuppose that the activities of culture-bearers relate to, reflect, transmit, even symbolize the native's cosmography and culture. On the other hand, the self-evident truism of this "truth" is precisely what conceals a lack of critical reflexivity and a denial of the historical constructedness of social realities. Instead there is only the flagrantly presumptuous assertion that *they* themselves *have* transcended the errors of science and popular culture in their penetrating discovery of the true and original mountains in the Maya mind. Thus, their narrative of "Three Thousand Years on the Shaman's Path" (subtitle of the work) seems to have captured the authentic Maya heart and sacrificed it on the mountains of science.

City of Wax: Lost Wax and Lost City

The *discovery* of the Maya in the nineteenth century is an originary event in the invention of Maya culture and civilization. How was it that Chichén Itzá became a *lost city* to be *discovered* by Anglo-American and European protoarcheological travelers as one of many embodiments of Maya culture? And, how did this discourse of discovery articulate with statements on the Maya circulated in Spanish, particularly, by the Yucatec and Mexican intelligentsia? The material condition for the possibility of the nineteenth-century discovery of pre-Hispanic indigenous civilizations is, of course, the devastation wrought on indigenous societies by the Spanish invasion and conquest. Pre-Columbian cities were abandoned by force or completely refashioned as and buried underneath Spanish habitats. As well, these cultures and civilizations were transfigured but lived on in the discourses and practices, Spanish and indigenous, that remembered them. That they lived on, that they retained an immediate and vibrant power, is obvious from both the fervor of the missionary vengeance on the Indian who seemed to return to idolatry—for example, Bishop Landa's Inquisition (see Clendinnen 1987)—and the Crown's suppression of "anthropological" or sympathetic investigation of Indian ways of life, especially religious forms (Bernal 1980: 102). These civilizations were not "lost": they were known to exist and to exist in specific sociopolitical and historical locations, which the colonial regime sought to contain into a subordinated and "past" place. Destruction, in central Mexico, or allowing, in the Maya world, the jungle to cover over the cities, were strategies by which these monuments and memories for resistance were strategically confined within colonial rule. The unevenness, therefore, of Spanish conquest and domination of indigenous peoples was transcribed differently in creole discourse across the Americas. For example, during the seventeenth century, when Sigüenza y Góngora was writing the blueprints of a Mexican nationalism based on idealizations of the Aztec, Yucatec missionaries were writing firsthand accounts of "initial" contacts with and conquest of still independent Maya polities deep in the heart of the Petén and Belizean forest (see Jones 1989; Bernal 1980). I think it accurate to say that the colonial endeavor everywhere was ambivalent and anxious about its rule, but this was forged differently at every point according to the particular cultural and historical modes of resistance.

In Yucatán the prophecy-histories of the Maya that foretold a future return of Maya autonomy forged a particular anxiety and ambivalence of colonial domination and discourse. As much as this indigenous cultural form has instilled fear of rebellion, it also, as Jones (1989) has pointed out, has been *mimed* so as to be used as the means to motivate, justify, legitimate, and enact conquest. Whereas from a Maya perspective, the prophecy-histories were read from a will to escape domination, Spanish and creole read and imitated these from a will to colonize/dominate (see Mediz Bolio 1987; Peniche Barrera 1986; Cáceres Carenzo 1990; Abreu Gómez 1983). Thus, what could not be effected through force was accomplished through the discursive fabrication of a fictitious wedge between the identity of contemporary Indians and the memory of self-rule that operated, on the one hand, as a *legitimization* of colonial rule and, on the other hand, as a *forgetfulness* to assuage the colonizers' fear of rebellion in the hope that the Maya too would forget their prophecies of resistance. The jungle was a natural manifestation of this wedge growing between past and present. Only in the late eighteenth and early nineteenth centuries, with the birth of the idea of a nation-state, independence from Spain, and the growth of liberalism, did the need emerge to root domination in a *historical progression from primordial Indian origins* through which a national community could be imagined. It is in this context that the architectural remains of Maya polities became *lost cities* to be *discovered* and *explored*. In this archeologizing move (see Pratt 1992), the jungle growth that covered pre-Hispanic cities shifted in meaning from a wedge between Indian past and present to the sign of an amnesia. But such discovery is not so much of a city as of a site of contestation in which national communities would forge images of themselves and others. Whereas the Aztecs had already been appropriated by the intelligentsia of New Spain in various *neo-Aztec* discourses (Keen 1990; Lafaye 1974; Pagden 1990; Bernal 1980; Klor de Alva 1992; Paz 1985), colonial Yucatán was caught in the well-grounded fear of indigenous rebellion and could not afford to transmute contemporary and ancient Maya into cultural patrimony until after 1821, when it initiated its own national agenda (see Campos García 1987, 1989; Morales Valderrama 1987, 1988; cf. Pratt 1992).

Lost in this suppressed memory, the Maya of Yucatán would be invented as archeological vestige, not by regional intelligentsia, but by Anglo-American and European discovery. The former did their job, not in the rude and uncivilized jungles, but in and through a forest of historical records and documentation. The latter were motivated to explore the "American Egypt" of Yucatán (Arnold and Frost 1909), to explore but also to appropriate it and make it *American* in a specifically national way (Hinsley 1984, 1985; Campos García 1989; Ramírez Aznar 1990; Sullivan 1989). Patterson (1986) has charted aspects of the political economy from which Americanist archeology emerged and how it fits into hemispheric agendas of U.S. elites (cf. Willey and Sabloff 1980; Trigger 1985; Lagemann 1989; Haraway 1989: 120–32, 203–6). Here we need only note that John Lloyd Stephens was able to pursue his career as founding anthropologist-traveler of the Maya because of his political and economic positioning. He was commissioned as U.S. consul to Central America. Stephens thereby initiated another tradition in that he was the first of three leading U.S. archeologists that had overt or covert political agendas as they conducted their studies: Edward Thompson was the U.S. consul to Yucatán at the turn of the century and Sylvanus Morley was a covert naval intelligence officer during World War I. But the key point here was that the Yucatec intelligentsia used these foreign agents as the means to initiate a new discourse on and about the Maya; thus, Stephens's discovery was part of a broader *local* reinvention of the Maya as archeologized civilization and as the degraded but living descendants of the ancient Mound Builders (cf. Pratt 1992: 132–41, 172–97).

A genealogy of this reinvention would require a comparative study of nineteenth-century creole discourses in Guatemala, Chiapas, and Yucatán, at least. Instead, I want to revisit the narrative and imagistic invention of the material site of Chichén Itzá that Stephens and Catherwood, his artist traveling companion, provided. What was their vision of these ruins on which the conjoined projects of the Carnegie, the Mexican government, and the Yucatec archeologists built their own ancient Maya *sight*?[8] This mapping lends an originary point (a partial beginning) in understanding why this and not another pile of rubble became targeted for the future Museum of Chichén Itzá.

Catherwood's map of the site (see figure 1) shows three types of ruins, or what can be referred to as memory loci of exhibits: "ruined mounds," whose indistinguishable conditions are such that they warrant no comment in the text; "well-preserved buildings" of artistic/ architectural interest; "piles of buildings" whose architectural characteristics can be discerned but are not of interest. Stephens offers a narrative tour of the "principal buildings" whose circuit is guided by an unmotivated logic in that the hut at the Hacienda where he had lodging is his point of departure: Akatzeeb (*sic*); Monjas; Eglesia (*sic*); Caracol; Chichanchob; Gymnasium or Tennis Court, including "Stohl" (*sic*; Temple of Jaguars) and "upper building" (Ball Court Annex); Castle; and finally the columns only of what is later to be named the Thousand Columns (Stephens 1963: 204–38, plate xxvi). Two locations are ambiguously left out of the description, the Deer House, which is shown on the map as a building in good condition and will later become a tertiary exhibit, and the "pile of buildings" to the south of the Monjas, which then and today remains uncleared and unrestored, thus, a nonlocation within the museum. But many other future locations of memory are literally mapped as "ruined mounds," even though they are not brought into the narrative:

> I have now closed my brief description of the ruins of Chichén, having presented, with as little detail as possible, all the principle [*sic*] buildings, of this ancient city. Ruined mounds exist, and detached portions of sculpture strew the ground, *exhibiting curious devices,* which often arrested us in wandering among them, but which I shall not attempt to give. They [the principal buildings]...had additional interest in our eyes from the fact that the broad light of day beams upon their history. (Stephens 1963: 236; emphasis added)

It is almost as if Stephens were expounding on the classical rules for images and not the allure of ruins: they need to be "striking" without too much, or too little, light so that these memory devices can give up their contents. Or, is it better to understand that this use of a classical art of memory as the travel logic of Stephens's guide to Chichén is necessary because it is what invents the ruins that are to be toured? The ancient city is an architecture of memory—a giant wax slab of the mystic writing pad, as will be explained shortly, composed of multiple wax tablets, some in use and some waiting a future inscription. Note that, for Stephens, these memory loci are only buildings, yet, as if remembering the future Museum, he anticipates the possibility that dispersed sculptural debris are also future locations of memory as artifact exhibits. Note further that this memory architecture does not include, but is rather bounded by, two "senotes" (*sic*): At the very end of the chapter preceding the guide to the ruins, he describes his party's attempts to ward off villagers so they may swim in the Cenote Xtoloc (201–2). At the end of the guide chapter, two pages after formally finishing the tour, he mentions that, just before leaving Chichén, he visited the Sacred Cenote where human sacrifice was performed (238). Thus, this wax architecture of memory is circumscribed by two giant holes filled with the water of underground rivers that metaphorically insinuate civilizational depth and historical connection with only a terse recounting of the centuries of legends and sacrifices that course through those specific cenotes. The opening device to the visit of Chichén is an exegesis of the place name (200–201), followed by complaints of the Pisté villagers watching the foreigners swim in the buff. Then, in closing the tour narrative, he epitomizes not only his rhetoric, but the topography of this study: "From the words used, it may be understood that the discovery was then made of an actual existing city, but it is a fair construction of these words to suppose that nothing more is meant than a discovery of what the words Chi-chen import, viz., the mouth of wells . . . an event worthy to be noted in their history" (237–38).

In the years immediately following Stephens's travels, the Caste War deterritorialized Pisté and the cattle Hacienda of Chichén; and, without cattle grazing among the ruined mounds, the underbrush reclaimed the inscriptions of human activity, reclaimed as if erased in a gesture of lifting off a sheet of paper. But the Stephens and Catherwood mapping constituted a template, the wax slab, on which Chichén is carved from the jungle. Later nineteenth-century "protoarcheologists" expanded the memory locations by adding, in piecemeal fashion, the Venus Platform (LePlongeons) and the High Priest's Grave and the Sacred Cenote (E. H. Thompson). For its part, the Carnegie initiated its writings on the museum palimpsest with the Temple of the Warriors, the associated Colonnades, and the Caracol, while Monumentos Prehispánicos restored the Castillo, the Ball Court, and the

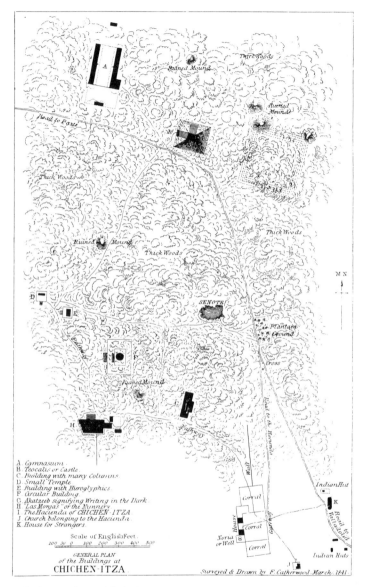

Fig. 1. Catherwood map of Chichén Itzá, 1841. Depicted here on what might be the first map of Chichén is that part of the city with the greatest concentration of monumental architecture. This area, the legally designated archeological and tourist zone or site, will become what is identified and referred to as Chichén, even though the city extended continuously seven kilometers in all directions. Interestingly, the future highway that leads east from the Pyramid of Kukulcan to Valladolid and west to Mérida is already inscribed in the jungle. It is this road that will come to spatially

nearby temples and platforms of what would become Toltec Chichén.[9] As each of these building and artifact exhibits became the topic of a research endeavor, it also came into existence in a thick network of texts, not only the literal documentation of archeological notes, reports, synthetic studies, and guidebooks, but in the oral discourse of archeologists, local Maya who excavated and restored the ancient site to vision, guides who renarrate this archeological sight into language, and tourists who reimage the site in pictographic narratives of souvenirs and photos. Hand in hand with the invention of the Museum's ruins, a hypertextual, multimedia library was written. It seems, then, that Andrew Carnegie's philanthropic hobby of donating (the buildings for) libraries as a "road to (En)light(enment)" was fulfilled in the Museum of Chichén.

Invention of Maya Ruins: Monument to Modernity and Battlefield of Nations

> The Chichén Itzá project has differed from most archeological undertakings in the New World in that from its inception Dr. Morley has striven for three definite objectives over and above the usual single one of recovering specimens and information. These may be stated as follows: to conduct the work in a manner calculated to create a feeling of confidence by the Mexican government and people in the good faith of foreign scientific agencies; to handle the site in such a way as to make it a permanent record of the artistic achievement of the Maya; and to develop Chichén Itzá as a focal point for correlated researches. (Kidder 1930: 96)

---

demarcate and signal the historical-cultural division of the city into "new/Mexicanized" and "old/Maya." In the lower right-hand or southeastern corner of the map, Catherwood marks the Hacienda Chichén (I), which will be bought by E. H. Thompson and rented out to the Carnegie archeologists, and the "House for Strangers" (K), which will become the Casa Victoria or first posada at Chichén, named after and owned by Thompson's Maya-mestizo "wife" from Pisté. The unnumbered "Plantation Grounds" will be the future site of the Hotel Mayaland, opened in 1930 by the Barbachano family, after they bought the Hacienda properties from both Thompson and the Mexican government. Farther south, Club Med will construct a hotel in the 1970s. Unlike all later tours, Stephens's narrative tour begins here, in this southeastern corner of the central zone of the city where a community of Chichén Itzá lived in the first half of the nineteenth century.

In this passage from the annual report of the Middle American Division of Historical Research (CIW), Kidder succinctly defines key elements of the archeological *inventio* by which the nineteenth-century vision of the lost, ruined city became transfigured into the modern ruins of Chichén Itzá.[10] Impressed by the scriptural operations of restoration, the "raw" slab of wax that was Stephens and Catherwood's vision was erased ("lost") and reedited, revised, rewritten ("discovered") in the peeling back of the forest, the cataloging and drawing of stones, the excavating of earth, the sifting and hauling of rubble, the photographing and note taking of data, and the restoring of pieces to their proper place within a giant jigsaw puzzle that was being invented along the way.[11] The Carnegie invention was this puzzle, which must be deconstructed to disclose the logic and forces that shaped its construction. Let us consider Kidder's three factors in reverse order, even as they necessarily imply and intersect one another.

First, to best understand the importance of the third objective — "to develop Chichén as a focal point for correlated researches" — it needs be contrasted with what Morley's agenda was not: this is *not simply* the collection of specimens and data. This comment has two direct references; one is to the scientific difference between Morley's project and E. H. Thompson's "archeological work," which at that time was still under trial within the Mexican federal courts for the looting and plundering of cultural patrimony (Ramírez Aznar 1990; Willard 1926; E. H. Thompson 1932); but the comment also seeks to distinguish Morley's science from that which grew up hand in hand with U.S. museums. The archeological study of the indigenous past occurred, of course, in the aftermath of the genocidal removal of Native Americans in the United States and was sponsored by national and private museums in search of archeological and ethnological artifacts for their permanent collections; E. H. Thompson's dredging of the Sacred Cenote and supplying of the Peabody Museum was a practice revolutionary Mexico sought to halt. In the United States, the increasing (overt) politicization of the study of the Indian led to tensions when researchers were hindered in the conduct of "objective" investigations that did not support, or even critiqued, the ideological project of nation building: permanent collections and expos displayed Indian mannequins in museums as surpassed vestiges of savagery and as the cultural patrimony of an imagined community that was fashioning itself as the pinnacle of modernized civilization (Hinsley

1981: 64–79; cf. Jacknis 1985; Stocking 1985a). Thus, the professionalization of the discipline began when the university context established a different socioeconomic basis for anthropologists that allowed for a critical distance and difference to open up between the sciences, here anthropology, and the politics of the nation. However, the mistake is to believe that this space is neutral and objective in the usual, commonsense meanings as the new professionals professed.[12]

Although it is true that the period of "museum anthropology" had "ended," Morley, Kidder, and the Carnegie were actually renovating these relations between that institution, the discipline, and the nation.[13] This is clearly reflected in a 1929 statement by W. J. Holland, who was both the director of the CIW and president of the American Association of Museums: "The ideal museum should cover the whole field of human knowledge. It should teach the truths of all the sciences, including anthropology, the science that deals with man and all his works in every age. All the sciences and all the arts are correlated" (quoted in Donato 1979: 221–22). Hinsley has identified the scientific truth that this ideal museum sought to communicate: "While industrial museums and expositions displayed the superiority of civilization, museum anthropology made the same point by exhibiting the inferiority of other peoples. It contributed to the celebration of (the United States of) America's coming of industrial age by demonstrating relative racial and national accomplishment" (1981: 83–84). In other words, museums remake the "chain of being" into an evolutionary ladder that represents "progress" as an ascent from the cultures and races of others, past (Western) nations and (modern) civilization, to the essence of the enlightenment cosmos, which is construed in the image of universal, rational man, but modeled implicitly on an ideal community of the nation. Indeed, the truth of the museum is that all the sciences and all the arts are correlated with all the politics of all nations. And, they are all correlated in the institution of the museum, which stands as the testimony of this truth and as a monument to modernity. The first and second objectives aimed at the realization of this ideal museum in the topos of Chichén Itzá.

Thus, "Morley's" third objective can be understood not only as the will to create such a complex machinery of representation that could work these effects, messages, and politics. Of course, one of the key functions of the museum is to *conceal* the political implications, intentions, and forces that underwrite its operations of knowl-

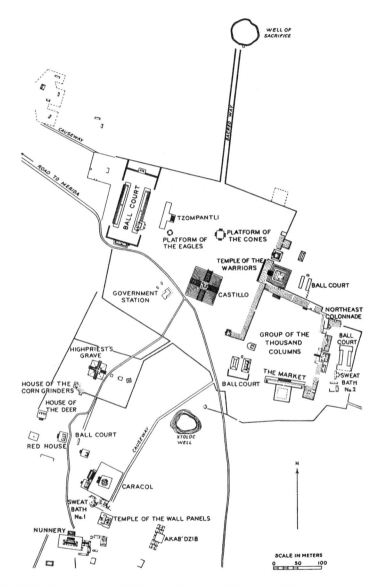

Fig. 2. The Carnegie map of Chichén Itzá by J. O. Kilmartin, 1920s to 1930s. Not only did the archeologists have their Maya workers peel the jungle off the buildings of Chichén, but Kilmartin also "peeled" the "thick woods" from the Catherwood map to leave only the measured lines of ruins reconstructed by science. Also erased from the previous map are the traces of any contemporary population: not only are the Maya huts, corals, and milpas not depicted, but the Casa Victoria, Hotel Mayaland, and Hacienda Chichén—all in use as lodging for archeologists or

edge. Although it is literally true that the Chichén project was different from these prior styles of archeological science, the political-modernist agenda remains. The distantiation from the collection of ossified knowledge/humans works to conceal the continued functioning of the same national politics both within and across the boundaries of the nation-state.

The "second aim of Dr. Morley, in his administration of the Chichén Itzá project, has been so to handle the site as to make it an enduring monument to the genius of the ancient Maya" (Kidder 1930: 97). Why should U.S. scientists and a U.S. public be interested in Maya genius? Here an appeal to the universal importance of the Maya and of knowledge for its own sake conceals a series of harmoniously conflicting and contesting motives. The Anglo-American motivation stems in part from the wonder that Maya mysteries effect in the perception of the Westerner: the Maya are comprehended as a special type of human group that reflects particular lessons about civilization and social collectivities and, hence, the scientific fascination of this non-Western other. But this is only part of the answer.

There is another constitutive irony of the creation of Chichén as Museum, for although its overt rationale would be to promote this indigenous civilization, the institution itself is a structure and strategy that controvert this intention in specific ways. Again, the Indian becomes a mannequin staged and stuffed not only by the Anglo-Americans, but by the Mexican government and the Yucatec archeologists who control the means and mechanisms to invent the modern Chichén Itzá as a Museum of Maya Culture and Civilization. The museum as architectural figure is already constituted as a site of engagement and contestation between nations: here, in this specific machinery of

tourists—are left off the map. Further, only the most prominent public architectural features are mapped: not depicted on the edges of the main plaza are the minor platforms and constructions associated with private residences. The Carnegie map accentuates a north-south axis to the city layout by including the Sacred Cenote as well as the path that leads south from the Monjas to other major and minor architectural complexes (which, however, are not shown on this cropped reproduction). This cropping off of all but the "north" and "central" parts of the site is a common procedure for the near-universal use of this map in guidebooks. In those rare cases where the "southern" or (really) "old" Chichén is depicted, the linking road will be the only ancient road shown on the map. These mapmaking tactics are among the many techniques that helped to produce an image and understanding of Chichén as a highly bounded and empty Maya ceremonial center.

knowledge, at least four nations/national communities—the United States, Mexico, Yucatec regional society, and Maya societies—are, in various forms and through different agencies, engaged in conflict. In this field of power, the Maya is the target of three distinct archeologizing strategies and the monument itself must be understood as a battlefield of nations waging a war in and through scientific knowledge.

In contrast to the Mexican and Yucatec archeologizing strategies, that of the U.S.-sponsored researchers was not oriented toward forging an image of the Indian as a subordinated subcommunity within a narrative of the Anglo nation. Rather, the interpretations of Maya society were shaped as instruments to delegitimize the new revolutionary government and to cause, as well as to exploit, ideological fracturing of the Mexican community along ethnic-cultural fault lines. In this regard, Anglo archeological interpretation of the history of Chichén has participated and continues to participate in an encompassing and older discursive production of Mexico in negative, devalued, and critical images. Although the history of political relations between the two nations provides enough context as to why this is the case, the Anglo use of the Maya as a foil to Mexican nation building has its own history: Sullivan (1989; cf. Reed 1964; Patterson 1986; Katz 1981) discusses Morley's role as a U.S. naval intelligence officer while conducting research as a Carnegie archeologist during World War I; his task was to make contact with groups that would rebel against Mexico if it sided with Germany.[14] When the Rebel or Cruzob Maya leaders approached Morley for assistance with guns and ammunition in order to continue their war with Mexico, Morley feigned ignorance and diplomatically played off these requests in pursuit of the greater good of objective and neutral science: he chose, that is, "to handle the site in such a way as to make it a permanent record of the artistic achievement of the Maya" and promote the genius of the Maya, not their *contemporary* claims to "national" autonomy and legitimacy.

The Yucatec archeologizing strategy is almost the reverse of Morley's, at least at its inception when the new socialist governor signed the agreement with the Carnegie allowing joint excavations. Gov. Felipe Carrillo Puerto was motivated by the need to develop a political class consciousness among the proletarianized and peasant Maya in order for the social transformation of the Mexican Revolution to take root in Yucatán, or at least to not be subverted (which it was). The restoration of Chichén Itzá was demanded by the Yucatec and

Mexican agencies as a condition for the concession to the CIW in order to provide a vehicle for the ideological mobilization of Maya solidarity against conservative forces in regional society (see Campos García 1987; Várguez Pasos 1989; Joseph 1982: 213–27). This was clearly a dramatic shift from the archeologizing that was initiated after 1821 by the Yucatec intelligentsia, which aimed at the consolidation of Indian subordination. Yet it is not in contradiction with either the nature of museums or this specific Museum as a site of contestation and engagement: the representation of subnational communities in museums always works an ironic logic of subordination and integration through promotion and celebration. By the same token, the tensions between the political objectives of the national and the regional centers can be grasped. The once autonomous nation of Yucatán has maintained, throughout the nineteenth and twentieth centuries, a staunchly regionalist society and ethic of distinction; although the sentiments of solidarity no longer constitute nationalism, they continue to cast regional society in the image of a "national" entity. This cultural nationalism is what defines Yucatán, even more overtly than many of the *many Mexicos* or regionalist states/societies, as a "world apart." The ideological integration of the Yucatec "nation" into the Mexican is facilitated through this monument to Maya genius by working the scientific interpretations of the pre-Columbian past into allegories of contemporary political legitimacies. In turn, it is this allegorization of scientific knowledge that provides the space of contestation in which both Yucatec and Maya national societies are fashioned in constrained images of delimited autonomy. And it is this space that is exploited by U.S. interests in the heterogeneous discourses depreciating Mexico. Thus, by celebrating Maya, the Museum of Chichén Itzá figures the imagining of several "national" communities and configures them in a condition of tension, contestation, and struggle.

These conflicts and engagements, some of which we shall later see enacted "on the ground" in ethnographic space, are a war of knowledge that is primarily waged through the interpretation of the history of the Maya generally, and of Chichén specifically. Thus, the Museum of Chichén is not so much the issue of conflict as a structure and means for the orchestration of the politics and struggles between these nations. A more subtle, insidious, and epistemological form of violence occurs in and through the scientific production of objective and neutral facts; because the agents or communities that are engaged in this battlefield do not so much put into question the production of this knowledge or the Enlightenment machinery (i.e., the museum) that economizes this knowledge production, the context, conditions, terms, and structure of the struggles are in a sense "agreed upon" or shared, to say the least. Rather, the overt contestation centers on the *interpretation* of the facts, which can therefore remain within the culturally constructed and specific notions of "objective" and "neutral." From this angle, the first of "Morley's" objectives as reported by Kidder — "to conduct the [archeological] work in a manner calculated to create a feeling of confidence by the Mexican government *and people* in the good faith of foreign scientific agencies" (emphasis added) — was well served. The comment does not *only* refer to the obvious possibilities of the generic exploitation of Mexico by U.S. business, scientific, and governmental agents, E. H. Thompson's covert pillaging of antiquities for a private museum in the U.S. (which Teobert Maler denounced), and Morley's covert political interventions (which Boas denounced).[15] It also refers to the more pervasive situation and organization of power and knowledge within the Yucatec and Maya contexts. Further, if we consider the great facility with which the Carnegie intervened throughout Guatemala, Belize, and Mexico to establish factories of knowledge, we must conclude that Morley's genius was indeed his diplomatic skill in convincing others of the good faith of science and scientific agents despite the incontrovertible bad faith and subterfuge.

Morley was also blessed with the ability "to correlate" research of heterogeneous sciences and scientists into a singular endeavor. Indeed, not only did Chichén become a factory of knowledge, but Yucatán became a laboratory. On the Yucatec topography was inscribed yet another landscape, whereby a scientific geography overlay the sociocultural topography. In this sense, we return to what the Carnegie projects were not — the simple "recovering of specimens and information." Instead, they constituted a massively scaled experiment in the Enlightenment project of the museum in which its cosmology of modernity is constituted in its most perfect form. In other words, the CIW sought to and was able to transfigure Yucatán into three of the four essential elements that Bacon listed as necessary for a "man of learning": a cabinet or museum, a library, a laboratory, and a garden.

The Carnegie intervention was indeed successful, not only in attaining Morley's three goals, but in having an *impact* on Yucatán.

I return now to the seemingly bizarre thesis that the impact of anthropology on Yucatán is tourism. This is, however, precisely what we can consider from the fourth of the Carnegie's objectives, which Kidder presents in a parenthetical manner within the second goal already discussed: "If Chichén Itzá can be kept both interesting and beautiful, it will without question become a Mecca of travel" (Kidder 1930: 99). Why is this a goal of science? Kidder continues, in the same sentence: "...and, incidentally, a most valuable asset for archeology which, like every other science, needs its 'show-windows'... [because] public interest must be aroused and eventual public understanding must be achieved if archeology is to go forward." Thus, from the very inception of the strategic restoration of Chichén is the desire of archeologists to create a "Disneyland" (cf. Kurjack 1989) that would be capable of attracting tourism, disseminating to the public the *genius* that is *both Maya and archeological*, and, thereby, producing funding sources through tourism. But, if Chichén was to be created as a Mecca of travel, then Yucatán was to be relandscaped as the laboratory composed of many archeological show windows. Indeed, such has been the impact of anthropology.

The invention of Chichén Itzá as a Museum of Maya Culture and Civilization is the *inventio* of a modern monument to Enlightenment science and cosmos: The museum's runes are ruins of modernity. But I have also argued that this Mecca of travel is therefore a battlefield of nations in which war is waged in and through the scientific and touristic production as well as practice of knowledge: the Enlightenment theater of memory is a theater of war conducted through knowledge. Thus, we must concur with Kidder, who provides the following caveat: "Chichén Itzá of all great Maya cities is the most accessible and the most healthy. And, with the possible exception of Uxmal, it is without a rival in the number, beauty and architectural distinction of its buildings. What Luxor is to Egypt, or Athens to Greece, Chichén Itzá is to Yucatan. *A heavy responsibility, therefore, rests upon him who excavates there*" (Kidder 1930: 97; emphasis added).

Before moving to the next section, I want to underline again the ethical matter of anthropological responsibility. As if consciously alluding to the struggles, contestations, and engagements that are enacted in this Mecca of travel, Kidder, in a thoroughly ironic—if not deceitful—comment, adds that "if handled in a manner so *obviously altruistic* it can not fail to produce a feeling on the part of the Mexican government and the Mexican people that American agencies can be trusted within their borders" (Kidder 1930: 99; emphasis added). The Museum of Maya Culture and Civilization should therefore also be understood as yet a third type of theater, that of a stage for the performance, as we see in the next section, of cultural, political, touristic, and economic dramas and, as we read here, of *scientific espionage*.

The "Mystic Writing Pad" as the Art of Museum

We must come to terms with the temporality of the wax slab.
Derrida, "Freud and the Scene of Writing" (225)

The rhetorical, occult, and rational arts of memory inhabit the museum as its inspiration and principles, but they are not adequate to describe the functioning of the museum. The art of memory describes the logic and practices of individual rhetors, orators, readers, and visitors of an architecture of memory, whether predominantly mental or physical. A model of the scriptural operations of the museum must be able to map the ethnographic intricacies that link heterogeneous practices by which memory is redeposited in and recalled from loci that are themselves reinscribed and reread such that both the permanence (repetition) and novelty (alterity), the individual and collective, as well as the presupposed and contested facets of memory-knowledge, can be comprehended. Such a model must allow us to understand how the museum is both the orchestration and the result of the multiple practices of heterogeneous arts of memory; there must be a model by which to understand the internal mechanisms by which there is continuity through inscription of difference as well as disjunction and novelty through reenactment of sameness, whether in meaning, form, context, or by agent of memory.

Freud's thinking on the unconscious, especially as filtered through Derrida's reading, provides an answer. As the latter points out, Freud fluctuated between a topographic—that is, literally spatial—understanding of memory that ultimately derives from the rhetorical arts, and a trace theory that fashions memory as a kind of writing (*archaewriting*).[16] Based on three analogies with the mystic writing pad (a type of palimpsest and children's game), Freud imagined the unconscious as a writing machine or a scriptural economy of memory events. This apparatus can also serve to describe the internal mechanics of the museum theater of memory.

The writing pad is composed of two layers. The bottom layer is made of an impressionable material—a slab of wax or resin—on which is permanently and literally inscribed the markings that are pressed into it through the top layer. The top layer is dual, being composed of two sheets attached to each other at one edge only.[17] The top sheet is a transparent plastic and the second sheet is a translucent wax paper that adheres to the wax bottom. Writing is effected not with the deposition of material onto the page, but through the force of contact. The stylus is used to impress or inscribe on the wax bottom by pressing on the top layer so that the middle or wax sheet sticks to both the bottom and the top at selected points; in this way, "marks" are made "on" the middle sheet that only exist through contact between the bottom and the middle and can only be seen through the top layer. In Freud's first analogy with conscious memory, the top retains no marks (no ink or other material is deposited on its surface) and resists the engraving of its surface; *it acts only to receive, transmit, and protect the force of impression.* The writing *appears* as if it were on the second, sticky surface, yet these marks are only the traces of an inscription that occurs even further below on the wax tablet. It is here where the writing is permanently retained as inscription on the surface of a material that can ceaselessly accumulate memory. The simultaneous depth and superficial engraving of memory on the wax slab suggested a second analogy to Freud; here was the unconscious. In this game and model, the legible effects of writing only exist with the retention and at the points of contact between two surfaces. Further, this visible writing exists as the trace (the representation) of another, different inscription whose visibility is dependent on this contact, which in turn is the material trace and manifestation of the gestures enacted on the blank, transparent top surface. Thus, writing (in the narrow sense of legible marks) is already and irreducibly a representation of its own representation of itself.

Tactility is the precondition of visibility and legibility: visible and legible meaning is constituted from the moment of inscription that established initial *contact* until the top layer is separated from the wax bottom. Lifting the top both "erases" visible marks by breaking contact and leaves the top "clean" for further writing by establishing a disjunction between the inner surfaces of the wax paper and the wax slab. The erasure of prior writing (i.e., separation or cessation of contact), however, is not the end of writing, but is actually its inception: Erasure is the necessary anterior gesture by which a momentarily "blank" space, a "page," is cleared sufficiently that writing can operate upon it. This is significant because the machine thereby satisfies the requirement of memory to be a "double system combining freshness of surface and depth of retention" (Derrida 1978: 217). On the one hand, writing thereby already presupposes its own erasure *before* it comes into visibility, legibility, and intelligibility through tactile contact: "writing is unthinkable without this repression" that is necessarily surmounted (ibid.: 226). Erasure is the forgetting that constitutes memory as retention. On the other hand, erasure is only a surface operation since all inscriptions are retained underneath on the wax slab that thereby conflates the temporality of different writings into a unitary and synchronous inscription of a spatial arrangement. The depth of the mystic pad is simultaneously infinite and superficial: the depth of writing becomes a topography of discontinuous, yet irreducible, layers of a differentiated operation.

This, then, raises the third aspect of Freud's analogy, that is, the *time of writing*. One hand, holding the stylus, performs the marking, while the other hand, periodically lifting the top layer, enacts the erasure for new inscription/impressions. Within this timing of these series of gestures, the operations already noted create permanence, succession, and simultaneity. Further, this complex temporality effects a spatialization, that is, time becomes space, spaced, spacing; not simply on a horizontal plane, but in a vertical depth of conjunctions and disjunctions. The topography of memory, then, is a complex stratigraphy in which "time is the economy of [this] system of writing" (ibid.). In other words, the temporality of the writing pad is the orchestrating logic by which gestures, images, meaning, visibility, tactility, and legibility are all regulated so as to constitute memory.

Regarding the museum theater of memory, then, this model specifies the scriptural operations that occur at each exhibit, or memory locus, and at the "architectural" level of the whole museum. In other words, the museum of Chichén as a whole can be considered a mystic slab of wax that has been divided by the archeological *inventio* into locations, each of which also operates as a wax tablet or "mini" writing pad. Both continuity and repetition, as well as disjunction and difference, are accounted for within a description of the practice of the museum by heterogeneous agents, all of whom perform from within the categorical position of a master orator-visitor. All who enter the museum operate the mystic writing pad at each memory locus with two hands, one erasing the visibility of prior inscription and the other performing the writing gestures of a new inscription and deposition of memory-meaning. But it cannot be forgotten that the rhetor-visitors, as they physically and mentally traverse the memory-architecture from locus to locus, *read the text of the image deposited in wax as they operate the machinery of writing in order to speak the discourse always already textualized, engraved in images and under erasure.* Thus, the "complete" gesture of memory is a series of reading-erasing-writing-saying and traversing of space to reenact the performance at the next locus. This structure of practice enacted by distinct agents constitutes a ceaseless *reinvention* of the artifact-image, the simulacra of Chichén Itzá as Ancient City, the Museum embodiment of Maya culture and civilization, the Enlightenment monument to modernity, and the multiform theater of war. This fabulous reinvention, like Freud's Derridean writing machine, is simultaneously repetition and alteration; that is, there is both a restoration of inscribed memory and a novel revisioning of the invented.

The writing pad provides a blueprint by which to comprehend vision as a practice in time and space. Not only is the artifact-image a function of the visibility, legibility, and intelligibility that is effected by the scriptural economy of the writing pad, but *so is the general field of vision* within this and any museum or tourist attraction. I suggest that this framework allows a new and fruitful analysis of the everyday experience of vision as a temporal practice of bodies in relation to discursive productions. Understanding the temporality of vision allows us to transcend research on the disembodied, ahistorical, asociological, masculinist, and essentialized "structures" of vision that have been all the fashion in the study of tourism under the topic of the "tourist gaze" (e.g., Urry 1990). Further, understanding the economy of vision in this way allows us to avoid the privileging of one term of a series of oppositions that derive from a mind/body split, such as in Taussig's (1991) prioritizing image over discourse, mimesis over allegory, corporal experience over conscious thought. The image in which memory is deposited and from which sentient knowledge is experienced is already caught up in a thick topography of oral discourses, texts, spaces, disciplined gestures, movements, and temporalities that constitute its perception and reception as an image. Thus, it becomes naive and ahistorical to make an argument, as Mascia-Lees and Sharpe (1994) have, regarding the immediate, sentient experience of Maya ruins as somehow existing in an unconscious that is prior to or outside of the discursive and textual matrix that has created those ruins in very specific ways within particular contexts so as to evoke a calculated effect. The image in which memory is deposited and from which sentient knowledge is experienced is already caught up in a thick topography of oral discourses, texts, spaces, gestures, movements, and temporalities that constitute its perception and reception as an image.[18] The exhibit of an artifact is both created and supplemented by these multiple other texts, discourses, times, and spaces that are inscribed on the surface of its display. This supplementation, in the Derridean sense, is necessary for the restoration of the image to vision, meaning, and communication; without this addition supplied through the traveling art of memory, the artifact would be excluded from the invention of the tourist sight.

The Scriptural Economy of the Museum: Practices

The archeological zone, or *la zona,* comprises the area that can be literally considered the wax slab of the mystic writing pad; this is the legally defined archeological patrimony. Arguing from this analogy, the archeologically reconstructed site is not visible or apparent and, in and of itself, it is not *legible.* Time (and jungle) will always erase the effects of human intervention; they will "separate" the top layer from the wax bottom to erase all or part of the ruins. Thus, to become a sight, the text of the Museum must be continually reinvented and reinscribed through heterogeneous practices of the museum-memory so that the ruins can become, first, *visible* (as material image), second, *legible* (as a signifying system), and, third, *intelligible* (as meaningful and communicable meaning). This statement is meant in both a literal and an analytic-metaphoric sense.

Consider that site maintenance work and conservation are two series of practices of the museum that explicitly function to retain the visibility of the inscriptions. In the case of maintenance, there is the daily work of *chapeo* (weeding) and *limpieza* (the cleaning of underbrush from monuments and paths), which is conducted primarily by the custodians of the INAH.[19] When I discussed work routines with one of these caretakers, he remarked that in the old days before unionization made the wardens "lazy," the custodians would work hard to maintain the whole site free of weeds and shrubbery. In those days they were fewer, but they kept the site as "clean from the jungle as when Morley had finished restoration." Although this vision perhaps makes an inaccurate claim about the past, the idea is that *limpieza* and *chapeo* are conceived, even if implicitly, as an editorial rewriting of the "original" archeological inscriptions. Contemporary archeologists, who are also employed by the INAH, perform consolidation work on architecture that is in danger of severe deterioration and deal with other issues of site preservation. For example, after the devastation of Hurricane Gilberto on September 14, 1988, the INAH began, in early 1989, a consolidation of the roof of the Annex to the Monjas in Old Chichén. This project was put on hold in June when fifty million old pesos (US$20,833 at 2,400/1) was allotted for consolidation of the Temple of the Magicians at Uxmal, which had also received hurricane damage. These projects were initiated following the visit of the then new director of the Secretaría de Turismo to Yucatán and were in response to extended criticisms in the newspapers about the dangerously dilapidated conditions of the ruins. Note that these two practices of the Museum, carried out by an agency of the federal government, are complementary: one preserves the traces of memory by restoring visibility; the other preserves visibility of memory by restoring the traces.

In Mexican archeology, the discourse and practice of conservation have become a key supplement, just as in North American archeology "salvage archeology," but also "ethnoarchaeology," are supplementary discourses and practices. For example, at the twenty-first Mesa Redonda de la Sociedad Mexicana de Antropología (October 15–19, 1989), there was a session moderated by Ruben Maldonado entitled "La destrucción del patrimonio arqueológico de Yucatán: Alternativas y soluciones para su preservación"; another session was devoted to the preservation and development of cultural patrimonies, such as culture museums. This discourse of site conservation is focused on a series of "problematizations," such as ecological destruction/ preservation, tourist impact/development, maintenance/creation of cultural patrimonies, and Maya farming rights. It is manifested in events and texts, that is, practiced, in various forms—for example, the 1989 "Conference on Eco-Tourism" held at Uxmal or a series of articles debating the "Disneyland" status and condition of Chichén Itzá that resulted from the 1989 *National Geographic* article on the "Ruta Maya" (Garrett 1989; *Diario de Yucatán* 1990a, 1990b).

In a figurative and in a literal sense, these practices can be analyzed as forms or systems of punctuation, typesetting, page layout, and so on, to borrow a whole series of analogies from the modern technology of writing. These arts of cleaning, site conservation, and salvage restoration are, clearly, not insignificant: they are a critical arena of microphysical power in which the larger political struggle over the images/imagining of the national community gets played out. There is an entire political geography and hierarchy of cultural patrimony. The archeology of Mexico City, for example, offers monuments of centralization and nationalism that Chichén cannot. In the national periphery, the political symbolism and knowledge allegories of Chichén do not as effectively reflect centralized power as they foment and disseminate contending *sub*national solidarities related to Maya and Yucatec identities and the politics of *inter*national groups in which Mexico, the United States, and Yucatec and Maya communities are engaged.

The more ostentatious arts of the museum are found, however, in the practices of the guide (guidebook and tour guide), artisanry production, and touring attractions, and of anthropological research. These are the dominant scriptural practices that comprise the economy of the museum: it is the arts of memory enacted by the guide, the artisan/vendor, the tourist, and the archeologist that reinvent the Museum of Chichén Itzá by *restoring* the visibility, legibility, and intelligibility of the modern ruins. By reading, writing, erasing other texts, discourses and images within the circuits of memory locations, an invisible and permanent stratigraphy is ceaselessly deposited on these runes of modernity that are named Chichén Itzá. The overlapping yet distinct, mutually reinforcing yet conflictual relations between these genres of human agency comprise the economy of scriptural practices that resuscitates the deathly machine of memory/knowledge.

Archeologists read and write Maya culture in their practices of excavation and restoration, thereby reinventing the spatial text of artifact-exhibits and the place of the museum as a strategic order of things. The tour guides, for their part, read the archeological texts, both books and the archeological zone, and write their texts, that is, invent Maya culture, in the practice of the Tour, which is a form of writing constituted by three factors (space, time, and word). The guide conjugates, within the regimen of the tourist timings, the explanatory word and textual space in order to create another text, which is literally a script *of and for* Maya culture. The tourist also reads and writes Maya culture, over the shoulder of the guides, as it were. The tourist, already familiarized with, if not steeped in, the signs of Maya culture via the publicity campaigns and propaganda associated with tour packages as well as travel and leisure literature, has a horizon of reading erected by the multinational promoters of tourism in Mexico. The tourist reads guidebooks and "reads" the explanatory tour of the tour guide, all in order to *understand* Maya culture as represented by this life-size simulacrum. In other words, the tourist, physically directed to the ruins, interprets the received explanation, thereby transforming the visible into the intelligible. Alongside this reading, other texts are invented: representations of Maya culture that are mostly cast in the form of a discourse of "encounter with the Maya or Maya culture." These texts are forged in discursive practices that derive from the history of travel—for example, tourist photography and collection (of art, artifacts, souvenirs).

Artesanos and *vendedores* read over the shoulder of the tourist, reading the tour guide, who is, in turn, reading the archeologist reading Maya culture. In this way, they get answers to the questions, What is Ancient Maya Culture? How do you sell it? What of it is bought by tourists? The artisans then provide their "answer" in the multiple forms of handicrafts by which the tourist can sign—sign as in signature and signal—the text of Maya culture that they invent. Returning full circle, the archeologist again reads over the tourist and the artisan. Concerned with questions of the preservation and conservation of archeological zones and ecological balance, the archeologist reads the "tourist impact" on Maya culture as objectively embodied in ruins.

In this economy of invention, a fifth figure intervenes, the ethnographer. Although practicing radically different anthropologies, they all devote themselves to reading, writing, and erasing a culture-text, text-culture of the relationships between anthropology, tourism, Pisté or local Maya society, and regional politics from which are invented the progress that was Maya culture (Redfield), zero-degree culture (Steggerda), political economy of traditional-tourist artisanry (Peraza López et al.), and a war museum. Here, then, is an imaginary machine that orchestrates its own invention through the orchestration of heterogeneous practices as its data.

4 / Mysteries of the Maya and the Marvelous Sciences of Survival

A "Dark Writing"

When Atlantis sank, Yucatán rose—and that's just one story. The mysterious Maya have inspired many.... The mysteries don't stop here. We know but two things about the Classic Mayan civilization. It evolved and then ended. All the rest is pure conjecture.

Antoinette May, *The Yucatan:*
A Guide to the Land of Maya Mysteries (1987: 3, 16)

Chichén Itzá, invented as a Museum in ruins, became a factory of knowledge. The product was Maya culture and the industry was Maya studies, one field within the professionalized discipline of U.S. anthropology. In addition, the Carnegie projects, by conscious design, converted Yucatán into a laboratory, a research lab in which the experiment was civilization itself. It is no surprise that anthropology was invented in the nineteenth and twentieth centuries in order to comprehend human being in "all" (or at least as many as possible) of its aspects, variations, continuities, transformations, and so on. Why? Although anthropology, in its modern incarnation, has been *the* discourse, practice, and apparatus of *culture,* this trope, or the substitutes it has marshaled in a Nietzschean army, has always worked in a necessary relation to another notion, which traditionally has been conceived in terms of, and is here glossed as, *civilization.* This latter term has perhaps reached the limit of its utility in the late-modern and postmodern eras as a dominant trope to comprehend self and other. In contrast, *culture* lives on in the postmodern world, not so much as the fiction of rarified discourses like anthropology, but as the hyperreal frame and popular forms of everyday life. Anthropology, like a properly sedentarized and civilized human, has planted this trope, but now others are cultivating the harvest. It seems clear that this (*culture*, that is) is a New World crop; at least that is what is implied by the many arguments that hold that this art of cultivation — anthropology — was invented in the encounter between the "European" and the "Indian."[1] The goal, here, is to sketch a history of the use of these two figures, *culture* and *civilization*, as they relate to the Maya. This is an archaeological excavation of a discourse by which Europeans have comprehended, represented, and colonized indigenous peoples of the western hemisphere. The stratigraphy (i.e., profile view of the sedimented layers and intrusions within a deposit of human occupation) that is mapped can reveal the continuities and ruptures within a series of tropes (e.g., cannibal, savage) by which the Maya have been invented: How does the trope of mystery come to govern the discursive formation by which Maya have become a culture and a civilization? The present task is to put mystery in reverse.

A Mysterious Invention

Like other archeologists, I have always been skeptical of the term "lost" for cities or civilizations. In general, even the most remote ruins are well known to the people living nearby. Not so with many of the Classic Maya cities, for in the end they were reclaimed by the very jungle that had sheltered them. Classic Maya civilization was truly lost *until the beginning of the 19th century, when brief notices of crumbling jungle cities began to appear in obscure publications.* Thus was born the aura of mystery that ever seems to attend things Maya.

> George E. Stuart and Gene S. Stuart, *The Mysterious Maya*
> (1977: 40; emphasis added)

This artifact of an episteme presents a hieroglyph whose decipherment can lead to the unraveling of the discursive formation in which the Maya are invented as a culture and civilization. This book marks a moment in the trajectory of the discourses when the trope of mystery was at its apogee of effectiveness and pervasiveness within the register of science. Here there is no irony and certainly no criticism in the use of the epithet; but, from this moment in the late 1970s on, the figure of mystery, if not the episteme that it supports, comes under scrutiny as a shift in paradigm that slowly began in the 1960s, if not the 1950s, began to allow students of the Maya to reflect upon the trope that governs the discursive formation in which we work. I focus on this passage because its message is commonplace in popular and academic discourse; and, more important, it can serve as a diagram of the operations that led to the invention of the Maya.

Let us begin with the obvious: Who is speaking and what audience is implied? Given that this textual shard is published by the National Geographic Society in a popular, coffee-table-style book, there should be no surprise that both author and readership speak/read from an imagined center of the universe into which all humanity naturally and rationally feeds: Western civilization. Yet this center of knowledge, technology, science, history, and so on, is imagined in a very specific nationalist, racial, and linguistic guise: this is the United States fashioning itself as the most modern heir of Western tradition speaking to itself about its Others. There is a cosmology operating in this archeological rune; the text spatializes three communities—the authorial self of the anglophone West, the Maya Other, and the silent and silenced Iberian/Latin others—in a hierarchic relation of parts whose unity comprises the totality, civilization, that is object of the subtext. This is a site of contestation in which a story of archeological knowledge about civilizations allegorizes sociopolitical relations between American nations: U.S., Mexican, Guatemalan, and Mayan.

These rational skeptics admit disbelief in the belief in "lost" cities. Why? On the one hand, to prove their scientific rationality and common sense they assert, *over and against the nineteenth-century belief and contemporary popular opinion,* that Maya cities are not lost; people who live there knew/know about them but they remained silent to the world at large *because they did not understand the scientific importance of these cities.* The target of this critique is the intelligentsia of Mexico and Guatemala, who remained "ignorant" about the historical past to the extent that the jungle did in fact remove these cities from memory. On the other hand, the Stuarts promote the anglophone discovery of lost ruins as an authentic, *true* event (this is not the work of Indiana Jones, yet), which becomes situated as the *direct* ancestor of their own work; truly, these cities were lost even to those who should have known.[2] Thus, their comments implicitly condemn the Latin nations to a less than scientific and less than fully civilized stage of social evolution even as they position the Maya as a civilization that can serve as a more adequate mirror reflecting the true civilization that the Anglophone West, specifically the United States, represents. We have already witnessed this logic in Redfield (chapter 1) and in the Museum (chapter 3), and we will witness it again in the equinox event (chapter 6).

Here, the Maya cities and civilization are *lost* yet known; and precisely because of this ironic condition, these artifacts of human agency become *mysterious*. In other words, these artifacts (cities) and the imagined totality to which they belong (civilization) are inscribed with mystery because that is the character trait and *essence* of those humans who produced them. It is not the physical condition of being lost or displaced that is mysterious, but the *consciousness* that attends to that which has been recovered from a condition of displacement that "births" mystery. But this fiction of a linear continuity between *lost* and *mystery* is motivated by the desire to narrate a scientific progress from nineteenth- to twentieth-century archeology. Instead, we should understand *lost cities* and *mysterious Maya* as two distinct, yet incestuous, tropes that have governed two different paradigms of knowledge. The former belongs to the discursive *archaeologizing* of Indians into emergent Latin nation-states as the savages were disinherited from their pre-Columbian heritage (cf. Pratt 1992); it is a figure and discursive practice whose genealogy passes through the antiquarianism of the nineteenth century to the fables of cities of gold, which in turn derives from the Atlantis mythology of the Mediterranean. The genealogy of the latter passes through the discourses on savagism and cannibalism, which in turn originate in the marvels of the East.

The former is a discourse on the Other with*in* the space of the Same; the latter is a discourse on the Other with*out*, in the space of "Elsewhere." Both are origin myths, but one is cast as a fable of diffusion from the selfsame while the other posits an exogenous alterity. The third and fourth paragraphs of Montaigne's essay "Of Cannibals" clearly marks this same distinction: the New World and its savage, he argues, cannot be comprehended within the ancient paradigm of a lost Atlantis. Yet they intertwine, not only in tourism, as noted in the epigraph at the beginning of this chapter. but in the sixteenth-century encounter with New World alterity (see Hulme 1986; Greenblatt 1992; Mason 1990). Their combination is also evident in narratives of ancient astronauts as the source of Maya, and other Amerindian, genius; but here the two tropes and discourses are thoroughly conflated, rather than intertwined. In a related, yet distinct calculus of these tropes, twentieth-century science has resolved the question of Amerindian origins through a figurative compromise in which the Atlantis discourse becomes subordinate to that of marvels: the matter of the Americas is a derivative phenomenon—diffused not from the *oikumene* of Western civility, however, but from the marvelous wellspring of Asia.[3] Colonizing discourse in the United States positions the North American Mound Builders as indigenous yet their material culture as marked by an implicit inferiority. By the same token, in the rarified discourse of Maya studies, the lost cities discourse becomes a subsidiary of the dominant trope of mystery, which marks the ambiguous positioning of the Maya as civilization. The rhetoric of lost cities is, thus, disseminated in scientific and popular debates on the origins of New World Indians generally, and the Maya specifically, but is posed within an encompassing romanticization of mystery (as in the opening epigraph) constructed as an unresolvable debate in which the contradictory premises are so contested that all of it appears as "pure conjecture."

On the Genealogy of Marvels: Cannibal, Savage, Mystery

Any "lost civilization" will inspire some sense of mystery as one ponders the fate of ancient cities covered over by desert sands or tropical forest. The Maya have a particularly strong claim to the alliterative epithet of "mysterious" that has been applied to them.
    Nancy Farriss, *Maya Society under Colonial Rule* (1984: 117)

Critical analyses of colonial discourse in Latin America (e.g., Hulme 1986; Greenblatt 1992; Pratt 1992) have shown how specific medieval tropes and discourses on the alterity of the Orient were reused to comprehend the New World and how these tropes of wonder, cannibalism, and savagery were reforged in new figures and discourses throughout the ongoing struggles since 1492. It is to this genealogy that the mystery of the Maya belongs, because, in the functioning of this hegemonic trope, the same mechanisms continue to operate, but in different contexts.

Campbell (1988) summarizes the elements of the Medieval Wonders, which we can take as a protoethnologic, and rudimentary, theory of otherness. The "ecology" of the East is conceived as a land of abundance because of its dangerous location so close to, yet so far from, God. The natives are of three types only, which are defined, whether to demonstrate God's power or not, by either (1) the hybridization of animal and human species, (2) the gigantism or miniaturization of body parts, or (3) the teratalogical multiplication or elimination of features. The *Wonders of the East,* that is, the text concerned with this topic, also comprises a theory of action. When approached, these Others either drop everything and flee in fear or they viciously attack with the purpose of killing and eating the flesh of their human "interlocutor." Internal "social" relations, however, are reduced to fecund procreation, eating, sleeping, lounging, and so on. These wonders provided the template for the social construction of marvels that came to inhabit the later European cosmovision of the Americas (cf. Mason 1990).

According to Greenblatt's (1992) deconstruction, a marvel was, first of all, something witnessed, *seen,* that triggered very specific events. What is seen is that the observed social fact (object, being, relation) is an aporia; in other words, that which is marvelous is that which is *perceived to be in essence a contradiction* of logic, reason, expectations, context, truth, and so on. The perception of the marvelous is concomitant with the experience in the beholder that it triggers: *wonder.* According to Greenblatt, this wonder is a momentary lapse or void that is immediately filled with a desire, specifically the desire to possess. The experience of wonder and its desire is simultaneously manifested as an epistemological/mental and a physical/corporal event. On the one hand, the negativity of wonder triggers an epistemological antithesis that takes the guise of *naming*; naming is a discursive and social act of power in which categorical and logical certainty is imposed on the marvel that causes wonder. A name and an order is imposed, not so much to erase as to dominate, domesticate, and control the alterity that is comprehended as aporia. On the other hand, the marvel induces a physical wonder that is felt as a lack and the desire to literally possess; thus the response to wonder is to *take physical* possession in a "positive," if political, act. A marvelous possession is less an object than a hermetically sealed event and set of procedures, complete within itself. As Greenblatt argues, this event can explain some of the microphysics of Spanish behavior in the encounter five hundred years ago. I suggest, further, that these marvelous procedures operate in the trope of mystery that strategically designates the Maya.

This marvelous discourse, however, did not survive the initial encounter as the dominant mode for comprehending the human otherness of the New World. The related discourse of cannibalism was much better suited to the task, as Hulme demonstrated. The wonder triggered by the marvelous cannibal was much less complicated in its epistemology. Here there was no crisis of knowledge; it simply induced fear and fortitude in the continued attack on the savages. Yet the immediate "experience" of cannibalism—which, Hulme proves, is only an encounter with a sign relation—also entailed the imposition of a name on the Other, which is the proper name of a total rejection of the human body as the quintessential symbol of the sacred. In this way, the cannibal justified European atrocities and war. But if this mode of legitimation could sustain the invasion, it could not justify colonization and colonialism, which, after all, targeted as the object of colonial rule *not the cannibal that remained on the outside margins of European encounters* but the cannibal's double, that is, the "good, domesticable savage" that remained within the colonial situation; the gentle, friendly Arawaks versus the irascible Caribs, the noble savage versus the treacherous Indian. It is on this savage, not cannibal, body that the debates and discourses about the status of the "Indian" are waged.

In the present context, these familiar and well-studied debates are significant for the way in which they frame the discussion about civilization versus its antithesis, savagism and barbarism.[4] The scholastic discussion of the Indian focused on the nature of the Indian being as a class of humanity in order to resolve their juridical status in both secular law and divine order. In this way, it was determined that the Indians were not natural slaves, but rather like children in nature; thus, there was no viable justification for colonization, except indirectly to the extent that colonial rule furthered that which was legitimate for the Catholic church, namely, Christianization. But, of course, the issue did not rest there. The debate of 1550 in Valladolid,

Spain, between Las Casas and Sepúlveda again took up the problem of legitimization and the justified means by which to enact it. However, the terms had shifted and here the status of the Indian as a *social collectivity* was more prominently at stake. In this, the Aztec was positioned as the synecdochic case of all Indians: Were the Indians *civilized*? Did they have *civilization*? Or, were and are they irrevocably *savage*?

The debate was based on a series of criteria that were then and are still well known, not so much because we all have read the protagonists' arguments, but because the 1550 debate effectively canonized an understanding about and valorization of the differentiation of social forms that continues to inform the scientific and popular mind five hundred years later. Thus, *we* (and I believe I generalize validly across all Westernized countries) have read and are reading versions of the arguments continuously; for corroboration, it is necessary only to take a vacation to visit a non-Western culture (see, for example, O'Rourke's film *Cannibal Tours*), or, to read Todorov's highly acclaimed book *The Conquest of America* (1984), in which he insidiously reinscribes the Indian as an inherently inferior human and not truly civilized. As the critiques by Root (1988) and Clendinnen (1993) demonstrate, Todorov reenacts, reproduces, and refines the colonizing operations, logic, and tropes of the colonial discourses that he analyzes. Although he reworks the binary opposition between orality and literate cultures, Todorov's denial of the *sameness,* civility, and equality of the Indian derives from what he erroneously postulates as the lack of *true writing.* There can be no surprise, then, that the episteme of Maya studies (as well as the discipline of archeology in general) is founded on the questions that are already mapped out in the early sixteenth century: Does the Indian have *civilization* as defined by the presence of *true* (1) sedentary life, (2) urban cities, (3) agriculture and technology, (4) commerce with money and markets, (5) personal property, (6) leadership of a political elite, (7) law and government, (8) religion, and (9) phonetic writing?

Within the Spanish context, these criteria were all conditioned on the idea that civility is the capacity to transform, that is, *cultivate,* nature as manifested in its multiple registers. In the context of Anglo-American colonization, the discourse on the North American Indian always strove to deny that such traits as settled villages, cultivation of crops, or creation of game parks as "permanent" transformations of nature that would qualify as *true* civility existed (see Pearce 1988); these same criteria were used to categorize Indians as incorrigible savages, which marked and legitimated the appropriation of their lands, genocide, and multiple forms of marginalization. Todorov, however, avoids such blatant misrepresentation by more subtle misconstruals, such as reconceptualizing the whole debate on the question of Indian mentality; the lack of what he asserts as "true" writing among ancient Mesoamericans locks the Indian into a mentality defined by orality, which prevented the Aztecs from *lying*. In other words, the Indian was too honest and noble to employ political strategies of deception. This difference from the literate mind is not only what caused their inevitable conquest by the Spaniards, but it asserts what Columbus long ago had suggested: the Indians do not have true language because the absence of the capacity to lie is the absence of representation and symbol (cf. Haraway's analysis of Hardy's argument of the natural-bodily lying of the female sex). Interestingly, this argument of the incapacitated mentality of the Mesoamerican Indian resonates with what Pearce (1988: 76–134) isolates as the way Anglo colonial discourse constructed the North American Indian as the "zero of human society" on the ambivalence that the essential virtues of savagery (oral virtuosity, egalitarianism, state of nature, etc.) were simultaneously the diagnostics of an essential inferiority.

In this way, Todorov subverts what Las Casas had won. Despite the problem posed by human sacrifice and its associated "cannibalism," he made the obvious case that the Aztecs had a civilization according to the criteria just listed. For Las Casas, even these problematic traits demonstrated the presence of an understanding of divinity, faith, religion, and thus civilization. As for the Maya, the question of civilization was not raised explicitly except in the birth of Maya studies at the end of the nineteenth century, which were constituted precisely as the extension of the 1550 debate to the Maya situation. However, a discourse on Maya savagism was not formulated within this field of studies as it was in Mexico or North America.[5] Significantly, the anomalous presence of these two savage traits (human sacrifice and "cannibalism") in a civilized context did not contribute to the forging of a hegemonic mystery either for central Mexican societies, which have never been characterized as mysterious, or for the Maya, whose bloodletting practices had been explained away as a result of the corrupt influence of ancient Mexican colonizers—or, as many have pointed out, simply erased from the database by not allowing evidence of them into the discussion (see Schele and Miller 1986). Indeed, the Maya and central Mexican cultures (Teotihuacán, Toltec, Aztec) have been opposed within the Carnegie paradigm on the basis of an analogy to the contrastive relations between Greek and Roman civilizations. In other words, whatever was *cultured* (art, science, calendrics, writing) in civilization, the Maya created and gave to the Mexicans, but whatever was *uncivilized* the Mexicans diffused back to the Maya origin (e.g., war, sodomy, totalitarian bureaucracy, human sacrifice). But not only were these negative characteristics the putative result of Mexican/Toltec influence, but other diagnostics of civilization itself were said to be central Mexican: true urban cities, commerce beyond ceremonial trade in luxury goods, true state-level government ruled by a political/kingly elite versus a theocracy of philosopher-priests. In short, the "Maya were considered the Greeks of the New World, and the Aztecs were seen as Romans — one pure, original and beautiful, the other slavish, derivative and cold" (Schele and Miller 1986: 21).

The study of the Maya that emerged in the twentieth century was grounded in a series of questions that framed Maya civilization as a contradiction in terms. The Maya did not have real cities, but empty ceremonial centers. They did not have true *settled* agriculture, but extensive and shifting swidden agriculture. They did not have true phonetic writing, but pictographic writing. Furthermore, this was not a true writing because it did not concern the history, politics, and economy of a civilized society, but the philosophically and religiously oriented study of astronomy, calendrics, math, geometry, and architecture. The Maya had no true polity with a political elite, war, and social problems, but a theocracy of priests devoted to mystic arts and sciences. Even their monumental architecture was viewed as anomalous, given that it consisted primarily of temples with seemingly few govermental buildings, markets, or residences. As for the economy, instead of a true or essential commerce in everyday necessities with markets, an elite trade in luxury goods for ritual/symbolic decoration is posited. These are the contours that constitute the Maya as an object of study. On this invention, other debates are enacted dealing with specificities and gaps of cultural history, most prominently with regard to the chronology and causes of the rise and fall of this mysterious civilization. The perspective that imposed these qualities con-

Fig. 3. View of the main plaza of "New/Toltec" Chichén showing inscription of tour routes onto the earth. (Author's photograph from the top of the western wall of the Ball Court)

strued the Maya as inherently contradictory and anomalous: noncivilized civilization. Mystery, then, configures a discursive formation in which the scientific will to know shapes Maya alterity as a mirror-other to Western civilization.

Here the possession that is performed through scientific knowledge is not that of incorporation, but of situating the Maya other at the margin of possible forms of civilization. From this angle, *lost cities* is a distinct trope belonging to a different political and discursive relation with the Maya. It belongs to a romanticized vision of the colonized other as archeological vestige to be plundered in a material, physical form and as cultural patrimony to be incorporated within the imagining of a nation-state. The North American image of Yucatán and the Maya as the "American Egypt" is transparent in its political economy, occurring as it does at the moment when the United States sought to replace Spain and impose its hegemony on Latin America. With the professionalization of archeology and the invention of museums of Maya culture not only at Chichén but at other sites such as Copán, Palenque, Uaxactun, and Tikal, the trope of lost cities, as well as the romantic vision it effects, became subordinated within the dominant configuration of knowledge ruled by mystery.

Marvelous Mysteries and Mysterious Marvels

*A central appeal of the Maya for us lies in their challenge to our
traditional vision of humanity. Lowland Maya Civilization is
therefore uncanny and romantic, and our perceptions of its
"mysterious" qualities have hindered serious empirical research on
subjects that until recently were in danger of drowning in
methodological quicksands.*
Grant D. Jones, *Maya Resistance to Spanish Rule* (1989: 2)

In a truly ironic mode, the trope of mystery has itself become a topic
of discourse, that is, a necessary trope in which scholars can distanti-
ate themselves from the "old" paradigm that was ruled by "textual
preconceptions" (Jones 1989: 1–2). This shift has been well publicized,
not only by its protagonists, but by *Time* magazine (August 9, 1994):
it is a break from the Carnegie vision whose principal authors were
Morley and J. E. S. Thompson and whose most monumental text
was Chichén Itzá. As the story goes, Morley followed the line inherited from the nineteenth century with regard to the nature and content of Maya hieroglyphs; however, under the intellectually dominating
force of J. E. S. Thompson, the assumption that this writing system
was pictographic (and not syllabic) and that it concerned esoteric
knowledge of a religious-astronomic sort (and not sociopolitical history of ruling elites) became the first premise of Maya studies. Coe's
(1992) version of the story is interesting because it depicts the paradigm or "age of Thompson" as a fifty-year lapse into stubborn error
and self-centered blindness, despite, of course, increased understanding
by a downtrodden, yet courageous, minority among whom he counts
himself as leader; for Coe, the great advances in decipherment that
began in the mid-1970s had greater affinity to nineteenth-century
views. In contrast to Stuart's account of the linear progress of science,
Coe narrates a major *hiatus* in rationality's onslaught. The difference
between the nineteenth-century and post-1975 visions, however, is
that the latter perspective turns on a linguistic approach. Thus, there
are three visions or discursive formations—the nineteenth-century,
the Carnegie, and the linguistic—that must be accounted for in terms
of mystery.

Interestingly, the attempts in the last century to decipher the Maya
hieroglyphs as a phonetic-syllabic script led to a series of highly imag-

inative interpretations that were easily refuted. Despite the often mystical, esoteric, or arcane content of the writing that was proposed in different speculations, *mystery did not prefigure* the decipherments premised on phoneticism. Again, it was the trope of *lost* that operated here: to crack the code required a Rosetta-decoder stone that would hopefully be recovered from the obscurity of jungle or archive. Since none was forthcoming, mystery infiltrated in two distinct ways into the thought and discourse of Maya studies. On the one hand, the failed decipherments became signs of Maya mystery since they represent how the Maya have eluded Western comprehension and triggered fabulous conjectures. On the other hand, the consolidation of the Thompson view that Maya writing was *completely* calendrical and astronomic calculations relating to Maya religion-science led to an aporia that Coe nicely phrases: "A people with writing, but without written history" (1992: 122). Thus, mystery is a popular romanticization of the Maya—styled in an Indiana Jones sensibility—that overlays a more trenchant epistemic operation within the enduring discourse of *civilization*. In this second mode, mystery is the categorical contradiction in which Maya are cast, comprehended, and investigated as a certain kind of object of knowledge.

Although the popular forms of Maya mystery have been variously pooh-poohed as philistine understandings by Mayanists, this second register of the operations of mystery has not been well acknowledged. This is not to say that since the dismantling of the Thompson-Carnegie vision some scholars have not denounced the trope of mystery in an attempt to move beyond and outside of it. Rather, what these brief, but good, reflexive critiques have discussed is how mystery has prefigured the research questions and interpretations that have been formulated about Maya civilization, but not how it invents the Maya as a civilization. This third register in which the figure operates derives from the second, as "normal science" does from the conditions of possibility that structure the normal practices of ongoing study. Thus, in terms of the structure of the text in which such scholars are constructing new research, the identification of mystery as the Western trope of the Maya functions as a kind of abstract history of Maya studies and gives a genealogy, however brief, of the author's own location within the production of knowledge of the Maya. My reenactment of this logic in this text might be evidence of the validity of the assertion.

Schele and Miller (1986: 18–33), for example, deliver a fifteen-page discussion of what they title "The Modern Invention of the Ancient Maya." Although they do not discuss mystery per se, their task is to define the old Carnegie paradigm of Maya studies and to point out its errors and aporias; in so doing, they map out the new vision of the Maya in which they are working.[6] Consider again how Freidel, Schele, and Parker (1993) provide a genealogy of Maya studies to argue that the old vision was a Western imposition, but that they have overcome their own and prior cultural constraints so as to penetrate the Maya mind and narrate a more truthful account of the ancient Maya.

Without rhetorical appeals to their work as the real truth, two historians have recently made parallel commentaries on the mystery of Maya studies against which they measure their own inquiries on colonial Yucatán, Peten, and Belize. Both Grant Jones and Nancy Farriss note the way "Western fascination with Maya civilization reflects a preoccupation with this culture as a symbol of the struggle of humanity against overwhelming odds" (Jones 1989: 1). Jones continues in terms that could lead into structuralist analysis of nature/culture, raw/cooked oppositions: "We are thus faced with an apparent contradiction between our popular belief that the natural order of the jungle is the enemy of the order of culture and the obvious success of the Maya in overcoming the supposed limits placed on cultural expression in this environment" (ibid.). In other words, without invoking the terms, he identifies the categorical anomaly of the Maya as a function of Western discourses of civilization and savagery; furthermore, it is this anomaly that accounts for the mysterious wonder that this subject generates, because "Maya studies, save for those carried out in distant villages by intrepid ethnographers, have been predominantly studies of *civilization*" (ibid.: 3). Jones then lists some of the major topics of debate that have animated the field and points out the Western preconceptions that have regulated the interpretations of the great mysteries: hieroglyphs, cities, agriculture, and the "collapse" of Maya civilization.

Farriss, in an earlier work, also pursues the source of mystery:

Even more than the cause of the Maya decline, scholars have puzzled over the questions of how this civilization ever existed in the first place, and how, by implication, it could have lasted as long as it did. Most especially they have pondered the question of how it could have existed *where* it did. For the level of social and political organization needed to sustain this civilization is alleged to be incompatible with the physical environment in which it developed. (Farriss 1984: 117)

Similarly, Farriss invokes the conceptual bias of peoples living in temperate climates; but, there is a divergence here between the two historians in which the latter makes a critique based on empirical and ecological grounds, while the former is grounded on discursive and textual deconstruction. In the next sentence, the difference is enlarged: "Still, there are aspects of the puzzle that *cannot be dismissed so airily* and which touch on some basic issues in human history: the nature of the social bond, the foundations of social stratification, and the origins of the state" (ibid.; emphasis added). Ironically, Farriss "proves" my point, which is that mystery is a trope that derives from Western discourses of civilization and that it has come to configure and regulate the production of knowledge of the Maya.

Without critical reflection on the discourses she invokes, she proceeds to root this more pervasive and generic mystery at the origins of the social in a rationalist, not romanticist, mode:

The forces that lead people to band together in more than casual, ephemeral groups will probably remain a matter for debate as long as belief persists in original sin, the selfishness of genes, or any other explanation of behavior based on the primacy of self-interest in human motivation.... If we assume that people require some incentive for sacrificing their freedom to pursue individual needs and desires—a restraint inherent in any social bond—it is not immediately apparent what this incentive may have been for the lowland Maya. (Ibid.: 117–18)

In the opposition between nature/culture, raw/cooked, savagery/civility, the motives that transform the human animal into noble savage are "pure conjecture." Unlike the marvelous and romanticist appropriation triggered by Maya mystery in the realm of tourism, Farriss proceeds to speculate in a historically particularist and scientifically rational mode on the basic building blocks of civilization among Maya. If mystery "of the" Maya first attracted her to this field of study, it is the mystery of civilized life in general that she uses to legitimize her intellectual endeavor. Thus, unlike Steggerda, who we saw as seemingly incapable of fathoming the sticky magic of the social bond, Farriss proceeds to speculate—admirably, without doubt—on the nature of the specific ephemeral quality and insubstantial quantity (call it "culture") that gave Maya the fortitude to *survive* and to survive as a *culture*.[7] She truly is a faithful believer in that ghostly entity and aporia we call "culture" (cf. Herbert 1991; Cottom 1989). It is this superstition that renders her portrayal of collective survival so compelling.

The breakdown of the Thompson-Carnegie paradigm renders the Maya as humans in a human society comparable to other such entities. This humanization depends on, first, the use of linguistics to decipher the glyphs and, second, cross-cultural anthropological knowledge to demystify basic processes of Maya society and polity. Nonetheless, I suggest that the operations of mystery have not been braked; the new interpretations continue to work within a mysterious episteme. Whereas the question of Maya *civilization* as true or not has been resolved, scientific questioning has shifted to *culture* as the dominant frame by which to comprehend the sameness and difference of the Maya. And here too mystery continues to operate in both the romantic and the rationalist mode.

The introduction of history and sociopolitical process into the new interpretations has effectively displaced the image of the Maya as a unified and monumental totality. The new image is of highly factionalized city-states ruled by kings who devoted themselves to exotic, shamanic ritual and constant warfare aimed at conquest. But notice what happens when the interpretation shifts from Mexicans having taught their southern neighbors violence to a Maya obsession with war and human sacrifice: Maya war is a thoroughly *culturally constructed practice* replete with the mysticism that Thompson so adored since it is governed by the calendrically calculated movements of Venus and attended by extraordinary practices of penis-perforation, tongue bloodletting, and alcoholic enemas. Here we witness a historic mystery in a rationalist mode transfigured into cultural exoticism in a romantic vein of historicizing.

I have no objection to the idea that everything within society is culturally constructed, including war. My objective is, rather, to point out the irony that attends this shift in perspective as well as the political contexts that motivate these interpretations. In the aftermath of the Mexican Revolution, North American archeology determines that the ancient Mexicans must have conquered and taught the peaceful Maya war; in an ironic maneuver, scientific discourse both acknowledges the legitimate hegemony of the contemporary Mexican state in Yucatán and critiques this domination as one of power mongers bullying defenseless quasi intellectuals and star worshipers. In the aftermath of the Guatemalan military's genocidal campaigns against the Maya, the Maya are now portrayed as always already obsessed with war, bizarre self-inflicted violence, and eternal factionalism. As Victor Montejo has argued,[8] this new interpretive framework operates as a scientific legitimation of ethnic cleansing in which civilized peoples (the Guatemalan government and its U.S. sponsor) seek to exterminate "savages" for the sake of constituting a so-called modern nation-state. Again, cannibalism proves itself an externalization onto the Other of the Self for legitimizing violence (Hulme 1986; Fabri 1994). This demonstrates that the discursive formation in which the Maya are constituted as an object of knowledge operates as a privileged mirror of contemporary national politicking between the United States, Mexico, Guatemala, and Maya peoples. Thus, the shift in terms from civilization to cultures is intelligible as a revisioning of the Maya into *subnational* entities of the past whose claims for national autonomy in the present or future are foreshortened through the production of very specific forms of scientific knowledge.

A civilization is an entity unto itself, complete and not part of a larger whole, for *it is the social whole,* especially in the totalizing sense of the word, as all humanity and human history. In contrast, a culture is an integrated, totalized entity, but a kind of cohesive, coherent whole that is a subpart of a larger civilizational entity or that exists in dynamic relation to other such partial social wholes that have not attained the qualitative transformation to civilization. To call *Maya* "civilization" already presupposes the validity of potential Mayan claims of legitimacy as an autonomous sociopolitical collectivity known as a nation. To call *Maya* "culture" is to put into question rights to national autonomy and self-rule, especially in the postmodernist, postcolonial, and *multicultural* worlds of the present. This strategy of defining, constraining, and ruling over the Other through the notion of cultures that are conceived as partial subunits of a larger collectivity of regional (civilizational) or totalizing (humanity) scope is actually quite old. It dates to the founding of anthropology in the nineteenth century. The concept of culture as a quality and categorical frame of all human collectivities emerges in the history of European colonialism precisely when the categories of alterity that situate the Other at or outside the margins of civility ("primitives," "savages," "the working classes") fail to guarantee the *shared ideological integration* of the Other within the fragile colonial society as *permanently* and *legitimately* subordinated subcollectivities. In the United States, for example, the discourses of savagism, as Pearce (1988) noted, begin to be replaced with other scientifically rational tropes when national policy shifts from extermination to incorporation of the fragmented Indian as a vestige requiring preservation (cf. Haraway 1989 on taxidermy). From this angle, a direct line can be traced from Morgan to Boas in that the planting of culture inaugurates a new, more "humanitarian" arrangement of power that coordinates the relations between communities subordinated within the emergent social form of the nation-state. The genealogy of culture as a scientific instrument of power would then be traced through multiculturalism and postmodernism as the popular modes and uses of this instrumentation; the relativism of both are variations of a generic cultural version and function within the contextual ground of the nation-state and late capitalism.

The Maya, no longer as a civilizational, but rather as a culture species of social collectivity, continue to operate within North American media as a special variety of cultural alterity that speaks some fundamental truth to "modern man" about what it is to be civilized and to have civilization. Two examples can lead us to a conclusion.

First, the August 9, 1993, cover of *Time* magazine states this clearly in its title: "Lost Secrets of the Maya: What New Discoveries Tell Us about Their World and Ours." The article begins with a prophecy-like announcement of new archeological discoveries and paradigm-breaking interpretations: "But what researchers have now found among these haunting irruptions of architecture may be, among other things, reasons for admonishing today's world: At a time when tribal fratricide is destroying Bosnia and farmers are carving through the rainforest, the [new] reasons [for the mysterious collapse of civilization] yielded by the Maya have a disturbing resonance" (Lemonick 1993: 46).[9] Instead of ecological exhaustion, revolt of the masses, and so on, the current interpretation holds that the classic Maya "collapsed" because of the centuries-long failure of kingly elites to create a panregional philosophy of kingship that would allow for the legitimation of colonization and permanent political incorporation of one city-state into another.[10] Here again, the Maya are cast into a categorical contradiction of their civilization in that theirs was not built on an expanding political state, or empire; theirs was a highly civilized culture in the High Tradition sense of the word, not a *political* culture—a culture in which war and politics were conducted by astronomy and by kinky kings in ecstatic states induced by bloodletting and alcohol enemas. The message is that culture, especially bizarre cultural beliefs of mystical or religious dimensions, gets in the way of dealing with what is *real* and *pragmatic*, and stifles the true progress of civilization—integration. This is what is being offered to the North American audience as an explanation for the human devastation that often occurs when non-Western peoples with radically opposed religious views enter into struggles with other similar groups to control their nation-states. It also tells us that it is local farmers stuck in anachronistic cultural traditions—not, of course, transnational corporations such as McDonald's—that destroy the ecology. Here is where the dam breaks that is holding back the massive intervention of development projects and ideologies that seek to intervene on indigenous land ownership through modernization tactics of colonization.[11] Here the farmer who is "destroying" the forest with centuries-old agricultural practices joins hands with the *teporochos* in the puddles of Pisté's streets and with the *artesanos* of Chichén who in their ignorance destroy the cultural patrimony of Humanity's ruins.

Reading the discourse on the Maya as an allegory for geopolitical relations between nations reveals that the Maya are constituted as an object of study so that they might serve as a site of contestation. Maya are both the target of a will to know and a battlefield of national politics waged in, through, and as scientific discourse. This discourse can operate as such because it "speaks" certain "truths" about what it is to be civilized, to have civilization, and to be a culture. Thus, the political messages or morals that are to be communicated through knowledge of the Maya bring us back to the mysteries of civilization in both romantic and rationalist modes. Furthermore, as the comparison to Bosnia, as well as the invocation of ecological rape, illustrate, the discourse on the Maya offers lessons not only about the past but about the future, and thus participates in that discursive formation that Haraway (1989) calls *survival literature.* Her analyses of primatology show this field of knowledge to be concerned with constructing the nature/culture interface in order to provide moral stories about how and who of humanity can and should survive. To call Maya studies survival literature incites a horrific and multilayered irony, because the morality here is to learn how the Maya necessarily survive against the odds and then are *again overcome* by one or another dominating factor to somehow survive yet again. The mysteries of the Maya endlessly accumulate in this logic of prophetic submission-survival: They overcame the savage jungle to create civilization, then they succumbed to a revolution of the masses, ecological overload, political/military inferiority, or bizarre cultural traits. Yet they survived the "collapse" of civilization only to "succumb" again to European invasion. But, mysteriously, after disappearing twice already, they survived only to confront modernization, which once more augured their demise according to twentieth-century theories of acculturation.

The Maya are indeed survivors. It is not simply a Western, anglophone, discourse. Rather, this lens of survival through which the Maya are comprehended in different social guises is, ironically, a disguised appropriation and recasting of the stories that the Maya have been telling about themselves for centuries. In other words, the Western metanarrative of survival has its analogue in the Mayas' own narratives of prophecy-history, such as those found in the *Books of Chilam Balam*. Such borrowing of Maya stories for Western purposes has a long history: Jones (1989) found this transculturation operating in the way Spanish missionaries and colonial authorities used indigenous prophecy-history in undertaking the final conquest of the independent Tah-Itzá Maya in 1697. But this is a two-way event: According to some interpretations of the *Chilam Balams*, the sage priests who wrote these books already foretold the coming of white men, cars, electricity, airplanes, telephones, and many other artifacts of Western technology.

It is here, in the articulation of a profound and transcendental knowledge, especially of astronomy and time, with the theme and plot of survival, that is located the second example of how Maya cultural alterity speaks to "modern man" about civilization. There is an extreme fascination with Maya among New Age and gnostic spiritualities in which the mysteries of Maya civilization and culture are taken to a transcendental or religious level of allegorical meaning. The social guises of civilization and culture in which the Maya are cast shift into their most abstract reference to humanity to produce from the elements of Maya culture and civilization allegories in which Maya stands as the universal human life force. The New Age theol-

ogy of José Argüelles (1987, 1989) exemplifies this religiously romantic mode of allegorizing Maya mystery. This mode is manifested in
such events as the Harmonic Convergence, in which thousands of the
spiritually (self-)select(ed) traveled to the indigenously sacred places
of the earth (such as Chichén or Stonehenge) to welcome the new
spirit-guardians of the earth that were calculated by Maya calendrics
to change on August 17, 1987. Here New Age spiritualism sits together with ecological developmentalism.

These multiple moral and political lessons for contemporary living that are forged in the Western comprehension of the Maya are,
indeed, a wonder. It is a marvel to see how these heterogeneous discourses and social practices converge, overlap, conflict, and reproduce
within an economy mysteriously emanating from a trope written in
the dark recesses of the scientific production of knowledge.

5 / Con/Tour(s) of the Museum

Ventriloquism, Citing Vision, and the Temporality of Tourist Site

> *In modern Athens, the vehicles of mass transportation are called
> metaphorai. To go to work or come home, one takes a
> "metaphor"—a bus or a train. Stories could also take this noble
> name: every day, they traverse and organize places; they select and
> link them together; they make sentences and itineraries out of
> them. They are spatial trajectories. In this respect, narrative
> structures have the status of spatial syntaxes.... Every story is a
> travel story—a spatial practice.*
>   Michel de Certeau, *The Practice of Everyday Life* (1984: 115)

Even before the termination of the Mexican and Carnegie research
projects, tourism at Chichén had already begun and the first guidebook of the museum had been written (Erosa Peniche 1948 [1937];
cf. Andrade 1927; Cirerol Sansores 1951; Ocampo 1941). Embodied
in the guidebook of the archeological site is a strategy of knowledge:
the concise narrative description of the "principal" buildings is a testament and artifact of the interpretive models, theories, debates, research
paradigms and practices, problems, methods, objectives, sponsorship,
and organization of a multidisciplinary and international investigation.
    Invented in the very heart of this anthropological strategy of
knowledge is the tourist deployment of the Maya. At the conjuncture
of the criollo political economy of Maya culture and the anthropo-

logical study of Maya civilization stands Chichén Itzá: the historical construction of this place as a tourist attraction is prefigured by the conjoining of these two series. It was necessary for Chichén to become monumentalized as an attraction in order to provide an objective referent and material reality to these discourses of cultural patrimony and civilization. According to the explicit Carnegie and socialist strategy, Chichén would become a "Mecca of travel." In turn, the nineteenth-century travel-tourism of the Maya is the condition of possibility for the emergence of these two discursive formations. Clearly, there is no exteriority between anthropology and tourism, but a complicitous interdependence of borrowing, appropriation, practices, discursive intertextuality, and historical conditioning. The tourist spectacle of the Maya is inscribed in the sacred artifact of archeological reconstruction. In this light, the various forms of pollution and danger that tourism represents to the discipline and some practitioners of anthropology are only a symptom and sign of the intimate history and interdependence of the two.

In this scriptural economy of the museum, guides (both guidebooks and guide service) are strategic practices in the quotidian reinvention of Chichén Itzá as an ancient Maya city, and of Maya culture and civilization. Both guidebook and tour reinscribe the ruins as a mystic writing pad through their spatializing enactments and discursive practices of anthropological knowledge. The aim of this chapter is to perform an analysis of guides and of the Museum in which vision is shown to be a function of the scriptural operations of time, body movement/travel, spatialization, and discursive/textual production of images.

Maps of the Museum: Envisioning Chichén (by Guidebook)

In the first guidebook of Chichén Itzá (Erosa Peniche 1948 [1937]), a genre is enacted and a vision is inscribed. In an introduction, a framing device narrates historical and cultural contexts and general information about the site while interweaving diagnostic features of the guide. A map is narrated so as to situate the sight in a tourist geography and in the timing strategies of travel. Subsequently, a graphic map of the archeological site is depicted, an altered copy of the Carnegie master plan drawn by J. O. Kilmartin (see figure 3). This representation, which is notoriously limited and incomplete, only charts the central core of the site in which are located the "principal" buildings. Accompanying the map is a list of the names of these numbered memory loci. Not only is the number of "arresting" monuments augmented substantially from Stephens's map and the cenotes included as ruins, but a hierarchized classification and historico-cultural prioritization has constituted a new display of the ruins, a new inscription on the wax slab. The numbering on the map and its legend in the Erosa Peniche guidebook replicates the order of the tour enacted in narrative. The guidebook begins with Toltec Chichén, that is, the "new"/north part of the site that is differentiated only by the road built in 1936: (1) the Castillo and its substructure, (2) the Ball Court, including the Temple of the Jaguars, (3) the Tzompantli, (4) the Temple of Eagles (and Jaguars), (5) the Sacred Cenote, (6) "the Mausoleum #3" (i.e., Venus Platform) are listed as separate exhibit locations; completing the circuit is the complex exhibit of the Thousand Columns, which is composed of (7) the Temple of the Warriors, (8) the "Tables," (9) the Market and its Annexes. Then the narrative turns to the south, "old" Maya Chichén, in an order that follows the physical path south from the Pyramid of Kukulcan: (10) the Temple of the High Priest's Grave, (11) the Red House and the House of the Deer, (12) the "Caracol" or Observatory, (13) the Nunnery and its Annexes, (14) the Akab-Dzib, and (15) Cenote Xtoloc and its Temple (Erosa Peniche 1948: 8). The order is not linear, although it does represent a reversed historical trajectory back into the mythic waters of origin represented by Xtoloc. Memory locations are now not just single building-images but complex topoi, being either compound exhibits composed of equally paired buildings (11), hierarchical topoi with a principal building and annexed memory locations (2 and 13), or a series of multiple building exhibits (7, 8, 9) considered as a unit.

The description of the museum proceeds through the cumbersome articulation of two series: on the one hand, selected fragments from the historical discourses of conquering Spaniards and criollos and, on the other hand, the material fragments of buildings reproduced through archeology. These two series are not yet effectively linked in a sign relation where the former is the *depositio* of the latter. The excessively objectivist and rationalist description of stones, architecture, sculptures, and motifs operates as a representation by itself that is so realist that it seems unable to function as an image capable of storing and evoking anything but the archeological techniques (survey, excavation, cleaning, cataloging, restoration, and reconstruction) that brought the image to light. When the historical discourses are evoked from the narrativization of the visual there is a tremendous disjunction; the images are too rationalist for these discursive fragments to be tied to those locations, except by chance.

This seemingly iconic and transparent representation of a reality, the remains of an ancient city, is created by eliding even this *depositio* of an archeological way of knowing that produced the monuments as material exhibit. Erased from the guidebooks, this strategy is documented elsewhere, in the different Carnegie and Monumentos Prehispánicos monographs, reports, and notes, and contributions, books, and conference papers about Chichén. In inverted proportion to the texts of guidebooks (for exceptions, see J. E. S. Thompson 1963: 1–41; Hunter 1986; INAH 1965), the archeological discourse of the Carnegie is constituted through the detailed reporting of the scientific procedures, objectives, methods, results, and interpretation of the excavation of each building and complex. Even before they are written in guidebooks, the remains of Chichén are already textualized as data; like an exhibit for a court case, each artifact must be documented in a multiplicity of texts to become (archeological) evidence. In this regime of truth, the exhibits, by themselves, cannot be seen; their image is visually obscured. "Los datos que damos sobre las ruinas de Chichén Itzá son brevísimos, con el objeto de que el visitante, *guía en mano, pueda observar los monumentos*" ("The data that we provide about the ruins of Chichén Itzá are very brief, with the objective that the visitor, guide in hand, can observe the monuments") (Erosa Peniche 1948: 4; emphasis added; my translation). The task of the guidebook, even as demonstrated by Gilpin's (1948) photographic guidebook, is to bring the ruins into view, but through language and writing.

The ruins are invisible or hidden from sight because of a fundamental lack of language: the stones are mute and out of sight. It is this lack of speech that precipitates the guidebook, which is a mouthpiece for the archeological discourse that invents the artifact in the first place. This discourse, like an inquisitional practice, makes each stone or ceramic shard confess the history of the Maya to the archeologists, iconographers, and epigraphers; and only these specialists of knowledge can read and write the significance of the stones. They transform carved and mute stone into hieroglyphic runes that are made to speak through the ventriloquism of the expert. The physical dimensions and attributes of objects are ceaselessly narrated, and then only on this transmission of the image into language can any other part of the rhetor-archeologist's *inventio* be deposited. To the lay public, the artifacts are mute when narrated into visibility, but not silent; they are pregnant with a meaning to be revealed through the rarified knowledge of the experts. The ruins require a supplement, which, with its discourse of details, brings the monuments into common language and, therefore, into view. In a Nietzschean reversal, the ruins are the product of and supplement to the ever-expanding number of guidebooks of touristic, archeological, epigraphic, even spiritualist genres of explanation that write on this palimpsest. The ruins are inscribed in wax by archeology, but on the contact surface of the mystic writing pad the runes of other texts are written by tours, guidebooks, and tourists that substantiate the archeological inscription and its fables. If it is archeology that has reinvented Chichén Itzá, it is the guidebooks that reinvent both Chichén *and archeology* in a supplementary series of scriptural operations.

Language is the condition of visibility and legibility. The narration of details inscribes the ruins in the field of vision as legible, that is, visual, images:

> The total height is approximately twenty-nine meters and [the height] of the truncated pyramid, from the terrace to the top platform, is twenty-four [meters]. . . . Each one of the four staircases has ninety-one steps and the top platform or the base terrace of the building forms a step shared in common between the four staircases, for a total of 365, a number equal to the days of the year. (Erosa Peniche 1948: 10, 11)

Through this ventriloquism, the stones speak and the sign of significance is thereby written onto the material artifact constituting it as an image that comes into view as a surface on which multiple texts are performed. In this way, the artifacts of the Museum are not simply vestiges of the Maya, but the pre-text and subtexts of other texts. The Museum exhibit is constituted as this intertextual economy that operates between the legible artifact and the texts that are written and read on its surfaces.

Another discourse of historical fragments runs concurrently with this description of near "zero-degree" interpretation of the objectness of artifacts. There are only a few authors, the most renowned of sources, cited in the guidebook: Landa, Carrillo y Ancona, John L. Stephens, Bernal Díaz, Maudslay, Morley. These authorized fragments are patches of cultural-historical information whose relation to the narrative visualization of artifacts is problematic. Although specific fragments are in a sense "triggered by" specific images, they generally do not refer to the immediate vestige or to the ruins, except through an oblique semiosis. In typically *firsthand* accounts or quotations of such, these fragments describe, comment upon, or explain *other* artifacts, practices, events, and situations than those narrated. Premised on analogy or similitude, the juxtaposition of this discourse at each visualized image simulates an explanation of that exhibit. In other words, the juxtapositioning of these two disjunct series of descriptions in this early guidebook operates by an allegorical and cosmological principle derived from the occult theaters of memory: the museum logic of representation operates here by a complex of synecdoche, metaphor, and metonymy to deposit fragments of heterogeneous discourses on Mesoamerica at each image location in order to forge a totalizing representation of a greater form. Through this cosmological and occult operation, a rational order of archeological knowledge is invented.

For example, the structure at Chichén that has rows of skulls sculpted onto its facades is already called the "Tzompantli," which is the Nahuatl (ancient Mexican), not the Yucatec Maya, word for the sacrificial "skull rack" (Erosa Peniche 1948: 30–31). Following an objectivist description of the structure, a quoted passage from Bernal Díaz narrates his eyewitness account of a *tzompantli,* which he saw in the summer of 1519 in central Mexico. While each of these two artifacts signifies a culture (Maya and central Mexican), the conjoining of their narratives fabricates a single sign that refers to a civilization (Maya-Toltec or Mesoamerican, the latter being is a twice-removed abstraction). No explanation, no interpretation, of the rack of skulls at Chichén is actually made; nothing is explained and no meaning of it as such is devised. On the surface of this articulation of two discourses is "pure" description: two particular *tzompantlis* are described and become material examples of a general case. The pair of objectively narrated images and allegorized accounts forge a synecdoche for Maya civilization that is simultaneously represented and invented as an intertextual construct at the point of contact between the two discourses.

These two discourses are braided together along the spatial trajectory of the guidebook's itinerary through the memory topoi of Chichén. It is this braiding that constitutes the place of Chichén Itzá as an ordered, demarcated unity. Rune by rune within each ruined building and ruin by ruin, the archaeological site comes into vision, that is, becomes a sight, as it becomes written in its being read. Thus, the site of Chichén is constituted as a material referent (the ruins) within the simultaneous inscription of a encompassing textual system (a rune) in which Chichén represents an exemplary ancient Maya city. This ancient city is an imaginary, textual object comprising the totality of architectural structures, spaces, building phases, and historical periods of extension and contraction. In surveying, excavating, restoring, and reconstructing only a selected part of this imaginary totality, the archeologists constructed a representation; by focusing vision on only the "most significant" of this already scientifically reduced selection, the guide (book or person) constructs an even more condensed metonymy. In turn, this rune of an ancient Maya city becomes a synecdochic representation of all Mayan culture and history and Mesoamerican civilization. The narrative movement from exhibit to exhibit simultaneously constitutes the ancient Maya city as its own representation of itself and of Maya civilization: the Museum, then, is an art of memory embodied in its own theater of memory.

While Maya civilization is represented through synecdoche at each textualized exhibit, the ancient city is represented through metonymy in the trajectory to and from each intertextual braid. From the perspective of both the legible artifact and the totality of the sight, Maya civilization is represented through its reduction in a metonymy and metonymic trajectory in space. The triple inscription in stone, vision, and writing constitutes the *legibility* of the ancient city, but it is this dual reduction of civilization that fabricates its *intelligibility*.

Between the ancient sight and Maya civilization, a third, mediative narrative emerges, that of interpretation. In Erosa Peniche's guidebook (1948) it is almost absent. The introductory frame is devoted to quotation of historical fragments and the mapping devices of tourism. In the spatial trajectory of the tour, interpretation (in the popular sense) is restrained and tentative. No discourse of interpretive procedures is applied to the exhibit-text of details to reveal meaning (i.e., "the meaning of"); instead, the deposition of historical fragments at each locus provides significance, but not meaning. When interpretation (in an explicit sense) is forged, it is based on historical knowledge extracted from a discursive field that is elided from the narrative; the "facts" are attached directly to the details while the discourse of history is reduced and discontinued: "365 [steps of the Castillo represents the] days of a year" is stated without further discussion or explication of the calendrical complexities of Maya thought.

In contrast, later guidebooks (INAH 1955, 1965; Ellis and Ellis 1964; Díaz Bolio 1972; Bloomgarden 1974; Mallan 1986; Hunter 1986; Piña Chan 1987; Brosnahan 1989) reverse this calculated ratio of meaning and significance. The central operation of the guide becomes the extraction of meaning from the exhibits and its designation as culture. This is a dual inscription of writing meaning onto the legible surfaces of artifacts and reading those meanings synecdochically as Maya culture and metonymically as the interpretation of that culture. Thus, the narrative of culture and its fabrication, Maya culture, remain submerged and sporadic in the first guidebook. With the narrative and textual shift to culture in later guidebooks and tours, civilization becomes invented through a different semiotic. Historical knowledge is provided in anonymous, nonauthorized discourse. The primacy given to the textual construction (invention) of culture forces the invention of Maya civilization to hinge upon the discourse of the former: it too is "reconstructed" in the runes of an ancient Maya city on the modern ruins of Chichén Itzá.

Tours of the museum also function in this way as guidebooks. Both are spatial practices of narration that reinscribe the place or visual order of Chichén Itzá and its representational stratigraphy through the reading and writing of the museum exhibits. Existing in different material forms, guidebooks and tours operate the same mechanisms in the invention of Maya culture and civilization (see figure 4).

The Art of Weeding: Ventriloquism

Guide service is a practice conducted in a strategic calculation of time. The timings of the tourist body constitute a landscape of sights, attractions, shops, and service sites, a landscape that unfolds as the temporalized trajectory of movement. Within this tourist geography, guides (as well as vendors, waiters, artisans, etc.) are deployed in

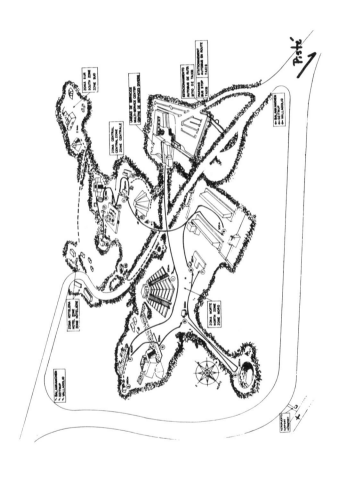

Fig. 4. 1988 CULTUR relief map of Chichén Itzá showing a suggested, but uncommon, tour of the site in three languages. Also indicated are the old road that divides "New"/north and "Old"/south Chichén; the *desvío* where the road from Pisté is diverted around the northern part of the site toward Valladolid and Cancún; the Unidad de Servicios that opened in 1987, which includes the Parador Turístico and the Tianguis; the hotel zone, which includes Club Med, Hotel Mayaland, and Hacienda Chichén; and the "back entrance" where artisan vendors set up stalls on the southeastern part of the old road.

time to practice their spatializing arts of explanation. These arts are constituted in a tactics of time and its tactical manipulation of an economy that operates from the major temporal cycles of the season (high/low), the month, the week, the day; through the local schedules of work routines, charter group itineraries, transportation, daily rounds, localization of movement, and designation of activity; to the micro-intervals and durations of distance, space, gestures, drinking, resting, taking a photograph, buying, talking, walking, reading, listening, and looking. Most important, in this strategy of measuring, multiplying, extending, squeezing, deferring, and dividing of time, vision is constituted, as legible objects, as a place, as an ordered field, as a practice, and as experience.

A tour is to last three and a half hours, according to the official dictum of SECTUR (the federal Secretaría de Turismo). Charter groups from Cancún, Mérida, or Cozumel receive a two- or three-hour tour; the variation depends on the amount of time given to the tourists to rest, the restaurant where they will eat, time of departure from hotel, the distance and mode of travel. The free-agent guides of Chichén (the *bolsa* or "bag") as a rule give one-and-a-half-hour service. Here another series of variables intercede. With regard to the tourists: What nationality and age are they? What languages do they speak? What economic type are they, budget backpackers or luxury travelers? Are they a charter group with no guide or independent tourists? What attitude did they show when told the price? Did they haggle over it or do they look like good tippers? Do they seem interested in the Maya or would they prefer getting a good tan while climbing the monuments? Do they want a "complete" or a "short" tour? With regard to the guides: Whose turn is it among the twenty-two to twenty-five guides of the *bolsa*? To what union does the guide belong and what languages does he or she speak? What season, month, day of the week, and hour of the day is it? How hot is it, or is it raining? Who is next in turn and what are the prospects for hooking another *entrada*? Whether a complete or a short tour is bought, the guide calculates these elements to determine whether it will be conducted in good faith or be a *haranchak*. (This term, derived from agricultural work, means "quick, superficial weeding.")

Although the term *haranchak* is used by the guides to refer to a fast, unenthusiastic tour, it accurately captures two aspects of guide service that need to be underscored. Typically, a tour is speeded up or foreshortened as a tactical maneuver to take advantage of another opportunity "to enter" (the zone): the moment is used better elsewhere. Thus fewer exhibits are seen and those that are explained, are seen less. In the Parador Turístico, the guide plays a game of glances, approaches, and gestures to "hook" a group of tourists. A tourist who declines the first guide in turn may be open to the offers of those next in line. The guide is always on the watch, waiting to "jump" the list of turns; it is an art of poaching on the tourist body as the tourists move through a wide corridor of the Parador from ticket counter to turnstyle. *Haranchak,* then, can be the name for these tactics of hooking and ventriloquism that make the runes speak their secrets through a "quick weeding": guides weed/read memory. Recall that in the maintenance of the site, *chapeo* and *limpieza* (weeding and cleaning the pyramids and paths) is the principal activity of the INAH wardens. This practice forms a kind of typesetting and editorial service in the scriptural economy of the museum; in this way the original archeological reconstruction is kept visibly (re)inscribed. In a complementary practice, the tour itself is also an art of "weeding" memory: the tour weeds the field of vision with the tools of language so as to bring the ancient city into the sight of the ruins as discourses, texts, images. Reciting and resighting their speech, the guides reweed these runes.

The Vision Tour: Space/Word/Time

It is 2:25 P.M. on Wednesday, August 3, 1989. It is the middle of the summer high season and the flooding waves of tourists have substantially ebbed for the afternoon. However, a charter from Club Med Cancún is expected by guides, INAH workers, Tianguis vendors, and other merchants. After landing at the airport, the group is shuffled off by a team of taxis from Pisté directly to the steps of the Parador Turístico. Some five minutes before 5:00 P.M., these same taxis will shuttle the group back to their airplane so that they can arrive at the Club Med between 6:00 and 6:30 P.M. At 2:45 the corridor is filled with the scoping glances of all those in the area as a group of thirty to forty tourists enter past the ticket counter. Even before they buy the tickets, the conductor is busy greeting everyone. Several guides approach the conductor and everything is arranged: the charter is to be divided into an English and a French tour; two guides are needed and they are paid. The guides sign their receipts and are introduced to the tourists. Only eleven minutes after entering, the two groups are already being led past the turnstyles into the sight. While the conductor gets into conversation with different merchants and Tianguis vendors about commissions, the French group heads into Old Chichén and the English group is taken to the north. We are concerned here with the construction of vision in the conjugation of word, space, time; therefore, we let pass without comment the two *inventios* implied by these two different nationalities and starting points in the art of memory-weeding as we follow again the English tour by Edy.

It takes less than four minutes to walk up the main path into the southwestern edge of the central plaza. Along the northern and southern perimeter of this western side are stopping locations, where groups sit to rest or stand to see the explanations of the Castillo. The English-speaking guide takes his group to the far west of the plaza on the grass near the Ball Court where the old road from Mérida met the Castillo. This location is selected for its sight line of the northern staircase: the inscribed image is the legendary Castillo.

At 3:00 P.M. Edy, the guide, slices right into the main artery connecting culture, civilization, and the ancient city and demands the deposited memory: Quetzalcoatl arrived in Chichén from central Mexico "to settle the second period, which is running 900 to 1200 A.D." There is his temple:

> When we see the pyramid this way, we can notice the edge of the corners, the terraces... they coincide with the ramp of the stairway all the way down. This is what makes the twenty-first of March and the twenty-first of September with the position of the sun. There on the back... the *sol* [sun] light illuminates the whole facade and then *sol* light comes through the corner, and the triangles that we see coming out of the wall of the stairway they will also get illuminated, giving the idea of a snake moving down... and light on the ground also illuminates the head of the snake that we see just behind the girl in the red, I mean green, shorts. And it only happens twice a year. According to the archeologists, the building is oriented in this way.

In case the tourists are blinded by that serpent on the balustrade, Edy calls their attention to the number of stairs, 365, which makes "the temple built in the name of the sun god... in honor of the sun;

yet we still see the snake with feathers, which is the symbol of that Quetzalcoatl, the feathered serpent also known as Kukulcan, same thing." In a symbiotic relationship, the sun and the snake bring each other into light, into vision. While they make each other legible, it is the guide who writes their images onto the surfaces of the pyramid for the tourist to see: "when we see"; "we can notice"; "we see just behind the girl." The guide points to the surfaces bathed in the afternoon sun and writes on the tourist's imagination a shadowy idea of a shadow that is a shadow of an idea of the feathered serpent. Vision is communal: "we see." There is corroboration of the spectacle of the Maya. In a dual verbal gesture, meaning is legibly drawn on the contact sheet and wax so that the tourists can read it as if they were merely seeing what is obvious, hearing what is merely oral.

This introduction concludes, in six minutes and thirty-five seconds, with spatial gestures that both mark off a map and the itinerary of the tour: Further behind is the Temple of the Warriors, which is to be seen later. Over there is the Ball Court: "Notice the ring from here . . . We'll find inside two rings. . . . And there on the wall we are going to find carvings . . . [representing] sacrifice. Let's take a look inside." As the group moves to the second location, a question emerges from a tourist as if the person, also demanding the deposit of the images, spontaneously remembered a centuries-old debate: If the culmination of the ball game was sacrifice by decapitation, which side (winner or loser) was decapitated? The answer is quick, but calculated: "We still don't know."

Mystery is brought to the surface, but the laughs in response keep it concealed. "Also, the referee was sacrificed." Within thirty seconds of walking and questions, the tour stops at the two three-meter-long fragments of carved stone in the weeds outside the wall. These are feathered serpents that had adorned the wall (and that had arrested Stephens's tour): "but they had just fallen down; this is how they first found Chichén Itzá, all covered by the vegetation. . . . Archeologists cleared this jungles [sic] out. They put all the stones back together. Notice the little stones in between the blocks. . . . That is where the archeologists placed them in between to hold [together], reinforcing the construction." In a repetition of an "original" founding act by Quetzalcoatl, that famous Toltec who rebuilt the "Pure Maya city," the archeologists found another city, that is, reconstructed the ruins of this dual city (Toltec-Maya and Pure Maya). Like the hyperreality identified by Eco (1986: 1–58; cf. Baudrillard 1988: 166–84), the archeological reconstruction is a simulated reality that maintains authenticity through the traces of its reinvention: "Everything is original, except where you can see the little stones." In a reversal of causality, the traces of archeological artifice indicate not the modern fabrication, but the purity and authenticity of the original that stands in a simulated full presence: "Really wonderful work [of reconstruction], because you almost see everything original. You can see every single block with few exceptions in which you see little stones." The little stones are traces of restoration that mark and re-create the authenticity. But this reinvention is authentic, not staged; authentic simulacrum, not only because it was socially constructed, but because the masons, contracted by the (Yucatec creole or Anglo) archeologist, who reconstructed this artifact were all Maya. There is more irony: many of these contemporary Maya masons hired by the archeologists were from the town of Oxkutzcab, the figurative descendants of Uxmal, Chichén's archenemy in the politics of the tenth to the twelfth centuries, as is explained at the Sacred Cenote.

In the two minutes devoted to the two serpents, Edy notices another group entering the Ball Court, where he was headed, and that the Annex (Temple of the Jaguars), which opens to the east, is empty of tourists. He detours the group: "Let's take a look inside this way." This tactical addition is balanced with a subtraction; later, the Temple of Eagles and Jaguars is bypassed. It's 3:09 P.M. and five minutes will be spent examining the details of the carvings that take up three entire walls of the Annex. First, through gestures and words that focus attention, identify, and interpret details of the carvings, a scene is written on the engraved wall. A visual text is inscribed onto the surface of an already carved artifact. Second, the speech of the guide shifts from description to historical narrative and transforms the visual images from a scene of action to an event in a story of Chichén Itzá, and then to a story in the history of a civilization. The gestures and speech of the guide produce at least three texts (scene, event, story) that intercept each other to form a single explanation:

This was one of the most [well preserved wall carvings]. It shows warriors in a procession. Notice the profile. Very exact. You can see the nose with a form, you see also a woman, you see a headdress of green and red feathers. We see his chest plate. Notice the shield and also a spear right here. He is a warrior. We see all the royalty right here. That one is really interesting because the headdress if you find the face you can almost tell that it's the headdress of a Centurian of Old Rome; anyway, the man has a bob through the nose which is usual in the natives of this ground. We have those warriors, among them nobles, and they are all coming toward this man, who is the central personage of the whole scene. We see quite clearly his, ah, chest plate; notice his belt, both feet down here, and here is his face, eyes, nose, mouth. You see that, ah, it is considered here a beard on the man so that this and the snake with feathers with the mouth open up there, so that this one is the famous Quetzalcoatl, the feathered serpent, the priest who has established the second period of Chichén Itzá, the one who settled around the 900s of the Christ of Chichén Itzá. There is a very interesting relation [*relación*, i.e., historical account] that says that Chichén Itzá, ah, in the Old City of Chichén Itzá, ah, settled his residence, a man, so powerful that people from Mexico, from Guatemala, from Chiapas, from all the surrounding, they sent presents in sign of peace and friendship. That will give you an idea of how powerful and important would be this man known as Kukulcan or Quetzalcoatl. A man, ah, outsider coming from the central plateau of Mexico—according to the archeologists this could be the coming in of the barbarians, so-called Chichimecas back in those days, that made the Toltecs lose its city, [pushing them] out and along with them this personage who started the worship of this Quetzalcoatl, the snake with feathers. So we see all of them with the offerings, known as the fruits, the flowers, the *flora*. This man in the attitude of giving the offering to this man identified as a priest. . . . And, ah, the throne for the man was that: the jaguar we see in between these two columns was the sitting [*sic*; i.e., throne] for this priest identified as Quetzalcoatl, Kukulcan, the feathered serpent. Let's take a look in for the Ball Court.

The timing of the wax tablet reveals a thick stratigraphy of inscriptions. And the travel in wax culminates in the totalizing image of Kukulcan.

The walk into the center of the Ball Court takes two minutes (see figure 5), including a pause to allow the rear of the group to catch up to the front. While waiting, the guide gives a rule of memory: he mentions how the changing sunlight during the day allows for different details to be seen on the stone carvings. This also gives time for the earlier group to move away from the carvings that compose the

Fig. 5. View of at least five different guided tour groups within the Ball Court of Chichén Itzá. Groups in the middle distance to the right and to the left are standing before the central panels of carved stone that depict the players of two teams, one supposedly Pure Maya and the other supposedly Toltec-Itzás, lined up facing each other across the sacred Skull-Ball as the leader of one team decapitates the first in the row of the opposing team. The Ball Game is read allegorically as a representation of the Itzá conquest of the Maya city of Chichén. There, in the center of the Ball Court, one can see where guides demonstrate the acoustics with a hand clap, which illustrates both Maya science and spirituality via the seven echoes. (Author's photograph)

primary memory stop for the Ball Court. In *seven* minutes, he details the central panel: the two teams, the ballplayers, the accoutrements, the paraphernalia, the position of bodies, the decapitation. From the details of the ballplayers that make the carving legible, the narration slides into the historical events that make it intelligible. Memorialized here is the arrival of the Toltecs under Quetzalcoatl and the establishment of their dominion over the Pure Maya. Through the text of details (the exhibit), the guide reads a historical text (the ancient city). These become a pretext for another and are read in the name of a written text that authorizes Maya culture, the Popol Vuh:

> The man there has his head cut off so that out of this carving we can tell that commemorating what is said in the Popol Vuh they have sacrificing somebody and it could be that idea of the good and the bad because, according to some of the historians, the

game itself had a meaning of the universe. It was a fight of the forces of the universe and the pass of the ball through the ring, it would be a good point, a positive part of the universe itself, the conjuncture, and so the going on of the world itself. So maybe that is how they played it. And the game itself would be given in honor of the gods.

Here, then, we are told, is a foundation act of the Maya cosmos. And the guide's repetition, in the mode of recitation, of the archeological understanding is yet another reinvention of the archeological *inventio* of that cosmography in the wax replica of Chichén Itzá. But the show of ventriloquism does not yet end; as if reciting the "central truth" of tour guides, Freidel, Schele, and Parker (1993: 34–37) become the (rarified) mouthpiece for the *inventio* of the guides: "the words and actions of the Maya themselves ... [such as] Chichén Itzá raised in its final glory are essentially forms of the same thing. They are all symbols of the Creation of the cosmos" (37). The acoustics of this mystic Ball Court are indeed mysterious.

It is now 3:22 P.M., and, after this seven-minute explanation, the guide moves the group on, through the northeastern entrance to the "back" side of the Tzompantli. During this two-minute walk, Edy mentions that the audience sat on top of the walls. Keeping watch of the time, he has decided not to illustrate the acoustic marvels of the Ball Court, which can be enacted in two ways. One is to stand in the middle of the court and clap. The guide then asks the tourists to listen: There are seven echoes, which correspond to the seven streams of blood from the headless necks that are carved in the form of six snakes and the vine of a water lily. What this or other symbolic correspondence *means* is usually left unstated so as to invoke the totalization of cosmos—and the emptiness of signification. Seven, after all, is magical and potent not only in Maya thought but in Occidental and Oriental numerologies. If there is plenty of time, other guides, and most guidebooks, direct the group, upon entering, toward the room at the southern end of the court; one tourist is sent to the northern temple and asked to talk in a normal voice. The group is then told to carry on a conversation with that person. In both performances, the acoustic function—an artifice of space, in any case—*is made visible* by finding its imprint on the wall carvings or by enacting in a bodily practice the spatial arrangement of the memory location. These reenactments simulate a resurrection and re(sus)citation: at the heart of the Ball court, where the players were sacrificed, the walls are made to speak in an act of ventriloquism.

As the group exits en route to the Tzompantli, a one-minute pause is made at the walls of the court. Notice the construction, the thickness, the angle, precise carving, and so on. The guide points out the catalog number on a stone. Another trace of archeological restoration. Edy stops at the southeastern corner of the Tzompantli, but he speeds up now; he only identifies some of the figures carved on the waxy wall—jaguars, warriors, eagles, serpents, skulls. Heart sacrifice is depicted and described. By 3:27 P.M., the group begins the eight-minute walk to the Sacred Cenote. Halfway there, Edy breaks the silence and points out the construction of the *sacbe* (ancient "white road") on which the group walks to a new memory location.

At the Cenote, guides shift narrative style. Narrativization is no longer to render visibility, but to evoke the invisible. This memory image is deposited with history: the history of dredging and exploration of the Sacred Well, the colonial accounts of sacrifice, the legendary pilgrimages and prophecies of the rain god Chak, the treacherous politics of Hunac Ceel, the Trojan-like love story of the League of Mayapán, and the history of Chichén's founding and abandonment. Other texts authorize discourse through citation of sources: Landa, Edward Thompson, the CEDAM, *National Geographic*, and the *Chilam Balams*. The ritual of virgin sacrifice is demythologized by the description of the male skeletons dredged out of the well in the 1960s by the National Geographic Society and of the cumbersome mechanics of Thompson's winch that he used at the turn of the century to explore the Sacred Well (see Willard 1926; E. H. Thompson 1932; Dávalos Hurtado 1961; Littlehales 1961; Folan 1970; Coggins and Shane 1984; Ramírez Aznar 1990). The mythology of the Well is first historicized in the recounting of events and then naturalized by descriptions of the Yucatec topography, the problem of water, the wars between Maya polities that "flow" through the Well. Typically, guides allow fifteen minutes at this location, about ten minutes of words and half again for rest and rehydration at the *palapa* at the mouth of the Well. Edy allows only six minutes for the group to contemplate the still waters, and the explanation is continued as the tourists walk back along the *sacbe* to the main plaza. Edy pushes the tour forward in order to keep time.

He silently passes "behind" the Venus Platform to a location between the Castillo, the Temple of the Warriors, and the Venus Platform. Already it is 3:51 P.M.: two-thirds of the site remains to be toured and half an hour must be provided for the tourists to wander on their own. In six minutes he brings these three exhibits into language with only gestures toward these memory topoi. In other words, twenty to thirty minutes, including walking, are cut out—weeded—from the tour.

While the Cenote is the topos for history, the Venus Platform is a place of astronomical and calendrical explanation. The calendar systems based on the sun, moon, and Venus are described. The interlocking of these three systems in the Short Count of fifty-two solar years is highlighted and read into the architecture devoted to Venus and Kukulcan as well as pervasive rattlesnake iconography carved on most balustrades of the Toltec Chichén. The detailed measuring out of the calendrical cycles and their multiple overlapping simultaneously charts out a scientific rigor and knowledge unsurpassed except for one civilization and a system—call it Maya culture—of sacred meanings and gods that supervise time. Thus the Venus image leads back to a new angle on an already visited location, the Castillo, but now either demanding another acoustic show or an account of the Chac-Mool, "messenger of the gods."

It takes five minutes to cross the central plaza and the old road that inscribes the divide between Maya/Old and Toltec/New Chichén. The guide has been moving the group quickly since leaving the Cenote and stops at the Temple of the High Priest's Grave, only to relieve the tourists from the pace. It is now 4:10 and the group, after an hour and ten minutes, has tired; no questions are asked of the guide during this walk. Another four more minutes of walking brings the tour to the Observatory.

Here in the heart of the "Pure Maya" City, there are only four sight locations: the Observatory, the Monjas (Nunnery), the Church, and the Annex of the Monjas; the Deer House and Red House, which Stephens mapped, are left out of virtually all tours by all guides. Here everything shifts. Significantly, the extent of undergrowth increases; there are more weeds and they cover more of the restored buildings. In the "old" part of the sight, the INAH wardens put less effort into weeding. Space is diminished, not only by this visual limitation, but by the physical and architectural layout of the sight itself; the buildings are smaller and their facades close in upon themselves. Here also, the tours do less weeding of the ruins, and the descriptions are themselves weeded. In the explanatory discourse of this section, the historical commentary and subtexts are left aside. Only the details of art and architecture are made visible through the gestures of attention. Cosmological sciences and the religion of Maya Chichén are given primacy over politics and the social history of Toltec/Mexican Chichén. History is reduced to the history of building phases and art styles or the phases of archeological excavation. Time is also limited to the movement of astronomical bodies as charted by architecture. Thus, the Western *inventio* of the Maya as priests/shamans/kings is re-inscribed against the image of ancient Mexicans as military/merchant bureaucrats. Here the Maya are taken out of time at precisely that moment when the tour becomes squeezed into time (charter group time). As if to simulate an exhibit of a museum culture, time is stopped and space is contracted.

The Pure Maya is trapped in a museum diorama as the philosophico-theocratic savage. The discourse of the tour also becomes an art of mapping the surfaces of features: Here is the Monjas, look at the geometric design on the facades; it is the rattlesnake. To the left is the Church; see the four *bacabs* (Guardians of the four corners) on the facade? Those on the corners are Chac masks. In the courtyard, there is a Buddha-like Maya Priest at the top of the entrance; you can climb up the Monjas to see the Castillo or walk around, take photographs, but remember the site closes at 5:00 P.M. To return to the bus, follow that path straight ahead. The path over there leads to the Temple of the Tables and that one to the Ak'ab Dzib or House of Night/Dark Writing, but be careful, there are snakes—real serpents that bite, not those feathered snakes that center the universe. It's 4:33, and with these final comments and spatial orientations the guide takes his leave. Several tourists approach to give a tip. It is here where the paid tours of the *bolsa* guides end; but other tours, those given off-duty by certain "guides," or by some of the young and male INAH wardens to interested female tourists, continue along the obscure path to the south and behind the Nunnery that leads eight hundred meters to the Temple of the Phallus, where a different image of the Maya is inscribed in the waxy stone. I walk back with the guide to the Parador as he explains his timing decisions and tactics.

Fig. 6. View of "Old" or "Pure Maya" Chichén showing the Observatory or Caracol with the Pyramid of Kukulcan to the north in the central background. Visible in the foreground are the traces (more trees and underbrush) of the archeological inscription of selective *chapeo* that renders this part of the sight "older" and more "mysterious." The touristic rewriting of this archeological vision is engraved in the grass and earth as paths that privilege certain exhibits, such as the Caracol and Monjas, but de-emphasize others such as those that attracted Stephens. To the left, the back of the Red House or Chichanchob can be seen. To the right, in the foreground, a path leads past the Iglesia out of the framed image to the Ak'ab Dzib. Behind the photographer, situated on the stairway of the Monjas or Nunnery, one can find a path that leads a kilometer south to the Temple of the Phallus and even more mysterious ruins, for they combine elements of "Pure Maya" and "Toltec Maya" but nonetheless are diagnostic of "Old Chichén" for their southern location.

He asks for my opinion on the content of his tour as he comments on how it differs from those of other guides, especially from Mexico, who romanticize and speak *pendejadas* about Maya origins.

Mysteries of the Rune and the Mystic Ruins

Within the regimen of the tourist timings, the guide inscribes the surfaces of spaces with the images and texts of a multiplicity of discourses. Within this stratigraphy of memory Chichén is reinvented as Maya city in ruins and *this rune* is simultaneously inscribed as another topos and trope: the Museum of Maya Culture and Civilization. The conjugation of time, space, and discourse constitutes this hetero-topia as a strategic field of vision; vision exists only through the bod-ily practices and temporality of a practice embedded within a scrip-tural economy. The tour, as well the guidebooks, practiced in the shadow of the feathered serpent and in the scorching sun of Yucatán, are truly an Ak'ab Dzib, that is, a "dark/mysterious writing": By marking the spaces of the sight with the shadow of language, the ar-tifacts become legible images, that is, they enter into the light of vi-sion as blank or white spaces that can be imprinted with a multiplicity of texts that designate the intelligibility of the exhibit. In the quotid-ian practices of tourism, the Museum of Chichén, which is the strate-gic order of knowledge embodied in the ruins, is continuously rein-vented as a sight, as texts, as photographs, as postcards, as tours, as souvenirs, as an encounter with the Maya, as memory of a culture and a civilization. From this perspective, Maya culture and civiliza-tion do not refer primarily to some people out there, but to an effect of a scriptural economy. At the heart of this discursive apparatus and anthropological strategy of knowledge are the ruins of Chichén Itzá: a machine that functions to read and write the Maya. The ruins are a mystic writing pad, a rune whose writings are marked by mystery and whose scriptural operations are themselves mysterious writing.

Charter or large group tours never see the Ak'ab Dzib. Because it is rather isolated from the main sights in Old Chichén, few tourists see it. Guides, whether of the *bolsa* or from Cancún and Mérida, do not include it in their *inventio*. Usually only the most interested of "travelers," who have not been told to fear the snakes, lead themselves with guidebook in hand to this location. Otherwise, this topos might be visited on those special tours given by an off-work guide, an INAH warden, or other local who is seeking to make friends with tourists. "Considered one of the older Maya structures at Chichén Itzá, the Akab Dzib (Obscure Writing) is reached by taking a very short walk east of the Iglesia [or Church]" (Hunter 1986: 301). "On the south side over the doorway is a figure of a priest [writing on] a vessel in front of him covered with hieroglyphic writing. These unknown words give the building its Mayan name" (Bloomgarden 1974: 25). "In other rooms, traces of red hand-prints are still visible" (Brosnahan 1989: 486). These are the markings of Itzamatul or Itzam-Kabul, the earth/serpent deity or "Heaven's Hand."

This rune stands as a machine at the heart of Chichén. Local knowledge has it that at midnight—some assert under a full moon at this hour, when *aluxes* (spirit-owners and winds) travel about— the inscriptions become luminescent and glow. Shining from their magical light at night, this "dark" writing becomes legible, even if the meaning is not always intelligible to those intrepid visitors who would read its secrets. The dark writing of the day becomes a clear, bright writing of the night. Local Mayas usually do not bother to become enlightened through this dark writing, largely out of fear of the aluxes and other "spirit-owners" of Chichén. The mysterious play of light and dark is a dangerous mystery best left for others to encounter.

6 / Vernal Return and Cosmos

That Serpent on the Balustrade and the New Age Invasion

Twice a year the sun crosses the equator and night and day are of equal length all over the world. These spring and fall equinoxes usually occur on March 21 and September 23. On these dates, an incredible solar phenomenon occurs in Chichén Itzá — the setting sun creates the form of a serpent down the side of the main pyramid there. Thousands of people gather each year to witness this event that the Mayans had scientifically calculated many years ago.
Cancún Tips (summer 1989): 126

Licenciado Arochi deserves the good graces of archeology and I propose him as a candidate for the Medallion of Yucatán; well, even though he did not discover the Serpent of Light, he did make the days of the equinox become a great romería [Roman-style carnival/pilgrimage] at Chichén Itzá with thousands of visitors that year after year increase in number such that they no longer fit in that part of the plaza from which one can contemplate the spectacle; visitors, not only from Yucatán and the Mexican republic, but from such faraway places as Japan. For all of this, I have told him that he is the champion of the Serpent of Light.[1]
José Díaz Bolio, *La Serpiente de Luz de Chichén Itzá* (1982: 8–9)

Endless Equinox Every Day

As if it were any other day, the March equinox epitomizes everyday life in Chichén and Pisté. Everybody will tell you, "It's no big deal." Meanwhile, elaborate preparations are in full gear at all levels of society.

Preparations begin months before the actual event. The Ayuntamiento of Mérida sends a brigade of approximately forty persons to Chichén for another semiannual round of *limpieza*. CULTUR renews contacts with the police, military, Boy Scouts, newspapers, and emergency medical services to organize infrastructural services for the event. Travel agencies, hotels, and restaurants finalize arrangements for special equinox charter groups. Even more behind the scenes, diverse persons, some politicians or aspirants to office, unionized workers, artisans, and handicraft vendors organize events or confrontations, which are strategically planned to serve political and economic interests.

Like any other day, the equinox is a day of conflicts between and within the different sectors involved in the tourist apparatus. But, more auspicious than any other day, it provides the occasion for tactical maneuvers against political, social, or economic adversaries that could result in a strategic or tactical advantage. The contemporary ritual event of the equinox no doubt equaled the ancient Maya ritual for complexities in political, social, cultural, and economic intrigues, implications, and effects.

Traditionally, a few days before and the day of March 21, CULTUR runs an advertisement in the *Diario de Yucatán* for the equinox events at both Chichén and Dzibilchaltun. These are composed of pictures of the main pyramid of each site where the two different events occur. A simple caption invites the reader to attend either of the "natural phenomena." This naturalization is a dominant trope with multiple ramifications. The architectural and astronomic knowledge that allowed the Maya to construct a building according to astronomic calculations is demoted from the realm of culture to that of "raw material" in both a staged Maya event and a tourist construction. To the extent that it is construed as a phenomenon of Maya agency and culture, the Maya are located as agents of Nature in a stage beyond a primitive humanity that the touristic staging simply *frames*.

In Pisté, everybody is concerned about and discusses the upcoming day, or at least some pressing issues with which it is then linked. Gossip is overflowing with ongoing events in local and regional politics, local social life, and the issue of what to sell this time round. The preparations are extensive, and often require arrangements with relatives to work together or to pool resources to make an investment. Many persons, even those not normally dedicated to commercial enterprise, stake claim to two to four square meters of territory alongside the highway and entrance road to Chichén. As if it were part of the phenomenon itself, small piles of stones or stakes begin to dot the recently cleared brush all along the sidewalk that connects Chichén and Pisté. Here pole-and-plastic-sheet stalls are set up on land rented by the *ejido* authorities for the sale of tacos of *cochinita* (pork), roasted chicken, soda, ice slushies, juice, T-shirts, blankets, *huipiles* (traditional women's dress), stone, idols of wood, ceramic, or concrete, film, and even parking space.

This is everyday life; it is like any other day in the life of Chichén. But, all activity—activities that happen year-round—is intensified and condensed on this day. From union strikes to the public fights between archaeoastronomers, from the staging of incidents by politicians to the intense skirmishes over space by local vendors—everything that ever happens, happens during the equinox. Yet, somehow these disparate struggles of local and translocal concern become connected and seem to be articulated into coherent strategies of control and conflict. A casual reading of the newspapers suggests that not only regional and national but international politics and events seem to intensify from January until the end of March; this was especially the case in 1989, when the equinox was preceded by omens (the sky turned bloodred), a local assassination attempt, community-wide political protests, official visits by high-ranking PRI members, public denunciations of fraud by the director of the state's program to promote traditional artisanry, scandals among vendors over the rights to sell artisanry in the Tianguis, protests over the increasing "tourist impact" on cultural patrimonies, and so on. Everything seems to be in motion and accelerating toward a collision with the setting sun of the vernal equinox.

The event of the equinox is in the first case a tourist ritual whose objective is to promote Yucatán and its cultural patrimony as commodities for touristic consumption. Through a celebration of the Maya "genius" put on for a thoroughly *international* audience, the state tourist industry stages a massive publicity event. This staged ritual began only in 1984, even though attendance had escalated, according to government census materials, to tens of thousands during the previous six years. Of course, the tourist event itself had only been invented eleven years earlier, with the publication of Luis Arochi's book in 1974. Since around 1987, the newspapers have systematically reported an attendance of thirty to forty thousand, although others have estimated twenty thousand; there is no accurate record keeping on this day because no entrance fee is charged and tens of thousands enter the zone en masse on the service road.

The equinox event is a ritual by which hegemonic interests imagine the Yucatec community as a whole, in its parts, as a historical entity, and in relation to both its internal and external Others. The equinox is the exemplary event of memory in the Museum of Maya Culture as well as the occasion for battle and the battlefield in this theater for the discursive war of nations.

The centerpiece of the government program organized by CULTUR is an "official" explanation of the equinox phenomenon as it occurs, but it also includes two or three hours of traditional Yucatec song and dance preceding the main attraction. In past years, the traditional central Mexican *volador* or "flying pole" dance was performed, but not since the inauguration in 1987 of the new Parador Turístico that belongs to the state government. Thus, in spite of the fact that March 21 happens to be a national holiday in honor of the birthday of Benito Juárez—which also happens to be an important factor in the impressive national attendance for this event—there is virtually no symbolization or promotion of national culture. In other words, this event of the museum is not about imagining the national identity of Mexico, but of the "national" communities of Yucatán and its subnational other, the Maya.

The Invention of the Maya as Culture and Civilization: A New Age Performance of Enlightenment Cosmology

On March 21, pamphlets containing the same tropological photo of the phenomenon at Chichén were distributed by CULTUR at the Parador Turístico. The text briefly explained the phenomenon and provided the entertainment agenda for the 1989 "Program of Art and Culture":

> EQUINOCCIO DE PRIMAVERA. *Chichén Itzá.* 21 de marzo 1989. *El Equinoccio.* In accord with the setting sun, it produces a wavy line that very gradually forms isoceles triangles, which begin [to form] at the first and second platforms and move toward the serpent head until seven perfect triangles are drawn in a luminescent play of harmony. The big [sculpted] heads [at the foot of the Pyramid] are no longer mere adornments, [but become] alive with

the light of the sun, in the moment that the spectacular body of the serpent can be contemplated. The shadow encroaches to cover the head, which is the last triangle to form and the first to disappear; one by one the triangles return according to the continued setting of the sun, until the last triangle disappears into the body of the serpent before the sun finally sets on the horizon.

12:00 [Not in order of actual performance.]
1. Regional Dance by Youth and Infant Ballet.
2. "The Prophecy." Theatrical performance. Passages from the play *Canek*. Theater Company of the State. Adapted by Enrique Cascante.
3. "The Vaquería Yucateca." [Performed by] the Folklore Ballet of the State, Director Alfred Cortés A.; Orquesta Jaranera del Mayab, Director Santiago Sosa.
4. "Song of the Legendary Maya." Autochthonous music [by the] International Center of Art and Folklore, A.C., Director Juan y Rodolfo Magaña.
5. Orquesta Típica de Yucalpetén. Director Manuel Gómez Betancourt.
16:00 Explanation of the Phenomenon of Light and Shadow. Archaeoastronomer Adalberto Rivera.

In addition to this formal, organized schedule of activities, the 1989 event included an extraofficial series of activities by a heterogeneous group of spiritualists, which erupted in conflict just prior to the climactic descent of Kukulcan. The aim of this analysis is to recount these events, especially with regard to the discursive production of messages about Maya culture, as an illustration of the ways contesting images of national solidarities are effected and disseminated in the museum theater.

The conflicts occur at several levels of experience: Not only is there an "actual," physical conflict, but there is also a symbolic struggle of control over the representations that different orator-visitors put into circulation through discourses, images, music, song, and dance within the equinox event; as well, there is a battle between the contesting forms and styles of knowledge that, finally, also enact an epistemological violence against Maya. In the historically fortuitous conjuncture of the scheduled and the ad hoc ritual I discern a strategic logic of representation that structures the discursive appropriation of the Maya through which the heterogeneous invention of Maya culture and civilization occurs. This strategic ordering of discursive production, practices, and conflict is what I called the Museum of Chichén Itzá.

The actual ordering of events in the official ritual (in contrast to the official program just listed) provides a first clue of the hierarchizing operations of the museum. Every year (not just 1989), the ritual is divided into two parts: staged performances that only indirectly relate to the phenomenon and the phenomenon itself, which is accompanied by an explanation by a CULTUR-appointed archaeoastronomer. Once again, the logic of the guide operates here in that discourse must bring the image into visibility and sentient knowledge. The staged ritual begins at midday with the Orquesta Típica de Yucalpetén performing traditional music in the early part of the day as tourists and charter groups stroll by touring the site. Following this, first the youth and then the adult dance troupes performed regional pieces of the *jarana* tradition. The musical accompaniment was taped. In 1989 this was followed with the performance of passages from a play dealing with colonial history. Completing the entertainment portion of the state ritual was the performance of pre-Columbian Maya music. The staged ritual ends before 4 P.M. when the phenomenon begins to appear and the explanatory discourse begins. This surface mapping of the ritual event indicates an evolutionary trajectory, but in reverse: there is a progressive moving "backward" in time, as if from one historical stage to the prior stage, in a presupposed unitary evolution of Yucatec society. Here is an archeologizing logic that operates in the performative imagining of a national solidarity by which primordial origins are established for the community as it is being fashioned. The representations move from hegemonic cultural forms of contemporary Yucatec society to that of nineteenth-century and colonial Maya, and then to that of the ancient Maya.

In this sequencing of the ritual, an organizing center is implied and constructed as the conceptual pivot against which this "historical" trajectory of national solidarity can be measured. Let us call this ritual axis the categorical position of self since the purpose of the analysis is to isolate the construction and contestation of identities postulated for the communities that are imagined in specific relations with one another. In the Museum of Chichén Itzá, the identity and manifestations of the Maya genius are both the representational pivot or self and the target of heterogeneous discourses that seek to fashion, that is, invent, the Maya in specific forms related to the sociopolitical motivations of the speakers of those discourses. Likewise, in this ritual occasion of the celebration of Maya genius, the sacred center is the identity of the Maya self against which other groups and national communities enact their politics of knowledge.

Barring an in-depth analysis of the music, song, and dance of the event, I only discuss these forms in terms of identity formation and sentiments of belonging. All three aesthetic forms are fundamental elements in the imagining of the regional society of Yucatán. They are diagnostic markers of and vehicles for the self-fashioning of Yucatec identity and belonging that are constantly and everywhere being performed at public events. They have also become markers of state identity in that many different types of government functions include these *traditional* art forms that date from the henequen days of economic prosperity. Thus, they have become somewhat folkloric and tinged with nostalgia, which is perhaps what allows for these forms to be a staple in the tourist market: every night of the week one can see and hear these musical and dance performances in Mérida as different groups perform in a circuit that includes the major plazas of the town.

Yucatán's troubadour musical tradition is a cultural complex that primarily has its roots and identity in white Yucatec society; the Spanish and Cuban sources of this attest to a non-Indian cultural form. In contrast, the regional dance, called the *jarana,* is a symbol of Yucatec identity premised on the *mestizaje,* that is, the mixture of races and hybridization of cultures; it derives from a combination of Andalusian and Maya forms of dance. The *vaquería* is a set of choreographed dances performed by the youth of the town or village during the festivities in honor of the patron saint, which also include bullfights and carnival-type activities. It symbolizes Yucatec identity and solidarity in a kind of dialectic: this symbolic synthesis of identities is based on a mixing of forms as well as an erasure and an overwriting of the racial differences and cultural oppositions so that a new presence/identity can be constructed. As such, this cultural performance (in Spanish, "representación cultural") re-presents Maya, that is, includes Maya community and identity within it, directly through metonymy. In contrast, the musical tradition is a white and urban cultural form associated with the lifestyle of the upper classes of the towns and cities. This cultural form is an image and vehicle for Yucatec society in which Maya identity is incorporated or "belongs" through a hegemonic imposition of the dominant culture; here identity is a more fragile synecdoche forged by metaphor. The *jarana* stands, as it were, as an "authentic" and "true" representation of the Maya self no doubt because it is a cultural form that has been reappropriated by the Maya for their own public celebrations—the *vaquería*—of the patron saints of the towns of Yucatán and is not simply an urban, Spanish derivative. But it is fundamentally a symbol of *mestizaje* not only as indicated, but in political terms as well. As a sentient image of society, the cultural hybridization communicates an effaced message of the sociopolitical subjugation of Maya community and identity by the dominant white culture. Somewhat differently, the musical traditions seem merely to assert their identity as an emblematic representation of Yucatec society and within that entity of Maya communities, leaving implicit and unstated the fact that it is the cultural and economic elite being referenced in and through this aesthetic form through synecdoche, while the reference to Maya is only through the fact of political incorporation into the neocolonial state. Thus, if these images of the Maya are considered a sign of Maya genius, of the categorical self around which the ritual is constructed, the referent of the sign relation construed in these symbolic/aesthetic forms is *mestizado* or hybridized identity and an *already subordinated* position within the Yucatec community being forged.

The tourist ritual proceeds from this musical/dance imagining of and nineteenth- and twentieth-century Yucatec society to the colonial society. The vehicle for this shift in the ritual narrative or trajectory is the play version of *Canek* (Abreu Gómez 1983; Cáceres Carenzo 1990; cf. Bricker 1981). The rebellious and prophetic Maya of the colonial and nineteenth-century eras is the theme, and thus the ritual moved antithetically and in "historical reverse" from harmonious visions of the contemporary Yucatec national community to a prior period of struggle and contestation that must necessarily be recast in aesthetic terms that can communicate the legitimation of the current state of affairs. This story/play is supremely fitted to the task. Canek is not only a regional but now even an internationally known figure of indigenous resistance and struggle, but also of capitulation "in the final analysis" to Spanish, criollo, mestizo hegemony.

The Quisiteil rebellion of 1761 is probably the most controversial Indian uprising in postconquest Yucatán...it has fired the imagination of many Ladino authors and historians who have regarded it as an attempt to revive the ancient Maya kingdoms destroyed by the Spaniards in the sixteenth century. The man who figures prominently in all the histories, legends, and novels that describe this uprising is an Indian named Jacinto Canek. (Bricker 1981: 70)

The figure of Canek is heavily invested with the contradictory values of illegitimate and legitimate domination of the Maya and is thus a powerful trope of colonial discourse. He is the embodiment of Maya history-prophecy in which the violent end of autonomous Maya society is foretold in the same moment as is foretold the violent revindication of Maya peoples. He is already a repetition and a transculturated image: Western histories concur that the Indian who supposedly crowned himself king of an independent and rebelling Maya polity was actually named Jacinto Uc. The question, however, is whether this Jacinto gave himself the name Canek, which is the name of the last Maya King of the Tah Itzá that submitted to Spanish colonial rule in 1697, according to the irrepressible logic of Maya calendrical cosmos (see Jones 1989). In other words, was he the leader of a rebellion? Or, was the name imposed by the colonial agents on the scene in the manipulation of the historical record in order to first fabricate a rebellion by a presumptuous *indio* who supposedly assumed a dangerous name and second to legitimate an excessive military action against a drunken Indian who did nothing but carelessly trigger the paranoid brutality of the colonial regime? It is telling how a scholar such as Bricker (1981) can explain how there is very little solid evidence for the rebellion of Canek and then proceed to transform the questioned event into an unquestioned piece of evidence for the relentless cultural logic of Maya prophecy-history and rebellion. Ah, these are mysteries of the Maya, no? Canek is the proper name of the Spanish, Ladino, and Yucatec mestizo, on the one hand, fear of the Maya as well as of their horrified collective guilt, and, on the other hand, of their dream of the total domination, if not eradication, of the Indian Other. Canek is a foundation and primordial origin of non-Indian society in Yucatán. To return to the equinox, passages that concerned Maya prophecies were performed from a most recent poetic reinterpretation of this event of colonizing discourse.

The subsequent performance was the *Mayab Legendario*. In this, the signifier in the sign of Maya culture shifts to the ancient or legendary Maya, as suggested by the title of this section of the show. The songs here are simulacra in a strict sense. They are Western facsimiles and approximations of a musical tradition that is virtually lost and unknown: there is only one surviving Maya song that is purportedly authentic, but "authentic" to what is not clear; the implication that has been pressed upon me by Yucatec ethnomusicologists is that it dates to at least the sixteenth century. Based on this song and the study of more robust source materials for pre-Columbian central Mexico, a Maya tradition of music has been reconstructed, which is this program of the *Legendary Maya*.

In this context, so heavily shaped and controlled by non-Maya interests, the lyrics of the songs and poems returned again and again to this theme of Maya prophecy as the vehicle by which to legitimate the colonial and post-Independence Yucatec society. These songs were generally written (with the exception of the putatively authentic first) by Yucatec criollos beginning in the early twentieth century as part of the literary intelligentsia's attempt to incorporate the Maya patrimony into an image of a racially unified society. This is the romantic and aesthetic archeologizing of the Maya that went hand in hand with the restoration of Chichén and other sights. Logically enough, the music began with the one Maya song—however, with the Spanish translation *first* and then in Mayan. Following this song was another written by a Yucatec Creole in the voice of an imaginary Maya nostalgically foretelling the end of Maya society and culture, but now no longer in the ironic and contestatory mode of the *Canek* prophecies: "Light of Love, Light of Love, where are you? Come here, because soon here in our lands they will be. There will be many dead and our race will disappear by the men that will come from far away to stay here forever." Further along in this song, as in all of the other lyrics and poems, the imagined voice of a pre-Columbian Maya laments the setting sun, which is used as a trope for the coming extinguishing of Maya peoples. Even this extraordinarily pessimistic rendition of the conquest through the metaphor of the sun insinuates the possibility of a Mayan comeback; yet these songs *do not* include lines devoted to the rising/returning sun/Maya, which I suggest effects a censorship on the reader/listener, who is distracted away from reading that corollary and positive message into this image of Maya identity.

It was at this point that a different rebellion began to intercede on the scene of the government-sponsored ritual. All of a sudden, a man dressed in pre-Columbian Aztec clothing appeared on the platform in front of the Temple of Kukulcan and began to ritually greet the corners with an arrow held up between both hands in a gesture of sacred respect. Two more poems were read with musical accompaniment as this *Azteca* began, in the accepted convention of a serpent, his zigzag descent down the north staircase of the pyramid. The poems continued their ironic exaltation of Maya genius by typifying the *indio* as a peasant automaton, as awestruck by nature and the supernatural spirit world, and as unavoidably susceptible to the guiles of females. The concluding song imaged the Maya as an echo of the sacred ritual drum that is in search of rebirth in the corporal form of an insignificant yet pretty bird. Thus, the overall thrust of the aesthetic celebration of Maya is as always already dominated, subordinated, weak, mindless, part of nature, and ephemeral.

By the end of these last two poems, the *Azteca* spiritualist had descended the stairs, where he was greeted by two other *Aztecas*, who then together ritually greeted the four corners. They were also met by the head INAH custodian or Encargado, several of the ranking police officers, another custodian, and the leader of the Boy Scouts. The head custodian, the late Felix Salazar, son of the first Encargado appointed in the 1920s by Monumentos Prehispánicos, proceeded to inform these *Aztecas* that they and their entourage of some fifty to eighty New Age spiritualists were illegally performing ceremonies and disrupting the equinox event.

Here, we need to interrupt and back up the narrative with a character sketch of the agents involved. Who were these folks? Actually, there were four different groups of religious pilgrims on that spring equinox of 1989. One was a group of neo-Aztecs, whom I refer to as *Aztecas*:[2] These are countercultural, typically urban mestizos who have turned to the pre-Columbian Mexican heritage as a source for creating a new, spiritually authentic, anticapitalist, and nationalist community. This movement is quite developed in Mexico City, where a Mexica college based on the pre-Columbian model has been formed where the traditions are taught—of course, through the filters of anthropologists and their predecessors; instruction focuses on dance, music, and religious-spiritual knowledge. There is a Fraternidad Blanca de Quetzalcóatl (White Brotherhood of Quetzalcoatl) from which the three *Azteca* leaders on this equinox day were graduated: they had attained the level of spirituality at which they became reincarnations of Quetzalcoatl. This *Azteca* movement is quite common in central Mexico, where for several years they had been conducting religious ceremonies of cleansing and propitiation at different archeological-sacred sites, according to their understanding of the pre-Columbian calendar. This was only the second occasion that such a group had visited Chichén Itzá, as far as I was aware. (The first was the previous fall equinox, when roughly the same group, which had been protesting for the return of Moctezuma's pendants in the streets of Austria, had come to dance in the zócalo of Pisté.) Since then many other groups, some affiliated with this Brotherhood and others not, have made the pilgrimage to this *gran romería*. Although my own information is weak on this point, I have been told that this extremely nativistic and inverted version of the state-sponsored *indigenismo* emerged in the aftermath of the 1968 massacre of students at Tlatelolco, the Plaza of the Three Cultures in Mexico City.[3]

A second group was composed mostly of Anglo-Americans who had joined a chartered pilgrimage tour of Yucatán that was led by Hunbatz Men (cf. Hunbatz Men 1990; MacAdams, Hunbatz Men, and Besinger 1991) and Helen Leembal. The former is a man of Maya descent from a town near Valladolid who is a kind of *h-meèn*, or Maya spiritualist; the latter is a Californian woman of whom I know nothing except that together they formed this charter group of persons who had paid (I was told) two thousand dollars to undergo spiritual training as "a Maya shaman" or *h-meèn* during the course of a ten-day excursion to Palenque, Uxmal, Mérida, and then Chichén Itzá on the equinox. This was the literal goal: for these Westerners to learn the spirituality and knowledge of "the Maya" in order to become *Maya* themselves.

The theology that undergirds such an idea was explicitly developed in a comprehensive New Age theology by José Argüelles, a California Chicano (see 1987, 1989). One of the many ironies to be discovered is that this theology is based on Maya calendar systems, religion, and history, which means both that it is necessarily filtered through anthropological paradigms and interpretations and that "Maya" here refers to the pre-Columbian, not the contemporary, "cling-ons," to use John L. Stephens's phrase. To quickly encapsulate Argüelles's theology: he explains that the tenth-century "collapse" of the Maya was actually the moment when all the Maya priests realized that their time on earth for spreading the Truth about the universe was over; thus, all wise and true men transformed themselves into other types of "light beings" and traveled to other parts of the galaxy, where they already had or had not yet been. In other words, the Maya calendar, hieroglyphic, and stelae systems were all gnostic-type texts that had captured the Truths of the Universe; thus, the Maya Long Count of history is actually about the comings and goings of different *spirit-owners* conceived of as pure-energy wavelengths who control the course of all human, animal, and natural life on earth by sitting on guard, as it were, at various places on earth construed to be sacred according to an appropriation of different religions. The famous Harmonic Convergence of August 17–18, 1987, was based on and disseminated through Argüelles's calculation of the next changing of the guard by these universal energy-spirits.[4]

An irony of this New Age theology is that one of its underlying goals is to forge a unifying orthodoxy for a movement primarily defined by its unorthodox mix of heterogeneous spiritualities (cf. Fuller 1989). Argüelles spends a lot of time arguing how the Maya calendar is a kind of structuralist variation on the Chinese I-Ching, among other forms of Eastern religious and spiritual thought. He also poaches from similar Western forms, such as gnosticism. One of the readerships that follow Argüelles is an international community of gnostics, which is quite strong in Mexico. This is the third group that arrived on this fateful equinox of 1989.

Living in Cancún are many practitioners and believers of alternative spiritualities, to whom I shall give the umbrella label "gnostic" because it is one of the prominent religious forms. My understanding of gnosticism in Mexico is that its practitioners are devoted to the individual or small group study and discussion of different spiritualities through an eclectic set of texts. Spirituality through individual knowing/knowledge of the true essence of the universe is the operating principle; here balance between the bodily and mental dimensions of knowledge and spirit is key. This contrasts, then, with Anglo-American New Agers and *Aztecas,* both of whom tend toward collective ritual performances; further, the former privileges bodily/sentient spirit and the latter privileges public display and performance. Thus, while the *Aztecas* and the would-be *Mayas* of the Hunbatz Men pilgrimage enacted group activities, the Mexican gnostics at this and other equinoxes separated themselves to perform individualized meditation and prayer in privacy. This, however, did not prevent the gnostics that I knew in Pisté (including the highest representative of CULTUR at Chichén and the archaeoastronomer) from attending the less public spectacles of group ritual such as that which occurred the night of and before March 21. Thus, in terms of the event under analysis, the presence of this third group was important but is not central to my argument because their activities were not collectively organized.

The fourth group lies somewhere between the two styles of individual worship and collective ritual performance. It consisted of a contingent of persons who fall within the rubric of the Rainbow Family, a broadly based, heterogeneous, and seasonal U.S. group of spiritualists. This group's participation in the *Azteca* and *Maya* rituals was on an ad hoc, individual basis. Its spiritual functions were conducted not inside the archeological zone, but at their chosen campsite and base, which was a commercial nature reserve established by an owner of a handicraft store in the Parador de Chichén, on the nights of the twentieth and twenty-first.[5]

This *mixed* alliance of the first two and fourth groups of spiritualists was the group being confronted by the state and federal authorities for illegal worship and religious activities in the modern Museum and Patrimony of Humanity. But this conflict on the twenty-first had already been foretold on the twentieth when these groups had converged on Pisté and Chichén Itzá to begin "purification" rituals at the principal temples; these group activities included silent prayer, handholding, burning copal, and "traditional" music. In the main plaza near the Castillo, the Encargado confronted the spiritual leaders of the *Aztecas* and the *Maya* pilgrims in order to extract them from Chichén. Interestingly, the Encargado personally had known the father of one the *Aztecas,* a Mexican archeologist who was famous for his discoveries at Palenque, and therefore also knew the son, the *Azteca* leader. According to gossip, the Encargado, who was Maya, asked the son if he was not embarrassed to go running around dressed like an *indio* and observed that if his father knew he would roll over in his grave, which happened to be in Palenque. Meeting head-to-head in this immemorial event was an encounter between two styles of appropriating the indigenous past within the imagining of Mexico and of two nationalist projects: the rational, objectivist archeologizing and the romantic, spiritualist revivalism. That night, in the Hotel Misión where the *Maya* pilgrims and the *Aztecas* were staying, the spiritualists conducted an *Aztec* foot-washing ceremony in the hotel garden at 1:00 A.M. But, prior to that, the leaders held a long debate on how best to organize a large-scale public ceremony that would not be interrupted by the authorities of hegemonic rationalism and the agents of both an illegitimate nationalism and an alienating capitalism: They were determined to manifest the true spirituality that the phenomenal event of the appearance of Kukulcan-Quetzalcoatl demanded.

In this debate, Hunbatz Men suggested elaborate ideas for highly symbolic activities that resonated with Maya notions of numbers, time, and space. In contrast, as if by stereotype, the *Aztecas* argued for a more pragmatic approach that could incorporate bystanders, which would deter police intervention, and that could be simply communicated and orchestrated within the chaos of a plaza filled with twenty to thirty thousand tourists. Although insignificant in itself, the *Azteca* plans were roundly accepted over the *Mayas'* and it was decided to slowly gather together by 2:00 P.M. around the base of the Pyramid of Kukulcan and at the signal of four conch-trumpet blows, they would form a human chain and make four turns (down from the original thirteen) around the base of the pyramid in a clockwise fashion; this would be accompanied by music and bystanders would be encouraged to join the circle. In this way, they would harmonize with the energy of the universe and of the sun as it is embodied in the sacred temple and in the phenomena of this special day. They swayed to and fro, against and around the Pyramid of Kukulcan, to the trumpet blasts of the caracol conch shells as they "ooohed" and "aaaahed" in a form they deemed appropriate for spiritual communion with their vision of Quetzalcoatl, the serpent-sun god.

This upset some people. The Boy Scouts, for example, had sought to clear everyone away from the pyramid starting around 2:30 P.M. and to establish a perimeter around its base so that an audience could sit behind this and maintain a view of the site. The spiritualists, circling around the pyramid and playing drums, whistles, flutes, conch, and so on, made this task of imposing order on the event difficult. The audience closest to the pyramid, which appeared to be predominantly Mexican, was quite upset; at 2:30–3:00 P.M. they had begun to gather right underneath the Temple of Kukulcan, and they were not pleased that these countercultural, *indio*-hippies were usurping their hard-won front-row seats. The Encargado, for his part, was livid;

the spiritualists were explicitly defying his authority in addition to making a ridiculous scene, in his view. Greatly encouraged by the nearby vocal audience, he, the police, and the Boy Scouts attempted to throw them out. The spiritualists made passive resistance and sat down just to the west and in the middle of a line between the north staircase and the Venus Platform. All of this hustling, shouting, and protesting occurred right under the pyramid while the main performances continued without interruption. Most of the thousands of spectators were unaware of this commotion up front until the one of the *Azteca* priests of the White Brotherhood of Quetzalcoatl appeared at the temple top during the *Mayab Legendario* and began his serpentine descent of the north staircase after making his greetings to the four corners. Below, two of the other *Azteca* priests—*but not Hunbatz Men, the Maya h-meèn*—had pulled away from the Boy Scouts and were waiting with open arms for this supposedly reincarnate Quetzalcoatl at the bottom of the stairs.

The Encargado was not pleased. By this time, the police detachment had arrived and the California *Maya* was negotiating with them about being allowed to conduct their ritual worship to "the sun god." The priest incarnation of Quetzalcoatl came down the stairs, greeted the four corners, prayed silently, and danced, while throughout the Encargado and the police exhorted the spiritualists to leave.

The *Aztecas* and New Age *Maya* finally settled down and were, it seemed, about to complete their activities and abide by the police directives. It was just before 4:00 P.M., during the intermission between parts one and two of the government program, that the master of ceremonies included in his lost-child announcements the authoritarian proclamation that "the brothers, the persons who are doing this religious practice, do not have any permission whatsoever. We ask you to stay seated so that everyone can see." Intended, no doubt, to impose order on the chaos of a pre-Columbian revivalist performance, this comment had the contrary effect; an aggressive faction of the audience, upset at the police and the Boy Scouts for having imposed the New Agers literally on top of them as they sat in the front, began to push back against the *Aztecas, Maya* pilgrims, and even the police and the Boy Scouts as they shouted and cursed with increasing threats of violence. The police, for their part, were getting ready to use force to assure compliance with their vision of order. Tensions were explosive, when all of a sudden the aggressive members of the audience

Fig. 7. New Age spiritualists and Aztec revivalists at the 1989 equinox. A high priest of the White Brotherhood of Quetzalcoatl (i.e., a reincarnation of Quetzalcoatl) descends the north staircase of the Castillo in serpentine (zigzag) fashion as Helen Leembal, a leader of the Maya Pilgrimage, negotiates with the police and Boy Scout leaders over the spiritual versus illegal nature of the religious practices being conducted on federally designated cultural patrimony. (Author's photograph)

and the authorities lunged forward toward each other. Caught between these antagonistic forces, the spiritualists' response was to shout, in Spanish, "MÉJICO! MÉJICO!"—A shout that within twenty seconds became mixed in with persons English shouts of "MEXICO! MEXICO!" (pronounced with English "x"). This general shout quickly intensified as the pronunciation converted into an explosion of "MESHICO! MESHICO!" (Nahuatl pronunciation) together with loud blasts of the caracol, drums, flutes, shells, and rattles. All the while, the master of ceremonies continued with his messages in the background. Up front near the pyramid, this blast of energy occupied everyone's attention and lasted for ten minutes or so, long enough to achieve a "pax romana"—that is, a "Mayan Harmony" of sorts—in the chaotic waiting for that serpent on the balustrade to begin its descent.

With a triumphant crescendo, the *Azteca* chant of "MESHICO!" ended and the voice of one of the leaders was heard over the calm: "Let's sit here and wait in silence for the descent of Quetzalcoatl."

Fig. 8. The reincarnate priest and dancing priest of the White Brotherhood of Quetzalcoatl perform the ritual greeting of the four corners upon the descent of the priest as the Encargado or chief supervisor of the National Institute of Anthropology and History exhorts them to desist from their illegal religious practices. The cameraman in the left foreground is a member of the Aztec revivalists and was documenting their pilgrimage to Chichén. (Author's photograph)

With this, the anxiety and tensions dissipated and, indeed, everyone did sit down in silence and waited for Quetzalcoatl, *rather than K'uk'ulcan,* as well as for the Feathered Serpent, as the official explanation of the equinox phenomenon began.

This spontaneous conflict and its resolution, this explosion and ebbing of tension, crystallize the symbolic structure and logic of representation of the whole event and of the Museum. The convergence of heterogeneous discursive practices, their multileveled conflicts, symbolic productions, and resolutions can be understood as a fortuitous event; or, in this historical contingency in the performance of an annually staged ritual, a strategic orchestration of the appropriation, reading, erasing, and rewriting of Maya *signs* might account for the conflicts and contestations between meanings, messages, and images performed in these Maya meanings and culture-texts.

Consider the following: In the actual rituals and activities of the *Aztecas* and the *Maya pere-grin(g)os,*[6] or New Age *Maya* pilgrims, the leadership of the former group had managed to take over the show. They had converted an Anglo-revivalist Maya ceremony into a neo-Aztec nationalist revivalism. This was the result of several factors, all of which comply with the stereotyping of the Aztec/Roman, Maya/Greek analogy that the Carnegie disseminated as scientific truth. Because of the greater experience and managerial abilities in conducting similar ritual events at central Mexican archeological sites and of negotiating with the authorities, the *Aztecas* were much better organized and had greater skills in commandeering not only the more than a hundred foot soldiers of the serpent, but the symbolic production of New Age images and messages. Furthermore, I was told in private by some of the pilgrimage participants that they were rather dissatisfied with Hunbatz Men, who seemed to be not as authentic and significantly less spiritual than expected, especially in comparison with the *Aztecas*. In other words, there was a kind of practical, symbolic, historical, and definitely ironic, nearly comic, repetition of the relationship between pre-Columbian Mesoamericans — a relationship construed and *known* through the anthropological apparatus of knowledge. Here was a New Age *Azteca* conquest of New Age *Maya*. Moreover, it is a structural and complementary repetition of the way the state government and its agencies *reconquered* the Maya through their reinvention of the Yucatec *nation*/national community as based on the prophetically unavoidable submission of Maya to the ritually imagined regional society as its underclass and archeologized patrimony. But, whereas the solidarity that is ritually performed, disseminated, experienced, and consolidated is a *Yucatec* identity and belonging, the *Aztecas'* performative repetition of the narrative/plot of Maya submission to central Mexico is directed toward an imagining of a different national community, which is not simply Mexican but an oppositional, countercultural, anti-imperial, spiritually and nativistically authentic *Mexica* nation. Let us call it, as they do, *Anauak*.

Thus, the New Age intervention in the Yucatec ritual *reinscribes* the politics of nations that the state government and its agencies sought to erase: Here is the symbolic performance of the tension between a Yucatán nostalgically dreaming of a lost national autonomy and a centralized Mexico in the pursuit of a hegemonic nation-state. Recall that on this national holiday, the state thoroughly eliminated representations and images of the Mexican nation that would forge Mexican solidarity, identity, or sentiments of belonging; in Yucatán, *espe-*

cially on this birthday of Benito Juárez, one can almost forget that one is in Mexico. The nearly violent physical conflict is a performative embodiment of these struggles between contesting visions of the national community. In this, the authorities, in both federal and state denominations, and the *turistas nacionales* (Mexican national tourists),[7] concurred that the neo-Aztec, countercultural version of community was not legitimate and needed to be silenced.

Now we can really appreciate the national *bomba*[8] that the New Agers detonated as if they were Aztec warriors on the verge of starting a flowery war against the Spanish colonizer, as well as the Yucatec nation, the Mestizo-Mayas, the *Maya peregringos,* and all other sons of Malinche. This shout of "MÉJICO! MESHICO!" is the shout of Tlatelolco reinvented in a battle: this was the chant of resistance and defense that was used by students against the paramilitary forces during the massacre of 1968 in the Plaza of the Three Cultures. Unlike its earlier deployment, here it was successful, that is, it broke down the antagonism just before breaking into violence. In a sense, *pax Azteca* was established in this *Mayan carnival* of truly *Roman* proportions.

The message of the Yucatec staged ritual, as I have argued, is that the Maya are always already *(re)conquered* by their Other who invades, dominates, and subjugates the Maya self. The *Azteca* spiritualists corroborate the message in two ways, in the practical engagement with the *Maya* pilgrims and in their reinvention of the shout of Tlatelolco, but also add to this message, or expand the terms of its analogy, with the symbolic implication of regional subordination (of Maya, of Yucatán) to the national center (Mexico City). In symbolic terms, the power and popular culture of the national community intervened and demonstrated its hegemony. Manifest in this is a principle of hierarchization that operates in any museum and that here orchestrates the representation of the Maya vis-à-vis all other sociohistorical groups that enter into display. More concretely, these messages and images of a mysteriously inevitable Maya subordination to the Other (Toltecs, central Mexicans, Spaniards, etc.) is already inscribed within the ruins and circulates within the scriptural economy of texts, discourses, photographs, tours, and other images through which the Maya are invented. The spatial division of the ancient city into a north and south Chichén Itzá is silent testament to this logic of representation: this spatial arrangement, an enduring invention of the Carnegie and Mexican inscriptions, is invested with the significance of a New and an Old stage of Chichén that corresponds to a later Toltec-Maya polity and an earlier Pure Maya culture. This fabulous distinction even marks the historicization of Maya civilization into Late Classic and Post or Terminal Classic periods (see Lincoln 1986, 1990). In fact and in stone as well as in text and in image, the restoration of Chichén Itzá in part and in whole was invented to argue this contestable supposition. This *was* the archeological *inventio* that was inscribed on the jungle; on the profane space of the Yucatec landscape, a modernist cosmology with a vision of the Maya as its sacred principle was founded according to Enlightenment science and national politics.

But this fortuitous performance that so nicely illustrates and corroborates the strategic and scriptural operations of the Museum has greater resonance, perhaps, with the symbolic structures of ritual that Bricker has analyzed in the ritual humor and dramatic performances of history among the Maya of highland Chiapas. The symbols, images, and textualized discourses of these rituals are graphic representations of the successive conquerors or would-be dominators of the Maya and are used to explore the difficult tensions between illegitimate domination, resistance, and de facto subordination. The difference, of course, is that those are Maya rituals, whereas here in the Museum and in the equinox, these are Western mythologies. Thus, what this comparison recommends is that there is an inexorable logic and practice of the *transculturation* of cultural elements across borders that are constituted by this mutual appropriation and hybridization of borrowed elements. In other words, if Mesoamerican peoples "syncretized" their religion with Catholicism, Western peoples engaged with the former also "syncretized" their cultural forms; here, specifically, is a transculturation in which Maya notions, visions, and styles of time became hybridized with Western modes of historical representation of the Maya.

Turning, finally and briefly, to the official explanation as performed by Adalberto Rivera, the same museum logic and practice of representation were at play. There is no need to inspect closely his description of the equinox phenomenon, which in general terms is pretty much the same as that of the other archaeoastronomers (see Rivera A. 1989; cf. Arochi 1974; Díaz Bolio 1957, 1972, 1982; Vergara and Martín Güemez 1988). Rivera's framework is couched in the style and practice of contemporary Western gnosticism, which bridges Eastern spiritualism with Western individualism in a way not unfamiliar to U.S. New Ageism. There are important differences, of course, such as the relation to gender and the sexes; gnosticism—at least its Mexican varieties—seems rife with phallocentrism. However, this is not the place for a close reading of his text, nor for a comparative analysis of gnosticism and New Age spiritualism, so I limit myself to two comments.

First, this archaeoastronomer, just like the New Age *Maya* pilgrims and José Argüelles, creates an empty signifier of the term "Maya," that is, he empties it of any real reference to Mayas at any point in time or space. In his hermeneutics of Maya iconology, Kukulcan becomes the marked title of a category of being designated as *Halach Winik* ("true man" in Yucatec). Although it is common knowledge among Maya and anthropologists that this term referred to those of the highest political and religious standing in the political landscape of eleventh- to sixteenth-century Yucatec Maya states, Rivera pushes this sense of the word to mean a person who has absolute and true knowledge of the universe and who, therefore, has transcended the seven states of human being. He does not specify what seven states are being referred to, although it is likely to be modeled on Eastern religious thought, such as the chakras, but modified with Western gnostic thought. For Rivera, Argüelles, and Hunbatz Men, *Maya* is the Self that one must comprehend in its own individuality in order to un-other oneself in relation to "true being"; for Rivera, *Halach Winik* is the proper name of this condition of true knowledge of self and universe. This *true being* is a key element of the uniqueness of Rivera's as opposed to other archaeoastronomers' hermeneutic of the equinox. This totalized, true condition of being is embodied in the image of the solar-serpentine-phallus, which, for Rivera, is the divine spirit or essence of all the universe that Kukulcan signifies. Thus, the spiritual and aesthetic *inventios* of the Maya are premised in the romantic mode of construing Maya mystery: here the Maya represent universal and authentic being as the pinnacle of human development, but it is cast, like most of New Age spiritualism (at least in the United States), in an extreme individualism that the Protestant church fathers might have appreciated. An ironic convergence, thus, should not be surprising: the New Age interpretation of that Serpent on the Balustrade is the romantic and individualistic version of the most recent scientific interpretations of the Mayan archeology that understand Maya kingship as a form rooted in shamanic mysticism and altered states of ecstasy.

Second, consider one of the theses Rivera stresses, seemingly as a way to differentiate himself and his interpretations from his competitors and detractors. He asserts that the real and true *Mayan* (!) name of what is glossed in English as "feathered serpent" is "Quetzal-Kan." This is a very curious proposition. The word "kan" is definitely a Mayan word, meaning "yellow," "heaven/above," and "snake," depending on its pronunciation. However, there is no question in the minds of linguists or the average Yucateco, that "quetzal" is *not* a Yucatec or Mayan word and is in fact a central Mexican word. *Kukulcán,* then, is the hispanicized word for the Yucatec Maya *K'uk'ulcan,* or feathered serpent, which in its sociohistoric specificity is a different personage than the central Mexican Quetzalcoatl. This linguistic violence that Rivera imposes repeats the shout of Tlatelolco by the *Aztecas* in itself and encapsulates a logic and practice of the violent appropriation of the Maya in the museum of Chichén Itzá.

Mysteries and Curiosities: Quotidian Critique and Spectacle

This ritual celebration of Maya genius does not really offer much for Mayas. All of the ritual practices of the equinox event—whether sacred or secular—are based on an expulsion and exclusion of the Maya (ancient and contemporary) from positions of respect, status, power, and legitimacy. Instead, to the extent that Maya are included within the symbolic, discursive, and performative productions, they are referenced within a dynamic that seeks to effect various modes and forms of subordination. It is not surprising, then, that the locals, Mayas, and other Yucatecos, are not really "into" the phenomenon or its event, which they view as something completely foreign. Everybody knows exactly what it is about, and they make sure to take advantage of this *romería* of forty thousand tourists to sell their Coca-Cola, *tacitos de cochinita*, touristic artisanry, parking spaces, T-shirts, and whatever else can fetch a dollar. Some—but actually very few—people from town do enter the archaeological zone on the equinox to see the spectacle, to see what the noise is all about. They see it not as a sign of Maya genius, but rather as a *curiosity*. Whenever I have sought to elicit opinions on the equinox, I have been confronted with astounding blank looks and hedgings, even by my best friends. For them it is a curiosity—it occasions no wonder, no mystery. On the other hand, as I was walking home from the event in 1988, I stopped to chat with a *vendedor de artesanía* about his sales. This man, a twenty-four-year-old grandson of one of the masons who worked on the "original" reconstruction of the Castillo, asked me, as he closed his *puesto*, "Why do all of the *gabachos* [Western foreigners] come to watch that *pendejada* [bullshit]?" Another man, who has been known as a witch, who has helped National Geographic Society explore the Sacred Well at Chichén (see Littlehales 1961; Dávalos Hurtado 1961; Folan 1970), and who is currently a leader of the Pentecostal church in Pisté, commented to me as follows: "It is pure scam by the government. What *pendejo* [asshole] would pay to see his shadow? Do you know how much the government makes?"

While these "mysteries" of the Mayas remain unresolved, these two Mayas from Pisté (*yete u weet kahalo'ob t'P'izte'*, that is, "their neighbors from Pisté") continue to sell tourist art and artisanry from the pueblo, Puebla, Guerrero, and Oaxaca under the shadow of the pyramid of Kukulcan *chen chan p'iz tak t'Chich'ene'*, that is, just a short but very well measured distance from the Lost Sacred City of the "Magicians of Water."

The War Museum

Chichén Itzá is a battleground of discourses. It is a field structured by encompassing social, cultural, political, and economic histories that have settled upon this place, reconstructing it to be a representation of Maya culture and civilization. In this Museum, a blueprint for a classically Maya ceremonial center, discourses defining, designating, and determining what is Maya culture contest each other according to a logic of poaching and appropriation. It is a discursive field and a war field.

On the premise or pretext of pronouncing on the "Maya," discourses are deployed that work to invent other cultural forms. For example, the state government consciously attempts to fabricate Maya culture and Yucatec society in representations that will effectively sell to tourists both a controlled vision of society and a vision of a controlled society. Other interests work to effect the symbolization

of national cultures, both countercultural Mexican and a more traditional variant of the Mexican nation-state. In order for the countercultural discourses to operate, they must in fact define what it is that
they are countering; in this, the business of tourism in the peninsula
assists a great deal since it generally seems to be organized around
the opposition between "Mexican" and (North) "American" cultures.
At the same time, variations on a religious worldview and series of
practices are being actively invented through strategic deployment
and symbolic uses of the "Maya" that ultimately refer back to variations of modern religious forms in both the United States (New Age
spiritualism) and Mexico (gnosticism), which seek to address problems of spiritual and social anomie in the context of postindustrial,
postmodern, postcolonial indeterminacies.

These discourses, deployed against the Maya, are nonetheless organized by a notion, that is, the sign, of the "Maya." The Museum of
Chichén provides this framework that regulates these discursive practices dedicated to the invention of Maya cultures. These textual inventions attest to a more encompassing vision or worldview. Recall that
a text is a coherent system of representation and that I have taken culture to be such a system that works to symbolize a social order. From
these premises and the analysis presented in this chapter, it is possible
to see the contours of a global culture, that is, the symbolization of an
international order, that uses the Maya as its subtext. These Maya
culture-texts that are invented in the Musuem of Chichén speak not
so much of flesh-and-blood Maya as of the possibility of a global culture — that is, of a world history and civilization — that may exist in spite
of the increasing threat of the fragmentation of meaning. The museum
is a cosmology in which are deployed — however contested — visions
of a whole and unified world. This is a world in which meaning is not
indeterminate or fragmented, but given according to a history and a
logic, whether it is the accumulation of capital, the spiritual transcen-
dence of being, or the scientific study of history and society. Nonetheless, the discourses producing these visions of the world are deployed
against each other as well as against the Maya. At the same time that
a coherent meaning is being constructed, it is being contested and
disputed. In the Museum of Maya Culture, the modernist project of
holism, transcendent meaning, and the progress of enlightened rationality are left standing in ruins by this war of discourses.

Fig. 9. The equinox event and the phenomenon of light and shadow, 5:00 P.M. view of the forty thousand witnesses to the descent of Kukulcan on March 21, 1988. As the official performance and explanation end, some of the audience claims the stage (front left under tree) for the height above the crowd that it offers in gaining a view of the disappearing and ascending triangles of light as the sun continues its deathly descent in the west. (Author's photograph)

The "ruins" invented by rational science as a monument to the Maya are already a monument to modernity. The erosion of competing interpretations seems to function as part of the monument. As if they were the little stones left by masons or the weeds along the path, these are traces that mark off the authenticity, truths, reality, and superiority of modernism and modern civilization, especially as measured against the Maya cultures and civilization that are ceaselessly reinvented in the tours of the museum theater of war. The project of modernity is left in ruins, but still standing in what might be viewed as a postmodern condition and spectacle in this contemporary city of Chichén Itzá. In this palimpsest, conflict and contestation are not external events, but are a part of the strategic orchestration of recolonizing practices and representations.

Part II

War and Its Topography

7 / An Everyday Guide to the Orchestration of Practices

The Apparatus of Pisté/Chichén

A place is the order (of whatever kind) in accord with which elements are distributed in relationships of coexistence.... The law of the "proper" rules in the place: the elements are beside one another, each situated in its own "proper" and distinct location. A place is an instantaneous configuration of positions.... [In contrast,] space exists when one takes into consideration vectors of direction, velocities, and time variables... [and] is composed of intersections of mobile elements.... [It is] the ensemble of movements deployed within it.... In relation to place, space is like the word when it is spoken... space is a practiced place.
      Michel de Certeau, *The Practice of Everyday Life* (1984: 117)

The Localization of Practical Sites

Within the place of Chichén-Pisté there is a series of three locations designated for three types of consumption; these are formed by the coupled procedures of *seeing/watching, buying/selling,* and *consuming/serving* (food or beverage). These three figures of action articulate tourist and touristic practices into complementary pairs through which the production, exchange, and consumption of tourist products occurs. The apparatus has a definite spatial arrangement that is oriented on an axis composed of seeing/watching and consuming/serving as its poles. In other words, posed facing each other—as if across a town plaza—are two dominant types of locations within the place of Chichén-Pisté; these are primarily constructed in relation to vision (the Museum) and food consumption/service (food establishment). Between the Museum and the restaurant, the space analogous to a plaza is given over to the procedures of buying/selling objects—commerce in handicrafts and souvenirs. The proper location for such exchange, which can be referred to by the figure of the market, is *between* the locations identified by the figures of the museum and the restaurant. This order is a spatial and temporal distribution in which procedures overlap and intersect as persons pursue their own strategies.

Locations of Seeing/Watching

The primary location for seeing/watching is the Museum of Chichén Itzá. Here, through the discursive practice of guides that reinscribe the Museum, visitors operate procedures of seeing in their enactment of tourist practices. While the tourist sees the sight, the police and the wardens of the INAH watch the site and the tourists' movements in it. Besides these institutionally authorized enactments of vision, there are informal practices of surveillance through which the tourist body is constantly watched. Although a semblance of panopticism remains, the lines of power are inverted: The tourist, situated in the center of a field of vision, gazes at the exhibit-displays of the sight; deployed all around this figure are police, wardens, guides, vendors, artisans, site maintenance personnel, and other locals who watch the tourist, *and each other,* in order to calculate a maneuver that will result in a commodity exchange or interaction. These parasitic procedures of watching poach on the formally designated practice of seeing the sight.

The Museum itself provides a hierarchized series of locations, primarily defined by the exhibit. A location is constituted by a subject-object relation between tourist and display, which is constructed in the form of a gaze mediated through tour guides and guidebooks. This properly situated line of vision provides a tactical site in which other lines of sight are multiplied as they poach on the formally designated gaze. Directly intersecting the tourist gaze is the watching eye of the independent tour guides. Their success as guides requires of them a peripheral vision that encompasses all the other guides and all groups of tourists that enter the sight. By sighting on the tourist gaze—that is, on the ongoing tours in the Museum—they answer critical questions: Who is working? In what order did they "enter" or begin working? What kind of group did they take or "enter with"? How many times has the guide worked and where is s/he in turn? And, for some male guides: Are there any attractive, available women to *pescar* ("fish") or to *vacilar* ("flirt with/hit on")?

The police and wardens, in the conduct of their rounds in the archeological zone, enact an art of walking and vision: walking, stopping to rest, pausing to chat with wardens, guides, or workers, they scope the sight and the movement of bodies within it. Formally, they provide "security" against both tourists who may disobey rules of behavior (vandalism, stealing artifacts, consumption of illegal substances, improper attire) and artisans who may illegally infiltrate the site in order to chance the sale of handicrafts to a tourist.

The occasional "delinquent" *artesano ambulante* (itinerant artisan) is parasitic: these artisans convert the place of the tourist gaze into a possible site for commodity exchange. Similar to sidewalk drug dealers, they scope an area unprotected by the surveillance of police and wardens in order to approach passing tourists with offers of (wooden or stone) *figuras* (figurines) that are "almost free" or "only one dollar." During the 1982–87 "invasion" of the archeological zone, three hundred *vendedores* and *artesanos* "illegally" entered the zone to sell their wares. Not only did this constitute a multiplication of the poaching on the visual field but it also constituted a parasitic infestation of procedures of buying/selling in a place formally designated for a different activity. The danger, pollution, and fierce struggles that were generated from the invasion attest to the order of the Museum as a sight and to the propriety of visual procedures as the designated activity for this place. Activities that are formed through other procedures, such as of exchange, can only occur in their delimited, enclosed locations; otherwise the spatial and social order is breached.

Throughout the day a variety of locals pass through the zone. Some, following the trajectory of the old road that leads to the Hacienda, are on their way to or from work at the Mayaland, Club Med, or the Hacienda. Others, who do maintenance, work for CULTUR in the transport of garbage or supplies to one or another *palapa*. They may on occasion stop to watch tourists or to chat with a friend.

Other locals, such as high-school kids on summer vacation, guides who have decided to stop working for the day, vendors who want a change of pace from slack sales, or even a resident ethnographer, enter the sight to watch "la movida." Of these persons, most of whom are male, some seek distraction. For others, the concentrated display of the female body, which is doubly other as female and foreign, provides a motive. Whether in a consciously designated act of surveillance or simply a wandering, unmotivated gaze that spots and locks in on a woman, there is a parasitic, male vision that is constantly sighting on the female. This engenders the visual field and situates the tourist gaze within a field of power: articulated to this gendered optics are rich discourses about self and other whose central trope is the body in national, racial, cultural, gendered, and class guises.[1] Unfortunately, this phenomenon cannot be analyzed here, except to note that the tourist, specifically the *body* of the tourist, is central to the visual procedures even as the principle of panopticism seems to be inverted. Just as the prison warden, situated in the central tower, is incarcerated along with the prisoners, tourists, situated in the primary relation of gazing at the sights of the Museum, are caught in the panoptic power of the apparatus. From this vantage point, it is no surprise that many tourists often sense themselves as being trapped or harassed by the eyes and bodies of a multitude of short, brown Mayas. This is a feeling that is perhaps expressed in somewhat belligerent or obnoxious attitudes when bargaining with locals.

Locations of Consuming/Serving

Food-service establishments are the primary location for procedures of consuming and serving food and beverage. As already noted, the spatial arrangement of the apparatus hinges on an "axis" that has consuming/serving as one of its poles, which, in a more general sense, can be identified with Pisté itself. In other words, the proper place for this type of consumption is away from the tourist sight proper, in Pisté.

There are five basic types of such establishments: charter group restaurants (both hotel and independent), independent noncharter restaurants, beverage stands, *loncherías,* and itinerant food vendors. Of the thirteen restaurants that serve charter groups, nine are located in Pisté,[2] three just to the east — *outside* — of the zone[3] and one inside the Parador Turístico. Among these, seven are operated through hotels, of which four are distributed in Pisté and three (Hotel Mayaland, Villas-Club Med, and Hacienda Chichén) are adjacent to Chichén. This distribution — that is, the high number of older room-and-board establishments within the boundaries of the archeological zone — attests to a prior configuration of space and social practice in the history of Chichén Itzá as a tourist site. At the same time that these older establishments have a certain privilege of rank, in a very real sense they also are seen to break with the proper spatial order of the recently configured apparatus. They are seen to inappropriately appropriate what would otherwise be a "normal" flow of the tourist body. This is evident from the attempt by a variety of sectors to close the back entrance that allows this clientele to enter the sight.

There are other such sites within the Museum sight: located on paths in the zone are two *palapas* that house beverage and snack food stands and, in the Parador, there is an ice-cream shop and a charter group restaurant that profits essentially from the sale of beverage and quick food. Further, poaching on these parasitic procedures are other sites for consuming/serving, but these are oriented toward the servicing of those who work in the Museum. The invasion of 1982–87 opened up this market to sell food to vendors, guides, INAH wardens, police, and the maintenance/supervision crews of CULTUR. During the height of the invasion, one or two dozen women — many from neighboring villages over seven kilometers away — assisted by any number of their two- to eight-year-old children, could be found doing rounds in the zone selling tamales, tacos, panuchos, soft drinks, water, atole, oranges, guaya, pineapple, and other fruit, to tourist and vendor alike. The imposition of a disciplinary regime or control to put a stop to these "illegalities" executed by "delinquents" reduced the number of *in*formally sanctioned — better, *tolerated* — food vendors to two women. By turning the eye of power on them, they were allowed to set up *loncherías* to service the four hundred-odd persons who work at Chichén. Even on these quasi-sanctioned, parasitic food vendors situated on the margins of the back areas of the Museum other persons poach in order to sell tacos, soda, fruit, and freshly squeezed juice. As might be imagined, all of this infiltrating of the territory of others inflamed a "food war" within the invasion of the *artesanos* and the general war of smiles that tourism constitutes.

In Pisté, another battlefield emerges on the proper locations for consuming/serving food. Here it is not a question of smaller establishments (beverage stands, *loncherías,* and noncharter restaurants) poaching on the larger ones. Certainly the smaller ones could only exist in Pisté because it is a high-volume market as the service center for the tourist attraction; in this sense, the *loncherías* and small restaurants are dependent on the charter restaurants. Instead, it is another phalanx of the heterogeneous invasion by free-roaming street vendors and artisans. The space between the door of the charter bus and the door of the restaurant becomes a site for buying and selling handicrafts in which vendors battle each other to make a sale in the twenty seconds that they have access to the tourist's attention. Generally, there are three types of vendors. First, there are female vendors who are alone or typically accompanied by their children or nieces/nephews of sufficient age (about six or eight years old) to be vendors themselves or by other adult female relatives; these tend to station themselves in designated sites to sell, more often than not, nonlocal artisanry. Second, there are adult male *artesanos* who locate themselves in specific sites but group together with other male family members (close or extended) as they travel from selling site to selling site in front of Pisté restaurants according to the temporality and volume of charter buses; they sell their own wood handicrafts. The third type consists of "bands" of six- to fourteen-year-old boys who peddle the "stone" idols (made of cement and limestone) that they themselves produce as they traverse the same spaces as their elders, but usually in advance of them. Caught off guard as they descend from the bus, tourists are often surrounded by half a dozen or more vendors, predominantly adolescent and younger boys, screaming over the crushing drone of the bus. In the opportunity of the moment, these kids shout "one dollar" and "almost free" as they forcibly position two or more stone or wooden idols in the tourist's face. This tactic of selling, which is a tactic of resistance to the decorum of the spatial-political order that reigns in the Tianguis, triggers a tactic of defense on the part of the tourist: depending on temperament and other factors, it may be a quick run to the restaurant or an overwhelmed purchase from the seemingly desperate and (from Western and Maya cultural perspectives) *pushy* kids.

Within the restaurant, other procedures besides eating and serving food are exercised. On a graduated scale from the major hotel/

food establishments to the independent restaurants serving charter and noncharter tourists, the decor moves along a continuum from modern and Occidental to the otherness of the Maya world. This decor, intimately linked to the names of the establishment—Parador Maya, Pirámide, Picuda, Sacbe, Xaybe, Nicté Há, Cunanchen—offers a visual extension of the museum. There are of five types of decor-exhibits: (1) murals depicting Maya princesses and heroes, temples and pyramids, gods and goddesses, pheasants and deer,[4] cenotes and sacrifices; (2) photos or facsimiles, maps, and drawings of archeological zones and artifacts; (3) a variety of the authentic artisanry of Pisté (wooden and stone chac-mools, serpents, masks, corn god idols, etc.); (4) a live performance of the *jarana* or traditional Yucatec dance during lunch by youth dance group; and (5) architectural decoration such as sculpted concrete replicas of serpent columns, jaguar and warrior bas-reliefs, stone chac-mools constructed on facades and as interior elements. These means of representing the Other operate on the same principles as the museum and submit to the museum effect of the apparatus: they are loci of a Maya memory—of which, however, little demand for their cultural deposits is made.

The restaurants whose interiors are saturated with these visual icons of the Other are placed at the "lower" end of the spectrum in terms of the official quality rating systems; they can also be ranked by the volume of tourists they service. The exception to this generalization is the historically prior and more luxurious (higher rated) hotel-restaurants of the Mayaland, Villas Club Med, and the Hacienda, where the use of the Maya as decoration is limited in quantity and in type. These, in contrast to the medium-sized, unrated, independently owned restaurants, have the social distance between Maya and modernity to exploit otherness as part of their advertising strategy. The "cheaper" establishments, which are owned and operated by local Maya, have no "choice" but to play on the cultural imagery and iconography of the Maya. Not only is it part of their *authentic* heritage, but the owners fully realize that it is the lure, the "mystery" of the ancients that attracts tourists to Pisté in the first place. This Maya semiotics is hyperreal culture, no doubt, but, as patrimony of the Maya and the local community, there is no false authenticity felt even as it is recognized that the semiotics is primarily for tourist consumption.

All of these murals, photos, artifacts, architectural features, and dance shows function as signs of Maya culture and civilization. By the same token, the menus (both written text and food) of traditional, regional cuisine operate as silent signs and images of otherness: All these signs of Maya culture and civilization provide *mute* exhibit displays. In contrast to the sights inside Chichén that are buried under the ceaseless verbiage and spoken textualization of the tour guides, these museum displays are not re-covered in endless explanation. Only the occasional legend or signature of the artist provides a written text that serves to verbally contextualize. Even the dance group begins its dance of the *jarana* virtually without any introduction and absolutely no explanation of its rich symbolism. This rule of thumb is valid, even if countered by the occasional questioning of a tourist in which the guide is asked the "deposited" significance of these images.

This informal extension of the Museum into the restaurants is a kind of poaching and creates a continuum of types of tourist sights in terms of their discursive-visual textualization. Halfway between mute and verbose, in the momentary battlefield between museum proper and restaurant, other exhibit displays in the form of traditional handicrafts and artisanry are being produced and sold in the streets, stores, and market of the apparatus.

Locations of Buying/Selling

Stores and traditional markets called *tianguis* compose the proper locations for procedures of buying/selling. These are situated between the two places specifically designated for the functions of seeing/watching and consuming/serving. The commercial exchange of handicrafts and souvenirs is properly located as a supplementary procedure to the activities of seeing the sight and taking care of the tourist body's consuming necessities. It is an activity that by nature must rely on a parasitic strategy. The competition, forced to sell exactly the same thing that all the other merchants carry, must *go to the tourists to trap them* in an exchange; or, they must devise mechanisms that bring already trapped tourists to the product. Of course, the highly capitalized souvenir merchants can purchase, at a pretty price, a location that ensures a constant clientele through commissions paid to guides. Thus, outlets of national and regional corporations can be found in the Parador Turístico. Other stores (devoted, for example, to jewelry and large, pure silver statues) are owned by private capitalists, who also own business in Cancún, Mexico City, and Mérida.

To maintain the categories pure between the cultural acts of sight-seeing, commercial exchange, and food consumption, specially demarcated spaces are alloted for private capital within the primary periphery of the museum site.

A significant result of the resolution of the 1982–87 invasion is that the petty handicraft merchants and producers were conceded both the right and the space to sell artisanry within this margin; however, this location is even more marginalized in that it is on the margin of the capitalist store owners located within the Parador Turístico. Thus, the Tianguis, adjacent to the Parador as its extension, was built and designated the proper location for all those Mayas that were in this business of trafficking in artisanry and souvenirs. This building, as if both a monument to the war and the architectural embodiment of the "treaty" that resolved the crisis of the invasion, cuts a sharp line between forms of selling in terms of legalities and propriety.

Not all of the vendors accepted the terms of the "treaty": they did not accept the terms devised by the state government and enforced by CULTUR, whereby their rights to sell artisanry would be respected and sanctioned only within the specially built handicraft market, the Tianguis (see Peraza López et al. 1987; Peraza López and Rejón Patrón 1989; Morales Valderrama et al. 1989). Of the three to four hundred invading vendors, only 120 entered the Tianguis. A few simply gave up the business of selling and turned to other occupations. Although many continued to try to sell in the zone on the sly, many others staked their claims on the most advantageous spaces outside the museum. Others entered the Tianguis and sent family (a husband, wife, son, daughter, or other relative) to occupy another site located on the margins. A group of twenty-five to forty vendors occupied the road between the Hotel Mayaland and the back entrance to the zone, which guarantees control of the tourist flow from Club Med, Mayaland, and the Hacienda.[5] Four other groups of ten to twenty each occupied sites in front of three high-volume charter restaurants in Pisté (Cunanchen, Fiesta, Xaybe-Misión) and the *desvío* or fork in the highway where the access road leads to the archeological zone. These para-sites of buying/selling are spatially demarcated in relation to the tourist traffic and are hierarchized in an informal ranking in terms of that volume, which is in turn a function of the eating/serving locations on which these improper, *illegal,* and parasitic procedures poach. These four parasitic selling locations are, of course, differentiated internally into *puestos* or stalls of varying sizes, shapes, and prime spots according to the relative seniority, political status, *surtido* (range of commodities sold), and type of worker/assistance of the individual *vendedores.*

To conclude this summary of the arts of distribution of touristic practices in the tourist apparatus of Chichén-Pisté: there is a definite logic and order that are manifest in this spatial arrangement of activities around three proper locations. The Tianguis, differentiated as the margin of both the Parador and the Museum proper, is an enclosed and legally differentiated place for the procedures of buying/selling. The localization of practical sites is a method of disciplinary power through which the touristic apparatus appropriates and differentiates an area from the surrounding environment in order to establish the domain in which specific practices can be enacted, surveyed, regulated. This method of disciplinary power establishes a social order, like a secular cosmology, in and through the spatial arrangement and distribution of procedures. Transgressions of this order are marked as illegalities, not only because they break the law but because they are held to be ecologically disruptive, aesthetically unpleasant, distasteful to the tourist, and economically threatening to the vested interests of dominant groups. These are the four tropes or problematizations that government, capitalist, guide, anthropology, and tourist actors use in their discourse against the Maya of Pisté in the latter's struggle against this imposed orchestration of power/tourism.

The Regulation of Activities

The description of everyday touristic routines can be made in terms of the techniques of discipline that regulate activities and that thereby organize them into formal, separate, and contained social practices or work disciplines. These techniques are (1) the designation of a timetable for the daily performance of routines, (2) the calculation of the time in which activities are elaborated, and (3) the correlation of body and objects through specified sets of gestures. Four general categories of work disciplines and touristic practices are significant in Chichén-Pisté: (1) the service work of employees in hotels, restaurants, and stores; (2) the supervision and maintenance work at the tourist sight;[6] (3) the alternative services of producing and selling supplementary products such as artisanry, tours, or entertainment by self-employed, petty entrepreneurs;[7] and, (4) the services for the transportation of tourists and merchandise via bus, taxi, truck, and airplane.[8]

The Work Discipline of Guides

Without delving into the rich, highly inflammatory, and critically important history of guide work, it should be noted that during the fieldwork period of 1988–90 there were least four different types of independent guides (*guías libres*) that need to be distinguished for the variation in their practice.[9] Among those that work at Chichén are guides who belong to one of two unions (SINAL, Sindicato Nacional, and SINYUC, Sindicato de Yucatán), in addition to which there are two groups of "free" guides that are not affiliated with either union.[10] Although there is only one work system for the union guides, until recently the *guías libres* had formed two distinct work groups based on their union loyalties. In 1988–89 they consolidated the two groups to form a single *bolsa de trabajo* (or "work bag") of twenty to twenty-four persons, which is officially recognized by all the relevant organizations, businesses, and authorities. With regard to control and regulation of guides and service, the national and state unions are the primary, self-regulating mechanisms and are supervised by the national tourist office, SECTUR (Secretaría de Turismo). The other two types of independent guides are composed of nonunionized, unsanctioned, officially untrained, and often unlicensed individuals. The work system of these two groups is distinct from each other and from the unionized *bolsa*—the result of different historical circumstances by which they became involved in this line of work. One of these groups are a handful of Pistéleños who have trained themselves to be guides; the other is a recent arrival of Mérida-based persons who began to poach on the official guides. The competition and antagonisms that began in 1988 seemed to have resolved themselves in 1994 with the unions' and state's sanctioning of two *bolsas*; but fissioning soon began again with the development of a new outside group of guides.

Three elements enter into the construction of the timetable for the practice of guide service: the work system, the duration of tours, and the general schedule of tourist volume. The daily rhythm or schedule of the tourist influx can be broken into four major periods in terms of guide work: early morning arrival of guides (8:00–10:00), late morning wait (10:00–11:30), afternoon rush (11:30–3:00), and end of day (2:30/3:00–5:00). Within this general framework, the work system and the duration of tours establish a precise, if fluid, and overlapping timetable.

The work system of the *bolsa* consists of turns organized around a list. One's position on the list at the end of the day dictates the timetable for the following day's work. All those persons that "entered" (i.e., worked) are marked on the list; one mark is given for every turn taken. Those who worked less are placed at the beginning of the list for the next day in the same order as found in previous lists. The order of the list indicates who has the *right* or first dibs to try to *enganchar* (i.e., "hook") a tourist or group before another guide can legitimately approach the tourist. In this ideal model, everyone gets an equal turn to work and works an equal number of times. Those who are left over from the previous day get placed high on the list and are the first to come to work in the morning, usually around 8:00 or 8:30. Those in the second group arrive an hour or so later — approximately the time it takes for a tour — or roughly 9:00 to 10:00. Those at the end of the list may arrive in the late morning, in time for the arrival of the first charter groups — or, during medium or especially low seasons, they may decide not to come to work at all. A no-show places the person at the very bottom of the list, after all those who did work. By "reporting to work" before 11:30 A.M. and waiting turn for an hour and a half, one is able to leave and still get marked high on the list, as if one had not worked the whole day.

Within this frame for guide work there are two series of durations that fill in and complete the timetable. As discussed earlier, there are *haranchak*, official-length, and extended tours of the museum. In the tour, the guides make tactical calculations of time to maximize their work and profit. These tactics are the gestures through which body and object correlations are forged in the composition of the practice of the tour. Tours may extend ten or twenty or more minutes for tourists who are both appreciative and seemingly capable of providing a good tip; on the other hand, the duration of a tour may be trimmed so that the guide can return to the Parador to hook another group if it is clear that no tip — or at least a worthwhile tip — is forthcoming. Tours at the end of the day may last longer, because chances of more work are slim; or they may be trimmed, if the guide is anxious to go to a bar (as is customary) or to catch a bus to Mérida (if they live there and not in Pisté). Early morning tours are often highly prized, not only because the sun is less hot, but also because there is greater likelihood of hooking a private group that has stayed overnight and that has an interest in learning and may thus provide a nice reward for a more conscientious, longer tour. Guidebooks written for the more aesthetically conscious traveler always recommend morning visits to the zone to avoid both the heat and the charter groups. Afternoon service may not necessarily be *haranchak* tours, but the guides are all the more shrewd in their calculations of time. Seasonal changes in the volume of tourists create variation in decision making within this temporal economy.

The obverse time of the tour is that of waiting in turn. Other tactics are deployed according to one's position on the list. A low position during low season allows a guide to "hang out," chat with friends, read the newspaper, review a language he or she may be learning. On the other hand, the top five or so persons on the list are poised like wolves near the ticket counter waiting and watching tourists pass through. Every single guide, including those low on the list and ostensibly relaxing, is "scoping" all the tourists who come through the sight, as well as the movements of the other guides. These professional observers visually mark all groups and all interactions and store this information; it will be the basis on which they calculate their work, on which they poach on both tourists and the missed opportunities of other guides, as well as debate the order of the list for the next day. It is a war of smiles and no opportunity is missed to hook a group, because one is certain that the next guides will "move in on" the tourists after one has tried one's own hand.[11] Thus, there is a very open terrain of contestation over the tourist body that is constituted by subtle signs of social interaction: Has a group of tourists rejected the guide whose turn it is? Can they be approached? Is this particular tourist part of a group with whom the guide in turn is negotiating?

Jumping turn can legitimately occur when a special language (i.e., a language other than Spanish or English, such as French, German, or Italian) is required of the guide and the person whose turn it is cannot provide service in that language. In such cases, the group goes to the next guide in line who can provide tours in the language. At the conclusion of the 1990 field season, however, there was a movement among the guides to create a sublist for those who can offer service in French. Starting in 1993, only two guides gave service in German; in fact, one, a Maya and autodidact of English and German, now works prearranged groups in the latter language. A group of tourists may reject the services of the guide who first offers, but may then accept a guide farther down the list, who usually offers less than the official price. Also, the guide whose turn it is may reject a group of tourists because they appear to be belligerent or they refuse to pay the full quota.[12]

The tactics for hooking a group correlate body (the guide) and object (the tourist) in gestures of space, of language, and of authority. From the entrance of the Parador to the opening of the path in front of the Castillo, there is a strip in which the guides lie in wait. Those in turn hang out closest to the ticket booth or, alternatively, opposite the ticket counter at the official guide stand. Along the first three benches, the guides of the *bolsa* may be found sitting. Farther down the corridor, the second, most then-recent group of (at the time) illegal guides hang out and solicit in any order. Beyond the turnstiles all the way to the Castillo, two or three other guides, who refuse to participate in *bolsa* politics, work individually as they scope out their possibilities. Changes in the volume of tourists moving through incite a little spatial dance among the guides, who are pacing, walking, standing, listening, chatting, scoping. In offhand manner, as a tourist passes, they offer "guide service," "servicio de guía," in Spanish, Italian, French, and German. The *bolsa* guides will discuss what exactly is offered in the tour and the price. They may offer a short tour. If the tourist tries to negotiate below official tariff, most of these guides cut short the bargaining. They stand behind the official identification they wear on their shirts and do not go below the sanctioned quota.

In contrast, the unsanctioned *guías libres,* who did not organize into a work system or *bolsa* until after the fieldwork period, arrive early in the morning. Because these individuals are unlicensed or insufficiently trained, they form a group that poaches on the would-be clients of the *bolsa.* Their tactics are to arrive earlier and stay later; to charge less than the price of the official quota for tours; to "steal" or approach tourists out of turn; to pursue tourists and repeatedly offer an unwanted tour, that is, to "improperly" cajole tourists in order to sell the product;[13] to give tours in languages in which the guide might not have fluency; to shorten the tour, which technically should be four hours, to forty-five minutes or an hour; to solicit tourists outside of the space designated in the Parador by CULTUR; to solicit tourists inside the archeological zone, which is prohibited by the INAH.

The Arts of Selling: Vendedores, Artesanos, and Artesanía

More than two hundred persons make up the local class of petty merchants. Most are from Pisté, although up to a dozen vendors—more during high season—are from nearby towns such as Xcalacoop, San Francisco, and Tohopku, three to ten kilometers to the east; Xocenpich and Dzitas, seven to eighteen kilometers to the north; Yokdzonot and Libre Unión, ten to twenty kilometers to the west; and Yaxuna, twenty kilometers to the south.[14] Kinship plays an important, informal, yet fluid element as resource in the composition, organization, and even practice of the Pisté vendors. There are three categories of vendors: *artesanos* who make and sell their own artisanry and occasionally nonlocal souvenirs, *vendedores* who primarily sell mass-produced handicrafts but who also sell locally produced goods, and *vendedores de comida* who sell food and beverages. The present discussion is limited to the first two, who form a continuum: There are artisans who sell their own products (primarily "stone" and wood figures and *playeras* or T-shirts of various types), but many have been able to capitalize and also sell Yucatec and Mexican handicrafts. By the same token, there are petty merchants who supplement the sale of such nonlocal artisanry with the small-scale production and sale of their own handicrafts. Most vendors find it necessary to compete in this way, so that although vendors may not themselves be producers, someone in the immediate family is; or, they may buy local artisanry directly from an artisan and sell it on consignment. Another differentiation among the vendors and artisans is the location of their activities. There is roughly an equal distribution between those who work in the Tianguis—"lovingly" referred to as the "Yanguis"—and those who have created (para)sites at the Mayaland entrance to Chichén, at the *desvío* or crossroads to the zone, and in front of the charter restaurants and hotels of Pisté. The following description generalizes the combination vendor-artisan practice, but distinguishes the stylistic difference between practices located and enacted in the Tianguis and in front of Pisté's restaurants.

The timetable for selling artisanry, just like that of the guides, is framed and structured by the temporal economy of tourist bodies. However, for the Tianguis vendors, the timetable is deferred one to two hours from that of the guides. Although a handful of Tianguis vendors open with the opening of the zone in order to catch overnight tourists, the typical morning begins with arrival and setup activities (9:00–11:00), which continue through the midday wait, during which the majority of the charters arrive (11:00–1:30). The afternoon rush (1:30–4:30) when charters leave the zone for lunch is followed by the slowdown and closing up shop at the end of day (4:30–6:00/6:30). Only a handful of vendors (mostly one or another spouse of a married team remain) for the evening shift (5:30–9:00) to catch tourists going to the Light and Sound Show.

For vendor-artisans who work in Pisté, the spatial difference between the locations of the museum and the charter restaurants designates a temporal lapse or delayed timetable. Those who work the Xaybe-Misión site arrive around 9:00 or 10:00 A.M. and stay as late as 8:00 or 9:00 P.M. during the high season. The early starting time was matched by the Mayaland vendors before their expulsion, but is still the operative time in their new location at the crossroad; however, these vendors begin to leave their site after 5:00 and by dark or 6:00 P.M. are at home. Those who work other sites in front of the Cunanchen, Fiesta, and Picuda do not arrive at work until noon, or even 1:00 P.M. during low season, and can leave after the last charter group has finished lunch, which is anytime from 3:30 to 4:30 P.M.; by 5:00 the truck that transports their merchandise takes them home. This difference in timetable allows for males to work milpa or to produce artisanry and for females to do other economic, usually household, activities in the mornings.

The art of selling is composed of a series of tactics by which bodily gestures of the vendors constitute a practice that correlates the object-artisanry and the tourist in the production of desire for the consumption of the commodities. The following map of "elementary" tactics is based on my study of activities at an important charter restaurant located near the center of Pisté. The small concrete porch area in front and to the south of this restaurant forms the site of selling. The space is divided into two functionally equivalent halves, but is occupied by four functional spaces marked for waiting, walking, display, and loading. Brought by independent transports, the merchandise is loaded and unloaded from a truck temporarily parked alongside the east of the restaurant porch. The wooden crates, boxes, and bundles wrapped in plastic are stacked close to where the displays are set up.

Charter buses may either pull up along the road directly across the porch in front of the restaurant doors or park in the parking lot to the west. These two locations create a designated trajectory for tourists to walk when entering and leaving the restaurant.

Along this path, the vendors set up their individual displays, which measure one to two meters square, depending on which side of the site the display is situated. Displays to the east are larger (closer to the town square) and are stocked with greater diversity, primarily of nonlocal manufacture: stacks of Oaxacan blankets, T-shirts from Mérida, stone jewelry from Acapulco, Pueblan figures of stone, ceramic, and wood, and all variety of central Mexican ceramics. Displays are set up side by side and organized front to back according to size (smaller items in front). With vendors lined up behind and tourists in front, transactions are negotiated across the display. Handicrafts are grouped in their categories, although each vendor situates his or her pieces according to personal tastes and assessment of what is "attractive" to the tourist. Laterally, the displays are evident by the repetition of types of artisanry.

Against the front of the restaurant, to either side of the door, are windows set within the walls that serve the vendors as shady rest areas where vendors lounge in wait for the charter groups to arrive. The time is consumed in talk, although one of the men may carve an idol and adolescent children may read *novelas* (racy, comic-type books with soap-opera plots) when not being rambunctious. Unlike vendors at other selling sites, these do not eat during work because they arrive after 11:00 A.M. and work during mealtime. Besides, they are completely exposed to the main highway and a part of the *zócalo*, which precludes even minimal privacy for the consumption of a meal. Nonetheless, this exposure affords another line of sight, which the vendors rely on in exercising their arts of selling; with their backs against the wall, they master a field of vision—a temporal schedule— through which the tourist body moves.

In the legendary stillness of midday, the vendors first hear the charter buses approach down the one-mile strip between the center of town as they appear over the first rise in the road on the eastern edge of Pisté. Everybody is accustomed to the roar of traffic flowing through town and can distinguish buses from cars and trucks. The vendors already know, through discussion with the staff of the restaurant, how many groups will arrive that day, and when; the sound prompts them to cast a verifying glance. As the buses approach, the vendors also move to their displays. If there is a drizzle, but not rain, they uncover at least part of their displays from underneath a protective plastic tarp. They stand poised (though not necessarily behind the display) in case tourists are interested in stopping to browse. Most often, however, upon arriving the tourists head straight for the restaurant in search of shade, drink, and food. Forty-five minutes later they emerge, alone or with a few companions. As they begin to wander toward the displays, the vendors move into position, remaining very attentive to the tourists' self-presentation, language use, bodily gestures, and gazes.

In the space of one minute tourists can walk the path to the bus; it is up to the vendors to steer them off this designated trajectory and lock them into a visual relation with the artisanry. If successful, the vendors may extend that one-minute space to three or even ten minutes. In an initial play, vendors seek to both attract and direct the attention of tourists through a tactic that articulates verbal and visual gestures. A series of verbal "hooks" are used in a combination of English and Spanish.[15] Vendors may announce (as if it were a traditional market) items that they are selling, but only certain ones ("T-shirts/*playeras,* blankets/*zarapes,* figuras"). They often hold up an item to display and say "almost free" or "one dollar." The Spanish equivalent is not used since it does not work the same effect on the Mexican personality: national tourists know that prices must be cheaper at the place of production. This tends to hook American tourists into a dialogue, when they ask what is for sale at that price, and brings them into a more direct visual relation with the handicrafts. The vendors address the tourists who have approached and are now inspecting the various artifacts: "Sí, ¿cómo puedo servirle?" "¿Cuál le gusta?" "Yes, lady, which one you like?" If a tourist does not pick something up, turning it over and over to inspect it, the vendor will locate the object that seems to preoccupy the tourist's gaze and offer it. In the Tianguis, some vendors had me teach them how to say, in English, "It's free to look/touch"; "You can look at it for free"; "Pick it up." These tactics of attention-getting are fleeting, momentary tricks that operate within and against the sociospatial order. They work to take the tourist off the proper trajectory designated by the guide or conductor.

In an instant, a distraction is forged. In the space of this distraction the vendor must unfold a visual field that entices and engages the tourist. These tactics are disruptions not only of the formal itinerary and the place of food consumption on which the vendors poach, but also of the tourists' own notions of propriety with regard to commercial exchange that, for example, are manifested in the civility of malls and stores as opposed to markets. These notions are addressed by the vendors' verbal hooks, which seek to link the tourist to specific objects. The English words the vendors learn are selected precisely to counteract the operating assumptions of tourists. The most significant complaint of the vendors when there are no sales is that the tourists "just stroll by" (*chen puro maàn*) or "just enjoy looking" (*chen ku chaàntko'*).

The actual ideas and preconceptions held by the tourist vary extensively. American tourists, unaccustomed to the barter that goes on in these types of markets, operate according to foreign principles. They may only look as they stroll by displays; they may be "afraid" of language or racial barriers or hesitant to touch objects that may thereby submerge them in a dialogue they feel they do not have time for, do not want, or cannot control. Although some may relish the thrill of bargaining, their hesitancy is further promoted by the discourse of guides and guidebooks. For example, the winter 1988 issue of *Cancún Tips* warned against markets and street vendors whose prices are not fixed, *because bargaining rips off the tourist.*[16] The guides, for their part, take charter groups to a "special, very cheap" handicraft store where the tourists will get the "best prices and highest quality" and where, of course, the guides receive a 10 or 20 percent commission on all purchases made by their group. The guides deploy a series of tactics that steer "their" tourists away from vendors who refuse to participate in the commissions game.[17] The tourist body becomes a site of struggle and antagonism between vendor and guide, with the tourist tending to side with the guide, whose authority, credibility, and knowledge are confirmed by his or her role as the "pathfinder." The most constant complaint of all *vendedores* and *artesanos* is the fact that the leader of the "sacred journey" is able to mold the behaviors and attitudes of tourists.[18] The vendors are perplexed and concerned at the unthinking behavior of the charter tourists, especially Americans, who allow themselves to be herded like cattle by the guides. To the chagrin of the guides, European tourists are much more curious and independent, and go wherever their interests lead them. This does not necessarily help the vendors, however, who consider the Europeans to be the most *codo* (miserly, stingy).

The immediate objective of vendors' tactics of attraction (or distraction) is to provoke the tourist into responding with a query: "How much is this?" "What is this made of?" "Where is it made?" Although commentary between touring companions concerning certain handicrafts brings them into the temporary visual field, a full engagement with the display and the vendor in the tactical gambit of bargaining is not guaranteed. More often than not, the tourist is "spying," that is, trying to make innocuous inquiries as to the prices of things, collecting information, and deferring the game of souvenir hunting for a "better," more calculated moment in Mérida or Cancún or in the handicraft store that the guide swears has the lowest prices (and the best commission).

The price of an item depends on the object, the vendor, the day, the hour, and the tourist. The general rule in all commerce is that the selling price is twice the wholesale price. Here, the tourists' nationality and self-presentation are factors to be calculated in the initial offering. Americans and Canadians may be quoted more than twice the cost just so that the vendor "can see what falls" ("hay que ver lo que cae"), but Mexicans and Europeans will not be quoted an excessive price. Vendors know that Mexicans have a better sense of the real value of the items as well as that they tend to have less money — with obvious exceptions. Germans, English, and other northern Europeans touring Yucatán tend to be of the "hippie/backpacker" type and thus are known to be infrequent buyers. The French (as well as the Italians, though not as notoriously) are known for being tight with money and *muy especial*; there is no point in starting too high because they may respond rudely and walk away. In any case, where tourists respond with disinterest or repulsion at a price (whether inflated or actual) and leave the scene, the vendors' comment tends to be, "*chich u kuk*" (literally, "his elbow is hard," i.e., "stingy" or "tight").

Tourist response to price is, of course, varied. It may consist of a nod and a comment: "That's nice/pretty," or "Too much." This verbal reponse is accompanied by a bodily expression of a measured interest in the item. The vendor reads this sign and counters "How much do you want to pay?" Again, the vendor is deploying a tactic of engagement in which the visual relation between subject and objects on display is substituted for a verbal relation in order to forge a subjective value for the tourist. A vendor can usually recognize when the tourist is genuinely interested in buying, and will be stubborn in fixing a price that may be relatively high. Feigned disinterest in an item can easily be interpreted by the speed of interaction or the studied pauses of the tourist. On the other hand, if there is a real, but mild, disinterest, the vendor may be all the more motivated to bargain and entice the tourist with offers of lower prices or additional items at a "discount"; the manipulation of the objects on display then becomes a critical tactic in bringing about a transaction. Tactics must be attentive and engaging—yet not aggressive—if a round of bartering is to be initiated.

In the Tianguis—unlike the selling sites where families have grouped together—the competition between vendors is aggressive. At any moment, three to six other vendors are ready to steer the tourist away from their neighbor toward a nearly identical display only three steps removed. This becomes an important factor in bargaining. The tourist is quite prepared to disengage with any one vendor to look for a better price elsewhere; usually, in fact, tourists seek to visually engage with vendors as little as possible, preferring to let their eyes scan displays, which allows greater mobility. At the same time, the vendor knows who else may have that item and at what price they might sell it. Price-cutting to a wholesale level is considered unfair and threatening to everyone. The daily worry of going home without a sale is very real, so vendors do in fact undercut prices, even as they assert that those vendors over *there* do it, "not I." Yet this tactic threatens the stability of everyone's livelihood, because the cost of merchandise is not always recuperated. Some vendors strategically stock items that others do not have, precisely to avoid price wars.[19] Thus, when a rare item sells well, soon enough the market is flooded with that item or style of wood carving, in the case of the artisans.

One example from the Tianguis serves to illustrate the tactics of bartering. A man and his wife (U.S. nationality) stopped at a stall after inspecting several items; the man inquired about a two-foot silver knife with engravings. The price was 60,000 pesos or US$25 (rate 2,400). The man offered 25,000 pesos. The vendor knew he had the only knife in the market and thus fixed his price. After a minute of countering, the tourist continued to other stalls. When he returned seven minutes later, the vendor said, "Yes, my friend?" The same prices were offered. The man raised his offer to 30,000 pesos and the vendor dropped to 50,000 pesos. At this point, the man's charter group had already boarded the bus and the wife had come to retrieve her husband. They repeated the offers after the man told his wife that he would be there in a second. He offered 35,000 or US $15 as his last price just as he began to walk away. The vendor was solid at 50,000. When the man walked away, this was the cue for the vendor's wife to take out of storage an identical, yet smaller, knife and substitute it for the larger one. The vendor called for the tourist: "OK, OK, mister! Take it. Fifteen dollars!" The tourist returned, paid the money and took the smaller knife that had been wrapped in paper before his eyes. He did not notice the difference.

The Tianguis was all smiles over this tactical coup. The vendor explained to me why he, a very honest man, felt comfortable about the deal. Both parties were satisfied with the exchange. The man really wanted a knife, but not for more than the price he paid. He could not appreciate the value of the larger knife and thus received exactly the commodity that best fit his desire and sense of self. He could not offer more because his integrity was at stake in a confrontation and contest with an Other, the Maya vendor. Two conclusions can be drawn: (1) textualized field of vision is made to materialize by the vendor in the momentary spaces of a display of artisanry; (2) in this art of illusion, attraction, and distraction, the vendor deploys a tactical manipulation of objects, gestures, and body to create an exchange that can reflect the relations of self and other that are constituted in the tourist practices of sight-seeing.

The Calculation of Time

The tourist geography of Yucatán unfolds in time as a meaningful, symbolic, and practical landscape. The places and attractions within a tourist geography are practiced spaces that come alive only within a strategic calculation of time. At every juncture of tourism a fundamental question of time and timing must be addressed: When to go

Fig. 10. A child of one of the Mayaland *vendedores* watches a Maya *artesano* hand over a stone artifact to a tourist for inspection. In the background are rows of T-shirts strung on rope all along the road that ends at the back entrance to the archeological site near the Hotel Mayaland. (Author's photograph)

on vacation? When are there flights/buses? What to see or do implies, and is dependent on, a schedule: How long to stay? When are the museums and stores open and when are shows performed? Tourist businesses, with their production and marketing of tourist commodities, structure the range of possibilities from which individuals construct their tours and vacations, which in turn are structured by the definition of leisure/vacation in the capitalist cores. Leaving, arriving, doing, and returning are the basic elements that compose the durations of tours; these elements form a syntax of tourist practices. The timing of tourism is like language in performance that is forged in the interplay of local, regional, national, and international interests. It is through the control and regulation of time that tourism is constituted as a practice and a spatial-visual form. Tourists are made to speak this language when they submit to this strategic timing and control.

The calculation of time structures the activities and movements of tourists, and constitutes these as determinate tourist practices. Four basic mechanisms compose this method of disciplinary power: (1) ac-

tivities are organized according to successive and parallel durations;
(2) activities are ordered according to complexity, from simple to complex; (3) activities are grouped together and finalized as distinct routines; and (4) series of routines are multiplied to form overlapping
tours. What follows is a synopsis of the durations in which activities
are realized—that is, it provides a totalized temporal order of these
durations. It is not necessary to develop further a description of the
tourist practices in the apparatus in terms of how they are organized
by complexity into tours and how the encompassing tour cycles enact the tourist geography of Yucatán. The present, more limited goal
is merely to lay out the everyday temporal structure or schedule of
tourist routines in the apparatus of Chichén-Pisté.

Cancún charter groups depart for Chichén between 8:00 and
10:00 A.M.[20] Half an hour to forty-five minutes earlier, the buses
make the rounds to the hotels and pick up tourists. The three-and-a-
half-hour drive is interrupted with a bathroom stop, usually at a
handicraft store, which may be in the towns of Valladolid, Catzin, or
Tikuch, or Kilometer 80. Alternatively, the guide may postpone the
"shopping stop" for the return trip. The charters arrive at Chichén
between 10:30 A.M. and 1:30 P.M., with the rush being between 11:30
and 12:30. Mérida is only one and a half hours from Chichén, so
charter buses or minivans from there may depart that much later and
arrive within the same hours. Charters from Mérida drive straight
through without a rest stop. Independent tourists coming from Mérida
usually take the 8:45 A.M. first-class bus and arrive at 10:00 A.M. If
they spend the night in Pisté, most leave their hotel or posada for
breakfast between 7:00 and 9:00 A.M., with the idea of beginning a
tour of Chichén at 8:00 or 9:00, but no later than 10:00 A.M.[21]

Upon arrival, charter groups may be given ten minutes to go to
the bathroom, especially if there was no stop en route or if it was
brief. Cancún guides tend to bring their tourists directly and quickly
to the ticket booth and into the archeological zone. Officially, tours
must last four hours. However, the charter tours are timed for two
and a half to three hours. This may suggest that these chartered guides
work more than the independent guides, but the actual service they
provide is shortened to one and a half to two hours: the groups are
given thirty minutes to an hour to "explore" the zone (i.e., climb pyramids) by themselves or to return to the Parador to relax. By 2:30,
groups begin to return to the buses to go for lunch in Pisté, or they

walk back through the east entrance to the Club Med or the Hotel Mayaland. Tourists who came by first-class round-trip bus may have spent an hour or more resting, eating, and shopping in the Parador and Tianguis; by 2:00 they begin to wait on the steps of the Parador for the 2:45 return to Mérida. By this time, tourists who spent the night in Pisté have already returned to their hotel, had a quick lunch, and are already on the road to the Caribbean (Cancún, Isla Mujeres, Tulum, Playa del Carmen) or Mérida, or they are waiting for a bus in the center of town that will get them to their destination by early evening.[22] Few indeed spend two nights and usually only those who have made friends with a special local "guide."

Charter groups—whether they originate in Mérida or Cancún—have lunch between 1:30 and 3:30 P.M. An hour later, they are on the road home. Unlike the Cancún charters, those from Mérida do not stop en route at a handicraft store; Mérida guides have to find their commission in Pisté. The Cancún guides have a number of options: they may stop at half a dozen stores in Valladolid or in two other towns farther west (Tikuch and Catzin). In some cases, the charter groups have lunch in one of three restaurants in Valladolid. In order to eat during lunch hours, these groups must be on an earlier schedule; they have to calculate the forty-five-minute drive between Chichén and Valladolid. In these cases, the guides combine their commissioned shopping stop in Valladolid rather than farther down the road in Tikuch or Catzin. By 6:00 or 7:00 P.M., buses arrive in Mérida and Cancún, respectively; depending on hotel location in Cancún, however, the tourists may not get to their room until 8:00 or 9:00 P.M.

Within this daily schedule, particular activities are organized, punctuated with termination points, and grouped into series or routines. Our analysis proceeded by describing the small building blocks that are aggregated to form practices (selling handicrafts, hooking tourists for tours). A more usual descriptive procedure reverses the process; it assumes the tourist practice to be a unit that can be broken down into these routines and durations. The analytical procedure used here helps to identify the mechanisms and techniques that regulate the time and timing of tourism as power relations. Thus, through the tactical manipulation of tourists, their activities, and their movements, a strategic calculation of time is composed and put into operation that effectively controls and regulates tourism as an everyday series of practices.

The Configuration of Practices

Tourist and touristic practices are spatially and temporally configured by five techniques. First, there is a functional reduction of individuals (tourist, vendor, guide, waiter, artisan, warden, etc.) to a body in space. Second, the movement of the tourist bodies in space creates a seasonal, weekly, daily, and localized time, that is, a temporal economy of durations in which a panoply of tactical maneuvers is practiced. Third, other bodies are synchronized according to the travels of the tourist body as these are arranged in durations and locations in order to provide designated services. Fourth, this temporalization of tourist and touristic bodies, through the spatial trajectory, creates a composite time in which bodies and activities are configured. Fifth, in this configuration of practices, power relations are transformed into and are evident as signals that designate the proper moment for the realization of activities as spatialized enactments.

Différance of the Tourist Apparatus

Although the notion of *différance* developed by Derrida critiques Western metaphysics, it can be usefully applied to the description of practices in Chichén and Pisté. Based on a play of words, it refers at once to (1) differences, which are already spatially positioned to form a system or structure; (2) the act or event of differing, which creates and distributes differences; and (3) deferral, which implies both delay or postponement between differences/differing and submission to authority or power (Derrida 1981; cf. Culler 1982: 94–100). Thus, *différance* does not describe a structure of differences, or contingent events of positive creation. Rather, it describes *both*—the spatialization of event as structure and the temporalization of system as event. *Différance* is a systematic play of differences, or, in this case, of tourist and touristic practices and their sites of performance. *Différance* arranges practices in space according to a structure that is only manifest or evident as the event or enactment of practices, and it elaborates these everyday practices within a temporal economy determined by an event that is generated from the strategic configuration of practices. The tourist attraction, then, is constituted in a grid of disciplinary power, or apparatus, that is itself configured in and by a principle of *différance*.

As already indicated, the timetables of different types of work are directly scheduled according to the flow of tourists: *when* the tourist moves between two proper locations where formally designated activities occur, a space is created in which unofficial sites momentarily materialize for the exercise of "improper" and often illegal activities. Whether arriving from Mérida in the west or Cancún in the east, tourists begin the everyday routines at Chichén at the eastern side of the apparatus. From their residences in Pisté in the west, all types of workers move east toward Chichén to set up and prepare business in the opening half of the day. This movement is dictated by the tourist trajectory: spaces are first temporalized, imbued with value, and then hierarchized by the timing of the tourist body. By the same token, the closing part of the day consists of a return movement where tourists depart from Pisté-Chichén for Cancún or Mérida and workers return to Pisté in the west.

Beginning at 6:00 A.M., Pisté comes alive with the opening of shops, the market, and the street vendors. The latter locate their stalls in the plaza area and sell tacos of cochinita, roasted chickens, and other fast morning foods. By 7:00, the half-dozen taxis have cued up in the road alongside the plaza and across from the town hall. Until 10:00 A.M. they are busy moving Chichén employees and many of the Tianguis vendors to work as these arrive and group together to share a ride. Others, such as INAH wardens, CULTUR workers, and Tianguis vendors, ride bicycles to Chichén. Meanwhile, street vendors and vendor-artisans are preparing their merchandise, positioning six to ten boxes and crates near the road or in a doorway where the *transportista* can easily load it onto his small truck. These vendors are usually picked up and individually taken to their work site, although a few vendors, specifically family groups of one or both parents, two or more working children, and maybe an adolescent nephew or niece, are transported together if they all sell at the same site. Those who are situated at the Mayaland, the Chichén crossroads, and the Misión-Xaybe are moved in the early morning, between 8:00 and 9:30, while those working sites to the west (the Fiesta, Cunanchen, Picuda) are taken in the late morning or early afternoon. In an hour and a half, vendors have loaded the merchandise, unloaded it at the site, and begun to unpack the handicrafts and set up their displays. Once set up, they wait for the charter groups. Although they have set up a display at one restaurant, a number of vendors will load blankets or idols on a bike to follow a charter bus to another restaurant, according to information on the number of groups scheduled for each restaurant that is received by wait staff. With the last buses returning to their origin, the vendors begin the process of dismantling displays, loading boxes, and moving merchandise back home. Meanwhile, the taxi drivers are again busy bringing all the workers back home from the museum. Within the spatial continuum of the apparatus and according to a schedule of durations already discussed, the trajectory of the tourist determines when and where practices are deployed. This deployment—the east-west-east movement of workers—forms a complementary trajectory of bodies. In combination, the two trajectories of tourists and workers configure practices in space and time according to a logic and grid of *différance*.

The combination of disciplinary methods (localization of practical sites, regulation of activities, calculation of time, configuration of practices) forms an apparatus of power that has no single locus of control or authority structure. The disciplinary apparatus that coordinates bodies and configures practices has no hierarchy, although hierarchic structures and institutions intercede (unions, national and state tourist agencies, the different levels of government, federal department of education and its anthropology branch). Instead of forming a macroinstitution, institutions, organizations, collectivities, and groups become articulated to this grid of power relations. Thus, there is no subjective interest, whether economic or political, but a multiplicity of heterogeneous interests configured within a unitary and dominant will to power. This will to power, or mode and rationalization of control, corresponds to the strategy of time that constitutes tourism.[23]

Three Bodies and Tourist Routines

In the anthropology of tourism, visual procedures have been marked as the principal phenomena that constitute tourism (e.g., MacCannell 1976; Urry 1990). Thus, great attention has been given to the construction and rituals of the tourist *sight* as an *attraction* that compels, directs, and structures vision toward a symbolic construct that signifies authenticity. As Veijola and Jokinen (1994) and Q. Castañeda (1991) have pointed out, in these predominantly semiotic studies of the modalities of tourist gazes, vision becomes a disembodied, masculinist, and imperial "I/eye" in much the way Pratt (1992) has analyzed travel writings. Often it seems that an ontological essence to tourist activities is presupposed, whether in the act of seeing or in other sorts of activities. The mapping of touristic practices performed here was possible by considering the activities of buying/selling and eating/serving as organized within the same operations as sight-seeing. Fundamental to these analyses has been a concern for the body and the spatiotemporal order of the activities through which tourism exists. I have sought to chart the ways in which tourism is constituted as the orchestration of bodies and its tactical maneuvers. As a result, relations of power understood as a spatiotemporal order or economy otherwise not perceived came into "view." This necessitated a shift in terminology because the object of study has shifted. *Properly speaking*, the tourist attraction is just the sight, yet this analysis revealed that this visual complex is situated within a wider field shaped by the operations of power. Borrowing from Foucault, I have described this wider field as a disciplinary apparatus. Borrowing other notions from de Certeau and Derrida, I have analyzed organizational principles and operative tactics within the tourist apparatus. At the same time, this analysis has pointed out the nexus where power is linked to encompassing strategies of control. It might be possible to use this framework and method to analyze other types of tourist attractions.

8 / Panopticon as Tianguis

Tactics, Language, Strategy

During the last five years the archeological site of Chichén Itzá has been invaded by vendors of artisanry, wood carvers, and itinerant vendors ... It is possible to reach a definite solution to [the invasion]: Once the Tianguis is inaugurated, then the total displacement from the archeological zone of Chichén [can occur], including the two paradores [i.e., the INAH-operated and the rented palapas] existing within, as well as the vendedores that exhibit their merchandise in small, improvised stalls ...
        Peraza López et al., "La invasión de vendedores de artesanías
            en la zona arqueológica de Chichén Itzá, Yucatán" (1987)

Walking into the Parador to pee, walk past F., L., someone shouts, "Aaye! Ba'ax ka'waik espiaah?" ["Hey, what do you say, spy?"]. I passed on and greeted J.P. at info booth. He continues loudly to someone else, "El es el espía del Lic" ["He is the spy of the Licenciado" (i.e., the CULTUR coordinator of the Parador Turístico)].
            Q. Castañeda, field notes (October 12, 1988)

The Tianguis or "traditional" handicraft market of Chichén is a living monument to the invasion of the vendors, and like any monument it works to establish a unitary truth and history through the double neutralization of oppositional power and memories of resistance. Such monuments as this are also war treaties in that they establish or impose an order with rights and rules that define illegalities and improprieties. Built in conjunction with the new Parador Turístico, the "Yanguis" was conceived both as a complementary attraction to the sight of Chichén and as the vehicle by which to resolve the crisis of the invasion (Peraza López et al. 1987; Gobierno Estatal de Yucatán 1982a). As one of three dominant locations within the tourist apparatus of Chichén-Pisté, this market for commodity exchange, and minor attraction, is the architectural embodiment of a specific strategy of social control. This chapter aims to describe the major features of the strategy of power that regulates vending activities and disciplines vendors in the Tianguis and that constrained my own practice of ethnographic inquiry. The purpose is not so much to show the imposition and resolute force of this control as to identify the tactics of manipulation that are the means of both resistance to and reproduction of control.

Strategy: Panopticism and the Practice of Fieldwork

In conducting my research, I inserted myself in a grid of power/ knowledge relations in which the vendors of the Tianguis are also embedded. As it turns out, this strategy of power shaped my research strategy, that is, the strategic choices that guided my investigation. I thus enacted a fieldwork practice that reproduced certain operations of power and thereby regulated my ethnographic knowledge. As in all ethnography, the ideal research project, with its pristine and naive methodology written for granting agencies, is transformed in the fire of fieldwork: the immediacies and contingencies of the local situation foster certain inquiries and prohibit or delimit other knowledge. The interesting question to pose with regard to this application of a "universal" method is not how ethnographic knowledge did not reach scientific standards for truth and veracity, but how the practice of fieldwork, being constrained by specific conditions, can reveal those constraints as a field of power that articulates local knowledge and embeds action.

During three months of preliminary fieldwork in 1985 I was able to witness a key moment in the war of tourism at Chichén: regional struggles between guide unions were manifest in local fistfights and antagonisms; factions of vendors and artisans were sabotaging one another's merchandise; discord among local and regional INAH employees was expressed in factionalism and union strikes at Chichén;

political factions in Pisté were recuperating from an attempted lynching of the mayor the previous year; and a coalition of capitalist and state interests was sending the police, the military, and union organizers to expel the invaders from the zone.[1] On the basis of this experience, I designed, for the subsequent period of fieldwork, a research agenda around the politics of tourism. I wanted to work, from December 1987 to December 1988, primarily with the vendors and artisans—and then, in a later stage, with the wardens, guides, and taxi drivers.

When I returned to the field I found that although the invasion had ended, the war of tourism continued in less visible forms. The Tianguis had been inaugurated in March 1987 and the authorities had been able to enforce the evacuation from the zone of all the vendors. Of the four hundred or so persons, approximately a hundred entered the Tianguis, while fifty to a hundred relocated to other vending sites in the apparatus; the others devoted themselves to other occupations. I thus refined my objectives: to study the imposition of a form of social control within the tourist complex through an analysis of the forms of resistance embedded in the everyday practices of vendors, artisans, and guides and in their ongoing sociopolitical struggles. This would be studied through stories of the invasion and accounts of the practice of selling during that time.

While I continued my language training, I devised an initial strategy and refamiliarized myself with the different work groups, their factions and struggles. The immediate question was how to situate myself in the field of political struggles between the different groups; that is, with which group or groups should I associate? The work of the wardens and taxi drivers was the least problematic, to my mind, and thus study could be deferred. The work of guides was central to the investigation, yet to study them entailed certain problems: this group was the most educated, Spanish-speaking, white or ladinoized, belligerent to observers, and generally disliked in the community, in part because of their general nonlocal origins and habits. It was strategic to defer research with the guides until having mastered Maya and developed friendships with the guides before intruding on the secrets and skeletons of their occupation. In any case, my ethical, political, and intellectual interests lay with the vendors and artisans, who are predominantly local Maya. However, this occupational group is composed of a range of different economic classes and political interests (see Peraza López et al. 1987). In other words, this choice of where to situate myself in the war of tourism (with which economic group) did not resolve the problem of how to insert myself in the political field (with which factions).

Initially, I presented myself as a cultural anthropologist learning Maya and who later wanted to study the different work that people pursue at Chichén. This presented a contradiction in terms, which was resolved by their ironic categorization of me as an archeologist. To begin, the qualifier was confusing, as this category is not used for anthropologists in Yucatán: the anthropologists with whom these Maya were familiar are "social" not "cultural" practitioners, a distinction that goes to the origins of the differences between these national traditions. Stereotypically, Mexican and Yucatec anthropologists are concerned with political or socioeconomic aspects of regional society and not usually with language-based analyses of culture. Thus, my interest in Maya and my apparently being "gringo" made people very receptive to me, but only if I was unambiguously categorized as an unobtrusive and innocuous archeologist rather than an interventionist academic with suspected links to government agendas.[2] The warmth with which I was received was noticeably affected when I shifted my research and the way I presented my work. As a way to ask about the history of selling artisanry, I explained directly, if naively, that I wanted to study how they have struggled to work as vendors and artisans in the context of tourism at Chichén. This highly intrusive line of questioning and threatening presentation soon had me characterized as a government spy — after all, I told people that I was being supported by a grant from the U.S. government. These two seemingly miscategorizations were not based on simple misunderstandings but on historical experience.

Only later did I discover that the crisis of the invasion was resolved in part through the intervention of the INAH and the work of four Yucatec social anthropologists. They had been commissioned to study the causes and possible solutions of the invasion. Although their report, from which the epigraph that opened this chapter is taken, had not been read by vendors, it was experienced. These were the persons who took down the names of those artisans and vendors who wanted to and did enter the Tianguis. It need only be stated that the relocation had severe economic repercussions for those concerned. Regardless of the earnest intentions of the INAH anthropologists —

which are recognized by many locals and myself—they had served as the mechanism for a strategy of control. Ultimately, they were "spies"—that is, agents of nonlocal, hegemonic institutions—and this prefigured all understanding of my activities and person. It is common for ethnographers to be considered spies, but in my case there is a context, as I show, that grounds or validates that interpretation. However, beyond these specifics, there is something about ethnography itself that in fact constitutes spying, regardless of intentionality or political affiliation.

I relied on contacts from 1985 to establish myself in town. My most solid friendships were with a family of vendors from whom I rented a house.³ This situation seemed ideal because this was one of the first non-INAH families to sell artisanry and its history is linked to the Carnegie days. However, I soon became uneasy about exploiting it for purposes of research. This family was fairly "ladinoized" in both language (they code-switched to Spanish with me and their children) and material culture (they were very successful in the souvenir commerce). The combination of their economic success and the power plays that they had used to secure that success had aroused strong antagonisms within the vendor community. Although I decided to develop friendships and informant relations with persons from other vendor groups, I soon realized that this community was splintered into political and economic factions, which always followed the contours of kinship.

My fear of being associated with only one political faction, occupational group, or type of vendor/artisan turned into a strategic choice that complied with a research objective: to attain a comprehensive view of all the touristic practices as they are situated in time and distributed in space. My thesis that the tourist attraction is a type of "panopticon" led me to a panoptical practice of fieldwork.⁴ My attempt to stay above the cross fire among the vendors *was possible,* but only at the risk and cost of a different association with and to power. By trying to keep "above" the vendor antagonisms, I implicitly aligned myself with external or nonlocal political interests against which the vendors were (usually) unified in their struggles. The infrastructural circumstances of my presence, the categorization of my activities, the thrust of my questioning, and the shape of my practice all solidified the understanding of me as an agent of state power who had been sent to collect information on the efficacy of and resistance to the hegemonic order that had been imposed. Indeed, my practice articulated and reproduced the panopticism that I was inventing in analysis as a model of social relations. In a certain sense I embodied the figure of the warden in Bentham's prison, that is, my practice of ethnography located me in the grid of power as if I were a "warden" in the "central tower" of the tourist apparatus: I attempted to position myself as an "all-seeing eye" that could observe all of the activities distributed in the "periphery" and to document their temporal coordination.[5] However, unlike the warden in Bentham's prison, I was also under constant surveillance. There was, then, a mutual unverifiability in our reciprocal visibility: I never knew who precisely was watching me and no one was ever certain that the notes I was writing concerned *them* specifically or not.

These two aspects of Bentham's panopticon—observation and documentation—are tightly linked, as Foucault has analyzed (1979: 200–207): The control established through the surveillance of the warden allows for a detailed process of documentation of the inmates by the agents of the institution. In turn, the production of knowledge through documentation is a mechanism of power that facilitates and increases control as it reshapes resistance. Ultimately, as Bentham argued, the application of this dual mechanism in a panoptical architecture is a powerful means of transformation guided by rational and utilitarian notions. Prisoners could be reformed, students trained, patients monitored to health, or, in the present case, vendors and artisans disciplined to act as individualized, law-abiding, rational entrepreneurs. This utilitarian, and political, goal was the motivation of the state and federal authorities for the construction of the Tianguis; the two coordinators of the "Yanguis" were appointed precisely to carry out a program of discipline that would change and control the vendors. A kind of "panopticon" had been instituted, and the coordinators functioned as its "wardens." Further, the ethnographic endeavor that I was enacting—the task of describing vendor organization, history, social relations, and political struggles—constituted me as an agent of nonlocal, hegemonic interests. According to the Foucauldian model that I textually impose and create, I was a "warden," but to the people of Pisté, I was simply a government spy.

The irony is that this assessment of anthropology and anthropologists as spying and spies is sociologically and historically true and valid; this much we have learned from critical historicization of the discipline. If we want to rethink our ethical matter in relation to the production and dissemination of ethnographic knowledge, I feel we must begin from this fact that espionage is constitutive of our discipline.

A spy is "a clandestine agent employed by a state to obtain intelligence relating to its actual or potential enemies at home or abroad" (*New Riverside University Dictionary* 1984: 1127). There is always something secretive or clandestine-like about ethnography, because the "natives" never really know what anthropology "is" or what the ethnographer is "really doing" (as if the researchers really knew as well!), no matter how much effort is spent in sincere and elaborate explanations. It's not that the natives are dumb — after all, it takes undergraduates a semester to *begin* to vaguely learn these things according to our self-satisfying stories about anthropology. The insight that subjects of research often have (that we are spies) has simply been too accurate and loaded for practitioners to accept (until recently). The real question concerns the ethnographic *intelligence* that is produced: Who can or will make use of it? Who does or could it empower and disempower? It is no surprise that these were the questions I was always being asked by vendors, although in a different form: What is it that you are always *writing*? What do you do with the information that you write? Since I told persons that I had to send reports to the U.S. government, they wanted to know how often I made reports, what *they* do with the reports, and who exactly "they" are.

Understanding the thrust of these questions, I always (naively) expounded my desire to tell the stories of how the people of Pisté have struggled against outsiders and forms of domination to attain satisfactory lives. They may have accepted my good intentions (even at first), but remained skeptical about how this naive, young, and intrusive gringo could be useful to them outside of teaching them English — if he ever got around to it.[6] In the field, and even more now, in the process of writing the ethnography, it seems clear to me what must have been their concern. How could documenting and describing the often ugly details of their squabbles and political struggles help them? One controversial protagonist was very straightforward in posing the ethical question. I had been trying to interview him for over a year to get his version of some unfavorable stories told about him. His aggressive refusal was accompanied by the challenge: "Who are you to ask about these things?" He argued that if I really wanted to be of assistance to people, I would not write about the invasion and the local politics of the vendors. Clearly, a unitary or absolute solution is neither possible nor sufficient. One possible answer would be an ethnography written for the tourist market and popular readership, which would provide a heroic and/or mysterious depiction of Pisté and forge an *alluring image* capable of *attracting* tourist interest in Pisté. But, this guidebook is not that book; it is, rather, about this ethical dilemma.

By 1989, during my third field season, when I began actively to assist the community's political movement for municipal independence, my intentions and commitments became clear. Regardless of my intentions (good or bad vis-à-vis local interests and factions), however, I was a spy, even a "double agent." As an obvious spy, I was marked and associated with specific interests, specifically those that sought to impose discipline on the vendors and artisans. I was a spy and, by analogy, a "warden." Yet I was not marked with any official standing or authority. My *political* power was implicit (not authoritative) and symbolic, because it was constructed on a temporal gap and deferral of a potential effect. By collecting information, I posed a threat because its *future* use was in question. Although I was marked with high social status based on certain features (North American, money, education, English-speaker), these qualities did not give me "personal power," but rather targeted me as a resource to be manipulated and utilized through various tactics of reciprocity and power plays. But this was reciprocal, because participant observation is the "methodological" deployment of an ethnographic strategy, composed of "techniques" and "procedures" for the collection and elicitation of information. In other words, the subjects of research or "informants" and I were caught in a field of tactics and maneuvers that sought to control knowledge and its exchange. In my practice of fieldwork, the ethnographic task was always subverted, diverted, and distracted, whether by friendly discussions—for example, of AIDS and poverty in the United States—or by subterfuge. One privileged arena within this grid of power/knowledge relations is that of language; because it is simultaneously an economic resource, a context of interaction, a knowledge, a means of communication, a mechanism of power, and a marker of identities, it exemplifies the double bind of the ethnographer, which is to be both a spy and a target of power.

Language: The Arts of Selling and a New Writing Lesson

A critical goal of my research was to develop an understanding of Maya ways of knowing, viewing, and relating to Chichén Itzá, which could only be attained through their language. Thus, it was important to situate myself within this plural, hybridized, and polyglot society with Maya who speak predominantly Maya. At Chichén, Spanish, English, and Maya are almost "equally" used, although in different spheres. In Pisté, the monolingual Maya-speakers are few and tend to be strictly campesinos or older persons (above seventy years of age). The monolingual Spanish-speakers are restricted to non-Maya and those Maya that systematically "negate" having knowledge of it. I refer to women that in other parts of Yucatán, such as the Puuc area, would be called *catrines,* and to males (seventeen to twenty-four years old) who attempt to present themselves as having a superior socioeconomic status.[7] Most locals, however, regardless of economic class, are bilingual in Spanish and Maya; a surprising number are tri-lingual, with the addition of at least English; others command French, Italian, and/or German. People have a direct and pragmatic interest in foreign languages. Those working in any aspect of tourism have a variable command of English, from limited lexical items and essential sentences to fluency.

As a speaker of English, I had a valuable and sought-after resource at my disposal. Throughout my stay, people would approach me in any variety of contexts to ask that I teach them English, either free or for money. I would decline, protesting that it is not my vocation. This caused a lot of difficulties and anxiety. In itself, I felt that it would consume time "better" used to other ends; soon I realized that I was constantly put in a position to accept, or to legitimate my refusal and accept certain negative consequences of not accepting a gift relation. To decline such an offer from a recent acquaintance is to refuse a social relation and to assume an antagonistic stance toward the person. I was charged with egotism and self-centeredness for not teaching others my language. My protests that it would detract from my "work" and my learning Maya only further engendered this sentiment.

People would offer to teach me Maya in exchange for my teaching them English. Clearly, such language exchange can be both a tactic of research and a vehicle for establishing a more intense friendship. Unfortunately, these seemed always to be people whose Maya was less than ideal, whose economic situation put them outside my research interests or, simply, someone with whom I did not want to work (i.e., my selfishness). The best way for a male to learn Maya is perhaps to immerse himself with agriculturalists and work with them in their fields. I always felt and feared that this would take me too far from the business of tourism. Artisans and some vendors are primarily Maya-speakers, and for this reason, working with them was the ideal substitute. But these were persons who had the least socioeconomic space to take time either to train me in Maya or to arrange a formal language exchange outside of their work time. Thus, I resolved to learn Maya without a formal trainer, through conversation. In the course of participant observation, I would ask questions about syntax and lexicon from various persons with whom I developed friendships. In turn, these and other persons would always ask me for English translations of words and sentences that pertained to their own work.[8] This was a tactical exchange of knowledge — specifically, of language — that was essential for establishing friendships and informant relations.

My time in the Tianguis was often spent "hanging out," observing activities, and joining in idle conversation. It seems that I offered something of a relief from the dull moments during which there were few sales, as my friends would always invite me over to discuss English, U.S. society, Maya language, or simply to bum a cigarette. In such contexts of male talk conducted in a semiprivate "corner" of the Tianguis, conversation could become laden with sexual innuendo and an occasion for verbal dueling. Generally, dueling consists of taking advantage of another's speech in such a way as to assert a dominance over that person through a metaphoric association as a passive homosexual.[9] A common assumption among Yucatecos is that one has not learned Maya until one has mastered this type of talk or dueling; the corollary is that one must first learn to insult (*poch'* in Maya) and defend one's "face" in order to have effectively learned Maya. In part, this idea must stem from, or is manifest in, the way that Yucatecos who assert a lack of knowledge of the language are "tested": such persons are insulted through subtle sexual joking in order to see their response. Similarly, I was always "tested" and made the brunt of joking, sexual and otherwise. No doubt I presented a rewarding

Fig. 11. A view of everyday life, spatial arrangements, and displays in the Tianguis, Chichén Itzá. Maya women dressed in Western-style clothing in foreground are itinerant food vendors who are speaking to their child as a male artisan and female handicraft vendor wait to buy a snack or beverage; the vendor on the left keeps his eye on a tourist attracted to the objects and images displayed on his *mesa*, or one meter by one meter stall. (Author's photograph)

opportunity for such duels, in that a person could easily invert the apparent social statuses to mark himself as superior to the gringo. Except where a person seemed to be vicious or particularly vulgar, I always enjoyed these duels; not only do I find sexual punning humorous but I took it as an opportunity to learn Maya and establish friendships.

My jovial attitude and my inferior dueling abilities combined to make me a susceptible target for insults. However, I was not quite aware that I lost a certain degree of respect, at least in the short run, for being such an easy put-down. I felt that I never quite mastered the game or its rules. Half the time I was unable to respond adequately, and a fourth of the time I may have responded with an excessive or tactless retort. Usually, however, someone helped to "defend" me against such joking: If I were in a conversation with someone and someone else threw a barb at me as he walked by or joined the talk, the first would prompt me with a correct response in Maya. In this way, I could sustain a minimal duel—that is, I could be a prop for the duel of the other two persons. More often, however, I would not have a friend at my side to assume the role of my defender, particularly when I was wearing the ethnographer's hat.

In the Tianguis, unless one has moved to a more secluded space, three to ten other persons may be able to overhear any conversation. There is always an audience and people speak with the awareness that someone else is listening. It often happened that while engaged in a conversation, I would be insulted in wordplay. Not understanding the joke but observing the resulting smiles, I would ask the person to repeat his comment. Still not understanding, I would ask for a translation or explanation from the person, which would be refused. I would ask a nearby person to explain what had been said. That would be refused and I would be told to ask the person what his comment was and what it meant. If I insisted on understanding and asked the person again to explain, the humor and smiles would begin to disappear and people would often just walk away from the scene. At first frustrated with my lack of comprehension of the language, I would get more frustrated and at times angry at how such situations turned against me. In order to leave little concealed about me and my work, I always carried a notebook and wrote wherever the urge arose. I resolved to take as many notes as possible about such encounters, which repelled persons from me even more. I was unaware of how I had subverted the game, not merely by breaking the rules but by a more profound play of power. This, it seemed, was an everyday spectacle of power; and, it occurred to me while sitting in the Tianguis writing my notes that I should use such an incident as an exemplary trope in a chapter on the politics, language, and disciplining of the Tianguis.

I remember and read in my notes that on one day I was tense and frustrated and was with persons with whom I got along very well. It was late afternoon during low season and there was very little movement in the Tianguis. One man initiated a conversation, asking me pointedly what it was that I wanted to talk about today. A conversation developed about how Pistéleños "felt" about or identified with Chichén the ruins; it involved five or six persons who were semiengaged and at least another five were able to overhear. Someone directed a humorous comment to me at my expense that I did not understand. Everybody was laughing and I tried to ask what had been said in the manner just described. As I insisted on understanding, one person made a good-humored comment in Maya that I still had a lot to learn. The conversation quickly broke apart as persons walked away to re-form smaller groups a distance away. Intensely frustrated, I walked over to sit next to where four men had relocated and began to intensively take notes. My actions interrupted the new conversation as these persons became serious and concerned with my activity. One or another vendor who had not participated in the incident approached and, looking over my shoulder, asked whether I was writing in English, Spanish, or Maya? Why write so much? What is it that I was writing? At this point, one man with whom I have had a good relationship since 1985 asked me directly about my work. What was I studying and to what use would it be put? Why was I there and what were my intentions?

A new conversation developed along these lines, in Spanish, with a smaller, more serious group, but always within earshot of those interested in listening. The incident as a whole indicates how my fieldwork interactions were shaped by certain relations of power and knowledge. Although the verbal dueling broke down because of my ignorance, I subverted the game and pulled a play outside of the rules. By insisting on an explanation of the sexual innuendo or joking insult, I inverted the statuses and the process by which they are constructed: Instead of being marked as dominated or lower vis-à-vis another person, I brought to public attention how this person was tactless and rude for using vulgar language. Further, by implication I was negating Maya as a socially valid language. Maya are quick to attest that their language is good, poetic, profound, and more than adequate for polite conversation. Yet, by unknowingly highlighting my dueler's use of vulgarities I was making a negative statement on the language, the culture, and the people. Through my actions I was communicating what white Yucatecos say about Maya—that it is an obscene language used by dirty, lower-status, or inferior persons. Asking for the stupid joke to be retold was not merely in bad taste; it was unintentionally condescending in terms that go beyond the personal.

Besides turning the tables on the person, throwing out the rules, and denigrating the game, I transformed the scene into yet another, related struggle of power. My resort to writing was a tactic that enacted the grid of power/knowledge that had been imposed with the relocation of vendors in the "Yanguis." In the friendly situation of the verbal duel, my writing tactic made explicit what had been backgrounded: I was there to study and observe the vendors. Indeed, some incidences of dueling were directly motivated by this fact. People would use the language game as a way to deflect or divert my investigation, to avoid an encounter with someone they could only understand as a spy and a threat. The act of writing, constantly writing and observing, only solidified the threat that I posed and my position in the battlefield as an agent of external interests. The power of the act of writing notes and of its image had an even greater resonance because it embodied knowledge of different types (e.g., literacy, languages, secrets of vendor politics) and authority that the vendors did not possess. Writing then triggered an association with authority and the "outside" that blocked up the channels of communication. It reasserted the grid of power/knowledge that delimited knowledge between antagonized groups and categories of persons. I was aligned with the state and its "wardens," that is, coordinators, and could not be trusted with information. In the best of situations, I was interrogated about my ethical, political, and intellectual concerns; otherwise I was avoided.

Not surprisingly, I was caught in a double bind. On the one hand, I was associated with the "central tower" and enmeshed in tactics of knowledge. On the other hand, the authorities (the town government, the INAH, and particularly the state or CULTUR) would not trust me either because I was a foreigner and an unknown quantity. Thus, although I was given permission to work in Chichén, Pisté, and the Tianguis, I was not supported by the authorities with access to information that might have been "useful" to my research.

Tactics: Illegalities, Policing, and Resistance

Through the Instituto Nacional de Antropología e Historia and its predecessor, Monumentos Prehispánicos, the federal government has maintained legal jurisdiction over Mexico's archeological zones since the Revolution. In the late 1970s, the state of Yucatán sought an arrangement with the INAH to develop a Light and Sound Show at Uxmal and Chichén Itzá; this moneymaking endeavor was controlled and regulated by the state government through its Patronato de Luz y Sonido, which was created for the purpose. Although the Patronato was allowed to install lighting systems and build electrical facilities in the zones, the INAH remained the legal authority charged with the maintenance and conservation of archeological sites. For its part, the

INAH, as a branch of the Secretaría de Educación Pública, has full jurisdiction to mandate, but no real capacity to enforce, its laws with regard to the cultural patrimonies. Thus, the invasion of Chichén by vendors and artisans (1982–87) occurred in a curious kind of political vacuum, that is, in full view of a totally deficient and unempowered authority structure. Further, the inadequacy of authority was matched by the strength of local sentiment of ownership and identity with Chichén. Thus, even the resort to punitive force (police and military) or to co-optation (unionization) was not adequate to the task of disenfranchising the people of *their* recognized rights.[10] In this context, on March 18, 1985, the state of Yucatán, the INAH, SECTUR (Secretaría de Turismo), and FONATUR (Fondo Nacional del Fomento al Turismo) signed an agreement, "Coordination and Cooperation," through which a governmental junta was formed to design a juridical basis of control from which to legally and forcefully administer order.

On December 15, 1986, this legislation, literally a war treaty, was signed by the directors of the government agencies mentioned and the governor of Yucatán (V. Cervera Pacheco). Although the new Parador had already been designed and under construction since 1983, the supplementary Tianguis was not conceived as a necessity — that is, as a solution to the invasion — until this state intervention. The 1986 legislation established the Patronato de las Unidades de Servicios Culturales y Turísticos del Estado de Yucatán or CULTUR, which superseded the old agency in charge of the Light and Sound Shows. Teresa Borges Manzur, the director of the state's Department of Tourism (Dirección de Turismo), was appointed the first director on January 8, 1987. Although it seemed that she was going to be replaced the following year with the completion of Cervera Pacheco's term as governor in 1988, she was instead given control of yet a third agency dealing with tourism, the state's office of SECTUR. Although the problems at Chichén began during previous governorships, the resolution of the conflict was orchestrated by Cervera Pacheco, but implemented and continued to be managed by Borges Manzur until 1992–93.[11]

Before the new complex opened in March 1987, a coordinator of the Tianguis was appointed by CULTUR in 1986. This person was specifically charged with facilitating the transfer of the vendors and artisans to the Tianguis and instituting a discipline among them by which they could be controlled. It is not insignificant that this first "warden" was (*a*) a woman, (*b*) a native of Mexico City, and (*c*) an anthropologist (specialty in linguistics). Despite this occupation, she was not in any official capacity associated with the INAH or Yucatec anthropologists, because *anthropology as an institution was one of the protagonists in the ongoing struggles* and contestations at Chichén. These three aspects resonated with the will and power of external interests to dominate.

In both national politics and this local/regional situation, the metaphor of a disorganized and chaotic home was used as the rhetoric of persuasion by which order, authority, and rules were established. It was used by the representatives of the unions that had been called in to co-opt the vendors in the summer of 1985 and was then embodied in this woman: she would be the stern but caring disciplinarian who would "clean" and "put to order" the "home," that is, teach the poor Maya campesinos turned petit bourgeois how to behave and respect each other as disciplined citizens. She stood as "mother" to a symbolic "father," that is, the working representative of the detached, absolute, yet ultimately benevolent authority, the governor of the state. All the better that she was a Mexican, that is, a generally disdained outsider who could also symbolize the hegemony of the nation-state, a more totalizing, autonomous, and anonymous authority. It represented a threat to the regionalism of Yucatán, which had two genres, Yucatec-criollo and Maya "nationalisms." Her presence symbolized and embodied the coordination and cooperation of the four governmental agencies that sought to impose order on the uncontrollable and dangerous vendors. All the better that she was an anthropologist, trained to understand and deal with the "rude" mentalities of the less educated and impoverished Indians. Her specific personal traits indicated her transience and the substitutability of the person in the position, but also the permanence of external hegemony.

Initially, a female coordinator of the Tianguis and a male Encargado (supervisor) of the Parador were appointed. The Encargado doubled the relation between the *coordinadora* and the detached, absolute authority figure; he was a microcosmic embodiment of the authority of the governor, but responded to the state's female director of tourism. By the end of the summer or early fall 1987, only some six months after the opening of the new complex, these two positions were eliminated in favor of a single coordinator of both the Parador and the Tianguis. This can be understood as the normalization of authority and power relations within the Tianguis. The hierarchy of surveillance was and could be simplified to include only a single warden, because vendors themselves had "successfully" been "trained" to be their own "wardens." Instead of resorting to the old tactics of power deployed during the invasion, they adopted the mechanisms of the panopticon whereby the vendors maintain their own surveillance on each other and report illegalities to the coordinator. The next step would be internalization of surveillance, that is, self-censorship.

The creation of official and juridical authority in a space where none had previously existed entails the invention of illegalities, which transform the status of actions that had been everyday into formal crimes against the interests of the bourgeoisie (see Foucault 1979: 73–89, 257–91). The "Reglamento Normativo para Concesionarios del Tianguis de Chichén Itzá" (see Appendix) is the set of rules by which such illegalities were created. In this document can be read the state of affairs that prevailed during the invasion, because the articles are carefully prepared to illegalize the customary activities and behaviors of the vendors and to impose specific norms that befit the ideals, aesthetics, and economic interests of those who control the regional tourist industry. Certainly, these goals are two sides of the same coin—the realization of one implies the other.

In an interview in January 1988, the first and by then ex-coordinator identified to me what her objectives and mission had been. These general objectives encompass the specific points of the "Reglamento": to individualize vendors and train them to act as autonomous agents in the tourist market (see Appendix, articles 6, 8, 10, 11, 13, 15a–g, 16c, 16d); to domesticate vending practices and eliminate the customary rights by which vendors occupied the zone according to a Western ethic of property and business (see articles 3a, 11, 15b, 16e, 16f, 16g); to effect a control of vendors through the organization, arrangement, and regulation of space, particularly the spaces of display and activities (see articles 3a, 11, 15b, 16e, 16f, 16g); to instill a consciousness of individual responsibility and rights through the designation of one-to-one relations of functions to the "concessionaires" and CULTUR (see articles 10, 13, 15a–g); to train vendors to internalize a Western aesthetic of responsibility toward the ecology and the ruins as cultural patrimony (see articles 10, 13, 15b, 15f, 15g, 16e, 16f, 16g); to train vendors to practice a self-surveillance or internalized policing of illegalities (see articles 15a, 15d, 15e, 15g); to eliminate outsiders (nonlocal Maya) from among the vendors and artisans as a way of preventing a reinvasion of the zone (see article 7); to exclude non-Yucatec artisanry from the merchandise sold in order to purify Maya culture in the tourist promotion of Yucatán (see article 7). Only with the realization of these goals could a "traditional" market be invented (see articles 3b, 4, 5, 7) and managed for the general good of the state and the interests of tourism (see articles 1, 2, 3a, 3c, 9, 12, 13, 14, 15a–g, 16a–g, 17, 18, 19).

In this disciplinary regime, space is the critical mechanism and target of power: the imposition of a spatial order is the means not only to constitute a sociopolitical order, but to realize the ultimate, if implicit, goal of modifying the subjectivity of the Maya as vendors. A revised, shorter list of rules for the Tianguis, distributed by the second coordinator (a male) on February 16, 1988, makes these points:

1. Avoid the display of merchandise (blankets, hats, etc.) outside the concession area of the *puestos* [i.e., "stalls," which are of two types, one by one-meter *mesas* or tables, and *locales,* two by two-meter areas on the wall perimeter of the building].
2. Change the lightbulbs that correspond to your stall.
3. Do not:
   a. Bring cassette players or music that alters the original [electrical] system installed in the building.
   b. Arrive drunk or under the influence of alcohol.
   c. Bring and deal with personal issues or family problems in the Tianguis.
   d. Play cards or dominos during work hours on the "tables," in the "locales," or on the floor.
   e. Eat inside the areas of the stalls or in the Tianguis, *because this looks very bad and it makes things dirty.*
4. Maintain the area that pertains to you clean; sweep it and clean it.
5. Pay the rent on time. (Author's translation; emphasis added)

Under the first coordinator, rule 1 was strictly interpreted and enforced. Merchandise, specifically blankets, hats, and wooden or concrete idols, could not be placed on the floor in the aisles directly beside a stall. Nor could any type of shelving or apparatus for hanging merchandise be built on top of the tables or on the walls. All materials had to be displayed horizontally on the few meters of space that were rented. This amounted to a direct attack on the vendors, who had strung ropes for up to ten meters along a path to hang cloth products and had set up, along this full length, plywood and crate tables loaded with all other types of products. By severely restricting the merchandise that could be sold and minimizing the attractiveness of each vendor's display, the interests of the large handicraft merchants and guides had been served. In the zone, the vendors as a group seemed to have cut deeply into the profits of the artisanry stores and into the guide commission that was paid for bringing charters to these stores. This extreme rule about displays was a punitive measure that was relaxed under the second coordinator.

Even if temporarily enforced, its effect was critical for vendors, whose commerce is in a highly elastic market. In the zone, vendor use of space was a tactic of competition (the increased appropriation of space to display would push out competitors); the first defense against such a maneuver was to counter with the same tactic (arrive earlier than the competition to stake the space). Attempts to legitimate a permanent occupation and usurpation of a selling space with a stall would be destroyed. Verbal threats, vandalism, stealing, intimidation, and violence were the tactics of enforcement. Disputes easily escalated into factional struggles as the only way individuals could protect or further their interests. With the imposition of civility, authority, and order, such power tactics were strictly out of place. Instead, the vendors could wage their antagonisms through policing the illegalities of the competition.

The new rules of display hurt everyone in the Tianguis. Yet, if one or another person were to break the rule in a frustrated attempt to increase sales, it would directly jeopardize the sales of that vendor's neighbors; view of and access to other displays would be blocked by bulging clothes or hats hanging in the corridor. The motivation to retaliate was strong, but the old tactics were no longer viable. Thus, vendors would resort to the sanctions imposed by CULTUR and report any illegalities of one's enemies. The vendors became trained to police themselves and to enforce a rule that in the long run would be catastrophic to their individual and collective interests.

Other prohibitions (rule 3) on improper activities and use of space were created. This both consolidated the training in self-surveillance and worked to break customary practices that were deemed improper for a "traditional" market. The market was to be a place of business, not of diversions (drinking, cards, dominos), family affairs (children, gossip, personal problems), or food. These illegalities were gendered and engendered a male-female antagonism that was propagated by the vendors themselves. If the men could not amuse themselves, then women with children could not bring them into the Tianguis. In other words, vendors, who already knew to watch each other, learned to *police* themselves in the reporting of newly constituted illegalities to authorities. To counter the report by women of the improper use of space for alcoholic diversion, the affected males reported the impropriety of children. This policing broke down old factions into more localized struggles around the displays of *mesas*. In turn, new sets of alliances and antagonisms were generated. Warnings and threats of expulsion were levied by the coordinators, but the illegalities continued with increased discretion or behind the Tianguis in less visible, "back" spaces; and the denunciations persisted: the tactics that facilitated the insertion of external control were also the tactics of resistance to it. Official warnings and threats of sanctions became hollow. Enforcement of unfair or unappreciated rules was always fraught with the counterthreat of reinvasion.

The prohibition of food contributed to a tension of genders and class, but the main target was both more concrete (food vendors) and more abstract (vendor consciousness). Although both handicraft and food vendors had invaded the zone, the former were "given" the Tianguis, and the latter were simply outlawed. There was to be no peddling of food. Under the concerted demands of the handicraft vendors, guides, INAH workers, policemen, and employees from all of the stores in the Parador, an exception was made for two food establishments; they were given informal concessions by CULTUR to set up a few tables and a small *palapa* on a secluded dirt road behind the parking lot. Thus, vendors had a designated place to eat, but this compromise differentiated between those rich enough to *buy* their daily lunch and those who could not afford it; it also differentiated between men who had greater privilege to move in public spaces and more traditional women—specifically women with children—who would or could not leave their locales and necessarily had their lunches brought to them by their husbands, an adult child, or another relative. At any rate, of those who could afford to buy lunch, none could really afford the time away from their stalls at the most concentrated moment of tourist bodies. Put simply, people preferred to eat in private and to bring food to their stalls and share with relatives or paid workers, called *chalans*.

The illegality of food can thus be understood to be intimately linked with the juridical status of the vendors. The state, through CULTUR, owns the building complex and has granted space concessions to the vendors for them to display and sell handicrafts. In the legal contract they must sign, the vendors are designated as *concesionarios* (concessionaires) who pay a monthly *fruto civil* (levy or fee). Significantly, it is *not rent*. This legal labeling is a tactic of power that exploits a critical ambiguity between the legal status of renters that was being imposed and the communal sense of ownership and use rights of Pistéleños.

The vendors and artisans, as people from Pisté, but also from other nearby villages or hamlets such as Xcalacoop and San Francisco, have an internalized sense of identity with the ruins; Chichén *belongs* to them. As members of these communities, they have communal rights of property: it is *their* history, culture, *ejido* land, and community patrimony. It is on this premise that the invasion was possible in the first place, that the vendors remained entrenched in the zone for so many years, and that the vendors can continue to threaten a reinvasion as a last resort against disempowerment by the state. Note that all of the INAH workers had lived inside the zone and when they were displaced from their homes they were granted certain privileges: in the form of a cooperative store, INAH workers were given a *palapa* on the path to old Chichén where they could sell handicrafts, food, and beverages. Further, the Tianguis was only effective as a war treaty under the condition that these privileges were withdrawn because they unfairly disadvantaged the mass of vendors, who had an "equal" right to Chichén. If the vendors could not sell inside the zone, no one could, they argued, including INAH workers and fruit peddlers.[12] Although the vendors had no institutional backing of their interests, the wardens did, and it is said that the *coordinadora* lost her post in the struggle to enforce the expulsion of the INAH *cooperativa* from the zone.

The wording of the contract, then, avoided direct confrontation with the traditional rights of property and ownership. The orally transmitted convention was eroded gradually by the authority of the written laws, which targeted space as a problem. Vendors entered the Tianguis with the mistaken sense that they "owned" their stalls, that they were given to them as part of their "rights" to sell at Chichén. The legal designation of improprieties and responsibilities forged a new understanding of what it meant to "own" a stall in the Tianguis. At the same time that one was exhorted and constrained to change one's lightbulbs, clean one's stall, and maintain the public bathroom (see article 13, Appendix H), unwanted (and sometimes unwarranted) prohibitions were imposed: no drinking, no cards, no dominos, no children, no eating, no personal problems.

What sense does it make if one owns one's stall but an *outsider* prohibits one from eating in it? The appeal to a presumably shared aesthetic — "it looks very bad and it makes things dirty" (rule 3e) — is clear enough. The vendors are renters, not owners. Further, as if they were children, they must be *taught* to behave in the capitalist marketplace as law-abiding and individualized entrepreneurs. Ultimately, the question of training ("Westernizing") the petty handicraft merchants to be responsible free agents in the tourist market has a strategic goal: to strip the vendors of any economic advantage they had enjoyed in the zone and to force them to play by the rules that capitalist interests are able to control in their favor. Specifically, the name of the game is commissions, the gratuity paid to the guides by the artisanry stores so that a steady flow of charter groups is brought in to buy. In this juncture of power, the vendors of the Tianguis are caught in an either/or option: operate as individual agents or mobilize in the form of a collectivity. Thus, the disciplinary regime (the subjectivity or consciousness of the individual vendor) and of the politics of tourism (vendor mobilization) are extensions of each other. To close the present chapter, I return to this issue and to the political struggles surrounding commissions.

When I arrived in Chichén in late 1987, the vendors were still in a critical transition period. They were seeking new alliances among themselves under CULTUR's informal prohibition against unions and other collective forms of action. In this context, my ethnographic practice once again indicated that I was policing the Tianguis. Generally, blocked from information about the invasion, I inquired about contemporary political struggles and the problem of the guide commission. My questions sounded suspicious: How were the vendors dealing with the loss of clientele that resulted from their relocation? Who wanted to form a collectivity to pay commissions? Who were opposed to this and why?

To reiterate, the spaces of this "traditional" market were to be maintained free of excess and inappropriate behaviors, things, and persons. An ordering of space, by which it was divided, arranged, designated, and distributed, clearly inscribed the automatic and autonomous hegemony of an imposed control. In this situation, my presence as an ethnographer was highly problematic. Perhaps more than is usually the case for the field-worker, I was matter out of place—that is, dirty and dangerous. Physically, there was no place for me in the Tianguis. Even the simple act of observation was problematic. I wanted to observe the interactions of vendors and tourists, but where was I to stand to do so? If vendors were fighting each other over the position of stacks of blankets or hanging merchandise because they block access and lines of vision, where was I to stand to "scientifically" observe the interaction between vendors and tourists? Although I could move about, I was just as obstructive as a thick mound of *huipiles* (traditional female dress) hanging in a one-meter aisle. Initially, I learned more about displacing myself from the scenes I wanted to study than the tactical exchanges themselves.

When there were no tourists, I could stand, sit, or lean almost anywhere and converse with vendors. But when tourists entered, conversations had to be put aside as attention turned to business. To stand by a stall where tourists were shopping was distracting to either tourists or vendor, or both. Other vendors would position themselves near their merchandise either to engage tourists who came to look or to verbally hook a tourist passing by. If I stood away from the stall where a tourist was shopping, I would position myself in the way of the other vendors, who were waiting their turn to address tourists as they moved from stall to stall. My tactics of observation had to mime the movements of the vendors as they paced their stalls. During moments of high volume, I was completely in the way.

At first, I simply took myself out of the Tianguis to avoid antagonism and out of respect. I was well aware that vendors would lodge formal complaints with the coordinator against anyone who seemed intentionally to obstruct tourist access to their stalls. Because rush time is between 12:00 noon and 2:00 P.M., I took lunch then, after which I would return and continue with conversations. As I developed friendships, I was able to better position myself. I would stand against a wall to observe or "duck" into the locale of a friend. The key difference was that *they allowed me the momentary space* to stand and talk as if I were one of them.

On more than one occasion, vendors would utilize me as tactic to attract a tourist, particularly if it was noticed that I was not a tourist and not a Mexican/vendor. My writing, notebooks, and dress were all signs of difference; but the biggest clue was that I was hanging out with the vendors and speaking Maya with them. If a passing tourist was curious, the people I was with would typically engage the tourist in a discussion of Maya language. Although hooking a sale was a basic goal, another objective was manifest: by highlighting how this gringo had learned their language, Maya were making an explicit statement about the value of Maya vis-à-vis Spanish and Mexican/ Yucatec culture through an association between Maya and North America. Just as often vendors would tell me in Maya to talk to passing tourists in order to hook them for a sale. After an initial hesitation lasting several weeks, I realized that this was a kind of double classroom situation to which I had to respond.

I had become an exploitable resource. In itself this was not an issue, but it posed a strategic problem of method. I had decided not to do the kind of participant observation suggested by one of my advisers: to participate intensively with one family or set of persons by assisting in their work routines. To do so in this context would have been a radical interference, not in "native culture" but in the economic balance of the vendors. It seemed to promise a great relationship with a handful of persons, but major antagonisms with 115 others. It was this consideration that led me to opt for the "panoptical" strategy. This meant that I was always just "hanging out" in the Tianguis, moving around in the different areas and talking with ("informally interviewing") different persons or groups (and giving English lessons), but always watching and writing notes. Is it any wonder that I was considered a spy?

Certainly, my relationship with the second coordinator fueled suspicions. We developed a strong friendship based in part on our concern for Maya culture.[13] I spent many hours in conversation ("informal interview") in his office. No doubt this close association raised some questions concerning my status and purpose in the Tianguis. When asked by someone concerned, the coordinator would always affirm that I was making an *independent* and "important" investigation at

Chichén of Maya culture; his own understanding of my research was shaded by his own interest in cultural-mystical aspects of Maya traditions. However, the truth, even if believed, is not always as intelligible or meaningful as actions. In this regard, my attempt to observe his daily routines as coordinator resulted in a difficult situation.

He would make an afternoon tour of the Tianguis to maintain surveillance on activities, that is, to check on problems that had been reported earlier in the day, to be told of new ones, and to maintain a visible profile as authority. He would arbitrate problems — as, I suspect, his predecessor did — and conduct one-on-one business in his office; group issues, however, were mediated in the vendor territory of the Yanguis. Two months into fieldwork, I became aware of such problems, which were typically accusations of illegalities or of one vendor stealing merchandise from another. One afternoon I asked the coordinator if he would allow me to sit in on cases of arbitration for purposes of my research. He stated — correctly — that this would require the consent of both the director of CULTUR and the parties concerned, which did not seem likely. Instead, he invited me to go with him to the Tianguis. Entering on one side of the "V"-shaped, covered corridor we strolled through greeting everyone and stopping with one person and then another. He would introduce me as an investigator and ask a general question about the vendor's work that day. Soon enough, I realized that I was assisting him on his policing tour and that there was no way out of the trap. Although I tried to break from him by getting into a conversation and letting him proceed without me, he insisted that I complete the tour with him.

At once insignificant and pregnant with implications, an association had been established between myself and CULTUR that took months to dismantle. It seemed clear that I was some kind of agent working directly or indirectly with the government. It was yet another correspondence that situated me in the grid of power/knowledge relations that operate in the Tianguis. Despite explanations about the ethics and objectives of my research, I was intelligible as an ambiguous, thus dangerous, agent of external interests. In practice, my fieldwork appeared to everyone as a kind of policing. As a result, most people would not respond to my informal questions about the invasion or commissions; my requests for formal interviews were politely deferred. Nonetheless, I was able to collect other types of information as I waited for the mythical "big break" in fieldwork and data collection. It did not occur until September 1988 in the context of a failed attempt to organize the payment of commissions.

The *vendedores* have a long history of conflict among themselves. On the one hand, there were personal/family antagonisms and individualized struggles for space during the invasion. On the other hand, conflict and factions also derived from attempts at cooperative group action vis-à-vis the state, guides, and the INAH. Nonetheless, this internal discord and the multiplicity of invading groups that could unify or segment, depending on the context, gave the vendors a form of mass political power that took several years to domesticate and control. As the first coordinator explained to me, CULTUR's primary objective was to neutralize their political power through an erosion and reshaping of old antagonisms and alliances. Underlying the political differences, however, is a religious, social, and economic heterogeneity that has fueled conflict and opposition among vendors.[14] This heterogeneity congealed in radically different perspectives, attitudes, and goals on the business of selling. The displacement of roughly half the invading vendors into the Tianguis did eventually reduce the five or six major factions to two, which correspond to the two wings of the building. But, if the battle lines and alliances were effectively redrawn, it is only because the terrain on which the war of tourism was conducted was transformed. Half the vendors refused to enter the Tianguis precisely as a resistance to external control, a foreign work discipline, the economic game of commissions, and the market mentality of individual action.

Those who entered the Tianguis were willing to submit to these impositions, but only to a certain extent. A majority viewed these changes as enabling and empowering their economic pursuits; the incorporation of Western or capitalist ideas would allow them to take greater advantage of tourism. Others, the "traditionally closed-minded" Maya, experienced the new disciplinary regime as an attack on their mode of individuality. Both wage a war against their fellow adversaries, criticizing and blaming the mentality of the other for their worsening situation vis-à-vis guides, store owners, and the state. It is along these lines that the vendors divided into "new" bands in their political struggles and new forms of resistance to hegemonic control were developed and practiced.

It is critical to note that the imposition of an external order relied on the invention of illegalities, but that these disciplinary tactics were only effective to the extent that the vendors *used and manipulated* them as tactics of resistance. Whereas the imposition of authority can be represented in a top to bottom movement, the institutionalization of disciplinary control moved from the bottom to the top. The apparatus of power was pieced together from the bottom through multiple points of resistance. Thus, as Foucault has postulated, "Where there is power there is resistance" (1980: 95; also 92–98). It is this grid of power/knowledge relations, formed from tactical manipulations, that gave shape to the events of the invasion and continues to shape the ongoing political struggles in which the vendors are caught in a heterogeneous war of multiple dimensions.

9 / Departures from the Museum

Ethnographic Espionage and the
Topography of Culture

A Recipe for Travel

Guiding the analyses woven together in this text has been the work of
Michel de Certeau, among others. I turn to him again for a tip on where
to take this ethnographic description of tourism and anthropology at
Chichén Itzá as we are about to take leave of its Museum. In a brief discussion on the work of Foucault, de Certeau underscores the elements
that compose his art of making theory, that is, of "panoptical fictions."
De Certeau suggests that there is a kind of "recipe" to Foucault's art,
which leads him to offer a methodological principle and a hypothesis:

> Procedures are not merely the objects of a theory. They organize
> the very construction of theory itself.... In order to clarify the
> relationship of theory with those procedures that produce it as
> well as with those that are its objects of study, the most relevant
> way would be a *storytelling discourse.* ... In this hypothesis, a
> *narrative theory would be indissociable from any theory of prac-*
> *tices,* for it would be its precondition as well as its production.
> (De Certeau 1986: 192)

There's No Place like Home

This guidebook on anthropology and tourism at Chichén has not
sought to go "beyond" culture (Gupta and Ferguson 1992) as much

as to develop a conceptual frame that can comprehend, dissect, and theorize the heterogeneous and continuous *invention* of culture(s) as an ongoing activity and everyday reality, however sedimented in encompassing formations. The assumption has been that travel, understood as the intersection and divergence of textual, mental, discursive, and spatial trajectories in time, comprises a logic and practice by which cultures are invented, that is, *inscribed* in the imagination and imagined through inscription on bodies and the multiple media of social life. We have already seen how travel inhabits memory, not only in classical rhetoric, but in the modern museum and in the orchestration of tourism. From topos to topos, the traveler moves in time and mind, demanding the contents deposited in each figure located there at each stop to see, say, and reenact its inscription with a difference. And, as the traveler moves across this topography of identities, belongings, memories, places, practices, and discourses, this landscape is itself *mapped* in its being *toured*. Here, then, we explore travel as an art of culture by which communities are fashioned and by which imagined communities are traversed as cultures (cf. Clifford 1992). In this theory of practices or practice of telling stories, a culture and cultures are the artifice within economies of travel. By this I refer to the logic by which points of departure (places of self-identity) and destinations (places of the other) are differentiated as bounded entities and alternated. This concluding chapter is a story of an incident whose unraveling takes us crisscrossing a topography in fragments. The story begins in and returns to a question, which will be the place of departure and a destination of the narrative, because an "economy of travel requires an *oikos* (the Greek for 'home' from which is derived 'economy') in relation to which any wandering can be *comprehended* (enclosed as well as understood) [as travel]" (Van Den Abbeele 1992: xviii). But instead of complying with the teleology of travel, this narrative seeks as its "final" destination not a return home, but a return to the movement and gestures of travel itself.

"You Who Travel in All Places, What Do You Tell Us about the *Narco-Santánicos* of Pisté?"

This was the question posed to me one day in mid-June 1989 by the mayor of the town of Pisté, Yucatán, Mexico.[1] He had called me off the street and into his office as I walked home from a day of ethnographic fieldwork at the ruins of Chichén Itzá. I had spent the day interviewing artisans about their war with the government and restaurant owners who were trying to prohibit the *vendedores* from selling handicrafts on the streets in front of their restaurants.[2] But in that instant, the ethnographer became informant and suspect as an *eyewitness*.[3] Sitting on a wooden chair in front of the *comisario,* who was seated behind a teacher's desk discarded by the elementary school, I quickly sized up the two persons poised on the bench beside us. One was a campesino about sixty years old, in clothes worn to tatters by the milpa he cleared in the jungle; in the space between Robert Redfield's two books on Chan Kom, he had migrated to Pisté from that *village that chose progress*.[4] The other was a man in his early forties, but the taxi that he drove daily to the ruins had provided him with new, clean clothes and prominent silver chains and gold rings. He looked at me with "eyes (almost) like bees" (to use a phrase that once described the Carnegie archeologists who restored the ancient Maya city as a tourist sight). This man is known, however, not for his eyes but for his ears, as an *oreja* (ear), that is, a spy, of the town's resident capitalist. He was also the brother of the mayor who had resigned in 1984 under threat of being lynched. Why? To the town's displeasure, the brother had illegally sold a huge and very valuable piece of real estate to that very same capitalist. This property, on which was built the largest restaurant in Pisté and Chichén, figured prominently in this businessman's attempts to monopolize the market for charter-group lunches as well as in his plans to develop a hotel. These plans, needless to say, also entailed eliminating — with government help — the competition of street vendors that plagued his handicraft store.

"What should I say?" I thought.

I knew the town had a "devil" of sorts, at least from the comment of one *vendedor,* who promised me that "one day [his] balls would heat up and he would shoot that *hijo de puta*." Devilish, perhaps, but this man, whom everyone loved to hate, was too sober to be into drugs. In any case, his *vecino* (neighbor) and longtime rival (as both a guide and an owner of a handicraft store, and even as a suitor of the same woman) had crossed the street to visit him close to midnight that day in March 1989 when the northern sky became soaked in a deep and ominous red, and, wielding a hammer (for no apparent reason) as he pulled out his revolver, said, "Your hour has come; here ends your life!" Let me translate from the newspaper report, whose Spanish syntax economically illustrates the way travel, here of the body, reciprocally maps identities as it tours spaces:

> Alberto Hoil, by instinct raised his hands, receiving the impact with the index finger of his left hand, redirecting the projectile [from the heart], which finally penetrated at the height of the thorax, and fell to the floor. The aggressor left screaming, "You will never escape me because wherever you are I am going to kill you and nobody is going to do anything to me," as he finally directed himself to his house. Andrade Hoil, fifty-two years of age, was transported to this city [Mérida]. . . . [The would-be assassin] fled, and is currently finding himself in flight. (*Novedades* 1989)

I should add that Alberto — being alive and healthy now — is a man whose interventions in town hall have always led to problems. The mayor in 1989 — that is, my ethnographic inquisitor — was the target of an attempted lynching just a week before Hurricane Gilberto devastated Yucatán on September 14, 1988 (Burgos 1988b). Why? Allegedly, he was illegally selling valuable *ejido* lands to Alberto, who had assumed the suspicious habit of visiting the mayor in town hall at night behind closed doors. His subsequent absence from town clearly facilitated the increased unification of certain of Pisté's factions and aided the mobilization of the political movement that sought independence for the community as a new *municipio libre,* that is, the 107th county of the state of Yucatán. The attempted assassination occurred the very same day swathed in red — *chakchahih naaka'an,* they told me when I arrived in Pisté two days later on March 13 — when the town formally inaugurated the movement, called the Lucha 107, with a serpentine procession that led from the outskirts of Chichén Itzá to the center of town and that culminated in a public assembly in which speakers petitioned God, the governor, and the state congress in the name of their ancestral Itzá Maya (see *Diario de Yucatán* 1989a).[5] Thus, three months later, I realized again that he and his body were missing from the scene of interrogation. Yet, sitting there in that office, I sensed that his hand, or maybe that index finger, was still hovering above us as well as the entire tourist industry in Pisté. Certainly, his "ear" had remained, I thought.

"What should I say?" I asked myself as I glanced from the taxi driver to the campesino who migrated from Chan Kom, to the *comi-*

sario, to the opened door framing the road that led past the Evangelical Presbyterian Church to the Castillo of Chichén. But, now, here, in this archaeology of Chichén Itzá, I think all this travel (that is, dismemberment, diversion, and dispersion of parts to different parts, the returning to destinations, the reversal of roles, and the endless dissemination of ethnographic details) reminds me of "culture." It reminds me of the way culture is constructed in local contexts as complex textual "webs" (or assemblages of identities, practices, logics, values), and how, after departing from those scenes, the "webs" are transported and transcribed elsewhere, where they are destined to be rearticulated, respoken, reshaped, repackaged, and rewoven by other travelers in other contexts. But then such texts or cultures in fragments return home whole after traversing a topography inscribed in an economy of travel that marks the boundaries of the spaces it traverses.

"What should I say?" Really, I did not know what exactly or who they were talking about, although I did know, or recalled having known, about a satanic cult in Matamoros, Mexico, that had been reported widely in the international press; this devilish drug gang had abducted babies and Texan spring breakers and taken them to a secluded ranch for sex and sacrifice. Given the number of sightings in southern California, Texas borderlands, and elsewhere, it seems that the late 1980s were a busy time for Satan. For example, immediately following the reports of the Matamoros cult, an abandoned colonial hacienda very near Mérida was the subject of a monthlong exposé disclosing it as the privileged site of another group of *narco-satánicos* who performed ritualized sex, drinking, drug use, magic, and so on. It turned out, however, that the hacienda was only a place where the *juniors* (urban youth of the upper-crust bourgeoisie) took their dates so as to be away from the eyes and ears of moral and secular authorities. The allegations stemmed from local—and much lower-class—Maya who had complained to the police about the orgiastic debaucheries of the rich white folk's weekend fiestas.

I realized finally that my interrogation in town hall, like this "devil hysteria" in Mérida or the Valley (between Texas and Mexico), was a witch-hunt. After all, there was a political struggle afoot and the movement leaders needed to identify enemies within as "devils" and then expel the danger of the internal other, in order to purify and strengthen the community in a communal rite of social, economic, and political solidarity. But still, I wondered: *Who would be these "witches" of Chichén Itzá?*

Sensing my perplexity at his question about *narco-satánicos*, the *comisario* hinted at the doctor of the pharmacy and his wife, who are religious gnostics and practitioners of alternative medicines; the then coordinatoor of the Parador Turístico and his wife, who also are gnostics and spiritualists heavily inspired by Mayan mysteries; the guidebook-famous Calypso, a North American woman who came to live in Pisté at the end of the 1970s to study herbalism, crystals, and healing. Other non-Maya, semipermanent residents of Pisté were also implicated, not necessarily because of a personal association with these persons, but because of shared status as outsiders in terms of class, ethnic, and regional identities. The higher-level managerial positions or appointments of confidence in the six three-star hotels, eight of the ten charter-group restaurants, and nine nationally owned stores are often filled by central Mexican mestizos or white Meridanos who are brought in through family contacts with regional or national owners. These usually young, single, transient persons use their stint in the "boonies" as a step on their career ladder. All come with a definitive predisposition, sometimes racist and very antipathetic to the *indios* of Pisté, or just as often with a sympathic attraction to the ancient Maya. The careerists do not make for happy residents of the town and quickly seek to move on and up to their next job in Cancún. Those attracted to the ancient Maya typically develop a spiritual awakening or sensibility to the folkloric-shamanic aura of the ruins and the romanticized rural Maya lifestyle. This localized *foreign* "elite" of the tourist industry forms a sterile community that lives parasitically on Pisté with ambivalent interethnic/class relations much like a colonialist enclave. More than one such temporary manager, for example, has sought to "help" the town through interventions that ultimately center on teaching the "ignorant locals" how to behave (like mestizos) when selling artisanry, to respect the ruins of the ancient Maya, and to protect the tourist image of Pisté. Although it certainly would be worthwhile to expunge the town of such personages, it was not *these* persons of the managerial community, who pursue local politics for personal gain, who were being associated by the mayor with *narco-satánicos*. Rather, the would-be witches—who, indeed, *would be*—are those who become enthralled with the archeologized Maya for mystical and mysterious reasons.

At this moment in our travel narrative, we must map a parallel route to a place, a metaplace, both above and below this point, where the story can continue to be told in both ethnologic and ethnographic modes. Although the individuals comprising this managerial group share a general class affinity with the *bolsa* guides, the differences (transient versus permanent; Mexican or Yucatecan versus Yucatecan or Maya; urban versus rural backgrounds) only solidify a boundary of social interaction between these two subcommunities. Nonetheless, they both participate in and form part of an imagined community that I call *subterranean Maya culture*. This phenomenon is both local and translocal, that is, it exists in localized places but traverses and weaves together multiple locations in a discontinuous and fragmentary fashion. By this term, I refer to the *lived-in* "culture pattern" of Maya romanticization that occurs in everyday discourses and practices throughout Yucatán and even beyond the region by Maya, Yucateco, Mexican, Anglo-American, and European. Taussig (1987) provides a model for what I am seeking to isolate here when he discusses the way the Indian operates as a polyvalent and ambiguous image (trope and practice) for non-Indian and Indian alike as the authentic, naturalized source of healing. This *culture*—for surely it is such in the sense of traditional theory—of the appropriation and reinvention of the Indian as originary belonging has many *regional* variations: much New Age spiritualism in the United States and Mexico is blatantly such a way, logic, system, and structure of life that forges crisscrossing communities through the operations of an Indianized Wild Healer/Mystic. As discursive practices, these appropriations could be understood as the practice of and participation in a *survival literature*; the difference is that these reinventions of the Indian are not scientific discourses on "what is nature" or "what is civilization," but are *occult* practices of community formation constituted through discourses on "what is spiritual essence of being." Thus, in the Yucatec situation, the Indian is Maya and has become the pivot of a *survival culture*, if you will, which can be discussed as a subterranean Maya culture, one species in the invention of the Maya that contrasts with but relates to another, the state's archeologizing *culture of the pyramid*.

Certainly, the genealogy of this imaginary community traces back to the nineteenth- and early twentieth-century folklorization of the Yucatec Indian. Whereas we have discussed the archeologization of the Maya as the forging of ruins as a cultural patrimony for the national/

regional community, the folklorization here entails the transformation of Maya legends, myths, symbolism, history, spirits, healing practices, folk knowledge, and superstitions into a cultural belonging that inhabits the everyday life of Yucatecos, Indian or non-Indian.[6] This is the spirit world of *aluxes* and *xtabai* transculturated from the countryside into urban consciousness as the authenticity of being that has been/is being lost to Westernization. In other words, the imagining of Yucatec regional society as an integrated community composed of subparts and distinct from other Mexicos is built upon this fabrication of the Maya as its heart and blood. A metaphor by which to understand this culture pattern is offered by the karst topography of Yucatán, that is, the soft limestone whose erosion from rain produces a system of underground rivers, cenotes, caverns, and fissures that traverses most of the Yucalpetén ("Neck of the Land," supposedly the Mayan version of Yucatán). Although the region of the Maya has various names, such as "Mayab" and "Land of the Deer and Pheasant," it is the *subterranean streams* that connect up caves, wells, and even the pyramids and temples that give a special definition to the Maya landscape and its peoples. Cenotes in particular figure prominently in the imagining of Yucatán and of the Maya, not only from the academic fetishization of the problem of water in a riverless landscape, but as the home of Chak, the rain god; as portals to the underworld and the ancestral deities and heroes, these liminal topoi are populated by spirits, sacred beings, beauty, dangers, winds, and magical powers. For example, "folklore" collected by Redfield and Villa Rojas tells of how the Itzá fled from the Spaniards into the underground passage of Cenote Xtoloc and filled the portal with water to avoid being pursued; according to prophetic legend, it is from this subterranean world that the Maya will return to reclaim their legitimate rule of the land. The power of the subterranean is indicated in the saying that once a person drinks the water from a cenote, he or she will never leave the land of the Mayab.

Returning from this detour to the "home" of this talk—that is, my day in court—it became clear that this list of persons, all friends of mine, implicated me as well among the putative *narco-satánicos*. After all, I—and the "culture" of which I am among its bearers, that is, *ethnography*—travel, like the subterranean rivers, in all parts: I participated not only in the neo-Aztec foot-washing ceremony the night before the equinox and the group meditation in the doorway of the Caracol at dawn, but also in agricultural rituals, Catholic and Evangelical church activities, tourism in Cancún, and the political rituals of waiting for Pisté to become an independent municipality.[7] Further, "my culture"—call it "anthropology"—was also already deeply implicated in the history and contemporary life of the communities concerned (Pisté, the Mexican nation, Yucatec society, New Age and indigenist revivals). "My culture," which travels the world to witness and report on the cultures imagined in all possible communities, was always already there in court as accomplice, informant, juror, and reporter.

So, now I thought, "What *do* I say?" What could I say and, just as important, *how* could I say it so as to circumvent injurious scandal? Indeed, what do I *say* I said? "What do I *write down* to say I said" for reader and author to read? What indeed can and should be written about the ethnographic encounter?

Later, in the act of writing, it seems to me that this *duplicity* and *complicity* of *ethnographic espionage* are at the heart of the question, "How does culture travel?" What are the circuits by which *culture travels*? As it traverses the landscape of imaginary communities, how does culture constitute topographies—and topography, cultures? Ethnographic espionage, I argue, can be understood as that mechanism through which "cultures" are imported, exported, deported, transported, reported across cultural topographies. It is a mechanism of inscription through which communities are imagined specifically as *cultures*. This espionage—call it the discursive practice of culture— has been central to the historical settlement and reterritorialization of culture in Yucatán and elsewhere. Indeed, it may be a paradigmatic case of the economy of culture or what I have been calling scriptural economy.

Sending off, Signing off: A Dead Letter

A more traditional analysis of the story so far would continue to narrate the socioeconomic basis of conflicting factions and correlate these to the different religious/cultural/ethnic postures of the agents involved. In this alternative story that is not told here, the event of my cross-examination would be a key to an extended case study of how local politics is waged in an idiom of religion and ethnic-national antagonisms.

Having mapped such a code by which socioeconomic relations translate into religious-ethnic identities, the analysis would have then constituted an imaginary community in which an alliance of one series of factions brands another less powerful, but economically more successful, faction as *narco-satánicos*. The stage would then be set for the danger within to be exorcised, thereby inventing if not quite a homogeneous, at least an integrated and definitively modernizing, even if still traditional, community. This internal integration, of course, would be concomitant with an externalizing move or incorporation of the collectivity at three levels (the social community of the region, the political community of the nation, the global community of international economics). This plot is found in the story of Chan Kom told by both Redfield and his critics (Goldkind 1965, 1966; Stricken 1965). The master narrative of the Redfieldian and the anti-Redfield variations of this plot is organized by the *figure of the road* penetrating the jungles of tribal society and irrevocably Westernizing primitive life-forms (Villa Rojas 1977; Sullivan 1989; R. Thompson 1974; Press 1975; Sosa 1985): It paves the way for the massive intervention of the "outside," that is, modernity, whose effects are either orderly "progress" as in Chan Kom or cultural fragmentation, heterogeneity, corruption of language, loss of values, and abandonment of tradition as in the urban type of community. Whereas in the former scenario, there is national integration with the maintenance of cultural integrity, the latter entails national assimilation with a reduction of culture to a zero degree of mestizo ethnicity.[8] These are complementary stories that together, even the critical versions, comprise the narrative of the Folk-Urban Continuum. It is this vision that is inscribed in the Yucatec landscape and that continues to provide the dominant lens by which regional society is imagined.

The problem with this metanarrative of Maya culture is that it assumes that history started yesterday for the non-Western other; this is why it is saturated with an imperialist nostalgia. We have already seen that the historical complicity between tourism, anthropology, U.S. business and political interests, Mexican nation building, Yucatec regionalism, local Maya society, and Maya nationalisms goes back at least to the nineteenth century; Pisté and Chichén are living artifacts of that historical collusion. The problem with this form of analysis is based on an avoidance of that complicity and the traveling economy of culture, that is, the way space (textual and physical-geographic) are traversed and reinscribed as places within contested topographies. The problem with Pisté, then, is that it does not fit into the Yucatec landscape according to this narrative: it is a postmodernist zero-degree culture community. And, we shall find that in the space between the indifference of Pisté in the 1920s and 1930s and the political passions of the 1980s and 1990s, Pisté has progressed to zero-degree culture.

A Different Path: A Step Back

A sign that should alert us to the possibilities of a different reading and story is expressed by a key event: in contrast to other ethnographies of Yucatán, the plot thickens *not* when the road opens in 1936, but when, in 1983, the road that was built in 1924, from Mérida through to the archeological zone of Chichén, was closed. In Maya consciousness, the metaphor of closed roads connotes *war*, that is, communicative disruption, civil disorder, and struggle both within the community and between it and the outside world.

Remember that the closing of the road inaugurates the invasion of the archeological zone by three hundred vendors of artisanry and food. This tourist war escalates with the near death of an artisan during an interclan fight; a policeman is attacked by an artisan with a machete; the military and labor unions are called in to extract the *artesanos*. In 1984, the first state government-sponsored celebration of the equinox and the first of two attempted lynchings of Pisté mayors occur. In 1987, civil disorders—*inconformidades,* as they say—spread throughout the countryside as the opposition PAN (Partido de Acción Nacional) gains support and feeds the fire of discontent; the "traditional" handicraft market is built within the new Parador of Chichén, thereby ending the invasion, but the war continues (Burgos 1988a, 1988d; *Diario de Yucatán* 1988). The political and economic crises of the PRI and the nation crescendo in 1988. Millenarian omens and signs of change in the national culture flourish. Locally, the year-long antagonism against the mayor's faction that had come into power escalates in a physical attack in August due to his apparent attempt to privatize prized *ejido* land (Burgos 1988b, 1988c). Seven days later, Hurricane Gilberto destroys Cancún and mutilates the economy; the governor steals emergency aid and sells it to a regional chain of grocery stores. Carlos Salinas de Gortari assumes the presidency and sacks "La Quina," the scapegoat of Mexican corruption—officially rerouting the national economy from oil and debt to tourism and "swaps" in preparation for free trade. Salinas de Gortari promises to reform the political culture.

In this context, Refugio, the mayor of town, begins in January 1989 a series of petitions sent directly to the new president in which both emergency aid and the juridical transformation of the town to a county are requested. In the preceding months, the deterritorialization of the hurricane allowed the mayor's opposition to take de facto hold of the community; this was due, on the one hand, to the fact that aid was more directly forthcoming from the *ejido* (federal) versus the state authorities and, on the other hand, to the successful appropriation of leadership by the *comisario*'s opponents in community rebuilding and mutual help efforts. Among altruistic motives was Refugio's desire to regain his status as authority figure by championing a highly popular cause in the community. The success of the tactic in this regard can be measured by the way the opposition leaders of different factions did not long allow him to be the only voice requesting the legal change to *municipio libre*. Within a month a committee was organized for the purpose (Comité de Lucha 107) and various activities were planned, such as the procession from Chichén Itzá to the town plaza on the night of the assassination attempt (*Diaro de Yucatán* 1989f). A sense of the mayor's petitions can be gained from a letter written months later. On May 5, 1989, he asked Salinas de Gortari to pave the roads of Pisté so as remove both the huge mud puddles of the streets and the *teporochos* (drunks) that tend to lie in them from the sight of tourists; fix the water system, which in its broken condition only services 30 percent of the connected population; expand public electricity beyond the 40 percent then connected; build a baseball diamond for the youth; subsidize more government housing; install a reliable phone system as well as a post office; and, finally, send a specific kind of industrial saw that he, the mayor, can use in his carpentry shop so that he can help the poor people by selling his quality products inexpensively. The saw was important, he asserted to the president, because through it the mayor was then going to continue to convert the populace to the generosity and populist ideals of the PRI, which nonetheless he already insisted was 100 percent PRI-ista. Refugio ended the letter with his own sincere protestation of loyalty to the party and the person of the president.

In this telling expression of the practice of Mexican politics, we enter a destination of this ethnographic travelogue, a topic/topos of the story: what is at stake in this narrative movement to and from the question of *narco-satánicos* is not so much the *politics of identity* as the *identity of politics* and the multiple spatializations of culture in contested topographies. Across the Yucatec landscapes, the 1988 hurricane disrupted the usual structures of authority and procedures of control. In this temporary vacuum, the town of Pisté imagined and rewrote itself as a unified community, not under the banner of Maya culture, nor of Yucatec regionalism, not even of oppositional politics, but of the PRI. Putting aside the violent tactics of local factions, Pisté inaugurated a politics of waiting, of actively soliciting the intervention of the state and of patiently pursuing incorporation into the nation as a zero-degree cultural community. This in itself is interesting because it goes against our traditional ideas of nation building (the nation not as an expanding state, but as an interpellative discourse) and because it is specifically oppositional to the regionalism that Yucatecos are so fond of imagining. Beyond these two points, I argue that this strategy—that is, the conditions of its possibility, its representational practices, and the logic of its tactics—is present in an apparatus of power/knowledge that is embodied in the ruins of Chichén Itzá. This is what I have called the Museum of Maya Culture.

En Route: Waiting for Kukulcan in La Antesala de Chichén Itzá

At the end of his term as president of the republic, Miguel de la Madrid officiated the UNESCO inauguration of Teotihuacán as a Patrimony of Humanity. In the late spring of 1989, it was announced that Chichén was also given this status—without, however, any official ceremony, and only a back-page newspaper announcement. From that moment on, the ten-member committee, or Lucha 107, referred to Pisté as the "*antesala* of Chichén, Patrimony of Humanity" (*antesala* is the front room, the reception room of the house where visitors are entertained, but also where one waits endlessly to speak with a doctor or a government official). This describes not only the socioeconomic reality of Pisté, but also the politics of its struggle and the cultural identity of this politics. The figure of this politics is ritualized in the text of the annually repeated newspaper headlines and the event of the equinox: "40,000 Wait for the Descent of Kukulcan." This representation of the Feathered Serpent is composed by the setting sun, which projects a shadow on the balustrade of the north staircase, against which are also projected eight isoceles triangles of light. This phenomenon is also repeated on the ground. It is a figure of active passivity: passivity in the reception of a translocal and natural authority; active in the prior construction of the stage (the pyramid itself) on which authority is to be received and in the naturalization of the scene of descent (the ritualized event). Further, this naturalization hinges on a prior and automatically repeating erasure of previous writing on the space; this is a deterritorialization that constructs a place "as if" it were empty space, "as if" it were blank like a sheet of paper. It appears that it is the "natural" relationship between sun and earth that lifts the top sheet of this palimpsest by rearranging the relation between the sun and the pyramid. It is the heart of a scriptural economy through which heterogeneous discursive practices invent and disseminate knowledge of the Maya as culture/texts. My argument here is that this same logic of the equinox, this economy of culture, intercedes in the way politics is practiced and communities are imagined in Pisté.

A Topographic Map and a Journey in History

The archeological record suggests that the space where the contemporary town Pisté is located had always been a settled community, both as part of and as far back as the founding of Chichén Itzá. As a separate juridical, demographic, and political entity, Pisté per se probably did not come into existence until the early 1700s. Although insignificant during the colonial period, Independence in 1821 brought a prosperity to the community and region; Pisté grew to a population of eleven hundred inhabitants that was devoted to mixed corn and cattle production. The Caste War that began in 1847, however, transformed the region into a battle zone as semiautonomous indigenous groups farther east and south attacked and depopulated the region from Valladolid in the east to the older towns to the west of Pisté. The surviving population of Pisté fled north to Tinum and returned only sporadically in the subsequent decades. Continued military raids by the Cruzob or Rebel Maya, such as on Pisté in 1862 and in the 1880s, transformed the region into a permanent frontier zone until the pacification of the Cruzob in 1902. Although a military garrison was stationed in Pisté in defense of creole order, the war had dismantled the structures of authority and the people of Pisté—the majority Maya—on at least two occasions wrote letters to Valladolid requesting intervention by the state to stop the Mexican soldiers from stealing, raping, and otherwise abusing the community.[9] The absence of a strong regional or even national structure of authority lasted some seventy years in places such as Pisté before the state began its slow reterritorialization of the countryside.

Outside of the economic core of creole Yucatán, the infiltration of the state began after the "arrival" of the Mexican Revolution (Joseph 1982). Rural paramilitary squads were organized by the urban *liberales* to terrorize peasants and prevent their mobilization as a revolutionary force. As Redfield and Villa Rojas (1934) describe the history of Chan Kom, however, a countermilitia was organized by the *socialistas* from many towns in the region that waged a successful counterattack. From this moment on, Pisté and these related towns became socialist, 100 percent *socialista* according to the rhetoric of politically involved persons and octogenarians I have interviewed. Such claims, however, belie a long process by which the state apparatus became planted in the countryside primarily through the *ejido* land-grant system (federal) and the socialist leagues (state level). In Pisté there was a third arm of the state, the precursor to the INAH, that began to link the local to the "outside," specifically to the federal dimension of authority. But these links to the national and regional communities were weak and Pisté seemed to enjoy an "indifferent" kind of autonomy in the following decades as the host to the Carnegie factory of knowledge at Chichén. Unlike Chan Kom and twenty-eight other communities that had the requisite population size of five hundred adult males, Pisté was unable to take advantage of the 1917 Constitution that allowed communities to become a *municipio libre* or "free county." The irony is that it would be through this authority structure that promised greater political autonomy and economic viability to communities that the Mexican Revolution and its heir, the PRI, would be able to extend its control into the rural recesses of the nation. Pisté instead remained a *comisaría* in the jurisdiction of the county of Tinum. It was only later with the advent of mass tourism at Chichén that the community would unsuccessfully seek its "freedom" as a county in the 1960s, again in the early 1970s, then again in 1979–81 and in 1987.

Why did these early attempts fail? Listen to the public discourse of Lucha 107 in 1989 as reported by the press. Here is the *comisario ejidal*, the man who directed the opposition against the mayor in 1988, who maps out styles of national integration that correspond to imagined communities: "Patience has its limits and that of Pisté has finished. We are tired of living under traps and now we are going to struggle peacefully and without hatred so that the authorities realize that we have sufficient maturity to become a *municipio libre*." [10] Three kinds of patience operate here to define three political communities. First, there is the naive (or even ironic) suffering and tolerance of Maya villages that endure the corruption, lies, and containment strategies of the state government with childlike resistance. Pisté, the speaker implies, *was* one of these docile Maya villages that could not overcome the traps of containment. Second, there is the "patience"— rather, its lack—of enraged communities in which sporadically violent and rebellious Maya actively seek redress for local problems. This was a direct reference to much of the Yucatec countryside that in 1988 and 1989 was embroiled in various kinds of struggles over municipal power that were waged along party lines; this was the moment when the PAN extended itself from the urban centers of Yucatán into the rural areas by supporting and aggravating factional disputes. Third, there is the calculated patience of adult, rational, mature communities that have risen above the indigenous docility and barbarity to a non-Maya and non-Indian civility, that is, to a mestizo civility. This, then, would be Pisté actively waiting for its noncultural and nonoppositional maturity to be recognized by the reason of authority. These three figures—docility, chaotic barbarity, and active passivity—were used repeatedly to fashion a style of community politics, to imagine a solidarity of belonging through a history of shared struggle, to identify the community as such to itself, and, thus, to represent the collectivity to the public and the state apparatus.

These three figures map a topography of politics as cultural identities within a vision of the nation. The docile Maya dominated below but within, the dangerous Indian enemies and agitators on the borders, and the zero-degree cultural mestizo in the center of society. All three communities operate in and against the context of that which territorializes them: the governmental apparatus, specifically the revolutionary institutions of the *municipio* and the *ejido*. These complementary forms were originally conceived as vehicles for local empowerment, but they now operate as strategies of containment: they channel social unrest into dead-end movements of protest through the familiar tactics of buying off or intimidating leaders, fomenting factions, local espionage, patronage, false promises, and so on. The previous failures of Pisté to become an independent *municipio*, then, are attributed to these counterinsurgency tactics, which easily manipulated an unsophisticated, childish, and docile town of campesinos that was easily factionalized, bought off, and blocked from effectively imagining and fashioning itself as a unified community. Lucha 107 defined itself in opposition to both the community or campesino *communitas* that it once was and in opposition to those volatile communities elsewhere in Yucatán whose violence was fueled, no doubt, by both PAN and PRI agitators. Pisté proclaimed itself "mature" and, through its previous experience, able to see through and patiently endure the lies and traps of containment in a patient struggle to seize the local apparatus of government. Note that this political game is not like chess or other Western game and sports metaphors for war. Rather, it has greater affinity to the tactics of the Quiché Maya Hero Twins who are invited to play the Ball Game with the Lords of the Underworld. By sending their animal emissaries around the flanks of the Lords, they see through deceits; by using the natural elements of the scene of encounter, they short-circuit traps; by enduring tricks they escape, overcome, and, through their own ruse, decapitate and then incorporate the enemy. Let me now trace the two dimensions of this figure of active passivity in the politics of waiting.

The Waiting or Dissimulated Agency of Identity Formation: On the Road

There are three registers or spheres of action in which a *politics of waiting* is enacted: These spheres of action can be glossed as everyday economic, governmental and communitarian. First, in economic terms the town has settled into a condition of waiting ever since the construction of the modern ruins of Chichén in the 1920s. This waiting is for economic opportunities, not only in the form of employment, but in the seasonal, weekly, daily, hourly, and gestural *waiting for* the charter groups to arrive and in the *waiting on* the tourists with the

Fig. 12. "The Progress That Chose a Village": The long-awaited paving of the streets of Pisté began in late summer 1989. While the Comité de Lucha made its political stance by rejecting all *mejoramientos* offered by the state government as forms of co-optation, the leadership of the Movement 107 sought out special attention from the PRI at the federal level. In response to the stream of letters by the mayor and the Comité de Lucha, the federal government initiated some *mejoramientos* or urban

various services of the tourist sight. I have already described the temporal strategies that orchestrate the quotidian practices of tourism into a politics of waiting, which is premised on the tactics of active passivity. In a literal sense, then, Pisté is the *antesala* of Chichén.

Second, ever since the opportunities associated with tourism at Chichén began to multiply, the town has been waiting in a condition of *abandono* (abandonment) for the economic benefits to translate into social and urban *mejoramientos* (infrastructural improvements) such as those listed by the mayor. This state of *abandono* has been and continues to be a generalized condition of crisis for the underdeveloped margins of both Yucatán and Mexico, as the Maya Zapatistas demonstrated by their rebellion in January 1994. Pistéleños, though, have always asserted a special claim and a commonsense logic to have this situation redressed: It only makes sense, it would seem at first, to invest in and develop the service center on which the profits of Chichén depend, or else this "golden egg," as it has been called, might be lost. But, as elsewhere in Mexico, promises and projects for resolving basic socioeconomic problems have been empty campaign pledges; furthermore, in an imagined zero-sum game of tourist dollars, the urban infrastructural development of Pisté could shape it into a more attractive, overnight tourist site that might compete with other more heavily invested attractions of the region, such as Mérida and Valladolid. Thus, there is a general waiting in abandonment that has been attended by the kinds of patience the *comisario ejidal* outlined. In Pisté, this waiting has been aggravated by events stemming from 1981–82, when the state government planned and prioritized rural development projects for its counties. Several plans were projected for Pisté, yet the only ones that were completed were the closing of the road and the construction of the Cubertizo entrance behind the Ball Court. Thus began the invasion of Chichén Itzá and the wars of tourism that marked Pisté in government strategy not as a priority to resolve, but as a political "trouble spot" to avoid and from which to

---

development projects. On this day the bulldozers were set up in the street between the Presbyterian "Templo," from which the photograph was taken, and the Palacio or Town Hall, whose interior courtyard is seen in the background behind the wall. To the left is the center of Pisté, where nearly all the town came to greet the governor and other leading state officials who inaugurated the work as if they had been the ones to support and sponsor the federal aid given to a town that they had marked as a "political trouble spot" from which to withhold funds.

withhold needed services. Along with communities in two dozen other counties, Pisté was "punished" by successive governors, county presidents, and state deputies by being denied any *mejoramientos* whatsoever. The town entered a state of *political abandonment* in which politics became a jockeying game of loyalties and entreaties for government favors and services: As tourist *antesala*, then, Pisté was waiting to become (recognized, treated, developed) as the *antesala* of Chichén.

The economic waiting and political *abandono* of the town are related to a third kind of waiting inaugurated on September 14–15, 1988, by the deterritorialization of Hurricane Gilberto; this calculated waiting is an embattling diplomacy to end factionalism and to create an integrated community without giving up anything in terms of individual interests and group positioning. In the regional wait for emergency aid to rural areas, the internecine struggles that culminated in the September 9 assault on the mayor by the *ejidatarios* was put on hold. In the struggle to survive and rebuild, the *comisario* remained the nominal authority figure while new faces of the old power elite took over the everyday operations of local government. Inspired by the mayor's own decision to seek out the personal help of the president of the republic, this fragile alliance began petitioning state officials (the county president, state deputy, PRI leaders, state congress, and the governor) for *mejoramientos*. The weekly letters of protest and meetings with PRI officials, as well as constant newspaper coverage of the community protests, led to six weeks of deferrals, delays, and shuffling between offices as government offers of side deals to buy off the Pisté leadership were rejected again and again. Through the voices of its Comité de Lucha, the people of Pisté announced repeatedly their decision to reject any and all (token) development projects until it was given the juridical distinction of becoming the 107th county of the state of Yucatán. In the rhetoric of Lucha 107, Pisté had been waiting thirty years for the state government to take the town out of abandonment. In a statement in June, reported in the press, Pisté protested that the monthly budget granted by Tinum (the county seat) to pay for the police, electricity, water, and other basic expenses was a miserly three hundred thousand pesos (US$100); the community therefore proclaimed itself a de facto independent municipality and renamed itself "the *Municipio Libre de Chichén Itzá* with *cabecera* [county seat] in Pisté." Furthermore, as the self-designated *antesala* of Chichén, Patrimony of Humanity, Pisté announced again its patient wait for the arrival of state or federal authorities to sanction a new juridical status.

From these three registers of waiting, the everyday street discourse and the political rhetoric of the movement found a common voice that continually "protested" the residents' "lack of conformity" to the multiple forms of "abandonment" that "unfairly" "closed the doors" on Pisté and thereby broke the contract and rules of reciprocity by which the state claims legitimacy for its power to intervene. In this way, Pisté justified to itself as well as to the regional and national communities that it could legitimately reterritorialize itself as an autonomous county. The public announcements, protests, and declarations were the demonstration and the enactment of that rational, patient "maturity" capable of conducting a "peaceful struggle," that is, a *war of waiting*. On June 18, a member of the Comité de Lucha phrased it as follows: "The Pueblo endures everything. But we don't know what might happen if they [the government] don't attend to our demands." This is a waiting for the descent of the state, which is to occur in an official gubernatorial or presidential *visita* or tour during which the political "father" will "put his home in proper order."

Two quick comments here: First, this metaphor of the order of the home is a common idiom of Mexican political culture (at least it was used throughout the invasion of Chichén as a weapon against the invading army of artisans). There is no time here to exploit theoretically the coincidence of this trope in both the discourse through which the national polity is imagined (*casa*: the nation as home, home of the father, the law of the father, and father of the Mexican Republic who governs as a beneficent, but absolutist, patriarch) and in the economy of travel through which culture is inscribed (*oikos*: "home" and its "law," "order," "propriety," "property"; the topos of identity; the logic of travel; the figure and nonrule of *différance*). Second, the politics of waiting enacted by Pisté was *not* an isolated or unique case. Pisté anxiously followed Salinas de Gortari during his presidential tours of the country—that boundary-marking ritual that reinscribes the "nation" every six years with rhetoric and promises of improvement. During his visits to Chiapas and then Campeche, he "liberated" a small Indian pueblo (Cancuc) and a busy truck town (Escarcega) by declaring them independent counties. Thus, Pisté's strategy was to *construct the stage and the scenario by which the president could be received in Pisté and be persuaded to enact again the role of liberat-*

ing patriarch. As it turned out, the new president continually delayed and deferred his visit to Yucatán throughout the spring and summer of 1989. This, of course, was a clear sign that the governor was in disfavor. Why? Mostly because, like "La Quina," he was a dinosaur of the PRI who was under ferocious attack by internal enemies such as Xiu Cachón, a Yucatec deputy. By 1990 he was finally replaced, the second Yucatec governor to be sacked in ten years—leaving Yucatán doubly in *abandono,* both internally and in relation to the national center as a secondary center of power.

The Active Tactics of De-factionalizing Community: One Destination

How is solidarity fabricated in word, deed, and sentiment? I have been indicating throughout this story how the conditions, events, and contexts by which the generalized feeling of having been endlessly "screwed" (to quote the local phrase) by the corrupt government attains the threshold of common identity and alliance. The question is, How, in the blank spaces of *abandono,* does this imaginary identity become mobilized as a community of active passivity? What are the tactics of political mobilization that must necessarily erase the battle lines and scars of internecine war and rewrite on this palimpsest the fiction or disguise of a movement integrated as the mouthpiece of a community unified? Here we return to our *oikos,* the beginning of our courtroom story, and this event of its repetition.

There are three series of overlapping and intercalated tactics— or should we say, along with de Certeau, discursive practices of writing, reading, and performing space?—in other words, the tactics of spatial practices orchestrated in a scriptural economy. First, there are the tactics of exclusion and containment of the dangers within; second, of mobilization and practice of an internal alliance; third, of reciprocity with outside targets and their incorporation as allies. Together, these series form a strategy of war by which an "enemy" is targeted (the state government) and battled (individual subjects, whether a *político,* an *oreja,* or a discourse such as a "rumor" or a newspaper article) and deployed as a tactic (the politics of waiting). Such strategies of power/knowledge, as de Certeau points out, are what constitute place (as distinct from space) as the proper order of things and the contours of an identity: the topos of an imaginary community.

The tactics of exclusion and containment might be better understood as tactics of *silencing*, silencing not only of opposition but also of the self so that the ears that speak do not listen to talk. In this perspective, I mention two examples. One is the Comité de Lucha's ongoing struggle to make certain that all the bars in town stopped selling liquor after hours and on Sundays. This sobering attempt to make the town look more respectable by eliminating drunkards was specifically aimed at one restaurant owner, a non-Pistéleño by birth whose public discourse and association with the district deputy explicitly situated him as an opponent of the movement. He was known to sell information to the deputy, who operated as the point man for the government in its containment strategies; for example, in February 1989, under friendly pretense the deputy channeled *los inconformes* of Pisté toward the idea of becoming a *municipio libre*, all the while knowing perfectly well that in 1984 the state version of the Revolutionary Law had changed the requisite population size from five hundred to twenty-five thousand adults. It was not until late June that this trump card was played with the idea that it would break the morale and spirit of the community struggle (*Diario de Yucatán* 1989e, 1989f; de los Reyes 1989; Góngora Navarette 1989). Another example, closer to home, was the Comité's efforts to extricate the once-favorite taxi driver from its strategy-making sessions. It was discovered that, during trips to Mérida, he too was leaking information, but from his police-issue Impala taxi. Knowing this about the man on the bench beside me in the Palace of Pisté that one day, I thought about espionage and double agents and answered with my most ethnographically scientific intelligence.

Home Again

What should I say? I thought I had played smart—that is, answered "objectively" and "neutrally"[11]—but was surprised to find out a week later (after a short trip to the archives in Mérida) that I was now in danger of being kicked out of the country for *alleged* political activity. One of the would-be "witches" (the doctor) was told that I had spread a rumor that the doctor, in concert with others, was conducting New Age magic rituals in the nude inside sacred temples among the Maya ruins.[12] Naturally, the doctor was irate and initiated his own inquisition, threatening the fragile alliance between the resident foreigners and the Lucha, as well as exposing the double agents—the *orejas* of Hoil—who operated competing networks of intelligence gathering. When asked about the event of my questioning by the doctor, the mayor of course denied any such questioning had taken place; that is, the mayor told me he denied this to the doctor, but in such a way as to indicate that he actually did think I had said something scandalous about the doctor, his wife, and the coordinator of the Parador. As for me, when the doctor stormed into my home wielding a hammer of sorts to question me, well, I...sought to assuage his worries—and mine as well, because he threatened to have me deported for political activity as a foreign agent if I had indeed defamed his character. Although distance allows for the humor of the event to commingle with my anxiety and fear, the threat was alarmingly serious. Certainly, there was no culture of terror as in Guatemala (see Fabri 1994), but my participant observation and documentation of the Comité de Lucha during the previous two months had generated a climate of uncertainty as to me and the kind of actions that the opposing authorities might take against my person. My constant presence, questioning, tape-recording, and assistance were part of the everyday gossip; the press had even reported that a "Mexican-North American" was advising the movement (*Diario de Yucatán* 1989f). "What would the Fulbright Hays [my grant agency] have to say about this?" I thought. Thus the fear of reprisals that each member of the Comité 107 felt extended to me as I was constantly asked whether or not I was afraid and told not to worry, "because they would not hurt you, only confiscate all of your belongings and kick you out of the country." If the mayor's questioning me about the local *narco-satánicos* reversed my role from I-witness ethnographer to eye-witness informant, the doctor's threatening interrogation then positioned me as if on trial as a loose-lipped "spy," or at least a two-faced gossip and foreign agent.

Espionage of different types, stakes, and agendas is common enough in the history of Anglo-American anthropology in Yucatán. The grandfather founder of the field was the diplomatic representative of the United States to the Central American states at mid-nineteenth century. But the history of Maya studies reduces the importance of this to zero in statements that effectively assert that because there was no stable government with which to practice diplomacy, John L. Stephens did not "do" politics and simply went about his business as a true archeological adventurer. Edward H. Thompson's activities at the beginning of the twentieth century as U.S. consul to Yucatán are likewise rendered meaningless and not worthy of elaboration, even though his archeological "research" is often critically assessed as looting, destruction, and sale of precious artifacts to the Peabody Museum. Only Sylvanus G. Morley was critically targeted for his *covert* espionage, which does contrast with the *overt* political roles of his predecessors. But, again, Boas's critique of those anthropologists who conducted espionage for U.S. Naval Intelligence during World War I did not name names and thereby left Morley unsullied; even two years ago a reviewer of a journal version of this chapter protested the fact of his espionage as an untruth. Sullivan (1989), however, has amply shown that he not only used his archeological profession as a "cloak" for espionage during World War I, but he later used the ethic of scientific neutrality and objectivity as his "cloak" in purposefully misconstruing Cruzob Maya's diplomacy, which aimed at getting guns and ammunition from Morley to continue the war against whites.[13]

Whereas Boas protested the interweaving of nationalism and science as a corruption of truth and its scientific pursuit, I suggest the inextricability of (nationalist and other modes of) politics/power strategies in the scientific production of knowledge. Our (social) science(s) and our scientific practices—*even when at their most objective and neutral*—are irreducibly political, subjective, and biased. Thus, to indict one practitioner for mixing politics and science is to indict the whole field; the charges of *complicity cannot be dropped,* only *extended,* elaborated, and 'fessed up to as well. But understanding the historical and political complicities of anthropology should *not* be paralyzing, does *not* leave us without appeal to an ethic, or without ethics to which to appeal; rather, it provides us with multiple ethics and criteria by which to practice and contest ethnography. After all, whether or not Morley was able to convince only his U.S. business, scientific, and military colleagues of having dealt objectively and neutrally with the Cruzob polity, the Yucatec elite, and the Mexican nation, his diplomatic and scientific espionage did, and continues to, pass as such. This suggests a corollary: the complicity of power/politics and our scientific knowledge-producing practices does not prevent science from being "objective" and "neutral." In turn, this forces us always to ask, like the character Te Wheke in the film *UTU,* "Whose justice is being served by this court?"[14] If allowed to momentarily conflate objectivity and neutrality with justice, one of the morals of that story is that these qualities are culturally constructed, politically shaped, negotiated, performed, inscribed, and contested in the event of their expression.

A Step Forward: Second Stop

Moving on to the tactics of mobilizing internal alliances and identity, I mention four series of activities. First, the Comité de Lucha organized town assemblies in which the members of the committee would discourse on their various activities, with specific attention given to the three or four trips a week to Mérida for negotiations with PRI officials and allies. Meetings were also used to invoke unity and support and by asking the community about what course of action should be taken. Second, the town restructured itself by organizing previously constituted occupational unions and the semifamilial divisions of the town into work groups that would protest the condition of *abandono,* pledge public support to the movement, conduct mobilization activities, perform community labor (*fagina*), and improve the physical image of the town. Significant among these activities was the registration of every adult as a member of the PRI so as to establish a sectional headquarters of the party in Pisté. Third, after having declared itself an independent county, Pisté began to collect a monthly donation of at least one thousand old pesos from every adult in order to pay for the town's normal operating expenses and to finance activities of the Comité, especially trips to Mérida. Contributions in service and goods were also freely donated, such as labor to clean the streets of garbage, materials to repaint the town hall, use of vehicles, reduced taxi rates, food for fund-raisers, and supplies of refreshments to give to those who donated their labor. Fourth, between March 11 and May 9, with the aid of schoolteachers, the Comité conducted its own socioeconomic surveys. Census were taken of population size, of economic occupations and sectors, of professionals living and working in town, of business establishments and the amounts of state revenue they produced monthly, and of urban infrastructural necessities (Q. Castañeda 1991). During this time period, the document that was submitted to the state congress petitioning the juridical change was prepared; this included a social and economic history of Pisté as well as signed letters of support from Pisté groups and the authorities of nearby communities.

The tactics of reciprocity that targeted the "outside" either aimed at incorporation within (thus, territorial expansion) or the establishment of an ally or an outpost (that is, a home beyond the topos of community in the territory of the other). For the moment, I defer discussion of the former, but comment briefly on the latter. The Comité de Lucha brought neighboring villages and hamlets into a political alliance. Because these communities were also in a severe state of economic and political abandonment and for more than a decade were already oriented as a socioeconomic microregion "seated" around the *antesala* of Chichén Itzá, "diplomatic relations" were initiated that led to an alliance between Pisté and its periphery. The Comité de Lucha was constantly sending its members to speak in private with the leaders of these towns and to attend their public assemblies to promote solidarity. Reciprocally, these towns would send truckloads of their populace to rallies in Pisté, and even in Mérida. Not only were all five of the other communities of the county of Tinum (Chendzonot, San Felipe Nuevo, San Felipe Viejo, San Francisco, and Xcalacoop) publicly allied in support of Lucha 107, but four communities in other neighboring counties (Popolá, Yokdzonot, Yaxcaba, and Libre Unión) were prepared to reterritorialize themselves within the new *municipio* of Chichén Itzá. Not since the Mexican Revolution had there been this kind of grassroots mobilization that aimed at this sort of juridical, economic, and political restructuring of communities in this region of the state.[15]

Speculations/Destinations: Ethnographic Espionage and the Genealogy of Culture

It is very hard for me to assess my role in the Movement 107, which was at once trivial and significant. In mid-March I petitioned the Comité to allow me to participate in the movement by contributing secretarial and computer services. In exchange, I asked for permission to document the Lucha, that is, to be its journalist/historian. There was hesitation on the part of some because it was understood that I was a spy for either the Mexican or the U.S. government or both. That I was finally accepted as part of the Comité was not because they realized that I was not a spy, but that as a spy (of sorts) I was working with and for them. Just as I have sought to indicate in this text the historical importance of Lucha 107, my constant presence and persistent documentation of its activities conveyed to the members of the Comité and the community a transcendent significance to their struggle. But what "proved" my intent to aid versus sabotage the movement and convinced people of its historical import was the extensive census and economic data that I had collected on Pisté and had distributed to the Comité (see Q. Castañeda 1991: appendices A–F; Castañeda and Burgos Cen n.d. [1989]).[16]

As a result of this document, I was asked to coauthor, with the director of the high school, the written socioeconomic history of Pisté that would serve as the legitimating argument for the petition to become an independent *municipio* that was submitted to the State Congress on May 9, 1989 (Castañeda and Burgos Cen n.d. [1989]). Ironically, the previous year I had been struggling with the problem of how to transform a multitude of life documents, anecdotes, and other narratives that I had collected into a polyvocal text that could represent the social histories of Pisté in relation to Chichén. In April 1989, this academic problem was resolved when we invented *the* Social History of the *Antesala* of the Patrimonio de la Humanidad; although it was only one possible account among many and was always already *in contestation* with all other accounts, this *written,* synthetic version was authorized as an official history of the community, its representation to itself and to the outside world. The writing of this text and the text itself were a marked moment in the reinvention of the community of Pisté both in the rhetorical sense of *inventio* (determination of subject matter and arguments) and in a poststructuralist sense of the social invention of reality.

The historical text as object was the result of the crisscrossing and contestation of voices, discourses, interests, authors, logics, and cultural worlds that it synthesized; as an object of everyday discourse it became a pivot for the articulation of personal and family stories orchestrated by a master narrative of primordial origins. The text as historical event was the invention of a vehicle for the imagining of identity as an integrated, bounded whole, a topos, whose proper name was measured back in time to Uuc Habnal, Chichén Itzá, and the founding families of the nineteenth century, as well as forward into a future extension as the *antesala* and *cabecera* (county seat) of a new *municipio libre.* This imaging of community identity crystallized the common sentiment that Chichén is not simply the cultural patrimony of humanity or of the Maya in general, but specifically of Pisté as legitimate progeny of the Itzá and as their cultural descendants. Thus, what was known as *el historial* (the history) and *el libro* (the book, which included other documents, as noted earlier) became something of a modernized and hybridized *Book of Chilam Balam* in the value it was accorded. Few in fact read the book or even saw it, because the political leaders absconded with copies as they were reproduced to give to the state congress, the governor, PRI officials, members of the federal cabinet, and the president. Nonetheless, the book ignited the imagination of the town — as well as its allied neighbors — by mobilizing solidarity and forging sentiments into a spirit of community, which everyone was busily inventing, that is, making really real, through other tactics of writing culture just described. In this way, through a heterogeneous, multiple, and complicitous event, the *culture of Pisté* was (re)invented.

This statement requires clarification. Lucha 107 was constituting a political unity — that is, a solidarity of community identity in an overtly political register — in order to attain its governmental objectives. The social history of that struggle in a defined space, and of that topos as the continuity of a proper identity, articulated a sentiment of belonging to an imagined structure of feeling of pervasive and long-lasting quality: call it the culture and community of Pisté. The imaging of that structure has not been as a *culture* per se, but as the identity of a sociopolitical whole, "el pueblo de Pisté," that belongs to and within an encompassing *cultural continuity* — namely, "Maya culture/ civilization" — whose substance and shape are known and named through an apparatus of knowledge called "anthropology." Here, in this (written, edited, published) text, then, the analytical machinery of anthropology "completes" the trajectory (in an ironic and complicitous voice) by "writing the culture" of that imagined community *as culture,* in the guise of *culture,* which is a purely textual, yet nonetheless real, entity realized in text and textualized in the everyday practices in the space called Pisté. Thus, the distinction between what Linton called the "culture construct pattern" and the "real culture pattern" oscillates between opening, closing, and reversal in an economy of inscription in which "culture" is a complicitous practice of imagining communities.[17] Here, then, is an event, process, and practice in the transculturation of that superstition, aporia, and "thing" called *culture*.

My argument is that the culture of invention (anthropology) and the invention of a culture of Pisté provided a container, filter, and form by which to identify and imagine the political solidarity of the Movimiento 107 and the town. Yet, we still have to understand how this vehicle/vessel of the Pisté community becomes marked as a culture or, better, becomes *colored*—with all the implications—as and by a specific identity of ethnic/racial tone. A brief example can be useful here, which is also an example of that second series of tactics by which outside targets are incorporated as agents and allies on the *outside* of the community. This brief elaboration can serve as a stepping stone to a discussion of context in the next part of the story that concerns the ruins of the Museum of Chichén Itzá.

That very same Ides of March when I pledged allegiance to Pisté in a long council meeting of the Comité, a nationally renowned archaeoastronomer also affirmed his support to Lucha 107 and laid out a strategy of war by which he could be of help: through this man's contacts with important officials in the National Executive Committee (CEN) of the PRI and with the party's federal representative to the state government, Pisté was to court the president and his cabinet, especially the secretary of tourism. If containment of the movement stemmed from both the state government as authority structure and the network of corrupted officials within that apparatus of power, then the strategic move must be to outflank the enemy centered in Mérida through direct alliance with Mexico City. After announcing this battle plan to a council of forty men and women, the archaeoastronomer closed his discourse with a rhetorical invocation of Maya resistance, struggle, and the rights of the community of Pisté as descendants of the Itzá and as legitimate caretakers of this ancient city of Quetzal-Kan, the city and ruins of Chichén Itzá (see Rivera 1989). I looked around, amazed and bewildered: What would be the response to this incredible act of violence that we had already visited during the equinox? I was met with that famous stoicism of the Maya when enduring the impositions of *dzules* (whites, mestizos, and other foreigners): They *nodded*. In agreement with the strategy and offer of help, they nodded and sought to ignore or forget the atrocity of this mysterious wordplay: Quetzal-Kan. The irony of this trope of colonial discourse is that, as a figure of identity, it perfectly captured the tactics by which Pisté, as self-styled descendants of the Itzá, sought to ally itself with the PRI, itself characterized as the heir of pre-Columbian central Mexicans (cf. Paz 1985; Lafaye 1974). Although the assistance was accepted and became crucial to the progress of the struggle (discussed shortly), this rhetoric of inventing Pisté solidarity with an identity of Maya-Itzá descendants or neo-Toltec-Maya was not cultivated. Neither this grandiose self-fashioning nor the more politically pragmatic self-stylizing as an indigenous or as a campesino solidarity was used. Why not?

Pilgrimage Home: Zero-Degree Culture at the Mouth of the Well

One need only cite here the stereotypical image of the traveler, à la Rip van Winkle. . . . For the point of return as repetition of the point of departure cannot take place without a difference in that repetition: [which is] the detour constitutive of the voyage itself. Were the point of departure and the point of return to remain exactly the same, that is, were they the same point, there could be no travel. Yet, if the oikos does not remain selfsame, how can one feel secure in it . . . ?

Van Den Abbeele, *Travel as Metaphor* (1992: xix)

Early in February and March, Lucha 107 was still finding its voice. The rhetoric of patience that filled town assemblies and newspaper reports would often close with an invocation of the Itzá as a way to legitimate the struggle of this Maya community. The appeal to Maya rights and legitimacy, especially with reference to the rural, peasant context, has been a powerful trope and threat to the urban center of white power, but had become particularly forceful in the late 1980s, when other Maya communities, such as the renowned Xocen and Kanxoc, famous for its armed resistance to state intervention, were in a highly rebellious state. The crisis in henequen, on which the Yucatec economy had depended for most of the century, was becoming more serious as the evils of corruption were discussed as a motive for the structural change then occurring in the henequen industry; rural Maya communities were everywhere exploding in internecine struggles over the structures of local authority and in intracommunity fights over land ownership, tenure, and community boundaries. The 1988 election only further fueled discontent and forged a reputation for the Yucatec countryside as being strongly pro-PAN and antigovernment. Aligning the movement with the sign of the Itzá invoked a primordial claim to sovereignty charged with unyielding resistance to external forces even as it distinguished itself from similar struggles. Certainly, this achieved what was sought — public attention. Yet, as was expected, the ambiguously militant protestation of a pacific revindication of the town's rightful claims to municipal independence was met by the state with the usual tactics of co-optation. Nonetheless, the Pisté/Chichén situation piqued the interest of PRI officials at the federal level — perhaps because of the personal contacts of the archaeoastronomer.

Accordingly, the representative of the CEN-PRI to the State of Yucatán arranged to visit Pisté to listen to the community's petitions in an *asamblea* and to inaugurate a new strategy to attain justice. This meeting was more than appropriately held on March 28, 1989, that is, a week after the frenzied event of the spring equinox but still within the eight-day duration of the serpentine Phenomenon of Light and Shadow itself. The daytime meeting was a stirring success during which the PRI representative pledged his unconditional support and the town reciprocated by pledging allegiance to the PRI. From March 28 on, the references and rhetoric of Itzá and Maya rights were dropped; in their place, the Comité de Lucha, the unions, and other community organizations spoke only of the PRI and of being "100 percent PRI-ista." The movement was reborn as a politically legitimate struggle sanctioned by a faction of the PRI, which in turn became relegitimated by the Movimiento 107 as the rightful means and arbitrator of sociopolitical action. In a sense that requires further exploration, the movement changed "cultures," as it were; as if overnight, the community shifted from Indian to mestizo while the guise of its social action reversed from a politics of Maya identity to a zero-degree identity of (mestizo) politics.

Certainly, in terms of the "lived-in culture pattern" of everyday life, "nothing" changed. But with regard to the image, imaging, and identity of community solidarity — that is, the culture of Pisté that was being fashioned by the town through the tactics I have been mapping — the "culture construct pattern" became marked as a zero-degree culture; or, to use Rosaldo's (1989: 196–217) terminology, Pisté, led by its Comité de Lucha Pro-Municipio, was constructing its culture as a culture "without culture." In other words, the Movimiento

107 did not position itself as the true, authentic heir of the Itzá-Maya to conduct its struggle under the dual banner of Quetzal-Kan and the PRI. Instead, this process of marking, imaging, and self-constructing found a different style of transculturation to distinguish itself from other communities — the local subterranean culture of would-be *narco-satánicos*, the regional society of the Yucatec-Maya *mestizaje*, the rebellious Maya communities in *abandono*, the governmental culture of the pyramid, and, as we shall visit next, a panregional Maya community of protesting campesinos — and to forge a political alliance with that external community, the "core" of Mexican political culture. Thus, although there are different ways to travel, the *travel* of cultural fashioning already preinscribes a topography of communities and identities within which to imagine and demarcate the boundaries of "home," which for Pisté was a place of identity fabricated as zero-degree culture.

Cultures with Culture and Cultures without Culture

In December 1988, Gaspar Xiu Cachón, the umpteenth grandson of the Tutul Xiu, or King of the Uxmal-Oxkutzcab Maya, promoted the organization of the Congreso Supremo Maya. This was to be a nonparty and nonunion, yet state-sanctified, grassroots campesino and ethnic organization dedicated to lobbying for equal economic and political rights for the Maya. Unlike the Lucha 107, the movement behind the organization was a politics of identity. Although conceived as a nongovernmental entity, the interest that led the governor to support its creation apparently showed itself to be a desire to control the movement and its popular base. Instead of allowing for an independent leadership, Manzanilla Schaffer appointed one of his own political minions from the state *ejido* office and shaped it into a paragovernmental agency coordinated with the *ejido* authority structure. This appropriative move seemed to have the future in mind: not only was a major reform in the land-grant laws being promised by Salinas de Gortari, but the state reorganized the henequen industry around which much of the ethnic and campesino politics revolves (see *Diario de Yucatán* 1989d). Thus, it seems that the state supported the Congreso Supremo Maya as an ethnic-racial authority structure that would supplement and, if necessary, supplant the *ejido* authority. The originator of the idea of the Congreso Maya, Xiu Cachón, no doubt disgruntled by being left out of control, then mobilized his political networks as state deputy and PRI *político* to create another ethnic-campesino organization that would fulfill the ideals already noted: in early April the Alianza Maya was established under his leadership with representatives from communities primarily in the Puuc but also in the henequen regions. The politics that created both the Congreso Supremo Maya and the Alianza Maya can be understood strategically as moves in the ideological fashioning of the regional community as Yucatec and Maya and of the state as the legitimate heir of a Maya cultural patrimony.

On the night of April 21, during the height of the frenzied mobilization of Pisté, Xiu Cachón came to town to have a "secret" or closed-door meeting with the Comité and its most trusted assistants, including authorities from two allied villages and the present writer.[18] After a lengthy discussion of the general situation of municipal rebellion and the growth of the PAN in the Yucatec countryside, he offered an analysis of the Movimiento 107, offering his personal commitment and the support of the Alianza Maya. The discussion was electric; it filled the room and the plaza outside with images of a unified struggle of Maya that could overcome the political deadweight and oppression of so many years. An aura of historical and cultural significance was forged by the symbolic weight of this person, a descendant of the kings of Tutul Xiu, meeting with modern heirs of Chichén. It was as if the centuries-long antagonism between the two ruling elite lineages of the Maya world would be reconciled in the pursuit of justice. The irony of this symbolism, which was much felt and discussed by all, is that the antagonism that would be overcome was fundamental to the Spanish conquest. After having a kingly pilgrimage to Chichén slaughtered by the Itzá heirs, the Xiu allied themselves with the Spaniards in their colonizing and Christianizing endeavors. In contrast, the lineages that composed the Itzá have remained highly antagonistic to Spanish, later criollo, and contemporary mestizo rule; they have maintained militantly Maya cultural forms, such as among the Cruzob and in Yucatec communities like Xocen. For their part, the Xiu kingly lineage was maintained, if eventually in name only, but at the price of cultural assimilation over the centuries. Thus, the hybridized Xiu Cachón—heir of Maya kings and descendant of PRI politics—pleaded with the people of the *antesala* of Chichén Itzá to join forces as Maya in a Maya sociopolitical movement.

The inspiration of an authentic Maya solidarity and incorporation into a powerful yet patiently mature contestation of government
abuses spread like wildfire and raged in debates during subsequent
days. Yet the decision was made that Pisté could not jeopardize itself
by an out-and-out alliance with such an intensely antagonistic and
gubernatorially disfavored leader (*La Revista* 1989b; *Diario de Yucatán* 1989b). The analysis went as follows: Xiu Cachón was part of
a political bloc of the previous governor who was then the agricultural secretary in Salinas de Gortari's cabinet in charge of the *ejido,*
and the reform of the land reforms. The politics of the kingly heir
was part of a wider strategy to fuel the fires under the current governor, a PRI dinosaur who was not picked by Salinas, so as to have him
replaced by a reform-minded PRI that could adopt the president's more
flexible tactics against the PAN by confronting the social-economic
crises at the grass roots. Even though the ax did fall on Manzanilla
Schaffer as governor in 1990, Pisté could not wager on the results of
such higher-level gambits and thus chose a more solitary route as a
culture without a culture. The community chose instead the "mature"
and "patient" politics of waiting for the governor and, beyond him,
the president to bestow on their town a juridical status of independence. In this tactic of active passivity, Pisté chose to be a community
not of Maya or of Yucatec, and not even of mestizo, but of zero-degree cultural identity, that is, 100 percent PRI; it began to vocifer-
ously denounce Tinum as a hotbed of PAN-istas and to proclaim its
own loyalties to the ruling party and government.

The mobilization of Pisté and the towns that would be its subordinate *comisarías* of a new *municipio libre* of Chichén Itzá peaked
on May 9, when the *book,* complete with the *historial* and petitions,
was submitted to the state congress. A few days passed and the bad
news was unceremoniously returned: state legislation in 1984 had
changed so that not only was a minimum of twenty-five thousand
voting adult inhabitants required to form a new county, but also the
signature of the *alcalde* or county president was necessary before a
petition would even be considered. Thus began a long war of waiting
that would test the political maturity of Pisté. It was an active waiting that would extend through the summer in constant expectation
of a presidential tour of Yucatán; it was hoped that the Father of the
Nation would arrive and declare law the justice that Pisté sought, a
justice that the governor refused. While waiting, the Comité sought

out contacts and alliances in Mexico City and arranged for two of its members to slip Salinas de Gortari the book of the Lucha Pro-Municipal as they briefly shook hands with him in late summer as he passed into the Governor's Palace in Mérida. The advice and strategy from the key political allies in Mérida and Mexico City was: *Wait.* Because of the 1984 legislation, the only solution to Pisté's problem would be first to take over the presidency of the municipality in the 1990 state elections and then authorize the transfer of the county seat from Tinum to Pisté. Thus, a shift in objectives inaugurated a new phase of waiting that would last twelve more months.

Meanwhile, the governor was sacked and replaced by Dulce María Suari de Sierra. This was a promising omen: Her husband, an INAH sociologist who researched campesino politics and political parties, was a colleague and personal friend of many of Pisté's *batabs* (leaders). More important, Suari was one of Pisté's allies in Mérida, one whose counsel was always patience, not to do anything *antagonistic,* to remain neutral, and, especially, not to get involved with Xiu Cachón and the politics of Maya identity that was then embroiling the governor. This strategic advice was reasonable and compelling enough to guide the Comité de Lucha, but when juxtaposed to the governor's new style of running the state, it becomes a curious fact revealing something about the identity of politics. Advised, perhaps, by her anthropologically minded husband, she further elaborated and extended a governmental style of appropriating indigenous Maya culture. Troubadour music, *jarana* dance, and Maya *huipiles* (embroidered dresses) for criollo women had always been used as ornamental symbolism to the political and social rituals of the state, as evident from the equinox event at Chichén Itzá. But never before had there been a move to embellish such public functions with the *ritual* of Maya ceremonies performed by Maya *h-meeno'ob* (ritual specialists). For example, when the San Diego Symphony gave a concert in the Ball Court of Chichén on Columbus Day 1992, the government also arranged for thirteen *h-meèn* to perform an all-day rite of petitioning the guardian *aluxes* of the Sacred Cenote to allow the symphony to play. Similar Maya ceremonials were added to public functions in relation to visits to indigenous communities. This sort of "Maya Theater State" correlated with the governor's increased attempts to refashion a Yucatec community through relations to the Maya population in the area of *ejido* and campesino politics; instrumental in this regard was the Alianza Maya as the paragovernmental agency whose task it was to short-circuit the politics of identity being waged by the Congreso Supremo Maya. In short, a distinct tactical deployment of the Maya in the self-fashioning of the state as heir to Maya civilization was discernible under Dulce María Suari; distinct from but also an extension of the touristic use of music, dress, poetry, and dance of the Maya and Yucatec *mestizaje* that is so much a part of everyday life. This was less a relandscaping of regional society as *Mayan* than a *folklorization* of the state within an archeologizing logic that sought to consolidate the legitimacy of the PRI and the state. If indeed this was a conscious strategy of the governor and others of her group that advised the Comité de Lucha, it is not surprising that they did not want Pisté political culture to assume a Maya identity. In this re-archeologizing of the territory, the state would be the culture with culture, not Pisté. The complicitous web of power/knowledge that hangs over Pisté as a zero-degree identity is, indeed, thick. In this topography, Mérida, not Chichén, would be the Mecca of tourism and would dream itself the capital city of the future Mundo Maya tourist development.

Postcards from the Museum of Maya Culture: Writing Home

Although this strategy was short-lived, the complicity and collusion between tourism, the state, anthropology, archeology, and Maya communities on which it was forged has, as we have seen, a long historical trajectory. Dulce María Suari resigned in controversy as interim governor and Federico Granja Ricalde, another of Pisté's close allies and advisers, was seated in her place. Despite this changing of the guard in the seat of power, Pisté has not fared well. After winning the municipal elections in 1990, scandals erupted. The embattled mayor, the man who asked me so intently about the *narco-satánicos* of Pisté, was voted in as *alcalde* of Tinum. Thus began again another period of waiting that resulted not in the transfer of the *cabecera* to Pisté, but in the imprisonment of this new county president on charges of stealing federal monies, raping a fifteen-year-old girl, and other abuses of power. After being stripped of authority, he was sent to prison in Ebtun, the town from which Chan Kom's forefathers migrated—a demonstration of token justice for the *many* Maya communities in which charges of corruption on the part of elected leaders are constantly flooding the newspapers. Although everyone recognizes that he was capable of doing all that was charged against him, only his most die-hard enemies believe he is guilty of all charges. For example, a pregnant fifteen-year-old girl was hired to be the mayor's domestic and to charge him with rape; instead of stealing government funds, he probably *was* assaulted and robbed as the mayor claims, but just as likely mugged in the alley outside of the brothel where he supposedly liked to spend federal monies in aid of campesinos. What is painfully obvious to everyone is that he was a man whose ego was matched by his naïveté in that he not only let power go to his head but that he somehow let himself believe that his former enemies in Tinum had become his buddies overnight. Thus, by negating the hard-won support of the community, he succumbed to his own vices and fell face first into traps so clearly set by the power brokers in Tinum and Mérida. The real crime that took him to jail was different: he went against his political sponsors and superiors. Thus, the prophecy of municipal liberation yielded to a well-worn plot in which yet another community leader of a grassroots protest concedes to state co-optation. Nonetheless, the plot has a twist: the government intervenes and punishes the corrupt official in a spectacular show of the state's honesty, and the ex-mayor, onetime county president, and now political prisoner, operates a small artisanry business in jail as he awaits trial and the change of political climate that might release him.

As for Pisté, the shattering of the Lucha Pro-Municipal was a stunning shock that only briefly delayed a return to the factionalism of everyday life. As the patient waiting for some future seating of the municipal *cabecera* in Pisté passed into unfulfilled history, new struggles broke out. The archeological zone was reinvaded by the vendors in 1993 and a discontented faction of the Comité de Lucha organized the PAN for the first time in the history of Pisté: the 100 percent PRIista identity of the political community and culture was no more. And then there was the protest of the *comisario ejidal*'s apparent abuse of and profiteering from the commercial sale of *ejido* property for the construction of a superhighway. He and others fled to escape the violence that threatened them. Then, in late 1993, a tractor was kidnapped by *ejidatarios* as ransom for stolen monies. In this context and inspired by the Maya Zapatistas, the community turned decisively to the opposition, to the PAN, as a way to shape, define, and pursue its

Fig. 13. Postcard from the Museum: "A mysterious hieroglyph." Photograph of the visit of the Prince of Japan during his tour of Chichén Itzá (published in the *Diario de Yucatán*, August 2, 1992), occasioned by negotiations to increase Japanese tourism to Yucatán. Shown in the photograph, from right to left, are Dr. Alfredo Barrera Rubio (in back row with face covered), Director of the INAH-Centro Regional de Yucatán, who is also the boss of the governor's husband (not shown); Dulce María Suari de Sierra, governor of Yucatán and onetime supporter of Pisté, who is dressed in a most elegant traditional Maya huipil; the Prince of Japan, whose marriage had been recently announced; Peter Schmidt, Director of the INAH Regional Museum of Archeology in Mérida and director of the then current restoration projects at Chichén; and, posing as a tourist, the ethnographer-author of this book, who is standing underneath the arm of the archeologist-tour guide, who gestures north past the Platform of Venus toward the Sacred Cenote, where it is said that Mayas were sacrificed in order to retrieve Maya memory or prophecy-histories from the rain deity and underworld spirit-owners. In the background is the Temple of the warriors, which is remembered as a monument to the Toltec or Mexican conquest of the Maya of Chichén Itzá.

struggle for political identity and solutions to problems. The politics of waiting that Pisté played for the county seat turned into a waiting for the elections of 1994 (presidential) and 1995 (state) and is now a waiting for the politics of the *sexenio* of President Zedillo.

But that is another story.

Appendix / Reglamento Normativo para Concesionarios del Tianguis de Chichén Itzá

[Document provided by CULTUR]

Capítulo I: Del Objeto

Artículo 1. El presente reglamento tiene por objeto establecer la normatividad del uso de concesiones del tianguis de Chichén Itzá, para coordinar la administración, protección, aprovechamiento, mantenimiento y vigilancia de dicho tianguis.

Artículo 2. El presente reglamento encuentra fundamentación en el acuerdo de Coordinación y Cooperación suscrito el 18 de Marzo de 1985, entre el Gobierno del Estado de Yucatán, la Secretaría de Turismo, el Instituto Nacional de Antropología e Historia y el Fondo Nacional de Fomento al Turismo.

Artículo 3. Los objetivos generales a los que se ajustarán los concesionarios son:

a) El adecuado mantenimiento, conservación, protección, vigilancia y limpieza de las áreas concesionadas, conforme a los lineamientos y supervisión del Patronato.

b) El fomento y desarrollo de actividades artesanales relacionadas con la difusión y conocimiento de los valores históricos de la Cultura Maya.

c) La operación eficiente que permita la generación de recursos se destinará a coadyuvar los objetivos antes mencionados.

Capítulo II: De la Operación

Artículo 4. El Patronato dará a su juicio la concesión de los locales comerciales tomando en cuenta la disposición de los interesados para la promoción de artesanías.

Artículo 5. Los locales comerciales a los que se refiere el artículo anterior, sólo podrán destinarse al comercio de artículos compatibles con la función del tianguis, tales como, artesanías, indumentaria típica, grabados, pirograbados, pinturas, etc., especialmente las artesanías producidas en el Estado de Yucatán, quedando estrictamente prohibida la venta y el consumo de alimentos en el tianguis.

Artículo 6. Las concesiones de los diferentes locales comerciales, sólo podrán otorgarse a personas físicas, de nacionalidad Mexicana.

Artículo 7. Los locales comerciales se concesionarán preferentemente a:

a) avecindados de la zona;
b) productores de artesanías de la región;
c) y en general, a aquellas personas cuyas actividades considere el Patronato conveniente para el mejor funcionamiento del tianguis.

Artículo 8. Los concesionarios sólo lo podrán ser por un local comercial, aclarándose de que si se le sorprendiere que directa o indirectamente tiene dos o más, se le retirará inmediatamente la concesión otorgada.

Artículo 9. Los concesionarios deberán sujetarse a la propuesta del Patronato, para el acondicionamiento uniforme de los locales comerciales para entrar en operación; en el entendido que para futuro, los cambios de acondicionamiento o rediseño de los locales comerciales, deberán ser autorizados por el Patronato.

Artículo 10. A cada concesionario le corresponde mantener y conservar en el mismo buen estado el local comercial que recibió, así como la limpieza del mismo y sus alrededores.

Artículo 11. Los concesionarios tendrán que sujetarse a los espacios aprobados por el Patronato, para el desarrollo de sus actividades, y por ningún motivo invadirán áreas destinados a otros usos.

Artículo 12. Los dependientes no podrán portar por ningún motivo armas, ni almacenar en los locales comerciales ningún tipo de substancias tóxicas y/o productos corrosivos o flamables, incluyendo velas o veladores.

Artículo 13. La vigilancia de los locales comerciales y la limpieza de las áreas colectivos como los baños y pasillos, correrán por cuenta de los concesionarios, previo acuerdo bilateralestre éstos y el Patronato.

Artículo 14. Queda establecido que los horarios para la operación de los locales comerciales, serán las que fije el Patronato de acuerdo a la operación general del sitio arqueológico y de la unidad de servicios culturales y turísticos. Para el abastecimiento de las mercancías del tianguis, se hará por las tardes, los días [left blank]

Capítulo III: De las Obligaciones y Sanciones

Artículo 15. Las obligaciones de los concesionarios serán:

a) Destinar el local comercial exclusivamente a los usos y actividades autorizados por el Patronato, teniendo en cuenta que para tal efecto queda prohibido la contratación de empleados, la estancia de menores de edad en el local comercial y menores en actividades de atención al turismo.

b) Conservar el local comercial en su estructura orginal, sin alterar la pintura, fachada, logotipos, letreros e instalaciones eléctricas, etc., aprobados por el Patronato.

c) Pagar puntualmente las cuotas fijadas y en su caso, las que se determinen para mantenimiento en general.

d) Informar al Patronato o a la instancia que determine éste, de cualquier anomalía que se presente en el tianguis y sus alrededores.

e) Permitir a la instancia que designe el Patronato, el acceso para visitas de inspección a los locales comerciales, para verificar el cumplimiento de este reglamento y las condiciones impuestas en las concesiones respectivas.

f) Devolver el local comercial en las mismas condiciones en que fue recibido, al término de la concesión o cuando sea revocada por el Patronato.

g) Observar buena conducta y asistir en estado conveniente.

Artículo 16. Son causas de revocación de las concesiones, las siguientes:

a) Dar uso distinto al local del autorizado.

b) Dejar de cumplir con las condiciones impuestas en las concesiones o con lo dispuesto en este reglamento.

c) El incumplimiento del pago de tres mensualidades o las cuotas establecidas.

d) Engañar o transmitir por cualquier título parcial o totalmente, transitorio o permanente, los derechos derivados de las concesiones respectivas.

e) La instalación en los locales comerciales de cualquier aparato eléctrico sin la autorización del Patronato.

f) La venta de productos en sitios distintos al tianguis dentro de la zona arqueológica, incluyendo terceras personas; así como la venta de productos cuya manufactura contenga materiales o despojos de árboles conocidos como "pich" y "chacá", característicos de la zona.

g) Asistir bajo los efectos del alcohol, de alguna droga o enervante y realizar actos en contra de los miembros y las propiedades del tianguis.

Artículo 17. Las infracciones que se cometan a las disposiciones de este reglamento, serán sancionadas por el Patronato, quien señalará según la gravedad del caso, las medidas de amonestación y correctivas conducentes.

Artículo 18. De igual manera, la revocación de la concesión será dictada por el Patronato, previa notificación; y la resolución que revoque la concesión deberá expresar las razones y justificaciones de tal decisión.

Capítulo IV: Transitorios

Artículo 19. Las acciones no descritas en el presente reglamento, serán sancionadas por el Patronato, con el espíritu de una ágil y eficiente operación de la Unidad de Servicios Culturales y Turísticos de Chichén Itzá.

Notes

Guidebook to the Archaeology of Chichén Itzá

1. The reference is to Foucault's archaeological method for the analysis of discourses and discursive formations, which I adapt to other poststructuralist tools and methods. Generally, the spellings "archaeology" and "archaeological" refer to the Foucauldian concept, whereas "archeology" and "archeological" refer to the scientific discipline; but see Donato (1979), who argues for a shared epistemological matrix for both of these entities.

2. It is impossible to adequately cite the literature produced in and through the Chichén Project. Important for this study are Hay et al. (1940), Kidder (1930, 1940), Morley (1913, 1946), A. Morris (1931), E. Morris, J. Charlot, and A. Morris (1931), Redfield and Villa Rojas (1934), M. Redfield (1935), R. Redfield (1941), Roys (1920, 1943, 1957), Ruppert (1952), Shattuck (1933), Steggerda (1941), Thompson (1963), and Villa Rojas (1945). The Carnegie Institution of Washington (CIW) sponsored a series of numbered publications in which were included, first, a monograph series, second, a series of research papers and studies called *Contributions to American Anthropology and History*, and, third, an occasional series of field notes and reports called *Notes on Middle American Archeology and Ethnology.* The Carnegie also had two annuals, the *Cooperation in Research* series and the *Carnegie Institution Yearbook,* in which year-end reports of its sponsored research were published. The Peabody Museum and Middle American Research Institute began to publish extensively on Maya/Mesoamerican civilization after the Carnegie shifted its interests to the "hard" sciences. Bibliographies in Lincoln (1990) and Sabloff and Andrews V. (1986) provide a sense of the legacy of the Carnegie in Yucatán.

3. In 1847 some Yucatec Maya initiated a war against the white- or Creole-dominated Yucatec society. Although the shape, nature, and end of the war are contested, it nearly eliminated all whites from the peninsula and effectively created spheres of Maya political autonomy for the remainder of the century (see Reed 1964; Sullivan 1989).

4. There is no easy, common term to use for the Spanish-derived cultural forms and persons of Guatemala and Mexico. In the former, *ladino* is used to refer to persons of Western racial-cultural belonging, but in the latter nation, *mestizo* is used. The former is premised on or as the antithesis of "Indian" culture and race, while the latter is defined as the "racial" mixture of Indian and European. Thus, these two work in opposite directions: from the cultural category, a sociological construct of divided racial groups is derived; and, from the racial category, a construct of an integrative culture is forged.

5. There is much written on the black legend; in terms of its relation to contemporary identity formation, see Retamar (1989).

6. The feathered serpent is a notion, image, and trope that has been reinscribed by many different peoples before and after the sixteenth century; see Nicholson (1957), Carmack (1981), Piña Chan (1987, 1985), Carrasco (1982), Lafaye (1974), Tedlock (1983), Díaz Bolio (1957, 1972, 1982), Schele and Freidel (1990).

7. Victor Turner (1967) defines symbols as operating on a continuum between the sensory and the ideological.

8. My mother, on reading a draft of this essay, corrected my erroneous version of my autobiography. In any case, this mythology of my name indelibly inscribed ambiguity and ambivalence in my identity.

9. In his account of "How I Became an Anthropologist," Lévi-Strauss asserts that the profession oscillates "between a mission and a refuge" that results in "a kind of chronic uprootedness," psychological amputation, and homelessness (Lévi-Strauss 1978: 55).

10. Certainly my actions are situated between family predilections: although some of my family have been involved with Guatemalan politics, my father describes in his autobiography how in 1954 he chose not so much to be a Guatemalan as to be a philosopher, whose pursuit of knowledge was diametrically opposed in his mind to political action.

11. I never thought of becoming an anthropologist, not only because I did not really know what it was to be one, but because of the proliferation of anthropologists on my mother's side of the family (my uncle, his two sons, and two of the children of my aunt). When I finally decided to become an anthropologist, it was to get over the cultural shock of always being a tourist at home in Indiana, Guatemala, and Mexico.

12. Some archeologists have begun to develop awareness of the political and ethical dimensions of the discipline and their work.

1 / The Progress That Chose a Village: Measuring Zero-Degree Culture and Other Scandals

1. This analogy owes its inspiration to Pasi Falk (1991; personal discussion).

2. The major ethnographies are R. Redfield (1932, 1941, 1950), Redfield and Redfield (1940), Redfield and Villa Rojas (1934), M. Redfield (1935), Villa Rojas (1945), Hansen (1934, 1980), Hansen and Bastarrachea (1984). See Villa Rojas (1979b) for his views on his participation in this long-term, collaborative project.

3. Among the topics researched by Steggerda were milpa production, soil fecundity, animal husbandry, anthropometry, death rates and birthrates, metabolic rates, nutritional caloric content of food, growth patterns of adolescents, personality traits, and more (cf. Shattuck 1932: 109–11). When all tied together, they defined, for Steggerda, the Maya as a distinct racial group and civilization (Steggerda 1941).

4. MacCannell's term refers to "new" social spaces within postmodernity where a new continuum of sociocultural types (postmodern, modern, ex-primitive) interact. This simplistic typology does not account for Pisté, nor, I suspect, much else.

5. The oral history I have collected corroborates this interpretation. The diversity of family names of the central political actors attests to a lack of political dominance by one or two families or lineages. Unlike Chan Kom, economic and political power were separated spheres of influence.

6. See Q. Castañeda (1991: ch. 2, appendices C-D) for a demographic and economic history of Pisté.

7. Steggerda's appointment was not renewed by the Carnegie.

8. See Cottom (1989), Herbert (1991), Williams (1983), Wagner (1981), and de Certeau (1984, 1988) on the invention of culture as the object of ethnographic and historical discourse.

9. In a letter of November 5, 1931, Alfred V. Kidder (director of the Carnegie Division of Historical Research that was formulated as the umbrella for the Chichén Project in 1929) assuages Steggerda's concerns that "the Chichen staff harbors feelings in regard to you [Morris] and Mrs. Steggerda." Steggerda (1941: iii-vii) comments that he conducted research that would complement, versus replicate, Redfield's sociological studies. Certainly, their approaches are radically dissimilar, but this does not explain why Redfield does cite the physical anthropological data, but makes no comparative comments about the *community* of Pisté. After leaving the Carnegie, Steggerda became a missionary anthropologist at the Hartford Seminary Foundation.

10. Then and now Pisté is an unavoidable stopping place on the route from Chichén to anywhere else, such as Dzitas, another research site for Redfield. Thus Redfield must have had a firsthand experience of Pisté that led him to *not choose Pisté as a community to include in his study*. Perhaps he thought it already corrupted by the anthropological tourists.

11. That Redfield gives a slightly different version sixteen years later in the Preface to *Chan Kom Revisited* does not affect my argument. There, Redfield, now the single author, gives greater recognition not only to his own intervention — "At times during the years from 1930 to 1933 four persons, of whom I was one" (1950: ix) — but to "the people of Chan Kom, one especially, Sr. D. Eustaquio Ceme, [who] appears often in the pages" (ibid.: x) of the ethnographic sequel.

12. As in the "functionalist book," the initial chapters here are part of a scriptural machinery that seeks to constitute the object-culture of study as an isolate by creating imagined boundaries through various spatial and temporal tropes (cf. Fabian 1983; Boon 1982). Thus, Redfield and Villa Rojas (1934: 1–30) describe the spatial and temporal limits of the native's world according to twelve different criteria.

13. The identity relation between culture and spaces is a paradigmatic assumption within anthropology. Even the "borderland" metaphor spatializes culture, although differently than the traditional identification (see Fabian 1983; Clifford 1992; Gupta and Ferguson 1992; Anzaldúa 1987).

14. Cf. Derrida (1976: 101–40), Van Den Abbeele (1992: xxiv-xxv, 136 n. 28), and de Certeau (1988: 209–15).

15. Other appendices excluded from the abridged reedition are Nurse MacKay's report on midwifery, Villa Rojas's diary, Maya folklore, and an autobiography.

16. Sullivan (1989) gives an account of the Carnegie research from the perspectives of the Cruzob Maya and the ethical issues that confronted Morley.

17. First, there is the collaboration of three authorial interlocutors (junior and senior authors and the authorial voice of the primary informant), each of whom has independently contributed sections (Don Eustaquio's autobiography, Villa Rojas's diary, Redfield's theoretical overlays); the text as a whole, in content and form, attests to the dialogical intersection of these minds. At another level, there is the constitutive shadow dialogues with the discourses whose intersection constitutes the field of action in which the text is written: the legends, myths, and folktales of Yucatec society, the Revolution, science, sociology, the new education system of the Mexican government, Maya healing systems and agricultural rituals, archeology, Maya oral history, and so on.

18. See Pratt (1992: 1–11 passim): "Ethnographic texts [are] a means by which Europeans represent to themselves their (usually subjugated) others, [while] autoethnographic texts are those the others construct in response to or in dialogue with those

metropolitan representations" (7). Yet it seems that *all* ethnography is always already *autoethnographic*, especially since the *transculturative dimension* is also always *repressed*, such as the example of the creole reinvention of América that she analyzes.

19. "Each text is a machine with multiple reading heads of other texts" (Derrida 1979: 107).

20. Ethnographic details are in Goldkind (1965, 1966) and R. Redfield (1950: 88–112).

21. Not all Chan Kom's religious and political exiles moved to Pisté (see Goldkind 1966: 326–28, also nn. 3, 4).

22. This letter and the other correspondence cited below are located in the archives of the CIW, which I was graciously allowed to research in the summer of 1986.

23. The figures are as follows:

Year	Wages spent	Estimated number of workers
1927	$15,902.50	159
1928	7,357.79	74
1929	9,745.56	97
1930	11,496.78	115
1931	6,388.98	64
1932	15,319.47	153
1933	10,251.25	103
1934	4,241.60	42

The estimated number of workers was not supplied in this letter, but is my own calculation based on the 1925 and 1927 Estimated Budgets. Related expenditures are in Q. Castañeda (1991: Appendix B). It is also worth noting the explanatory or qualifying text that follows the data: "The figures are based on Chinese as well as Indian labor, in accordance with your request." Here is one of several similar telltale traces (of "postmodernity") that indicate just how weird the sociological situation of Pisté was perceived to be by the CIW personnel: What are *Chinese* doing in a *Maya* village?!

24. It needs to be made clear that my use of "freedom" is relative.

25. These are the topics of chapters 1 and 7 in R. Redfield (1950).

2 / Measuring Tourist Impact at *P'iz-te'*, "La Antesala de Chichén Itzá, Patrimonio de la Humanidad"

1. See Tyler's (1987: 10–20) discussion of the aporia of the arbitrariness of the sign.

2. There were field seasons at Chichén in 1939 and 1940. The project formally ended after the 1941 field season.

3. Archeologists have a tendency to rehire laborers who have demonstrated certain skills and capacities in archeological research. Many from Pisté made seasonal labor migrations to new sites as these were excavated and restored in the subsequent decades. For Pistéleños, this reached its peak when a Pisté man was killed in a fight with local workmen during excavations at Dzibilchaltun.

4. The phrase is borrowed from the exodus from the henequen haciendas when slavery and debt peonage were abolished after the Revolution.

5. One of his uncles, a master mason, was hired by a Frenchman to build a huge twenty-five-yard-long, eight-foot-tall feathered serpent, a replica Chac-Mool, and a mini-pyramid on his property, which has since been divided up among several owners, including the Hotel Misión and the Restaurant Xaybe. His mother was also employed by the Carnegie to do the laundry.

6. The low figure is based on the population sizes arrived at by the official census (INEGI 1991: 13). Two other sources provide data that are more consistent with other years. The 55 percent figure is calculated by using the 1989 population of Pisté as determined by the Comisaría in April 1989 and the 1990 population for the whole municipio as determined by the federal census conducted in 1989. The 1989 population of Pisté is corroborated by a 1988 survey conducted by Pinto González et al. (1989: sec. 3.1–3.3) and their growth rates from 1950 to 2005.

7. Peraza López and Rejón Patrón (1989) discuss this microregion; also see Peraza López et al. (1987) and Morales Valderrama et al. (1989) on handicraft production and sales in Yucatán.

8. This is an unpublished manuscript filed at the School of Architecture at the University of Yucatán and at COPLADEY (the state department of urban development); cf. Q. Castañeda (1991: ch. 4).

9. In April 1989 the Comisario de Pisté conducted a socioeconomic survey with different results as to the percentages and composition of the EAP. Further, the federal census provides data for earlier years that is at variance with both of these surveys. I have yet to consult the 1990 federal census on this issue.

10. The number of people active in construction, touristic services, artisanry production, and sales is extremely elastic based on tourist flows, which in turn affect construction activities.

11. For details see Q. Castañeda (1991: appendices E, F). The high figure reflects the major hotels and restaurants in the tourist apparatus.

12. Although figures on municipal incomes/expenses of Tinum and other counties for 1975–82 are available from INEGI (1987a, vol. 2: 1533–1640, cuadro 4.5.13.), this data is not very useful because of the years in question.

13. These calculations can be found in Q. Castañeda (1991: Appendix E) and are based on data from INEGI (1987b: 207–10) and the 1980 federal census.

14. These are tabulated in Q. Castañeda (1991: Appendix F). Baklanoff's (1980: 230–35) tabulation of the number of tourists visiting Yucatán and their expenditures for 1960–77 shows the increasing importance of tourism within the state economy: 31,783 visitors in 1960 increased nine times to 285,000 in 1970 and three times again by 1980.

15. There are two agencies in charge of the site, CULTUR, which has authority over the tourist dimension of the attraction, that is, the Parador Turístico, and the INAH, which has authority over the strictly archeological aspects; both agencies sell tickets, one to the archeological zone, the other for use of the Parador. Income for the INAH is limited to these ticket sales and is therefore inconsequential because of the policy of maintaining low entrance costs. The local INAH workers have a history of mobilizing strikes and work slowdowns to protest lack of sufficient custodians, among other complaints, which relates directly to this pricing.

16. Mérida captures about 65 percent of the overnight stays, Uxmal about 7 percent, Valladolid 13 percent, and Chichén 15 percent (see Q. Castañeda 1991: Appendix).

17. Yucatán is generally about thirty meters above sea level. Pisté would generally be called flat, but the variation in elevation across town was insurmountable by water propelled by this pump.

18. It must be admitted that even Mérida, with its antiquated drainage, becomes a black sea of city sludge during the heavy rains of July through October.

19. Baklanoff (1980) provides a useful map of the Yucatec economy, its history, and its problems of diversification up through the 1970s. For the political economy of Yucatán, see González Navarro (1970), Joseph (1982, 1986), and Moseley and Terry (1980).

On tourism, especially in relation to Cancún and Yucatán, see Jud (1974), Bassols Batalla (1976), Lee (1977, 1978), García de Fuentes (1979), Collins (1979), Peraza López et al. (1987), Morales Valderrama et al. (1989), Peraza López and Rejón Patrón (1989).

20. If we consider García de Fuentes's (1979: 95–109) conclusion to her study of Plan Cancún to the effect that this was actually *not* a cohesive, integrated, or focused development strategy, then the Yucatec efforts are more starkly laissez-faire. But see also Collins (1979), Lee (1978), and Baklanoff (1980).

21. A *palapa* is a pole construction supporting a palm thatched roof with no walls. The covered area can be of varying size and is multifunctional.

22. Although warrants for the arrest of the attacker and leaders of the putatively "planned assault" were issued, the police made only a token attempt to comply with the task.

3 / On the Museum's Runes, the Ruins of Modernity: A Genealogy

1. On travel, see Anderson (1991), Turner and Turner (1978), Campbell (1988), Van Den Abbeele (1992), Eco (1986), MacCannell (1992), de Certeau (1984), Hulme (1986), Greenblatt (1991), Mills (1991), Pratt (1992), Blunt (1994), Clifford (1992), Gupta and Ferguson (1992), Bartowski (1995).

2. Hooper-Greenhill (1992) seeks to test the correlation between Foucault's epistemes and museum institutions and precursors.

3. Hooper-Greenhill (1992: 91) discusses this aspect in terms of two out of three contributions that the Renaissance gave to the modern museum. The three are "programmatical" in terms of the building, "epistemological" in terms of a human-centered conception of the universe, and "organizational" in terms of the techniques of order and display. I collapse the second two but add a third—the emergent nation-centered politics of knowledge, representation, and polity, which she considers in a different way.

4. See Ortner's (1984) discussion of the theoretical impasses in the 1960s and 1970s.

5. See Tyler's (1987: 159) critique of the tropes of vision (seeing/museum), mimesis (saying/library), and kinesis (doing/travel) as the dominant tropes that underpin Western epistemologies.

6. Horne (1984) is one of the few in recent museum/tourism studies to accentuate the politics of national communities within the modern museum.

7. Here I am not using "arrangement" in the classical sense of one of the five parts of rhetoric. In that context, the term refers to the ordering not of information but of the actual oration in order to more effectively create persuasion.

8. Biographies of nineteenth- and early twentieth-century Mayan archeologists are abundant; see von Hagen (1947), Brunhouse (1973, 1975), Adamson (1975), J. E. S. Thompson (1963), Wauchope (1965).

9. Histories of the archeological activity at and interpretations of Chichén Itzá can be found in Ewing (1972), Lincoln (1986, 1990), L. Jones (1993), Tozzer (1957), Kubler (1962), Ramírez Aznar (1990), and Freidel, Schele, and Parker (1993). Annual reports by the Carnegie archeologists working at Chichén and elsewhere are published in the *Carnegie Yearbook* 1922–41.

10. The administrative organization in which the Chichén and other Maya studies were conducted changed over time. The CIW, which also legally became simply the CI,

initially had an "Archeology" section, which then became the "Section of Early American History," and then simply "Middle American Research" within its "Division of Historical Research."

11. Any student of archeology would confess that the basic principle is "to work from the known to the unknown"—and back again. Thus, archeological excavation is fundamentally and irreducibly a hermeneutic practice of movement back and forth between imagined parts and imaginary whole.

12. See Rosaldo (1989) on the Weberian ethic of social sciences.

13. On the "end" of "museum anthropology," see Hinsley (1981), Stocking (1985a), Clifford (1988), Hodgen (1964), Boon (1989), Willey and Sabloff (1980), and Trigger (1985).

14. Unfortunately, I can only point to the internal politics of knowledge within the United States as another pertinent context; see Patterson (1986), Hinsley (1985), Lagemann (1989), and Stocking (1985b).

15. I have not been able to investigate the connections, if any, between the Peabody Museum of Harvard and the Boston-based Peabody Cordage Company, which had been involved with monopoly control over the export of Yucatán's monoculture crop (see Joseph and Wells 1982; Patterson 1986; Hinsley 1984, 1985). Although the people of Pisté could not stop Thompson from buying the Hacienda, they did prevent him from purchasing land in the village that had been abandoned by a large landowner from Dzitas. Later, the Barbachanos bought this tract, which is behind the new Catholic church, and other plots.

16. My comments derive from Derrida's commentaries on Freud (see Derrida 1980, 1978: especially 221–28) in which he quotes at length from the latter's *Note on the Mystic Writing Pad*; on "archae-writing," see Derrida (1976).

17. Modern technology and capitalism have commercialized a variety of games with slightly different mechanisms. Freud's early twentieth-century version is no doubt the authentic one.

18. See Goodwin (1994) for an excellent analysis of the textual constitution of vision and scientific knowledge in the procedures of archeological excavation and documentation; his discussion illustrates that archeological knowledge and artifacts are constituted in a scriptural economy that begins in the smallest and seemingly purest act of observation, measurement, and coding.

19. The *ayuntamiento* or county government of Mérida also participates in the maintenance of the site by sending a brigade of workers twice a year to cut jungle growth. This seems to have begun in 1984 with the first state promotion of the equinox at Chichén as a tourist spectacle.

4 / Mysteries of the Maya and the Marvelous Sciences of Survival: A "Dark Writing"

1. See Todorov (1984), Pagden (1982), Klor de Alva (1988), and de Certeau (1988).

2. See Pratt's (1992: 111–97) "reinvention of América."

3. The subtext of the debates on human origins is about the relative evolutionary positions of Africans, Asians, and Europeans. See Bernal (1980: 19–34) on Amerindians as Asian derivatives.

4. This synthetic discussion is based on secondary literature, specifically Pagden (1982), Keen (1990), Todorov (1984), Root (1988), Hulme (1986), Pearce (1988).

5. The Maya claims to civilization were not in doubt. Certainly, after military defeat, most Maya in Yucatán submitted to both colonization and Christianization, even though resistance has never been extinguished. Those that did not submit simply moved out of the sphere of colonial control into the far reaches of the Petén jungle where autonomous Maya polities were viable (see Farriss 1984; G. Jones 1989). As Jones points out, these Maya lived beyond the "pale of civilization in conditions of savagism." Those who submitted as colonial subjects were ideologically constructed as docile and dangerous because of the ever-present threat of rebellion (see Bricker 1981).

6. These pages provide some details I leave out. Unlike my own use of the term, however, invention is inauthentic and ultimately false.

7. Farriss mentions how the Maya "case study" reflects upon the Khmer civilization. The comparison of Maya and Khmer as anomalous civilizations — a comparison Jones also makes — goes back at least to a 1961 article in *Comparative Studies of Society and History* by M. D. Coe in which transpacific diffusion is discussed for the origins of these marvelous social achievements.

8. In a talk delivered at the 1992 Meeting of the American Anthropology Association. I am unaware of any published postcolonial critiques of *current* archeological research on the Maya from indigenous, Anglo, or Latino/a academics. Maya and North American intellectuals have focused their revisioning of Maya studies on the ethnographic and historical registers of anthropology.

9. Lemonick is a frequent writer of travel articles pertaining to the Maya for commercial travel journals.

10. See the landmark anthology edited by Culbert (1973) and an early 1980s reassessment (Sabloff and Andrews V. 1986) that remains within the archeological approach. New views on "collapse" are informed by the linguistic/historical approach (Schele and Miller 1986; Schele and Freidel 1990; Freidel, Schele, and Parker 1993).

11. Jennifer Burtner and Abigail Adams have significantly aided my analysis of this ecological issue.

6 / Vernal Return and Cosmos: That Serpent on the Balustrade and the New Age Invasion

1. *Romería* refers to a European pagan ritual of the popular classes or sectors of society taken over by Christianity. It involved a vernal pilgrimage to Rome, or, if that was not possible, to a nearby sacred sanctuary just beyond the community perimeters. It was marked by the great consumption of food and beverage and was an occasion for sexual activity. It refers to a kind of Christianized bacchanalia, but one that invokes Rome as the pilgrimage site. For a discussion of the origins of the equinox event, see Q. Castañeda (1991: ch. 7).

2. This term is ironic in that it is a word contrived during the colonial period to refer to the peoples of central Mexico. Those who are known as Aztecs are more properly *Mexica,* from which the terms "México" and "Mexican" derive.

3. This movement shares a kinship with Chicano cultural nationalism that grounds its identity formation in the Aztlán mythos (Anaya and Lomelí 1989; Klor de Alva 1986; Anzaldúa 1987).

4. Argüelles (1987: 221) advocated that the spiritually open and true persons of the earth should form groups of twelve to go to the sacred places of the earth and propitiate this changing of the guard.

5. The *Aztecas* and the *Mayas* joined the Rainbow people on the night of the twenty-first for an event about which I have no information.

6. *Peregrino* in Spanish means "pilgrim"; "gringo" is slang for U.S. and Anglo Americans.

7. Logically, it only makes sense to assume that all of the tourists that were involved were Mexicans familiar with these *Aztecas*. Otherwise, why get so upset and antagonistic? Foreign tourists would most likely view the spectacle as "local color" (Mexican, Yucatec, or Maya) of varying *authenticity* and would therefore not interfere.

8. *Bombas* are a favorite Yucatec four-line rhyme of baudy humor that ends with the shout, "bomba!" (bomb).

7 / An Everyday Guide to the Orchestration of Practices: The Apparatus of Pisté/Chichén

1. Both males and females participate in the ongoing discourse on the tourist body and its alterity. This discursive surveillance can be sexual, economic, cultural, racial, or otherwise, but it always seeks to compare non-Maya alterity.

2. In 1988 an additional restaurant opened.

3. One only operates during high season.

4. The pheasant and the deer are totemic mascots of Yucatán, as is the ceiba tree.

5. The number of people involved varied according to seasonal fluctuations in the volume of visitors.

6. There are two government employers, the state's CULTUR and the federal INAH. Together they comprise the authority structure at Chichén dealing with the archeological patrimony and the archeological zone.

7. Music and dance comprise this alternative entertainment category (e.g., the *jarana* dance troupe that performs for chartered lunch groups).

8. There are two types of bus and of taxi service. The regularly scheduled bus lines service all the major towns, of which the most significant is the Mérida-Cancún line, and charter buses are operated by travel agencies in these two cities. The team of such charter groups is composed of the driver, a conductor, and a guide.

9. I do not include a comparative discussion of the Chichén guides with those operating charters out of Mérida, Cancún, and Cozumel.

10. The guide history revolves around political factioning of groups into antagonistic unions.

11. The antagonisms between guides begin as conflicts over tourists and arguments over the proper order of turns on the list. Violence has not been uncommon, even between the female guides, but especially when union bosses have called for it. CULTUR, in its establishing authority at Chichén, sought to bring both guides and the invading *vendedores* under control.

12. According to common knowledge of the guides, belligerent attitudes in combination with certain nationalities promise a poor tip.

13. The rules of propriety are established by the unions, but modified by the highly contested consensus of the *bolsa de Chichén*. By definition, the work practices of the non-*bolsa,* nonunion guides are improper and illegal.

14. These towns form an economic microregion of which Pisté is the center. These were the communities that joined the political alliance to constitute Pisté as a new county.

15. Maya and Spanish, as well as fluency in English, is the norm; many guides, including natives from Pisté, teach themselves German and French.

16. *Cancún Tips* is a free magazine distributed to tourists leaving airport customs; it is composed of tourist information and advertising, especially coupons. I have found this caveat against bargaining only in the issues for 1987.

17. Vendor antagonism toward guides is generalized, even though the *guías libres* of the Chichén *bolsa* do not control charter groups and thus are not economic adversaries with regard to commissions.

18. See the *Annals of Tourism Research,* especially the special issue on guides (Cohen 1985). The Turnerian dramaturgical-pilgrimage model of analysis is still hegemonic.

19. Vendors often complain of both the lack of sales and the "unfriendly" tactics of others. This should be understood as political rhetoric related to *envidio* (jealousy).

20. I do not discuss the charter groups that arrive by airplane. Chichén is on the Cozumel-Cancún-Mérida route. Flights arrive between 8:00 and 10:00 A.M. daily during high season or twice weekly. Taxis transport tourists to and from the airport.

21. Cancún Club Med flies in tourists once or twice a week for a two-hour tour in the late afternoon.

22. The Pisté bus station opened during the summer 1990 season. The movements and schedules of independent, noncharter tourists are just as stereotypical as the most structured package tour. The difference has more to with style and the sources of the structuring and guiding information.

23. Foucault (1980a: 92–98; 1980b: 92–108, 142–45, 187–98); de Certeau (1984: xviii–xx, 34–39, 45–49).

8 / Panopticon as Tianguis: Tactics, Language, Strategy

1. See Peraza López et al. (1987) and Q. Castañeda (1991: ch. 10).

2. For the first two weeks I was perceived as a tourist. Then I was confused with an Anglo-American who for years had made monthlong visits. Since he typically drank his time away, the town drunks have persisted in confusing me with their American "colleague."

3. The social organization and flexibility of work can be illustrated with this family. The father or ego, wife, two daughters, and two sons are all vendors. One daughter and both sons are married and these spouses are also vendors; the males have all worked part-time and seasonally as artisans. Ego, wife, two sons, and the son-in-law each owned *puestos* in the Tianguis and in front of their homes; the unmarried adult daughter worked for the wife in her market booth. Families of the wife's brother and the daughter's husband and are vendors. The wife's brother and his unmarried son are vendors, but his wife's brother's wife runs a *lonchería* and the two daughters are wage laborers. The relatives of the wife and the wife's brother's wife are merchants. The daughter's husband and his three brothers and their wives are all vendors in the Tianguis, but their father has been a hotel employee for twenty years; in addition, the brothers and father have sought to develop a cattle ranch as a corporate group.

4. See Foucault (1979) and Clifford (1983) on ethnographic panopticism.

5. On writing in relation to power, see Foucault (1979: 184–94); de Certeau (1984: 130–64); Lévi-Strauss (1978: 294–304; 278–80); Derrida (1976).

6. Eventually, I decided to give weekly English classes for a nominal fee. The attrition rate proved that I was not a good teacher of English.

7. In Pisté the word *catrín* has no currency, even though there are males and females (sixteen to twenty-five years of age) who are trying to "forget" their Maya and pass themselves off as having a "higher" status. Whereas older persons have all learned

Spanish as a second language in school or everyday life, it is not clear to me how or if this younger generation learned Maya. The common understanding is that they do know Maya but are faking a lack of knowledge; the test is to insult them in Maya and check the fluency of their response. I suspect that they have always used Spanish, although, having been brought up in Maya-speaking households, they have learned to understand Maya while developing an atrophied speaking ability. If this hypothesis is valid, it contrasts with the language-learning situation of some children today: according to the opinions of many locals, the generation of parents who are twenty to thirty-five years old speak only Spanish to their children, either completely devaluing Maya or asserting that it is something that is to be learned "in the street." Although public discourse protests the beauty of the Mayan language, there is also a regional lamentation of its being "lost" to Spanish. A political ethnography of language use and of the discourse on language is extremely urgent and necessary in Yucatán; Hanks's (1990) study of language practice is an important foundation for further research.

8. Besides translations of numbers and merchandise, vendors often asked for sentences with which to address, approach, and "hook" tourists.

9. See Hanks (1990: 115–23) for sexual punning among Yucatec Maya and Limón (1989; cf. Cummings 1991) regarding Mexican-American joking.

10. Similar "invasions" by *vendedores* occurred at Teotihuacán in the 1970s and at Tulum in spring 1994.

11. The role of the INAH is complex and heterogeneous. The social anthropologists who were charged with analyzing the situation recommended that the tianguis be built.

12. The trajectory of increasing state intervention peaked in the planting season (April-May) of 1989. After an untold number of years during which the INAH and white Yucatecos decried the destruction of archeological patrimony by agriculturalists, the prohibition against farming in the zone was finally and effectively enforced. *Milperos* who had prepared forest lands in the zone for planting were threatened with incarceration. They were allowed to plant and harvest that crop, but under an ultimatum to desist in the future.

13. The coordinator at the time was an archaeoastronomer who coauthored an explanation of the geometry of the Pyramid of Kukulcan in relation to the equinox phenomenon (Vergara and Güemez 1988).

14. There are two dominant religions, Catholic and Presbyterian; however, there is a small group of Pentecostals in Pisté who are mostly vendors. The group analogous to the "traditionalists" of highland Guatemala are a subset of the Catholics. Although all the vendors and artisans are petty entrepreneurs, most conduct or have conducted other economic activities, whether as campesinos, seasonal or temporary employees (in stores, restaurants, agriculture, hotels), owners of other businesses (food service, stores, transportation), or as self-employed, skilled laborers (masons, drivers, electricians). It is usual for the spouse and adult dependent children, who together with the vendor/artisan form an economic household, to work in different sectors of the economy.

9 / Departures from the Museum: Ethnographic Espionage and the Topography of Culture

1. *Narco-satánicos* could be translated as "drug-satanists." The question was asked in Spanish: "Usted que anda por todas partes, ¿qué nos cuenta de los narco-satánicos de Pisté?" The looseness of my translation of *andar* and *partes* is beside the point: I

seek to define a notion of travel that is not specific to types of movement or types of space as destinations.

2. See Burgos (1988a), Peraza et al. (1987), and Q. Castañeda (1991: ch. 10).

3. Although anthropologists realized long ago that their informants do not necessarily tell the truth, only recently have we more fully understood that our own reports are partial truths (see Clifford and Marcus 1986) — that is, that we are *not* the bearers of truth. As to my inquisitors' belief in me as a "sincere reporter," they were no doubt as astute as Montaigne (1958), who, in his essay "Of Cannibals," sought a common man as a more accurate reporter after dismissing the "cosmographers" as persons who know a lot about very little and who therefore *exaggerate* what they do not know from personal experience. On cultural exaggeration, see Boon (1983: 3–26; 1992); on eye/I-witnessing, see Geertz (1988), Pratt (1992). In other words, they wanted the stamp of my profession (the modern version of "cosmography") as the seal of scientific veracity by which to purport a "truth" they already knew, one most useful to their own individually and factionally distinct interests, which is the topic of this concluding chapter.

4. The family name is Pat. He and his family were among those forced out of Chan Kom at gunpoint because of his religion (Protestant).

5. The symbolic shape and direction of this march are important because they mime the political strategy of active passivity that I sketch later in this chapter.

6. Mediz Bolio (1987a, 1987b) would top the list of artists, intellectuals, and authors who have contributed to fashioning a Yucatec identity out of the Maya heritage.

7. The director of the high school and I coauthored the socioeconomic history that was submitted to the state congress in a petition to have Pisté declared the 107th *municipio* of Yucatán (May 9, 1989). Part of this was published in the newspaper (Castañeda and Burgos Cen 1989).

8. Sullivan argues in his discussion of the emplotment of Carnegie ethnographies (1989: 153–59) that Villa Rojas chose a romantic, whereas Redfield used a tragic mode of narrativizing their stories about modernity among the Maya.

9. Letters from citizens and the mayor of Pisté to state authorities, dated August 10 and 18, 1896, complained of the lawlessness of Mexican soldiers stationed in town (*Archivo General de Yucatán,* in "Valladolid Box 1885–86").

10. One month later I conducted an interview with the mayor's wife, a successful vendor of artisanry in the Tianguis, in which she narrated the interweaving histories of the politics of the town and the politics of tourism.

11. Scientific objectivity and neutrality do exist, but like any other sociocultural construction, they have very specific political orientations, biases, and ethical paradoxes that are presupposed by the rules for being objective and neutral.

12. This image of local nonorthodox spiritualists probably has as much to do with film images, such as the sex scene in the Monjas in *Against All Odds,* as it does with local male fantasies of making it with tourists in the Temple of the Phallus in "Old Chichén."

13. This discussion works from Sullivan's treatment of the ethical controversies surrounding Morley and Villa Rojas's work (Sullivan 1989: 131–59).

14. *UTU* concerns the violence of the collision of cultures and peoples that occurred during English colonization of New Zealand. As the leader of a Maori rebellion in 1870 and a renegade lieutenant in the English army, Te Wheke is court-martialed for the murder of several persons, which he was inspired to do out of a personal oath of blood vengeance. His assessment of his trial is that "some fat German woman

on distant shores" stands wrongly in judgment of his acts. Thus, he asks the question that applies here, "Whose justice is being served by this court?"

15. See Redfield and Villa Rojas's discussion of how an army of *socialistas* was recruited from Pisté, Ebtun, Cuncunul, Tinum, Chan Kom, and other towns to attack the Liberales located at Yaxcaba (1934: 25–27).

16. Census material is from government publications in archives of state and federal agencies in Mérida as well as from Steggerda's 1941 published and unpublished materials.

17. *Opening* is the separation of two culture-texts, one "here" being written by anthropology as read "out there," where it is always already written by its culture-bearers. *Closing* is the entextualization of the real, that is, the collapse of the distinction between the real world "out there" and the world as constructed in representation "here." *Reversal* indicates a transculturation where the anthropological text is appropriated (read) by the "culture-bearers" in their imaging of identity (rewriting of self).

18. See *Diario de Yucatán* (1989a) for press coverage of the meeting. As was my custom during these meetings, to which I had an open door, I not only took notes openly, but also tape-recorded the discussion. This tape-recording was permitted by the Comité; it prompted a lot of small talk and joking about my being a "spy," but this documentation also promoted a general sense of the historic importance of the struggle. People were concerned that I finish my book about them soon so that knowledge of their struggle would be disseminated in the United States and throughout the world.

Bibliography

Abreu Gómez, Ermilo. 1983. *Canek*. México: Dante.

Adamson, David. 1975. *The Ruins of Time*. London: George Allen and Unwin.

Anaya, Rudolfo A. 1976. *Heart of Aztlán*. Albuquerque: University of New Mexico Press.

Anaya, Rudolfo A., and Francisco Lomelí. 1989. *Aztlán*. Albuquerque: University of New Mexico Press.

Anderson, Benedict. 1991. *Imagined Communities*. London: Verso.

Andrade, Saul. 1927. *American Tourist's Guide Book for the States of Yucatan and Campeche*. Mérida: By the author.

Anzaldúa, Gloria. 1987. *Borderlands/La Frontera*. San Francisco: Spinsters/Aunt Lute.

Appadurai, Arjun. 1986. "Theory in Anthropology." *Comparative Studies of Society and History*, vol. 29: 356–61.

———. 1988. "Putting Hierarchy in Its Place." *Cultural Anthropology*, vol. 3: 36–49.

Argüelles, José. 1987. *The Mayan Factor*. Santa Fe, N.M.: Bear and Company.

———. 1989. *Surfers of the Zuvuya*. Santa Fe, N.M.: Bear and Company.

Arnold, Channing, and Frederic Frost. 1909. *The American Egypt*. London: Hutchinson and Company.

Arochi, Luis E. 1974. *La pirámide de Kukulcán y su simbolismo solar*. México: Panorama Editorial.

Asad, Talal. 1991. "Afterword." In G. W. Stocking Jr., ed., *Colonial Situations*. Madison: University of Wisconsin Press.

Baklanoff, Eric N. 1980. "The Diversification Quest." In E. H. Moseley and E. D. Terry, eds., *Yucatan*. Tuscaloosa: University of Alabama Press, 202–44.

Barrera Vásquez, Alfredo. 1980. "Four Centuries of Archaeology in Yucatán." In E. H. Moseley and E. D. Terry, eds., *Yucatan*. Tuscaloosa: University of Alabama Press.

Barrera Vásquez, Alfredo, and Sylvanus G. Morley. 1949. *The Maya Chronicles. Contributions to Middle American Anthropology and History* 49, vol. 10: 9–85. CIW Pub. 585.

Barthes, Roland. 1972. *Mythologies*. New York: Hill and Wang.

Bartowski, Frances. 1995. *Travelers, Immigrants, Inmates*. Minneapolis: University of Minnesota Press.

Bassols Batalla, Ángel. 1976. "El estudio de Quintana Roo." *Boletín de la Sociedad Mexicana de Geografía y Estadística*, vol. 124: 17–65.

Baudrillard, Jean. 1988. *Selected Writings*. Stanford, Calif.: Stanford University Press.

Bernal, Ignacio. 1980. *History of Mexican Archeology*. London: Thames and Hudson.

Bhabha, Homi K. 1994. *The Location of Culture.* London: Routledge.
Bloomgarden, Richard. 1974. *The Easy Guide to Chichen-Itza.* México: Litográfica Turmex.
———. 1982. *Guía fácil de Tulum y Coba.* México: Litográfica Turmex.
Blunt, Alison. 1994. *Travel, Gender and Imperialism.* New York: Guilford Press.
Bojórquez Urzaíz, Carlos. 1977. "El Yucatán de 1847 hasta 1851." *Boletín* ECAUAdY, vol. 5: 18–25.
———. 1979. "Regionalización de la política agraria de Yucatán en la segunda mitad del siglo XIX." *Revista de la Universidad de Yucatán,* vol. 21: 32–45.
Bolaños Cacho, Beatriz Gutiérrez. 1979. "Valladolid, Yucatán, centro distribuidor regional." *Boletín* ECAUAdY, vol. 6: 2–14.
Bolland, Nigel. 1977. "The Maya and the Colonization of Belize in the Nineteenth Century." In G. Jones, ed., *History and Anthropology in Yucatan.* Austin: University of Texas Press, 69–99.
Boon, James. 1977. *Anthropological Romance of Bali, 1597–1972.* Cambridge: Cambridge University Press.
———. 1982. *Other Tribes, Other Scribes.* Cambridge: Cambridge University Press.
———. 1989. *Affinities and Extremes.* Chicago: University of Chicago Press.
Bourdieu, Pierre. 1977. *Outline of a Theory of Practice.* Cambridge: Cambridge University Press.
Brannon, Jeffrey, and Eric N. Baklanoff. 1983. "Corporate Control of a Monocrop Economy." *Latin American Research Review,* vol. 18: 193–96.
Bricker, Victoria R. 1981. *Indian Christ, Indian King.* Austin: University of Texas Press.
Brosnahan, Tom. 1989. *Frommer's Mexico on $25 a Day, Plus Belize and Guatemala.* New York: Simon and Schuster.
Brunhouse, Robert L. 1971. *Sylvanus G. Morley and the World of the Ancient Mayas.* Norman: University of Oklahoma Press.
———. 1973. *In Search of the Maya.* Albuquerque: University of New Mexico Press.
———. 1975. *Pursuit of the Ancient Maya.* Albuquerque: University of New Mexico Press.
Burgos, Tomás. 1988a. "12,000 visitantes esta semana: Reiteran que en Chichén sí venden artesanías yucatecas." *Diario de Yucatán,* April 3.
———. 1988b. "Ejidales y municipales: Buscan una solución pacífica al lío entre autoridades de Pisté." *Diario de Yucatán,* September 20.
———. 1988c. "Inconformidad: En Pisté aún no se normaliza el servicio de agua." *Diario de Yucatán,* April 16.
———. 1988d. "Si se suspende la vigilancia: Que los vendedores podrían invadir de nuevo Chichén." *Diario de Yucatán,* August 20.
Cáceres Carenzo, Raúl. 1990. *Canek: Caudillo Maya.* Mérida: Instituto de Cultura de Yucatán.
Campbell, Mary B. 1988. *The Witness and the Other World.* Ithaca, N.Y.: Cornell University Press.
Campos García, Melchor José. 1987. "La etnia maya en la conciencia criolla yucateca, 1810–1861." Anthropology thesis, Universidad Autónoma de Yucatán, Mérida.
———. 1989. "Primera praxis anticuaria en Yucatán: 1835–1847." In L. Várguez P., ed., *Memorias del primer encuentro sobre investigaciones en ciencias sociales en Yucatán.* Mérida: Universidad Autónoma de Yucatán, 15–24.
Canclini, Nestor García. 1993. *Transforming Modernity: Popular Culture in Mexico.* Austin: University of Texas Press.

Cancún Tips. 1980. *Cancún Tips: Tourist Information of Cancún and Surrounding Areas.* México: Offset Multicolor.

Carmack, Robert M. 1981. *The Quiché Mayas of Utatlán.* Norman: University of Oklahoma Press.

———. 1988. *Harvest of Violence.* Norman: University of Oklahoma Press.

Carrasco, Davíd. 1982. *Quetzalcoatl and the Irony of Empire.* Chicago: University of Chicago Press.

Castañeda, Hector-Neri. 1986. *Self-Profile: Hector-Neri Castañeda.* J. E. Tomberlin, ed. Boston: Reidel Publishing.

———. 1989. *Thinking, Language, and Experience.* Minneapolis: University of Minnesota Press.

Castañeda, Quetzil E. 1991. *An "Archaeology" of Chichén Itzá.* Ann Arbor, Mich.: U.M.I.

Castañeda, Quetzil E., and Bernardo Burgos Cen. N.d. "Narración de la historia de Pisté, Yucatán: Historial del movimiento municipio libre #107." Delivered to the Congress of the Government of the State of Yucatán, May 9, 1989.

———. 1989. "Breve reseña histórica: En la época colonial, Pisté tuvo categoría de alcaldía." *Diario de Yucatán,* May 13.

Censo del Gobierno. 1980.

Cirerol Sansores, Manuel. 1951. *Chi Cheen Itsa.* Mérida: Talleres Gráficos del Sudeste.

Clendinnen, Inga. 1987. *Ambivalent Conquests.* Cambridge: Cambridge University Press.

———. 1993. " 'Fierce and Unnatural Cruelty': Cortés and the Conquest of Mexico." In S. Greenblatt, ed., *New World Encounters.* Berkeley: University of California Press.

Clifford, James. 1983. "Power and Dialogue in Ethnography." In G. W. Stocking Jr., ed., *Observers Observed.* Madison: University of Wisconsin Press, 121–56.

———. 1988. The Predicament of Culture. Cambridge: Harvard University Press.

———. 1992. "Traveling Cultures." In L. Grossberg, C. Nelson, and P. Treichler, eds., *Cultural Studies.* New York: Routledge.

Clifford, James, and G. E. Marcus, eds. 1986. *Writing Culture.* Berkeley: University of California Press.

Coe, Michael. 1992. *Breaking the Maya Code.* London: Thames and Hudson.

———. 1993. *The Maya.* London: Thames and Hudson.

Coggins, Clemency, and Orrin C. Shane III. 1984. *Maya Treasures from the Sacred Well at Chichen Itza.* Austin: University of Texas Press.

Cohen, Erik, ed. 1985. *Tourist Guides. Annals of Tourism Research,* vol. 12: 1–95.

Collins, Charles O. 1979. "Site and Situation Strategy in Tourism Planning." *Annals of Tourism Research,* vol. 6: 251–366.

Conley, Tom. 1992. "Montaigne and the Indies." In R. Jara and N. Spadaccini, eds., *1492–1992: Re/discovering Colonial Writing.* Minneapolis: Prisma Institute, 225–62.

Cottom, Daniel. 1989. *Text and Culture: The Politics of Interpretation.* Minneapolis: University of Minnesota Press.

Crapanzano, Vincent. 1980. *Tuhami.* Chicago: University of Chicago Press.

Crick, Malcolm. 1989. "Representations of International Tourism in the Social Sciences." *Annual Review of Anthropology,* vol. 18: 307–44.

Crimp, Douglas. 1983. "On the Museum's Ruins." In H. Foster, ed., *The Anti-Aesthetic.* Seattle: Bay Press.

Culbert, Patrick T. 1973. *The Classic Maya Collapse*. Albuquerque: University of New Mexico Press.

Culler, Jonathan. 1981. "Semiotics of Tourism." *American Journal of Semiotics*, vol. 1: 127–40.

———. 1982. *On Deconstruction*. Ithaca, N.Y.: Cornell University Press.

Cummings, Laura. 1991. "Carne con Limón." *American Ethnologist*, vol. 18: 370–72.

Dávalos Hurtado, Eusebio. 1961. "Into the Well of Sacrifice, Part I." *National Geographic*, vol. 120 (4): 540–49.

de Certeau, Michel. 1984. *The Practice of Everyday Life*. Minneapolis: University of Minnesota Press.

———. 1986a. *Heterologies: Discourse on the Other*. Trans. Brian Massumi. Minneapolis: University of Minnesota Press.

———. 1986b. "Of Montaigne: The Savage 'I.' " In *Heterologies: Discourse on the Other*. Trans. Brian Massumi. Minneapolis: University of Minnesota Press.

———. 1988. *The Writing of History*. New York: Columbia University Press.

de la Garza, Mercedes, et al., eds. 1983. [1579–81]. *Relaciones Históricas-Geográficas de la Gobernación de Yucatán (Mérida, Valladolid y Tabasco)*. 2 vols. México: UNAM.

de los Reyes, N. 1989. "¿Cumple Pisté con los requisitos para convertirse en cabecera municipal?" *Novedades de Yucatán*, May 11.

Derrida, Jacques. 1976. *Of Grammatology*. Baltimore: Johns Hopkins University Press.

———. 1978a. "Freud and the Scene of Writing." In J. Derrida, *Writing and Difference*. Chicago: University of Chicago Press, 196–231.

———. 1978b. "Structure, Sign, and Play in the Discourses of the Human Sciences." In J. Derrida, *Writing and Difference*. Chicago: University of Chicago Press, 278–93.

———. 1979. "Living On: Border Lines." In H. Bloom et al., eds., *Deconstruction and Criticism*. New York: Seabury Press, 75–175.

———. 1980. *The Post Card*. Chicago: University of Chicago Press.

———. 1981. *Positions*. Chicago: University of Chicago Press.

Desmond, Lawrence G., and Phyllis M. Messenger. 1988. *A Dream of Maya*. Albuquerque: University of New Mexico Press.

Diario de Yucatán. 1988. "Pocos productos yucatecos en el tianguis de Chichén." March 12: 1, 8.

———. 1989a. "La Alianza de los Mayas apoya la idea de convertir en municipio a Pisté, dice el Dip. Xiu Cachón." April 24: 4.

———. 1989b. "Manzanilla Schaffer me vetó para que no fuera a la CNC: Gaspar Xiu." May 1: 1.

———. 1989c. "Nuevas presiones para que la comisaría de Pisté se constiya en el municipio 107." March 12: 1, 4.

———. 1989d. "La Reordenación." 1, 12–13.

———. 1989e. "Según anticipó el PRI, Pisté no se convertirá pronto en otro municipio." May 30: 1.

———. 1989f. "Solicitan formalmente la creación de otro municipio." May 9: 1, 6.

———. 1990a. "Impulso al proyecto turístico 'mundo maya.' " August 24: 4, 6.

———. 1990b. "Sugieron expedir un 'pasaporte del mundo maya' para México y parte de Centroamérica." August 29: 1, 3.

Díaz Bolio, José. 1957. *La Serpiente emplumada eje de culturas*. Mérida: El Mayab.

———. 1972. *Instructive Guide to the Ruins of Chichén Itzá*. Mérida: El Mayab.

———. 1982. *La Serpiente de Luz de Chichén Itzá*. Mérida: El Mayab.

Donato, Eugenio. 1979. "The Museum's Furnace." In J. V. Harari, ed., *Textual Strategies*. Ithaca, N.Y.: Cornell University Press, 213–38.

Dorst, John. 1989. *The Written Suburb*. Philadelphia: University of Pennsylvania Press.

Eco, Umberto. 1986. *Travels in Hyperreality*. New York: Harcourt Brace Jovanovich.

Ediger, Donald. 1971. *The Well of Sacrifice*. Garden City, N.Y.: Doubleday.

Edmonson, Munro. 1971. *The Book of Counsel*. M.A.R.I. 25. New Orleans: Tulane University.

———. 1982. *The Ancient Future of the Itza*. Austin: University of Texas Press.

———. 1986. *Heaven Born Mérida and Its Destiny*. Austin: University of Texas Press.

Ellis, Allen R., and Phyllis T. Ellis. 1964. *Discovering Mayaland*. Glendale, Calif.: Arthur H. Clark Company.

Erosa Peniche, José A. 1948 [1937]. *Guía para visitar las ruinas de Chichén Itzá*. México: INAH-SEP.

Everton, Macduff. 1991. *Modern Maya: A Culture in Transition*. Albuquerque: University of New Mexico Press.

Ewing, M. Robert. 1972. *A History of the Archaeological Activity at Chichen Itza, Yucatán, Mexico*. Ann Arbor, Mich.: U.M.I.

Fabian, Johannes. 1983. *Time and the Other*. New York: Columbia University Press.

Fabri, Antonella. 1994. "Recomposing the Nation." Ph.D. diss., State University of New York, Albany.

Falk, Pasi. 1991. "Coke Is It!" *Cambridge Anthropology*, vol. 15 (1):46–55.

Fardon, Richard. 1985. "Introduction: A Sense of Relevance." In R. Fardon, *Power and Knowledge*. Edinburgh: Scottish Academic Press.

Farriss, Nancy. 1984. *Maya Society under Colonial Rule*. Princeton, N.J.: Princeton University Press.

Folan, William J. 1970. "The Sacred Cenote of Chichén Itzá, Yucatán." *National Geographic Society Research Reports: 1960–61 Projects*. Washington, D.C.

Foucault, Michel. 1970. *The Order of Things*. New York: Random House.

———. 1972. *The Archaeology of Knowledge*. New York: Tavistock Publishing.

———. 1979. *Discipline and Punish*. New York: Vintage Books.

———. 1980a. *The History of Sexuality*. Vol. 1: *An Introduction*. New York: Vintage Books.

———. 1980b. *Power/Knowledge*. C. Gordon, ed. New York: Pantheon Books.

———. 1986. "Of Other Spaces." *Diacritics*, vol. 16 (spring): 22–27.

Freidel, David A., Linda Schele, and Joy Parker. 1993. *Maya Cosmos: Three Thousand Years on the Shaman's Path*. New York: William Morrow.

Fuller, Robert. 1989. *Alternative Medicine and American Religious Practices*. Oxford: Oxford University Press.

García de Fuentes, Ana. 1979. *Cancún: Turismo y Subdesarrollo Regional*. México: UNAM.

Garrett, Wilbur E. 1989. "La Ruta Maya." *National Geographic*, vol. 176 (4): 424–79.

Geertz, Clifford. 1973. *The Interpretation of Cultures*. New York: Basic Books.

———. 1983. *Local Knowledge*. New York: Basic Books.

———. 1988. *Works and Lives*. Stanford, Calif.: Stanford University Press.

Gerbi, Antonello. 1983. *Dispute of the New World: The History of a Polemic*. Pittsburgh: University of Pittsburgh Press.

Giddens, Anthony. 1984. *Constitution of Society*. Berkeley: University of California Press.

Gilpin, Laura. 1948. *Temples in Yucatan: A Camera Chronicle of Chichen Itza.* New York: Hastings House Publishers.

Gobierno del Estado de Yucatán. 1995. "Asunto: se informe de la labor realizada por el Supremo Consejo Maya, de marzo de 1994, a julio de 1995." Mérida: Gobierno del Estado de Yucatán.

Gobierno Estatal de Yucatán. 1982a. "Plan de Desarrollo Integral de la Zona Arqueológica de Chichén Itzá." Mérida: COPLADEY.

———. 1982b. "Plan Municipal de Desarrollo Urbano: Tinum." Mérida: COPLADEY.

Goldkind, Victor. 1965. "Social Stratification in the Peasant Community." *American Anthropologist,* vol. 67: 863–87.

———. 1966. "Class Conflict and Cacique in Chan Kom." *Southwestern Journal of Anthropology,* vol. 22: 325–45.

Góngora Navarette, Noe. 1989. "Cuadratín: ¿Será Pisté el municipio 107?" *Novedades de Yucatán,* May 11.

González Navarro, Moises. 1970. *Raza y Tierra.* México: El Colegio de México.

Goodwin, Charles. 1994. "Professional Vision." *American Anthropologist* 96 (3): 606–49.

Gossen, Gary. 1986. *Symbol and Meaning beyond the Closed Community.* Albany and Austin: University of Texas Press for the Institute for Mesoamerican Studies.

Graburn, Nelson H. 1977. "Tourism: The Sacred Journey." In V. L. Smith, ed., *Hosts and Guests.* Philadelphia: University of Pennsylvania Press, 17–32.

Greenblatt, Stephen. 1991. *Marvelous Possessions.* Chicago: University of Chicago Press.

Gupta, Akhil, and James Ferguson. 1992. "Beyond 'Culture.'" *Cultural Anthropology,* vol. 7: 6–23.

Hanks, William F. 1990. *Referential Practice.* Chicago: University of Chicago Press.

Hansen, Asael T. 1934. "The Ecology of a Latin American City." In E. B. Reuter, ed., *Race and Culture Contacts.* New York: McGraw-Hill.

———. 1980. "Change in the Class System of Mérida, Yucatán, 1875–1935." In E. H. Moseley and E. D. Terry, eds., *Yucatan.* Tuscaloosa: University of Alabama Press, 122–41.

Hansen, Asael T., and Juan R. Bastarrecha Manzano. 1984. *Mérida.* México: INAH.

Haraway, Donna J. 1989. *Primate Visions.* London: Routledge.

Hay, Clarence L., et al. 1940. *The Maya and Their Neighbors.* New York: Appleton-Century Company.

Helm, June, ed. 1984. *Social Contexts of American Ethnology 1840–1984.* Washington, D.C.: American Anthropology Association.

Herbert, Christopher. 1991. *Culture and Anomie.* Chicago: University of Chicago Press.

Hervik, Peter. 1992. "Learning to Be 'Indian.'" *Folk,* vol. 34: 63–80.

Hinsley, Curtis M. 1981. *Savages and Scientists.* Washington, D.C: Smithsonian Institution.

———. 1984. "Hemispheric Hegemony in Early American Anthropology." In J. Helm, ed., *Social Contexts of American Ethnology 1840–1984.* Washington, D.C.: American Anthropology Association.

———. 1985. "From Shell-Heaps to Stelae." In G. W. Stocking Jr., ed., *Objects and Others.* Madison: University of Wisconsin Press, 49–75.

Hooper-Greenhill, Eileen. 1992. *Museums and the Shaping of Knowledge.* London: Routledge.

Horne, Donald. 1984. *The Great Museum.* London: Pluto Press.

Hulme, Peter. 1986. *Colonial Encounters.* London: Routledge.

Hunbatz Men. 1990. *Secrets of Mayan Science/Religion.* Santa Fe, N.M.: Bear and Company.

Hunter, Bruce C. 1986. *A Guide to Ancient Maya Ruins.* Norman: University of Oklahoma Press.

Hymes, Dell, ed. 1972. *Reinventing Anthropology.* New York: Pantheon Books.

INAH. (Instituto Nacional de Antropología e Historia). 1955. *Chichén Itzá: Official Guide of the INAH.* México: Departamento de Publicaciones.

———. 1965. *Ciudades Mayas: Guía oficial INAH.* México: Departamento de Publicaciones.

———. 1980–89. Libretas de Registro de ingreso al sitio arqueológico de Chichén Itzá, Yucatán. Archivo del CRY-INAH.

INEGI (Instituto Nacional Estadístico, Geográfico e Informático). 1987a. *Anuario estadístico del Estado de Yucatán, 1986.* 2 vols. Mérida.

———. 1987b. *Anuario Estadístico de los Estados Unidos Mexicanos, 1986.* México.

———. 1991. *Yucatán: XI censo general de población y vivienda, 1990.* México.

Jacknis, Ira. 1985. "Franz Boaz and Exhibits: On the Limitations of the Museum Method in Anthropology." In G. W. Stocking Jr., ed., *Objects and Others.* Madison: University of Wisconsin Press, 74–111.

Jones, Grant D. 1977. "Introduction." In G. D. Jones, ed., *History and Anthropology in Yucatan.* Austin: University of Texas Press, xi–xxiv.

———. 1989. *Maya Resistance to Spanish Rule.* Albuquerque: University of New Mexico Press.

Jones, Lindsay. 1993. "The Hermeneutics of Sacred Architecture: A Reassessment of the Similitude between Tula, Hidalgo and Chichén Itzá, Yucatán, Part II." *History of Religions* 32:315–42.

Joseph, Gilbert M. 1982. *Revolution from Without.* Cambridge: Cambridge University Press.

———. 1986. *Rediscovering the Past at Mexico's Periphery.* Tuscaloosa: University of Alabama Press.

Joseph, Gilbert M., and Allen Wells. 1982. "Corporate Control of a Monocrop Economy." *Latin American Research Review,* vol. 17: 69–79.

Jud, G. D. 1974. "Tourism and Economic Growth in Mexico since 1950." *InterAmerican Economic Affairs,* vol. 28: 19–43.

Katz, Fredrich. 1981. *The Secret War in Mexico.* Chicago: University of Chicago Press.

Keen, Benjamin. 1990. *The Aztec Image in Western Thought.* New Brunswick, N.J.: Rutgers University Press.

Kidder, Alfred V. 1930. "Division of Historical Research." *Carnegie Yearbook* no. 29 (1929–30). Washington, D.C.: CIW, 121.

———. 1940. "Division of Historical Research." *Carnegie Yearbook* no. 39 (1939–40). Washington, D.C.: CIW.

Kintz, Ellen R. 1990. *Life under the Tropical Canopy.* Chicago: Holt, Rinehart, and Winston.

Klor de Alva, J. Jorge. 1986. "California Chicano Literature and Pre-Columbian Motifs." *Confluencia,* vol. 1: 18–26.

———. 1988. "Sahagún and the Birth of Modern Ethnography." In J. J. Klor de Alva, H. B. Nicholson, E. Quiñones Kubler, eds., *The Work of Bernardino de Sahagún.* Austin: University of Texas Press, 31–52.

———. 1992. "Nahua Studies, the Allure of the 'Aztecs,' and Miguel León-Portilla." In M. León-Portilla, *Introduction to Aztec Culture.* Salt Lake City: University of Utah Press.

Kubler, George. 1962. *The Art and Architecture of Ancient America.* Baltimore: Penguin Books.

Kurjack, Edward. 1989. "Hay que evitar que conviertan las ruinas en un *Disney World* dice destacado arqueólogo" (interview with Ed Kurjack). *Diario de Yucatán,* July 10.

Lafaye, Jacques. 1974. *Quetzalcoatl and Guadalupe.* Chicago: University of Chicago Press.

Lagemann, Ellen C. 1989. *Politics of Knowledge.* Middletown, Conn.: Wesleyan University Press.

La Revista. 1989a. "El Gran Ausente ¿Por qué no viene Salinas a Yucatán?" August 16: 7–20.

———. 1989b. "Manzanilla Schaffer me vetó para que no fuera a la CNC: Gaspar Xiu; No aceptamos presiones de Xiu ni de nadie, afirma Espejo Peniche." May 1: 9–12.

Lee, Rosemary L. 1978. "Who Owns Boardwalk?" *Studies in Third World Societies,* vol. 6: 19–35.

Lemonick, Michael D. 1993. "Lost Secrets of the Maya." *Time,* August 9: 44–50.

León-Portilla, Miguel. 1968. *Tiempo y realidad en el pensamiento maya.* México: UNAM.

Lévi-Strauss, Claude. 1978. *Tristes Tropiques.* New York: Atheneum.

Limón, José. 1989. "Carne, Carnales, and the Carnivalesque." *American Ethnologist,* vol. 16: 471–86.

Lincoln, Charles. 1986. "The Chronology of Chichén Itzá." In J. A. Sabloff and E. Wyllys Andrews V., eds., *Late Lowland Maya Civilization.* Albuquerque: University of New Mexico Press.

———. 1990. "Ethnicity and Social Organization at Chichén Itzá, Yucatán, Mexico." Ph.D. diss., Harvard University.

Linton, Ralph. 1988. "Culture and Normality." In P. Bohannan and M. Glazer, eds., *High Points in Anthropology.* 2d ed. New York: McGraw-Hill, 199–206.

Littlehales, Bates. 1961. "Into the Well of Sacrifice, Part II." *National Geographic,* vol. 120 (4): 550–61.

Livesey, Herbert B. 1987. "Mayan Mexico: Rediscovering the Yucatán's Mysterious Ruins and Uninhabited Resorts." *Travel and Leisure,* February.

Lomnitz-Adler, Claudio. 1993. *Exits from the Labyrinth.* Stanford, Calif.: Stanford University Press.

Luxton, Richard N. 1982. *Mystery of the Mayan Hieroglyphs.* San Francisco: Harper and Row.

———. 1985. "Balam Dz'ib: The Itza 'Dreamwalk' into the Yucatán." *Anthropology,* vol. 8 (2): 99–126.

MacAdams, Cynthia, Hunbatz Men, and Charles Besinger. 1991. *Mayan Vision Quest: Mystical Initiation in Mesoamerica.* New York: Harper San Francisco.

MacCannell, Dean. 1976. *The Tourist.* New York: Schocken Books.

———. 1992. *Empty Meeting Grounds.* London: Routledge.

Mallan, Chiki. 1986. *Guide to Yucatan Peninsula.* Chico, Calif.: Moon Publications.

Marcus, George E., and Dick Cushman. 1982. "Ethnographies as Text." *Annual Review of Anthropology,* vol. 11: 25–69.

Marcus, George E., and Michael Fischer. 1986. *Anthropology as Cultural Critique.* Chicago: University of Chicago Press.

Mascia-Lees, Frances E., and Patricia Sharpe. 1994. "The Anthropological Unconscious." *American Anthropologist* 96 (3): 649–60.

Mason, Peter. 1990. *Deconstructing America.* London: Routledge.

May, Antoinette. 1987. *The Yucatan: A Guide to the Land of Maya Mysteries.* San Carlos, Calif.: Wide World Publishing/Tetra.

Mediz Bolio, Antonio. 1987a. *La sombra de mi ceiba.* Mérida: Editorial Dante.

————. 1987b. *La tierra del faisán y del venado.* México: Editorial Dante.

————, trans. 1973. *Libro de Chilam Balam de Chumayel.* México: UNAM.

Mills, Sara. 1991. *Discourses of Difference.* London: Routledge.

Mitchell, Timothy. 1988. *Colonizing Egypt.* New York: Cambridge University Press.

Montaigne, Michel de. 1958. "Of Cannibals." In *Essays.* London: Penguin Books, 105–19.

Montoliu, María. 1982. "Los antiguos Itzaes y otros relatos de Chan Kom." *Tlalocan,* vol. 9: 367–71.

Morales Valderrama, Carmen. 1981. "Delimitación y características de la región sur de Yucatán." *Yucatán: Historia y Economía,* vol. 5: 54–66.

————. 1987. "Prólogo." In *Los indígenas de Yucatán a través de historiadores, viajeros y anticuarios del siglo XIX.* Mérida: Maldonado Editores.

————. 1988. "Transformaciones en la concepción de lo indígena en Yucatán, siglo XIX." *Revista de la Universidad Autónoma de Yucatán* 166: 14–23.

Morales Valderrama, Carmen, et al. 1989. "Las artesanías del oriente de Yucatán." Primer Congreso de Mayistas, San Cristóbal, Mexico.

Morley, Sylvanus G. 1913. "Archaeological Research at the Ruins of Chichén Itzá, Yucatán." In W. H. R. Rivers, A. E. Jenks, and S. G. Morley, *Reports upon the Present Condition and Future Needs of the Science of Anthropology.* CIW Pub. 200, 61–91.

————. 1946. *The Ancient Maya.* 2d ed. Palo Alto, Calif.: Stanford University Press.

Morris, Anne Axtell. 1931. *Digging in Yucatan.* New York: Doubleday.

Morris, Earl H., Jean Charlot, and Anne Axtell Morris. 1931. *The Temple of the Warriors.* New York: Charles Scribner's Sons.

Moseley, E. T., and E. D. Terry, eds. 1980. *Yucatan: A World Apart.* Tuscaloosa: University of Alabama Press.

Mudimbe, V. Y. 1988. *The Invention of Africa.* Bloomington: Indiana University Press.

Myers, Fred R. 1988. "Locating Ethnographic Practice." *American Ethnologist* 15 (4): 609–24.

Nash, Dennison. 1981. "Tourism as an Anthropological Subject." *Current Anthropology,* vol. 22: 461–68.

————. 1984. "The Ritualization of Tourism." *Annals of Tourism Research,* vol. 11: 503–7.

National Geographic Society. 1989. Maya Traveler's Map. *National Geographic,* vol. 176 (4).

Nicholson, H. B. 1957. "Topiltzin Quetzalcoatl of Tollan." Ph.D. diss., Harvard University.

Novedades. 1989. "Pistolero prófugo lesiona a un comerciante rival en Pisté." March 13.

Ocampo, María Luisa. 1941. *Diez días en Yucatán.* México: Andres Botas, Ediciones Botas.

Orosa Díaz, Jaime. 1982. *Felipe Carrillo Puerto (Estudio biográfico).* Mérida: Fondo Editorial de Yucatán.

Ortner, Sherry B. 1984. "Theory in Anthropology since the Sixties." *Comparative Studies in Societies and History,* vol. 26: 126–66.

Pagden, Anthony R. 1982. *The Fall of Natural Man.* Cambridge: Cambridge University Press.

————. 1990. *Spanish Imperialism and the Political Imagination.* New Haven: Yale University Press.

Patterson, Thomas C. 1986. "The Last Sixty Years: Towards a Social History of Americanist Archaeology in the United States." *American Anthropologist,* vol. 88: 7–26.

Paz, Octavio. 1985. *Labyrinth of Solitude and Other Writings.* New York: Grove Press.

Pearce, Roy Harvey. 1988. *Savagism and Civilization.* Berkeley: University of California Press.

Peniche Barrera, Roldán. 1986. *La sublevación del brujo Jacinto Canek y otras historias violentas.* Mérida: Maldonado Editores.

Peraza López, María Elena, and Lourdes Rejón Patrón. 1989. *El comercio de artesanías en Chichén Itzá y algunos efectos del turismo en la región.* Mérida: CRY-INAH.

Peraza López, María Elena, et al. 1987. "La invasión de vendedores de artesanías en la zona arqueológica de Chichén Itzá, Yucatán." *Boletín de ECAUAdY,* vol. 14: 17–30.

Pinto González, Carlos, et al. 1989. "Anteproyecto del desarrollo socio-económico y urbano del pueblo de Pisté." Mérida: Facultad de Arquitectura, Universidad Autónoma de Yucatán.

Piña Chan, Román. 1985. *Quetzalcoatl: Serpiente emplumada.* México: Fondo de Cultura Económica.

————. 1987. *Chichén Itzá.* México: Fondo de Cultura Económica.

Pisté, Yucatán. 1989. "Estudio socio-económico de Pisté y pueblos circunvecinos." Official correspondence from the Comisaría y Comité Lucha Pro-Municipal de Pisté to the President of the State Congress of Yucatán. May 5.

Pratt, Mary L. 1992. *Imperial Eyes.* London, New York: Routledge.

Press, Irwin. 1975. *Tradition and Adaptation.* Westport, Conn.: Greenwood Press.

Ramírez Aznar, Luis. 1990. *El Saqueo del cenote sagrado de Chichén Itzá.* Mérida: Editorial Dante.

Raymond, Nathaniel. 1971. "The Impact of Land Reform in the Monocrop Region of Yucatan, Mexico." Ph.D. diss., Brandeis University.

Redfield, Margaret Park. 1935. *The Folk Literature of a Yucatecan Town.* CIW Pub. 456.

Redfield, Robert. 1932. "Maya Archaeology as the Mayas See It." *Sociologus,* vol. 8: 299–309.

————. 1941. *The Folk Culture of Yucatan.* Chicago: University of Chicago Press.

————. 1950. *A Village That Chose Progress: Chan Kom Revisited.* Chicago: University of Chicago Press.

Redfield, Robert, and A. Villa Rojas. 1934. *Chan Kom: A Maya Village.* CIW Pub. 448.

Redfield, Robert, and Margaret P. Redfield. 1940. "Disease and Its Treatment in Dzitas, Yucatán." *Contributions to American Archaeology and Anthropology 32.* CIW Pub. 523.

Reed, Nelson. 1964. *The Caste War.* Stanford, Calif.: Stanford University Press.

Retamar, Roberto Fernandez. 1989. *Caliban and Other Essays.* Trans. Edward Baker. Minneapolis: University of Minnesota Press.

Rivera A., Adalberto. 1989. *La pirámide de luz y sombra en Chichén Itzá.* Mérida: Editorial Itzaes.

Rodríguez Losa, Salvador. 1985a. *Geografía política de yucatán.* Vol. 1. Mérida: Universidad Autónoma de Yucatán (UAdY.)

———. 1985b. *Yucatan: División territorial, gobierno de los pueblos y población, 1821–1980.* Mérida: UAdY.

———. 1989. *Geografía política de Yucatán.* Vol. 2. Mérida: UAdY.

———. 1991. *Geografía política de Yucatán.* Vol. 3. Mérida: UAdY.

Root, Deborah. 1988. "The Imperial Signifier: Todorov and the Conquest of Mexico." *Culture Critique* 9:197–219.

Rosaldo, Renato. 1989. *Culture and Truth.* Boston: Beacon Press.

Roys, Ralph L. 1920. "A Maya Account of the Creation." *American Anthropologist,* n.s. vol. 22: 360–66.

———. 1943. *The Indian Background of Colonial Yucatan.* CIW Pub. 548.

———. 1957. *The Political Geography of the Yucatan Maya.* CIW Pub. 613.

———, trans. 1933. *The Chilam Balam of Chumayel.* Washington, D.C.: CIW Pub. 438.

Ruppert, Karl. 1952. *Chichén Itzá: Architectural Notes and Plans.* CIW Pub. 595.

Sabloff, Jeremy A., and E. Wyllys Andrews V., eds. 1986. *Late Lowland Maya Civilization.* Albuquerque: University of New Mexico Press.

Sabloff, Jeremy A., and Gordon R. Willey. 1967. "The Collapse of Maya Civilization in the Southern Lowlands." *Southwestern Journal of Anthropology,* vol. 23: 311–30.

Sahlins, Marshall D. 1985. *Islands of History.* Chicago: University of Chicago Press.

Satterthwaite, Linton. 1965. "Calendrics of the Maya Lowlands." In *Handbook of Middle American Indians,* vol. 3 (2): 603–31. Austin: University of Texas Press.

Schele, Linda, and David Freidel. 1990. *A Forest of Kings.* New York: William Morrow.

Schele, Linda, and Mary Miller. 1986. *Blood of Kings.* Dallas, Tex.: Kimberly Museum.

Scholte, Bob. 1972. "Toward a Reflexive and Critical Anthropology." In D. Hymes, ed., *Reinventing Anthropology.* New York: Pantheon Books, 430–57.

———. 1987. "The Literary Turn in Contemporary Anthropology." *Critique of Anthropology,* vol. 7: 33–47.

Shattuck, George C. 1932. "Medical Research in Yucatan and Guatemala." In A. V. Kidder, ed., Division of Historical Research, *Carnegie Yearbook,* no. 3 (1931–32). Washington, D.C.: CIW, 107–11.

Shattuck, George C., ed. 1933. *The Peninsula of Yucatan: Medical, Biological and Sociological Studies.* CIW Pub. 431.

Smith, Adam. 1980. "The History of Astronomy." In W. P. D. Wightman and J. C. Bryce, eds., *Essays on Philosophical Subjects.* Oxford: Clarendon, 31–105.

Smith, Carol A. 1991. "Maya Nationalism." *NACLA,* vol. 25 (3): 29–33.

Smith, Carol, ed. 1990. *Guatemalan Indians and the State, 1540–1988.* Austin: University of Texas Press.

Smith, Valene L., ed. 1977. *Hosts and Guests.* Philadelphia: University of Pennsylvania Press.

Sosa, John. 1985. "The Maya Sky, the Maya World." Ph.D. diss., State University of New York, Albany.

Spivak, Gayatri Chakravorty. 1988. "Can the Subaltern Speak?" In C. Nelson and L. Grossberg, eds., *Marxism and the Interpretation of Culture.* Urbana: University of Illinois Press, 271–313.

Stagl, Justin. 1990. "The Methodising of Travel in the 16th Century." *History and Anthropology,* vol. 4: 308–38.

Steggerda, Morris. N.d.. Unpublished field notes and census materials. Archives of the Hartford Seminary Foundation.

———. 1941. *Maya Indians of Yucatan.* CIW Pub. 531.

Stephens, John L. 1841. *Incidents of Travel in Central America, Chiapas, and Yucatan.* New York: Harper and Brothers.

———. 1963 [1843]. *Incidents of Travel in Yucatan.* New York: Dover.

Stocking, George W., Jr. 1985a. *Objects and Others.* Madison: University of Wisconsin Press.

———. 1985b. "Philanthropoids and Vanishing Cultures." In G. W. Stocking Jr., ed., *Objects and Others.* Madison: University of Wisconsin Press, 112–45.

Strathern, Marilyn. 1988. "Commentary: Concrete Topographies." *Cultural Anthropology,* vol. 3 (1): 88–96.

Stricken, Arnold. 1965. "Hacienda and Plantation in Yucatán." *América Indígena,* vol. 25: 35–63.

Stuart, George E., and Gene S. Stuart. 1977. *The Mysterious Maya.* Washington, D.C.: National Geographic Society.

Sullivan, Paul. 1989. *Unfinished Conversations.* New York: Alfred A. Knopf.

Taussig, Michel. 1987. *Shamanism, Colonialism, and the Wild Man.* Chicago: University of Chicago Press.

———. 1991. "Tactility and Distraction." *Cultural Anthropology* 6 (2): 147–53.

Tax, Sol, ed. 1952. *Heritage of Conquest.* Glencoe, Ill.: Free Press.

Tedlock, Dennis. 1983. *The Spoken Word and the Work of Interpretation.* Philadelphia: University of Pennsylvania Press.

———, trans. 1985 *The Popol Vuh.* New York: Simon and Schuster.

Thompson, Edward H. 1932. *People of the Serpent.* New York: Capricorn Books.

Thompson, J. Eric S. 1963. *Maya Archaeologist.* Norman: University of Oklahoma Press.

———. 1970. *Maya History and Religion.* Norman: University of Oklahoma Press.

Thompson, R. 1974. *The Winds of Tomorrow.* Chicago: University of Chicago Press.

Todorov, Tzvetan. 1984. *The Conquest of America.* New York: Harper and Row.

Toulmin, Stephen. 1990. *Cosmopolis.* Chicago: University of Chicago Press.

Tozzer, Alfred M., trans. 1941. *Landa's Relación de las cosas de Yucatán.* Peabody Museum of Archaeology and Ethnology, Papers, vol. 18.

———. 1957. *Chichen Itza and Its Cenote of Sacrifice.* Memoirs of the Peabody Museum, vols. 11–12. Cambridge: Harvard University Press.

Trigger, Bruce. 1985. "Writing the History of Archeology." In G. W. Stocking Jr., ed., *Objects and Others.* Madison: University of Wisconsin Press, 218–35.

———. 1986. "Ethnohistory: The Unfinished Edifice." *Ethnohistory,* vol. 33.

Turner, Terence. 1991. "Representing, Resisting, Rethinking." In G. W. Stocking Jr., ed., *Colonial Situations.* Madison: University of Wisconsin Press.

Turner, Victor. 1967. *The Forest of Symbols.* Ithaca, N.Y.: Cornell University Press.

Turner, Victor, and Edith Turner. 1978. *Image and Pilgrimage in Christian Culture.* New York: Columbia University Press.

Tyler, Stephen. 1987. *The Unspeakable.* Madison: University of Wisconsin Press.

UNESCO. 1976. "The Effects of Tourism on Socio-Cultural Values." *Annual Tourism Research,* vol. 4: 78–105.

Urry, James. 1984. "Englishmen, Celts, and Iberians." In G. W. Stocking Jr., ed., *Functionalism Historicized.* Madison: University of Wisconsin Press, 83–105.

Urry, John. 1990. *The Tourist Gaze.* London: Sage Publications.

Van Den Abbeele, Georges. 1992. *Travel as Metaphor: From Montaigne to Rousseau.* Minneapolis: University of Minnesota Press.

Várguez Pasos, Luis Amilcar. 1989. "Algunas ideas para el análisis de la cultura regional de Yucatán y sus transformaciones." At La Cultura regional de Yucatán (reunión de la Sociedad Mexicana de Antropología), Mérida.

Vásquez, Juan Adolfo. 1982. "Virgin of the Cenote: A Yucatec Maya Story." *Latin American Indian Literature,* vol. 6: 15–21.

Veijola, Soile, and Eeva Jokinen. 1994. "The Body in Tourism." *Theory, Culture and Society,* vol. 11: 125–51.

Vergara, Miguel Ángel, and Vicente Martín Güemez. 1988. *El mundo maravilloso del Mayab.* Mérida: Nolo, Centro de Investigaciones Maya.

Villa Rojas, Alfonso. 1945. *The Maya of East Central Quintana Roo.* CIW Pub. 559.

———. 1977. "El proceso de integración nacional entre los mayas de Quintana Roo." *América Indígena,* vol. 37: 883–905.

———. 1979a. "De la antigua sabiduría maya: Lo que dicen los arqueólogos sobre la hierofanía equinoccial de Chichén Itzá." *Enciclopedia Yucatanense,* vol. 10: 419–25. Mérida: Government of Yucatán.

———. 1979b. "Fieldwork in the Mayan Region of Mexico." In G. Foster et al., eds., *Long Term Research.* London: Academic Press, pp. 45–64.

von Hagen, Victor W. 1947. *Maya Explorer.* Norman: University of Oklahoma Press.

Wadgymar, Arturo Ortiz. 1976. "Diagnóstico económico del estado de Quintana Roo y estrategia para su desarrollo." *Boletín de la Sociedad Mexicana de Geografía y Estadística,* vol. 124: 191–281.

Wagner, Roy. 1981. *The Invention of Culture.* Chicago: University of Chicago Press.

Warren, Kay B. N.d. *Mayan Public Intellectuals and Indian Cultural Resurgence in Guatemala.* Austin: University of Texas Press.

———. 1992. "Transforming Memories and Histories." In A. Stepan, ed., *Americas: New Interpretive Essays.* New York: Oxford University Press, 189–219.

Wauchope, Robert. 1965. *They Found the Buried Cities.* Chicago: University of Chicago Press.

Willard, T. A. 1926. *The City of the Sacred Well.* London: William Heinimann.

Willey, Gordon R., and Jeremy A. Sabloff. 1980. *A History of American Archeology.* San Francisco: W. H. Freeman.

Williams, Raymond. 1983. *Culture and Society, 1780–1950.* New York: Columbia University Press.

Yates, Frances. 1966. *The Art of Memory.* Chicago: University of Chicago Press.

Zapata Alonzo, Gualberto. 1984. *An Overview of the Mayan World.* Mérida: G. Zapata Alonzo.

Index

Quetzil E. Castañeda was born in the United States of Ladino parents and developed an early appreciation of Maya peoples and cultures during visits with family in Guatemala and Mexico. His research with Yucatec Maya Indians, on the intersections between anthropology, tourism, Maya society, and national communities, began in 1984 and continues in the present. He has been an assistant professor in anthropology at the University of Houston since 1991, as well as a visiting professor at Princeton (1995). With attention to culture theory/studies, sex/gender, travel writing and practices, Castañeda teaches courses on the comparative histories of Indigenous and Hispanic/mestizo identities and community formation in and across the national boundaries of North and Central America. Castañeda has also been involved with the Fundación Cultural CECIJEMA in the creation of a cultural center in the Maya community of Pisté, Yucatán. Conceived as a means by which anthropological knowledge of the Maya can be reappropriated locally, the Centro Cultural is a combination of community outreach programs, research facility, gallery for Maya art and artisanry, and tourist attraction. In addition to sponsoring international events, such as conferences on Maya culture, the Fundación Cultural has been sponsoring an ethnographic field school in Pisté under Castañeda's directorship. His current projects include a history of community politics in relation to the nation and a historical ethnography of the equinox event at Chichén that takes the form of both a book-length study and a collaboratively produced video documentary.